SUCCESSFUL INTERIOR PROJECTS

THROUGH

EFFECTIVE CONTRACT DOCUMENTS

JOEL DOWNEY
ARCHITECT
PATRICIA K. GILBERT
INTERIOR DESIGNER

SUCCESSFUL INTERIOR PROJECTS

THROUGH

EFFECTIVE CONTRACT DOCUMENTS

A PROVEN SYSTEM FOR:
- Enhancing Project Team Relationships
- Administrating the Project
- Fulfilling Contract Requirements

JOEL DOWNEY
ARCHITECT
PATRICIA K. GILBERT
INTERIOR DESIGNER

Copyright 1995

R.S. MEANS COMPANY, INC.
CONSTRUCTION PUBLISHERS & CONSULTANTS

100 Construction Plaza
P.O. Box 800
Kingston, MA 02364-0800
(617) 585-7880

Southam
Construction
Information
Network

In keeping with the general policy of R.S. Means Company, Inc., its authors, editors, and engineers apply diligence and judgment in locating and using reliable sources for the information published. However, no guarantee or warranty can be given, and all responsibility and liability for loss or damage are hereby disclaimed by the authors, editors, engineers and publisher of this publication with respect to the accuracy, correctness, value and sufficiency of the data, methods, and other information contained herein as applied for any particular purpose or use.

The editors for this book were Suzanne Morris, Roger Greenlaw, and Diane Worth; the managing editor was Mary Greene. The production manager was Helen A. Marcella; the production coordinator was Marion Schofield. Composition was supervised by Karen O'Brien. The book and cover were designed by Norman R. Forgit.

10 9 8 7 6 5 4 3 2 1

Library of Congress Cataloging in Publication Data

ISBN 0-87629-383-6

TABLE OF CONTENTS

FOREWORD

Good projects don't just "happen." They are the result of careful listening, thorough planning, and competent execution. As economic conditions continue to tighten, the future of the design profession lies in our ability to listen to a client's needs, then deliver projects that exceed these needs, increase the client's efficiency, save money, and enhance the lives of those living with the project. This book helps you accomplish this by outlining step-by-step the keys to successful project delivery.

Successful Interior Projects Through Effective Contract Documents provides a thorough, comprehensive guide to completing successful projects. It outlines an *entire process* that supports continuity from one project phase to the next, rather than focusing on drawings or specifications alone. The authors effectively balance detailed "how-to" information with an overall focus on everyone's ultimate goal: producing a project that is a "success" in the eyes of everyone involved.

Each seasoned professional has developed his or her own project process. In a single volume, this book integrates many of the "keys to success" that have taken most of us years to learn. Design professionals at all levels stand to gain from this material. Beginning professionals will find a comprehensive overview of the design process, with insights into many project phases they have not yet encountered. Project technicians will find an in-depth study of Contract Document production. Experienced design professionals will find a useful checklist of items that will remind them of issues they may sometimes overlook.

All will benefit from the authors' overall focus on how a well-disciplined process contributes to the success of a design project.

The importance of Contract Documents must not be underestimated. They are the most powerful tool the design professional has to communicate his or her intent to the builder and client. Without solid Contract Documents, projects become full of accidental details, incur additional costs, and are ripe for litigation. Neither the client, the builder, nor the design professional is well served by the results. This book provides a rare common-sense approach to projects, striking a balance between the plethora of legal advice we all receive and the real-world conditions within which we must operate.

Gary E. Wheeler, FASID
President, The Wheeler Group
President, American Society of Interior Designers

ACKNOWLEDGMENTS

While the writing of a book is largely a solitary endeavor, we owe a debt of gratitude to a large group of individuals who have contributed to the process. Some have generously contributed ideas, advice, and constructive criticism that have helped shape our work. Some have, through professional association, taught us valuable lessons and sometimes unknowingly served as our mentors and helped to mold our thinking. Others have generously offered the support and encouragement that have sustained our efforts and made the task more rewarding.

Rather than attempt to detail each individual's contributions, which might become cumbersome and repetitive, we have decided to simply list those people in alphabetical order whose contributions have been invaluable to our work. They are: Wendy Beckwith; Keith Cochran, R.A.; M. Fran Colby, ASID; Diane Davisson; Brad Gray; Mary Greene; David L. Henderson, AIA; LuAnn Holmes, ASID; Kathryn Jolley; Melanie R. London; Sue Morris; Linda S. Smiley, R.A.; Clifford S. Sutliff; Robert K. Tench, R.A.; and, of course, our families.

In addition, we would like to thank two reviewers who reviewed the entire manuscript and offered many valuable suggestions:

Roger L. Greenlaw, ASID, President of Greenlaw Design Associates, Inc., in Montrose, California. Mr. Greenlaw has served the American Society of Interior Designers as Chapter President and as Regional Vice President on the National Board of Directors, and has taught at the Fashion Institute of Design and Merchandising,

Mount San Antonio College, and UCLA. Mr. Greenlaw is a contributing author to the ASID's *Professional Practice Manual.*

Diane B. Worth, ASID, IIDA, IFDA, a Management Consultant to interior design firms and an Adjunct Faculty member of Arizona State University's College of Architecture and Environmental Design. Ms. Worth is also a contributing author to the ASID's *Professional Practice Manual.*

CHAPTER 1

THE ROLE OF PROJECT MANAGEMENT

The purpose of this book is to describe effective methods for producing clear, concise, and comprehensive contract documents for interior construction, along with the management techniques required to achieve that goal. Interior design is a collaborative effort. Design projects often require the talents of many people to deal with complex technical issues—just as an orchestra comprised of talented musicians needs a conductor to produce a balanced performance, a design project needs a conductor to combine individual performances for a coordinated solution. Behind every successful project stands an individual who orchestrates the problem-solving and decision-making process that produces the design. That person is the project manager.

The project manager wears many hats. Because the project manager is involved in all aspects of the project, this person must possess a great many skills or be able to assemble a team that brings the requisite skills to the effort. Among these attributes are the abilities to deal with schedules, budgets, estimating, negotiating, organization, and, of course, design. The project manager must have leadership skills, effective communication skills, and a high degree of professionalism.

THE PROJECT MANAGER'S RESPONSIBILITIES

The project manager is called upon to perform a variety of duties, all of which are discussed throughout this book. These duties include the following:

- **Client Contact.** The project manager should be brought into the picture early to participate in contract negotiation. The project manager should help to determine the contract scope of service and should remain the primary point of contact for the client throughout the project.

- **Schedule and Budget Preparation.** The project manager is responsible for preparing the project schedule and budget and for constantly monitoring them to keep the project on track. This is probably the project manager's most important responsibility since the primary test for a successful project is that it is delivered on time and within the budget. Nothing else will be remembered if these goals are not realized.

- **Programming.** The project manager must analyze the client's wants and needs to arrive at objectives to be met by the design process. The project manager must also help the client to separate wants from needs and to understand the difference.

- **Team Organization.** The project manager must put together a team to execute the project, including the right mix of designers, technical specialists, and consultants. The project manager must also provide the resources required for the team to function efficiently and effectively.

- **Consultant Contact.** When outside consultants are engaged for the project, the project manager must establish their scope of work, negotiate their contracts, monitor their progress, and coordinate their work. It's important that consultants be made to feel that they are full partners in the process and encouraged to take an active role.

- **Record Keeping.** The project manager's responsibility for record keeping is absolute. The project manager must set up the project filing system and see that all pertinent information is recorded and processed in such a manner that all people working on the project have access to the information they need. In addition, the project manager must organize records so that they can be easily used for future reference.

- **Document Production.** The project manager is responsible for overseeing the production of bidding and contract documents. The project manager should be thoroughly grounded in the preparation of documents; however, if the manager's experience is lacking in certain areas, he or she should be able to rely on a team member who has these skills. While the project manager maintains overall responsibility for the project, it is important that he or she be able to tap the talents of other individuals to execute the work. It is here that the project manager's ability to communicate effectively and to delegate tasks is most important.

- **Construction Review.** Once construction is underway, the project manager becomes the owner's representative in dealing with the contractor. The project manager must regularly visit the site to review the progress of the work, resolve any conflicts in the work, hold periodic project meetings, review the contractor's submittals, prepare and process change orders, review and approve the contractor's Applications for Payment, conduct a final inspection, and oversee contract close-out procedures. Again, some of these tasks may be delegated to others, but the project manager must coordinate their activities and take responsibility for the entire process.

- **Evaluation.** Throughout the course of the project, the project manager is responsible for evaluating the work in progress in an effort to keep the process moving smoothly. The manager must be able to document methods that prove to be successful as well as recognize procedures for effective use of people, time, money, technology, and other resources.

To achieve a successful project, the design professional, consultants, the client, and the contractor must enjoy a positive working relationship. No one plays a more important role in fostering this relationship than the project manager. He or she has the responsibility for meeting the client's objectives within the project budget while meeting the project schedule. It is not a task to be taken lightly. Project management should be assigned to an individual who has strong organizational abilities, good verbal and written communication skills, and the ability to provide leadership for all members of the team. It is not a job to be undertaken by an already overburdened principal.

In some firms, it may be necessary to assign the project manager role to the best technician. Proven technicians often focus on their own areas of expertise; if the project's major thrust is in a certain technician's area of expertise, he or she may be a good candidate. The right person, recognizing his or her own shortcomings, will call upon others to achieve a balance that works well.

As we stated at the beginning of this chapter, project management entails producing effective contract documents as well as using effective management techniques to guide the project. For this reason, much of the text is addressed to the "project manager" who assumes primary responsibility for the project. When references to "the designer" or "design professional" are made, they are intended to apply to the design firm that is executing the project. It may mean the project manager when the specific reference addresses a topic that may be part of the project manager's assigned duties, or it may mean others in the firm who undertake more narrow, specific responsibilities. This depends on how the firm is organized and how it normally undertakes its work.

ORGANIZATION OF THIS BOOK

Interior design projects must progress through a series of well-defined phases, each designed to advance the project toward resolution. Because there is some overlapping of phases in what should be a logical process, it is difficult to lead the reader through a step-by-step sequence. Even the best-managed projects executed by experienced design firms go through an evolutionary process—design decisions are constantly challenged throughout production as new problems are encountered and new information becomes available. For this reason, we discuss topics in their entirety rather than try to divide them into components related to specific phases. While it should be profitable for you to read the entire book from beginning to end for an overview, it is not meant to be read as a novel. There are no characters to develop and no plot to resolve. If you find yourself skipping back and forth to elements that address points of particular interest, you will be using the book just as we intended.

The following chapters outline the primary areas of concern for the project manager. This is not to say that these issues are not the concern of the principal. The responsibilities of the project manager should be in concert with the principal's so that continuity can be maintained on a project no matter who "calls the shots." In a crisis, it may have to be the principal or a team member.

CHAPTER 2

CONTRACT NEGOTIATION

The foundation of every design project rests on the agreement between the client and the design professional. The contract sets forth the essential characteristics of the entire process; with a clear agreement that is responsive to the needs of the project and the client, the project is certain to be a positive experience for those involved.

Much has been written about the negotiating process, including such topics as what you should wear, the shape of the negotiating table, and how to read the body language of the other parties. While all of these issues may have some validity, we'll leave it to others to address them. We think that you should dress appropriately and you should be able to judge what that constitutes. We don't think opposing sides should sit on opposite sides of a table. That in itself presupposes an adversarial relationship that you should seek to avoid. As for body language, we believe that what you propose should be so clear that your intent will be easily recognized.

We believe in approaching each negotiation in a manner designed to produce what is commonly called a "win-win" arrangement. It is important to realize that for one party to win, it is not necessary for the other party to lose. Both parties should gain from the agreement. That may require mutual sacrifice, but, surprisingly, when both parties seek to reach an equitable agreement, both sides often gain more than they initially expected.

In all too many instances, particularly in larger firms, the principals on both sides conduct contract negotiation with little or no input from the people who will have responsibility for the project. Better agreements are invariably reached when the project manager and the client's project administrator — the people who must actually execute the project — actively participate in the process. When these parties are involved it is almost inevitable that the terms of the contract will enhance their efforts.

Contractual agreements have three major, interrelated elements: scope, time, and price. All three must be delicately balanced. If one element is out of balance with the others, the entire project will be adversely affected. For example, clear and concise communication throughout the project will be put at risk. We will begin our discussion by focusing on these elements, then move on to a discussion of areas of negotiation and common agreement types, concluding with some general propositions about negotiating strategy. The discussion in this chapter assumes that the designer has already been selected by the client and that both parties are now ready to forge an equitable agreement for those services.

SCOPE

An agreement to perform professional services establishes what is to be accomplished (scope of project), how the designer will execute the documents required to achieve the intended result (scope of service), how long it will take to perform the work (time), and how the designer will be compensated for services (price).

Project Scope

There are six general factors that take part in defining the project scope:

- **Client's Stated Objectives.** The client must give clear directions concerning what he or she wants to achieve; the designer must help the client separate wants from needs.
- **Construction Budget.** This may be the single most important determinant. Until the budget range is established, it is nearly impossible to address other factors.

- **Schedule.** This may or may not be a major determining factor. Obviously, if the time frame is too short, it may adversely influence all other facets of the project. Otherwise, it may play a very small role.
- **Design Complexity.** This depends mainly on one determination: whether the project incorporates simple, readily-available products that are easily applied or installed, or custom-designed or specially-ordered products that require sophisticated installation techniques.
- **Quality of Materials.** There can be a wide difference between products of a similar nature. You can, for example, employ carpet that costs just a few dollars a square yard or carpet that costs many times that amount. The general level of quality of the products used in the project must be established within this category.
- **Existing Conditions.** Since all interior projects, except for totally new construction, are executed within existing space, the conditions within that space play a major role in determining the scope of work required.

All of the above factors must co-exist in a mutually supportive relationship. If any one factor is out of step, an imbalance is created that must be resolved. This does not mean that all factors must arrive at the same level. It is entirely possible, for instance, to develop a very simple and elegant design using only a few very high quality materials. On the other hand, an extremely ornate and complex design can be put together with very prosaic products. Only after the six factors listed above have been carefully analyzed and brought into a workable balance can the designer arrive at an idea of the range of design service required.

Scope of Service and Time

Once you have identified the scope of the project, you can begin to address the scope of design service and the time available to provide that service. First you must have a clear idea of what service you are capable of providing, in terms of both available personnel and financial resources. One way to do this is to compile a comprehensive list of tasks that must be performed and relate each task to available personnel. With every task include a reasonable estimate of the time required to perform the task. Effective managers include every activity, no matter how insignificant, in this analysis. Small tasks can always be combined with related larger activities for budgeting purposes, but failing to consider them individually means that they may be overlooked. Some tasks will be absolutely necessary, while others may be omitted or revised without compromising essential service. An understanding of this distinction will help you to see where you have some room to maneuver when you negotiate the scope of service with the client. Altering the scope of service is the most flexible way to bring all factors into line.

Once you have established a list of tasks to be performed, you can begin to estimate the time required to complete them. To do this, you must rely primarily on past experience and time records from previous projects, keeping in mind the experience and skill levels of the personnel available for your current project. This topic is discussed further in *Chapter 3: Project Planning*. While that discussion focuses on scheduling after an agreement is reached, the principles apply here as well.

Remember that time is negotiable. Reducing the available time will reduce the scope of service and modify the price accordingly.

Price

Every task you identify has value to the client and represents a cost to you. In any negotiation, your goal is to maximize the value (either real or perceived) to the client and minimize the cost to you. If the client has a fixed maximum fee that he or she is willing to pay (and this is often the case), the only thing you can do is to match the level of service (that is, the scope) to that amount.

The Value of Design Service: Negotiating Fees

Numerous surveys have attempted to discern how both design professionals and their clients value design services. The studies invariably show that while designers place a high value on creativity, clients have a higher regard for more prosaic aspects of service. Responsiveness and the ability to adhere to schedules and budgets always top the list. Therefore, it may be unwise for the designer to stress the value of design unless the client is particularly sophisticated in matters of design. It is much more productive to sell the client on the ability to solve problems in a timely manner and deal realistically with costs. These are aspects of service that the client is likely to value highly and be willing to pay for.

The designer's fee scale is directly related to the level of competition in the marketplace. If your firm has several competitors and each is offering to perform the same basic service, potential clients will perceive all competing firms as more or less equal and will make a selection based primarily on price. That price will be dictated by ordinary costs for past work of a similar nature. When this situation prevails, competing firms typically respond by lowering fees, creating a downward spiral that can adversely affect your practice.

The only way to break out of this dilemma is to offer a service that has value to the client that is not offered by (or stressed by) others. Don't discuss fees until you can get the client to look at the cost of design services in terms of overall project costs. You should be able to convince the client that the initial fee is small compared with the total cost of the project over its expected lifetime. You should also be able to show the client how your design can save him or her money by reducing space requirements or increasing productivity.

For example, suppose a client approaches you with a program for a certain quantity of space (say 20,000 square feet) at a fixed rental rate (suppose $20 per square foot) over a five-year lease. With a little quick figuring we might expect that the construction cost would be in the neighborhood of $800,000 (assuming approximately $40 per square foot) and that you might be able to negotiate a total fee of about $80,000. Now examine how the total costs might be affected if, through good design, you can reduce the space requirements by just 5%. If you can deliver on that promise—and most good designers shouldn't find that to be an insurmountable task—just look at the impact on the total costs. The owner will immediately realize a reduction in construction costs of $40,000 and a savings in rent of $100,000 over the life of the lease. What is the value of your service? Do you think you might be in a position to negotiate a higher fee? Of course you are!

Look for other areas in which you can supply expertise that has value. Following are examples of expanded services frequently offered by design professionals to provide additional benefits for the client. These are benefits that command higher fees.

- **Energy efficiency.** Can you, along with your electrical and mechanical consultants, design systems that save energy costs that will be reflected in lowered utility bills?

- **Environmental issues.** Can you use materials that help conserve natural resources and minimize pollution? Many clients may have an interest in environmental issues.

- **Increased productivity.** Can you analyze the client's needs in ways that might increase productivity in the workplace? While you might do this normally, point it out and recognize that this ability has great value to the client.

- **Handicapped accessibility.** Become an expert in this area. All clients are required by law to conform to certain standards. If your ability to deal with these issues reassures the client, the value of your service increases dramatically. (See the *Recommended Readings* at the end of this book for titles relating to the Americans with Disabilities Act.)

- **Code compliance.** All designers have to conform to code requirements, but a thorough understanding of essential issues could uncover alternate methods that might save initial costs and reduce the cost of insurance premiums for the owner.

- **Real estate and financial services.** It takes a special orientation to be able to deal effectively with these issues, but if you can provide your client with sound advice about how to structure real estate deals and obtain project financing, you will have increased the value of your service immeasurably.

- **Fast track management.** Can you expedite the project in such a way that the owner can occupy the finished space much sooner than he or she may have imagined? If so, the savings may be great for both you and the owner.

- **Facility management.** What can you do to help the client in this area? If you have CADD capability, producing the project on CADD might represent a valuable management tool for the client, allowing his or her staff to create inventories and use the CADD base for future work.

Any of the above—or hundreds of other areas of potential service—can address issues that are translated by the client into increased value. If you can offer certain services such as these, you will quickly distance yourself from your competition – which will put you in the position to negotiate higher fees.

All of the foregoing should have persuaded you that while demand sets the ceiling on prices, cost sets the floor. Value increases both the demand and the potential for obtaining better quality work at commensurately higher fees. Sell value! Use your costs as a starting point but don't use them to justify fees to the client. To a client they are meaningless. He or she cannot evaluate the intangibles they represent.

There is the common belief that when a designer and client sit down to work out an agreement they are negotiating the fee. That's not quite true. They are negotiating *service*. Until the designer and client come to an understanding about the scope of the work, the schedule, the quality of the work, and, most importantly, the value of the work, there is no way the designer can commit to a fee.

A good way to start negotiating is to reach agreement on the scope of service first. If you have valued those services appropriately, arriving at the fee should go relatively smoothly. If you have correctly gauged the client's needs, you will know the relative value of the services you are offering. With this knowledge and the further sharing of objectives, you should be able to arrive at a satisfactory conclusion. Isolate those issues on which there is mutual agreement first, leaving until later the items where there may be some difference of objectives. In this way, when you get to those issues, each party will already have a stake in most points and will be more inclined to compromise, if necessary, to reach total agreement. Rarely will *one* point be important enough to stand in the way of successfully concluding the negotiation, but if the one difficult point is approached first, it may set the tone for the whole process and make it more difficult to come to an agreement.

Sometimes you will find that a client has a bottom-line number in mind and will not budge. When that happens, the only way you can reach agreement is to modify the scope or shift the responsibility for some services. The following discussion explores some of the ways that can be done.

Advance Payment Ask for a large initial payment. You may be able to sacrifice some of the total fee in return for this. It goes without saying that the sooner you are able to collect fees, the better able you are to manage all aspects of your practice. Being able to negotiate a larger advance payment allows you to conserve your working capital – this has considerable value to you and also locks in the client's commitment to the project at the very beginning.

Handling Submissions and Billing Limit the number of submissions to the client. You don't want to keep your client in the dark as the project proceeds, but a series of formal submissions for review at every stage is unnecessary. We've seen too many projects where a series of checkpoint dates has been set up for progress review. Rather than keeping the project on track and allowing it to proceed in a natural logical sequence, the designer is under some pressure to show uniform progress in all aspects of the project as it moves forward. To satisfy this pressure, decisions that might be better off delayed until more complete information is available are made in haste. When that happens, there is great reluctance to abandon positions that have been approved by everyone involved even when it's clear that some aspect of the project might be better served by moving in a different direction. All in all, too much time is wasted meeting artificial deadlines that cost time and money and, in many instances, sidetrack the project.

The foregoing is not to suggest that the client's right to know how the project is proceeding should be shortchanged in any way. It's simply a suggestion that formal presentations can be kept to a practical minimum. Suggest to the client that a simple calendar for submissions be established that coincides with the specific phases of the project when decisions must be made for work to proceed.

Try to simplify the billing procedure and shorten the billing cycle. Every design professional has probably experienced the problems created by poor cash flow. You don't have to be an accountant to realize that receiving x dollars each month is more advantageous than being paid $12x at the end of the year. Also, if you have to jump through hoops just to get paid by submitting minutely-detailed notarized invoices in quadruplicate, you'll spend far too much time on what is essentially a nonproductive (in terms of the project) activity. Ask to set up a simple procedure whereby you can submit a one-page invoice without backup on a monthly basis and get paid within a reasonable time — say ten days. If you are negotiating a flat fee arrangement no backup is ever required. If the contract arrangement is such that the client is entitled to some reasonable explanation of charges, try to have the client agree to accept a simple recap of items with no supporting data or detailed itemization of anything less than some reasonable, agreed-upon sum. You may have to give the client's in-house "bean counters" the right to look at your books if they must absolutely verify some charges. Usually your willingness to extend this right almost guarantees that it will never be exercised.

When discussing the billing cycle with the client, establish the mechanics that must be observed — for example, the project or requisition numbers that must appear on invoices, and to whom invoices must be sent for prompt processing.

If reimbursable expenses are to be charged, propose that a greater number of items fall into this category. Standard agreement forms typically identify a number of items that are reimbursable outside of the base fee, but there are many others that the client has some control over that are normally absorbed within the primary scope of services. Those items that can be shifted to a reimbursable status effectively reduce your scope and provide incentive for the client to be considerably less demanding.

Reimbursable expenses normally include the following:

- Out-of-town travel expenses
- Long-distance telephone calls
- Fees paid for securing approvals by authorities
- Cost of reproductions
- Postage
- Additional insurance coverage required by the client
- Expense of renderings and models requested by the client
- Cost of CADD equipment when required by the client

Beyond these categories, any requirement the client imposes that is outside normal basic professional service could be established as a reimbursable expense.

Some designers have the client retain any special consultants directly. Evaluate this option carefully; it has some drawbacks. You will effectively lose control over the consultant's performance while retaining most of the obligations relating to coordination of the consultant's work. In certain circumstances, however, this arrangement does have some advantages because it shifts responsibility back to the client and reduces the designer's exposure to liability.

Negotiating a Limitation of Liability Clause For the designer, professional liability insurance coverage is a significant expense of doing business. For interior design work, liability exposure is relatively minor—but in today's litigious society such coverage cannot be ignored. If you work with your insurance counselor to explore ways to reduce premiums, you're sure to find that a large step in this direction can be made by limiting your potential exposure to a manageable fee or some other limit that is more in line with your scope of service.

A limit of liability clause might look something like this:

> *"The Owner agrees to limit the Design Professional's liability due to any claim of any nature arising out of or relating to the performance of professional services under this agreement to not more than $ _____ or the Design Professional's total fee for services rendered on this project, whichever is greater."*

Don't just copy the wording above and assume that you've accomplished a limitation of liability. There are serious legal consequences involved. Seek advice from your own insurance carrier and legal counsel.

CONTRACT TYPES

There are a number of contract types that are regularly used in design work. They fall into two general categories: cost-based contracts and value-based contracts.

Cost-based Contracts

Design firms have traditionally used cost-based contracts, charging the client on the basis of how much it costs the firm to perform the service. The cost-based contract seems to have great appeal for the design professional, who is able to pass on all of his or her costs to the client and is thereby assured of making a profit—presuming that a reasonable profit is built into the arrangement. In the process, however, the designer is obligated to keep painstaking records to justify the charges. Under this type of contract, clients have the opportunity to question invoices and can demand an explanation for every minute recorded against their project. In the end, a serious breach of trust may be fostered and the design professional may have no incentive to control costs or increase efficiency. For this reason, clients are becoming more reluctant to enter into cost-based agreements and forward-thinking designers are less likely to propose them. Cost-based agreements seem to work only in circumstances where both parties recognize from the outset that an accurate scope cannot be established — and even then, only when provisions are established that give the client some input into how costs are incurred.

Types of cost-based contracts include multiple of direct labor, not to exceed, and percentage of construction cost contracts.

Multiple of Direct Labor Contracts *Multiple of direct labor* contracts have been widely used for many years. Under this scenario, billing rates for each classification of employee are established by multiplying the actual salary rate by a predetermined multiplier intended to cover overhead costs, indirect expenses, and appropriate profit. This contract type is entirely cost-based — the design professional simply sells hours and is compensated not for the value of services, but for the time expended to produce the work.

Generally, the client who proposes an agreement of this sort has determined that all design firms are essentially equal and is simply shopping for the lowest rate — which he or she may seek to control by insisting on a strict accounting of all time recorded to the project. When designers agree to work on this basis, they have no incentive to provide value. Their goal is only to maximize the amount of time spent on the project and to justify its expenditure. This type of contract should be avoided unless the scope of service cannot be defined. In this case the multiple of direct labor contract has some validity, but only until it can be replaced with a better form of agreement.

Not to Exceed Contracts A *not-to-exceed* contract is usually tied to some form of cost-based arrangement. On the surface it seems to give the client a convenient way to control the ultimate cost, but in reality both parties generally lose. The design firm's incentive is to use every penny of available fee and not one more, while the client seeks to keep the designer working beyond the limit to extract more service for the money. When this happens, the design firm may sustain an unprofitable project and ultimately both parties and the project suffer.

Percentage of Construction Cost Contracts The *percentage of construction cost* contract has been widely used, but is rapidly disappearing. It is similar to a value-based contract in that compensation is not directly tied to the cost of performing the service; however, there is very little correlation between the value of the service and the resulting cost of construction. In fact, the higher value (that of saving the owner money) actually lowers the resulting compensation. Although no ethical design professional would ever do so, a client may suspect that a project has been overdesigned to increase the designer's fee. Also, in times of recession, construction costs tend to be artificially low as competition increases and the designer is thereby penalized as a result of conditions he or she does not control.

Value-based Contracts

A value-based contract is one that recognizes that the value of the design professional's service is not necessarily a function of the time or cost to produce the work. For example, there is an old joke about a mechanic who was called upon to fix a piece of malfunctioning machinery. After scrutinizing the equipment for several minutes, the mechanic took a hammer from his tool box, tapped the machine, and the machine immediately began to operate smoothly. The mechanic sent a bill for $100 to the owner. Sensing that he was being overcharged for what was no more than several minutes of effort, the owner requested that the invoice be itemized. The mechanic promptly submitted a new bill, itemizing charges as follows:

Tapping machine with hammer	$ 5.00
Knowing where to tap	$ 95.00
Total	$100.00

Without belaboring the point, we think you can begin to appreciate the concept of a value-based contract.

Unit Price Contracts *Unit price* contracts, which are based on square feet of space or some other measurable unit, are becoming more common, particularly as they are pegged to workletter allowances reimbursed under the terms of a lease. They are value-based because they are not related to the cost of producing the unit of measurement. The greatest drawback of a unit price contract is that it can be intrinsically unfair when applied too broadly. When the number of units is dramatically reduced, the design firm is forced to spread the fee farther to underwrite activities that are common to all projects regardless of size. For example, the designer may be able to provide comprehensive service for a large project for several dollars per square foot, but the design of a single small space at the same unit price could mean financial disaster. The unit price contract works best when it is based on a graduated scale that sets forth a minimum fee followed by additional units in increments of descending cost.

Cost Plus Fixed Fee Contracts A *cost plus fixed fee* contract is a hybrid arrangement between a cost-based and a value-based agreement. As such, it carries with it most of the disadvantages of the multiple of direct labor type, with few advantages. Since this arrangement relies primarily on using costs as a measure of the work, there is little incentive for the design professional to focus on efficiency. It also allows the client to insist on excessive accounting of costs, which tends to create an adversarial relationship between client and designer.

Lump Sum Contracts *Lump sum* or *fixed fee* contracts are the most value-oriented agreements because they are aimed at achieving mutually beneficial results from the designer's efforts, regardless of the time expended. These contracts provide the incentive to do the project efficiently to increase the firm's profit without the conflict associated with having to defend costs. If incidental costs can be reasonably quantified in advance, those costs may be absorbed in the overall fee. Otherwise, separate billing for reimbursable expenses may be established.

The lump sum agreement requires a well defined scope of service broken down by tasks. The designer must have a reasonable assessment of how much time it will take to perform each task so that he or she can determine the approximate break-even point for each activity. Thus the designer can gauge performance requirements to the client and have a clear understanding of how each aspect can be negotiated.

CONTRACT LANGUAGE

For very small projects it may be appropriate to use a letter agreement that sets forth the terms in clear, simple language, but for most projects you should use a standard contract form such as those developed by the AIA or ASID. These contracts have stood the test of time and have been continually updated and revised to reflect the current standards and needs of the profession. If you wish to modify these standard agreements, or you are presented with a contract form with which you are unfamiliar, consult with your attorney to make sure it's not in conflict with the other contract documents. Never agree to perform services under a "purchase order" or similar instrument that the client may normally use for purchasing supplies or incidental services. It may be perfectly suitable for buying light bulbs or toilet paper but it is totally inappropriate as an agreement for professional services.

As you are attempting to tailor the agreement to best serve your interests, your client will likewise seek to insert language that will work to his or her advantage. In any true negotiation you should both be willing to make compromises and concessions to come to an agreement. There are, however, some seemingly innocuous provisions that you should vigorously resist because they may put you in a very undesirable position.

Ownership of the Design

The contract documents are *instruments of service,* and ownership should always remain with the design professional. Many clients, particularly those who are inexperienced, feel that the work produced by the designer is a product that they purchase and therefore own. Often language that supports this belief finds its way into the agreement. When this happens you should seek to have it removed. Your reputation and liability are at stake; you have no control over how your documents may be subsequently used if you surrender fundamental rights of ownership. At the very least, if the client insists on claiming ownership, get a clause included that precludes the re-use of your documents on any other project without your permission and the payment of an additional fee or royalties.

Responsibility for Budget and Schedule

Often a client will expect you to assume all responsibility for meeting both the construction budget and the schedule and will make the payment of fees, or some portion thereof, contingent upon your doing so. While you have a professional obligation to make every effort to do just that, in reality you do not control either budget or schedule — and cannot guarantee to do so. Seek to have such language stricken from the agreement; substitute other clauses acknowledging that budgets and schedules are shared responsibilities and that the attendant risks are also shared. If the client insists that you take responsibility, you should insist that you be given complete authority to make any decisions that may influence these items. Also, in any requirement for client response, insert a statement that "time is of the essence."

Approval of Shop Drawings and Construction Work

If you are presented with a clause that requires you to "approve" shop drawings, seek to modify it by inserting a qualifying phrase that requires you to "review submittals for design conformance only and to take appropriate action with reasonable promptness with the client." The word "approve" is often construed to mean *unqualified acceptance* and may put you in the position of endorsing the contractor's means and methods, which are clearly his or her responsibility alone.

Likewise, any reference in the agreement that requires you to "inspect" or "supervise" the work, or gives you the right to stop work, should be eliminated. Your role in the construction phase is that of "observing" the progress of the work for conformance with the contract documents, and rejecting nonconforming work and notifying the client, but you should not agree to any language that might appear to give you *supervisory* control that would drastically increase your liability. As for stopping work, only the owner is empowered to do that. If you accept that power, you could leave yourself open to damages, particularly if such action is not fully supported by the owner or otherwise proves unwarranted.

Preparation of Record Documents

If your agreement proposes to have you prepare record documents (as-built drawings), seek to delete it. Record documents are prepared from information that is controlled by the contractor and subcontractors — there is no way that you can assume any obligation for the accuracy of such information. Record documents are important—you should require the contractor to compile and record all changes to the documents. You should *review* such documents and ensure that the information is adequate and complete, but the responsibility for the accuracy and adequacy remains with the contractor. If the client is concerned about this issue and wants it covered in your agreement, propose a clause that reflects the proper assignment of responsibility.

Compliance with Codes and Regulations

Be wary of clauses that many clients (or their lawyers) like to incorporate that require the design professional to certify compliance with codes and governmental regulations. While all designers have an obligation to work in conformance with applicable codes, codes do change and they are subject to interpretation. Therefore, you cannot provide an absolute assurance of compliance nor can you "attest authoritatively" (the dictionary definition of "certify") that all aspects of the contractor's performance are in conformance. Try to soften the language to state simply that the designer will use ordinary standards of care of the profession to design all work to comply with applicable codes, ordinances, and regulations.

Definition of Individual Responsibilities

Most design firms, particularly those who use a team approach, rely on the talents and experience of their team members to be an important selling point when pursuing a project. The client has a right to expect the level of competence that is proposed. You should not, however, let the client insert clauses into the agreement that give him or her the right to approve the roles specific individuals may play. You are agreeing to provide the professional services of the firm, not that of particular individuals. While you should endeavor to use people with whom the client is comfortable, allowing the client to dictate work assignments gives him or her a stake in your practice to which he or she has no right.

Red Flags

Finally, before you sign the agreement, read it one more time to look for "red flag" words. These are words or phrases that carry a connotation of extremes or imply a promise of performance that is ambiguous or impossible to meet. Some typical terms are *all, none, every, best, highest, complete, adequate, safe, appropriate, satisfactory, insure, assure, guarantee, warrant, direct, oversee,* and *control.* In some very specific instances and contexts some of these terms may be acceptable, but look for them and evaluate their meaning before signing the agreement.

SUMMARY: PRINCIPLES OF NEGOTIATION

Once you have a clear idea of what you expect to achieve in an equitable agreement, understand where you can appropriately make concessions, and recognize the potential pitfalls, you are ready to embark on the actual negotiation. While negotiating an agreement is serious business, it can also be an enjoyable experience. It gives you a unique opportunity to establish a good relationship with your client — one that carries over into a successful project. Just be sure that the agreement clearly spells out what you can expect of each other. It is your first line of defense against liability exposure and it protects your right to collect fees due. It also assures your client that he or she is entrusting the project to a thorough professional. Don't take the task lightly. In closing, the following are some sound principles to use in the negotiation process:

- Negotiators on both sides must have the power to make decisions. Nothing can spoil a relationship faster than coming to essential agreement and then finding that someone who is not a party to the discussion retains veto power.
- Ask for what you want. The other side can't be expected to read your mind. If you don't ask for it, you won't get it. You may be surprised; what you feel is a sticking point may be perfectly agreeable to the client.
- Likewise, reject what you don't want. Do it gracefully and explain why you can't accept it. Again, points that you find unacceptable may not be very important to your client.
- Create a cooperative, rather than competitive, atmosphere. Look to create an equitable arrangement that benefits both parties.
- Trust your client. Assume that he or she is as interested in achieving a mutually beneficial agreement as you are. Once you've established trust, you've set the tone for the client to respond in kind.

- Seek to satisfy your own needs but also be open to ideas that fulfill the client's needs. Listen to what the client has to say. You can't begin to address your client's wants and needs until you understand what he or she hopes to achieve.
- Show a willingness to share risks. In every situation there are some unknowns. Don't seek to cover all of them in ways that eliminate uncertainties for you at the expense of the client.
- Be flexible and allow for the unexpected.
- Be willing to make concessions, but concede only those things that you can live without. Expect that a concession on your part will produce one from the other side, but don't keep score. Concessions don't necessarily have to be matched in kind.
- Give away later for now, little items for big ones, and ambiguous issues for clear ones.
- Understand that all concessions are tentative contingent upon reaching an overall agreement. If the client doesn't respond in spirit to what you've given, simply withdraw it.
- Don't establish anything as a non-negotiable issue. Even if it's something you can't give up, there's probably a way to re-structure or restate the item in a way that's more palatable to your client.
- Recognize that although you are trying to reach a mutually beneficial agreement, some arrangements will never work out. If you reach an impasse, it is often better to just shake hands and walk away. Nothing is gained by reaching an inequitable agreement that neither side fully supports.
- Collaborate! Try to remember throughout the process that you're trying to establish a long-term relationship — not a single project agreement — with a client. It may turn out to be a one-time deal, but even if it does, it is more likely that it will be a successful one that ends on a good note if you approach negotiation in this fashion.

Presuming that you and your client have come to a mutually satisfactory agreement, the next objective is to plan the project, which is covered in Chapter 3. In fact, by considering the elements of your contract (scope, time, and price), you have already dealt with the forces that shape the planning process — the foundation has been laid for effective project planning.

PROJECT PLANNING

The first step in achieving any goal of moderate complexity is to break it down into manageable, understandable parts. These parts may then be further subdivided until the result is a step-by-step plan of *what* needs to be done, *when* each task must be completed, *how long* each task is likely to take, and *who* will be responsible for the tasks, as well as what materials or resources are necessary. These principles apply whether one is planning a morning of errands, organizing a community event, planning a trip, or planning the interior for a 100-square-foot or 1,000,000-square-foot project.

In Chapter 2 we referred to the "designer" or the "design professional." These terms are meant to describe the design firm and all individuals representing the firm, regardless of their specific titles. In this chapter we refer primarily to the project manager, who alone has the major responsibility for the tasks discussed, including the preparation of budgets (with others' input).

THE WORK PLAN

The document generated by the type of planning described above is called a *work plan.* The work plan may take many different forms. For a small project, it may be as simple as a short list of essential tasks. For a complex project, it may include many interrelated bar graphs and schedules.

Developing the work plan at the outset of a project is one of the, if not *the,* most important functions of the project manager. The degree of accuracy of the plan is a critical factor in the success of the project, affecting many aspects, including:

- The amount of profit generated by the project.
- The ability to meet deadlines.
- The client's confidence in how professionally the project is being run.
- The morale of team members, which suffers from any disorganization or lack of leadership.
- The success of the design firm in smoothly handling multiple projects.

The work plan serves a variety of functions. Ideally, it should be developed *before* the design agreement is negotiated. From initial conversations with the client, the project manager outlines a general scope of work—broad categories of services that the design firm is prepared to provide—for review by the client. Often this step is part of the initial *proposal*, a document used in the marketing phase of the project to outline to the client what the design firm proposes to do. Once there is agreement with the client on the general scope of work, the project manager can begin to break down the overall scope into very specific tasks that will be required, the types of personnel that will be needed to accomplish them, and how much time each task will be likely to consume. By assigning a rough cost to each increment, an estimated fee can be generated. This is the total that is used when negotiating with the client—the comprehensive list of tasks, mentioned in Chapter 2, that is necessary for contract (agreement) negotiation. This list of tasks may look significantly different after it has been through the negotiation process and tailored to fit the client's budget and expectations, but the first list is of paramount importance in providing a starting point. The final list, which is incorporated into the agreement, is the basis of the design fee and establishes the final work plan.

As the project moves forward, the work plan becomes the yardstick by which progress is measured. By comparing services that are requested or required against the work plan, services that are outside the scope of work can be identified and brought to the attention of the client before they are performed. Giving the client the opportunity to authorize or reject additional work has two important benefits: the firm is more likely to be compensated for authorized extra services and the client's confidence and trust in the project manager is bolstered by this evidence of awareness, control, and professionalism. The value of a comprehensive, accurate work plan, conscientiously used, can hardly be overemphasized in terms of the value of maintaining a good client relationship.

Aside from identifying extra services, the work plan is also useful when it comes to billing for services rendered. Design fees are normally paid in increments based on the completion of either defined phases or a percentage of the overall work. The only way to determine how much work has been done is to establish ahead of time the percentage value of each task (or group or category of tasks) as it relates to the entire project. The percentage of work completed during each billing period is applied to the total fee, which determines the amount of each invoice. Even if this is not the basis for billing, assigning these percentage values to tasks affords two other advantages. It acts as a tool to compare work complete against fee expended and to monitor progress against the project schedule, which is particularly important when reporting to the firm's principals and explaining invoices to clients.

As we will discuss in more detail later in this chapter, one of the components of a work plan is an estimate of the duration of each of the tasks. This component is used not only to determine the cost and optimum fee for that activity, but also to assess the impact it has on the project schedule. Milestones and critical deadline dates are established based on the final completion date. Knowing how long each task is likely to take may affect what that completion date can be, when the milestones and critical dates must fall, and how many and which people are needed to work on the project at any given time. This is especially critical on large projects in large firms where efficient scheduling of personnel and allocation of resources influences not only whether people will be available when they are needed on specific projects but also the overall profitability of the firm. The complexity of this aspect of project management is further increased by the participation of outside consulting specialists engaged for the project. A work plan and resulting schedule that include realistic starting, checkpoint, and deadline dates for consultants are critical if overall deadlines are to be met. These deadlines must be included in contracts made with consultants.

A work plan can be extremely useful not only in developing and identifying a project team but also in promoting the effectiveness of that team. When team members are involved with the development of the work plan, and when they are consulted on issues affecting time allotted to tasks and deadline dates, the actual process of drafting the work plan has a dramatic bonus: the team's sense of responsibility and "ownership" in the plan. Rather than having to overcome a common human tendency to resist something thrust upon them (and the desire to prove someone in authority wrong), the project manager is instead steering a group of people intent on proving themselves *right,* working toward the success of goals they created.

Team effectiveness is also increased when each member's role is clearly defined and understood. A work plan developed and adopted by the team minimizes duplication of effort and encourages cooperation by reducing the tendency of some people to attempt to do too much (the "It's easier to do it myself" or "I'm the designer" syndrome) and of others to shift responsibility to others (the "I thought you were going to do that" or "You're the designer" syndrome).

With a sequential task list to refer to, organizing work for others as the project progresses is less time-consuming and instructions are likely to be more complete. In fact, a project manager can rely on a good work plan to greatly reduce the delegation process itself. An experienced team member can be assigned responsibility for a body of work, based on the work plan, at the beginning of the project (or whenever appropriate) and left to complete it without constant intervention by the project manager. Not only does this free up both the project manager's and the team member's time, but it can also result in a team of self-motivated, independent thinkers eager to live up to the challenge of the responsibility they have been given because they have the freedom to achieve results their own way.

Self-motivated, enthusiastic team members with a work plan to guide them do not have to constantly depend on the project manager to supply them with work assignments. They can often see for themselves what needs to be done and use their time to prepare something that will be needed in the future or assist another team member. They are in a much better position to support the project manager and each other when they are informed and involved. With a work plan in constant use, there is a sense of control over events. The project manager who can anticipate and control events can make informed decisions and can keep the project running smoothly. If problems are encountered and changes are required, those situations can be absorbed without trauma. The respect generated by this strength of leadership results in a hard-working, supportive project team.

It is not only the work plan as an end product that is valuable, but also the process of developing it. We've already touched on how it can cement a project team and bolster morale. Generating a work plan requires an in-depth, detailed mental "dry run" of the project. It can be an exhausting and time-consuming process but what percolates to the surface are questions and awareness of potential pitfalls which, when anticipated in advance, can help to eliminate crises or at least lessen their effect. A good project manager always has a "Plan B," the result of constantly asking "What if this happens (or doesn't happen)?"

When a work plan is used as the basis for recording time spent on a project, what you have at the end is a very good tool for measuring your performance on that project. How adept are you at developing an accurate work plan? On what tasks did you over- or underestimate the time required and why? In what areas does the team need to be more efficient? What were the special circumstances about the project that affected how much time was spent on certain services? With a good system for evaluating performance conscientiously applied, you will eventually accumulate some very enlightening "historical" data that will enable you to hone your ability to reliably evaluate future projects and to plan them and estimate production costs to a fine edge. And it all adds up to successful projects, satisfied clients, and higher profits for your firm.

Now that we've established the value of the work plan, let's move on to specifics. Just exactly what is a work plan?

Preparing the Work Plan

A work plan is basically a reference document that defines *what* is to be done, *when* it is to be done, *who* will do it, and *how much* it will cost to do it. In this chapter we will discuss each of these factors.

If you do the family grocery shopping, you prepare a simple work plan every time you make out your shopping list. The shopping list clearly defines *what* is to be done along with a recognition of *how much* it will cost, since it obviously has to observe the realities of your household budget. The *when* is usually the immediate present; the *who* is presumably you or another family member who is assigned the task. To carry this analogy a bit further, think about the shopping lists you make. For ordinary day-to-day needs you might stop at a convenience store to pick up bread, milk, and other minor staples. Your list will be short with very little emphasis on how you organize it. A work plan for a minor project has many of the same characteristics. However, if you are shopping for a special occasion, you may spend a considerable amount of time organizing and double-checking your shopping list to see that you've remembered every ingredient. You'll probably group the items into categories arranged in the sequence in which you will find the products in your favorite supermarket. If you need both milk and butter, for example, you'll group them together on the list since they will be displayed near each other in the dairy department. You will probably indicate on your list the products for which you have cost-saving coupons, and you might list some alternate products in case some of the items on your list are unavailable or don't live up to your expectations for quality.

As you can see, a work plan (shopping list) can take different forms. What works for a small project may be clearly insufficient for a major one, and an overly detailed plan for a minor project may be wasted effort.

The Task List The logical starting point in preparing a work plan is a summary of required tasks. To describe the scope of work, list the meaningful tasks and subtasks necessary to complete the project. Your agreement, if it's well drawn, should identify the principal activities.

Each task must be clearly defined, have a definite duration, and indicate what level of effort in terms of personnel must be expended to successfully complete it. Unless the project has an extremely limited scope, you can ignore items that are likely to be accomplished in a very short time. Since everything must be accounted for, lump minor activities together with similar or related tasks that may be undertaken simultaneously. Once you have a task list, evaluate it in terms of how it meets the stated criteria. Is each item a definite and distinctive unit of work? Does it have a starting and finishing point? Is it clear what effort and resources are necessary to accomplish it? Also, make sure that essential project management activities are listed. While they may not be separately identified in your agreement and may be easily overlooked, they are necessary to accomplish the objectives of the other defined tasks and must be included so that they are properly considered in scheduling and budgeting.

It is important to both recognize what comprises a significant task and understand the importance of its having starting and completion points. For this to occur, the stated task cannot be vague. To use a simple analogy, suppose you are making out a simple "to do" list for yourself that enumerates a series of household chores. To write down "clean the house" is too indefinite. What do you really mean? Are you intending to undertake a thorough housecleaning project or are you merely planning to do a bit of tidying up? "Vacuum the living room carpet," however, is specific and represents a significant task. It has a definite beginning and end, and embodies a measurable level of effort. Breaking it down even further is useless. Writing "get the vacuum cleaner out of the closet and plug it in" is simply not a significant task. Your project task list must use the same principles.

As you develop and refine your task list, realize that there are literally hundreds of factors that influence design and production that may not be anticipated in the agreement. Invariably they influence scheduling and budgeting, so it's important that they are recognized in both the contract negotiation and project planning phases. Many of these factors cannot be known in advance, but you can attempt to evaluate them on the basis of known conditions. If your firm is engaged in a large volume of projects that are similar in type, size, and scope, your own records will give you the necessary insight to accurately evaluate production costs for future work. Otherwise, one can only address these influences with reasonable awareness. Principal factors that influence design and production include:

- **Scope of Service.** Is the service you have agreed to perform of limited scope (and liability) or is it very extensive? Will you be responsible for extensive on-site review of work? Are you expected to perform tasks that might ordinarily be performed by the owner?

- **Project Budget.** Is the client's budget sufficient to support his or her expectations? Will you be required to expend a great deal of time investigating alternatives designed to contain costs? Do you have any input into setting the budget?

- **Project Size.** There are fixed costs related to every project regardless of size. The time spent on essential tasks, such as record keeping, filing, and project management, may be strikingly similar for all projects. Larger projects amortize these costs over larger overall values. Therefore, smaller projects may have proportionally more time devoted to these activities. It's like having a dinner party. Planning, preparing, and cooking dinner for four guests will not take half as much time as dinner for eight guests.

- **Project Quality Level.** A project designed with many custom features will require a greater degree of effort to design and produce than one that uses simpler means. Figure 3.1 describes four levels of quality. Refer to it to categorize what level of effort might be required for your project.

- **Project Complexity.** Aside from quality, how complex is the project? Will it require extensive research into unfamiliar products and functions? Have you done a similar project previously? Consider whether special technical functions are to be accommodated. They may include sophisticated systems such as mechanical, electrical, data, and audio-visual requirements as well as special functions such as radiation protection, handling of hazardous wastes, and acoustical control and isolation. All of these factors involve research and the involvement of outside consultants. On the other hand, spaces that are essentially simple and repetitive greatly reduce the complexity of the project.

- **Client.** How knowledgeable is the client? Is the client likely to expect a degree of involvement that might hinder the project? Will the client render decisions promptly? Be wary of having to deal with committees. Have you worked satisfactorily (and profitably) with the client previously? Does the client have clear goals for the project? Does the client have a history of terminating projects for lack of financing or a history of engaging in litigation?
- **Schedule.** Is the schedule adequate? Does it allow sufficient time for review? Can it accommodate unforeseen difficulties?
- **Design Firm Capability.** Do you have the necessary resources? Can your staff comfortably handle the project? Will you have to retain outside consultants? If so, have you worked well with them on previous projects? Are the production techniques regularly used by your firm?

Four Levels of Project Quality

A	Highest quality; very sophisticated with complex custom design, detailing, and built-in architectural features (marble; exotic woods; glass; silk wallcoverings; Oriental rugs; high-end or custom wood furniture).
B	Moderate design with some custom detailing and built-in architectural features and/or more specialized requirements (limited use of marble, woods, and glass; quality wallcoverings; medium-grade wood furniture).
C	Limited design with only certain target areas having some custom design, detailing, or special requirements (very limited use of woods and natural materials; primarily painted walls with some vinyl wallcoverings; primarily metal furniture with limited use of wood furniture).
D	Basic office interior, usually building standard theme with no additional built-in design features (low- to medium-grade carpeting; vinyl base; painted walls; standard lighting and ceiling; metal low- to medium-grade furniture).

Figure 3.1

- **Construction Factors/Climate.** Can you assess the local bidding climate? Might you be required to work with unfamiliar and potentially uncooperative contractors? Is there an abundance of similar construction projects that might inhibit competition? Is the scope of work such that many trades and/or subcontractors will be required? Will you have to deal with more than one prime contractor? Are requirements by inspection authorities clear?

Once you have refined your task list and evaluated the factors that may influence how those tasks are performed, you are ready to move on to developing the project schedule.

Scheduling

For very small projects of short duration, scheduling might be a very simple exercise. Suppose, for example, the project consists of choosing finishes and furnishings for a single space. For a project of such limited scope, a single person may successfully undertake all activities associated with the design and production of the work. The schedule might be reduced to a list of the tasks to be completed along with an approximation of the time required to complete each task. Since personal time management is the primary focus of this effort, there is really no need to employ sophisticated scheduling techniques.

For more complex projects, however, one must carefully prepare an extensive schedule that assigns realistic time allotments to a wide variety of tasks involving the participation of many people. How this is done is dependent on many factors; any attempt to reduce the procedure to some standard methodology for all projects is likely to be doomed to failure.

Predicting design and production time is very difficult. Even those experienced people who seem to have a knack for making pretty reliable schedules are quick to attribute much of their success to luck. There are a number of factors that enter into the process. Major ones that must be analyzed are:

- The client's expectations and deadlines.
- The length of time available to do the work to meet established milestone dates, and the staffing required to do the work.
- The experience and skill level of the staff assigned to the project.

- Familiarity with the project type and the production methods selected.
- Ability of the team to work together.
- Level of complexity of the project. Is it a project that will require a great deal of special detailing or research into materials or methods that are being encountered for the first time?
- Interest and enthusiasm for the project. Nothing inhibits production more than team members who would rather be doing something else.
- Type of contract. Does the contract include provisions that reward efficiency?
- Information available. Do you really know enough about the project or are there factors that may cause scheduling revisions? If so, a suitable contingency must be built into the evaluation.
- Time available for management. You must allow enough time for project management tasks as well as time for internal review corrections.

Once you have a feel for these factors, you can begin to develop a schedule. The key to successful scheduling lies in the ability to generate a comprehensive list of tasks to be undertaken and the sequence in which they must be accomplished. We will discuss several different methods of scheduling, but they all start from this point. Begin by listing every task or activity you can think of, no matter how small. Then try to arrange them in rough chronological sequence. You will probably find that the progression is not always apparent and that several activities fall in the same basic time frame. This is usually a sign that these tasks can be performed concurrently.

After you've arranged your task list in sequence, assign an estimated duration for each task. Records from previous projects and the opinions of those who may actually be doing the work are good places to start. Even if you are uncertain, assign some time to every task. Some you will overestimate and some you will underestimate, but overall they will tend to even out. Now consolidate your list to group together small related activities and narrow the list down to *significant* tasks (as discussed previously).

The Milestone Table The simplest form of scheduling is the *milestone table*. The table lists the major tasks and establishes the sequence and optimum completion dates for each task. Milestone tables are easily prepared and usually adequate for small projects of short duration involving few people. They tend to work for larger projects only when there are a number of tasks that can be undertaken independently and when those tasks do not depend directly on each other. For example, when a large project can be broken down into a series of smaller projects, each of which can be undertaken by one or two people, it may be possible to create a simple milestone table for each series as long as it can be completed without relying on the completion of others. Remember that activity start dates are equally important and must be fully accounted for to avoid overlaps in assignments.

For a small project of limited duration, a list of this type may be quite sufficient — again, this is particularly true if only one or two people are responsible for the project. In fact, in this instance, it is often satisfactory to simply list the critical dates on a calendar. For a large project, however, and particularly one expected to be produced over an extended period of time by a team comprised of three or four (or more) people, such a simple scheduling technique would not suffice.

Another drawback of the milestone table is that some individuals feel that it focuses on completion dates and tends to subordinate the points at which the activity must be undertaken in order to realize the projected completion point.

The milestone table shown in Figure 3.2 identifies the major activities at the beginning of a project. It indicates both a starting date and a completion date for activities undertaken by the design firm. For activities by the owner, only the required completion date is indicated. Note also that two or more activities may be undertaken simultaneously, such as doing a code search while measured drawings are being prepared.

The Timeline An advantage of the milestone table is that it can be easily converted into a simple *timeline* (see Figure 3.3) where task commencement and completion dates are represented at intervals along a continuous line. Because of its graphic nature, the timeline begins to point out the need to consider the duration of the various activities. It also begins to show the interrelatedness of the essential tasks.

This happens when two points fall close together on the timeline and one point can be concluded only after the other one is completed.

The Bar Graph While a timeline may be sufficient for scheduling some projects, it can also be easily expanded into a simple *bar graph,* which tends to render a truer picture because it more easily depicts simultaneous activities and shows tasks that may be interrupted at a certain point and continued at a time when related tasks allow them to proceed efficiently.

The bar chart (see Figure 3.4) is probably the most widely used scheduling tool. It is relatively simple to prepare and, if maintained, allows you to plot actual progress against projected progress. Its major disadvantage is that all tasks are listed in a manner that assigns each task equal importance and often yields no clues as to which activities can be delayed or must be accelerated to reach established milestones. For this reason, priorities may be inadvertently overlooked. Don't make the mistake of drawing all bars continuously. Recognize that some

Sample Milestone Table

Task	Start	Complete
Survey existing space	August 24	August 28
Code search	August 29	September 5
Prepare measured drawings	August 29	September 5
Prepare schematic plan drawings	September 6	September 22
Present schematic drawings to owner		September 25
Receive owner's comments and requested changes		September 29
Incorporate changes	October 2	October 6
Resubmit revised drawings to owner		October 9
Receive owner's approval of schematic drawings		October 13

Figure 3.2

tasks must contain gaps in time to insert related activities. For example, in preparing some documents it is necessary to obtain information from some other source; so the task is begun and executed to a certain level of completion, then it must be put aside until that additional information is received before it can be completed. Therefore, it is important to indicate the planned interruption by leaving a space within the bar drawn to represent the particular task.

The Critical Path Method A more sophisticated scheduling method and one that overcomes the inherent drawbacks of those previously discussed is the *critical path method,* or CPM. In this system, not only are the essential tasks identified and analyzed but their interrelationships are defined. Each task is compared with all others and their dependence on each other is charted. Essentially, three relationships are explored.

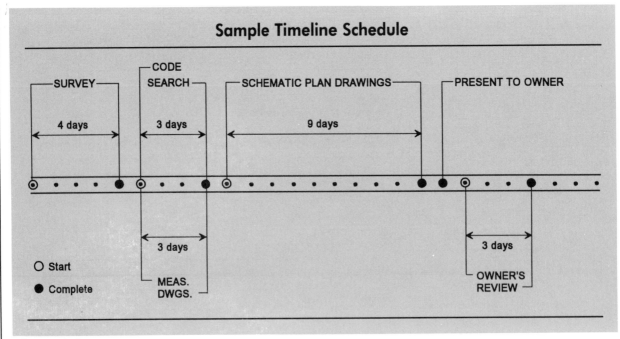

Figure 3.3

Sample Bar Graph Schedule

PROJECTED SEQUENCE OF ACTIVITIES	Sept.				Oct.				Nov.				Dec. ESTIMATED		
	1	2	3	4	5	6	7	8	9	10	11	12	13	14	15
Survey Existing Space	■														
Code Search		■													
Prepare Measured Drawings		■													
Schematic Plan Drawings			■	■											
Present to Owner					■										
Owner's Comments & Requested Changes					■										
Make Changes						■									
Resubmit to Owner							■								
Owner's Review and Approval							■								

Figure 3.4

They are:

- Tasks that must be completed before another task can begin.
- Tasks that must be started before another task can begin.
- Tasks that must be completed before another task can be completed.

An example of the first instance might be that power and lighting requirements must be established before the electrical engineer can begin to calculate his loads. In the second case, at least some decision will have to be made about types of finishes that will be employed before you can begin to choose specific finishes. For instance, it is only necessary to know that you will use ceramic tile, in a certain pattern, in a certain application, to design the substrate to receive the tile. Selecting the specific tile at this point is not required; only the basic decision that permits the other task to proceed is necessary. In the third case, basic hardware choices must be fully completed before you can finish the hardware specification.

As these relationships are identified, they can be set down graphically, taking into account their optimum duration and where—within each graphed duration—a related task must begin or be completed. Instances where one task may proceed to a certain point with input from another become immediately apparent.

The CPM method takes each task, estimates its duration, and analyzes both what related tasks must be completed before new tasks can begin and how each task influences other tasks. The CPM recognizes that although all tasks that make up the project are interrelated, some must precede others and, if delayed, can delay all tasks that follow. A critical path schedule plots activities in much the same way a bar graph does, with each task indicated by a rectangle or other geometric shape that bears some relationship to its expected duration, with arrows connecting it with other tasks in a way that illustrates direction of progress. It also normally includes tasks that depend on actions of others; these activities are usually denoted differently to call attention to the fact that the responsibilities of others may have an impact on the schedule. Figure 3.5 shows the basics.

The diagram in Figure 3.5 indicates that tasks B, C, and D cannot begin until A is complete. It also shows that E depends on C's completion and that E can *begin* before B and D are finished but cannot be *completed* before they are finished. Tasks F and G cannot begin before E is complete, and although F can be started before G is finished, G must be finished before F can be completed. The indication for task H is merely that it has to be done by someone else (as indicated by the circle), that it follows the completion of F, and that nothing else can be done until it is complete. It may, for example, represent an owner's approval process — if the chart is shown to the owner, it may graphically demonstrate how his or her action influences the rest of the schedule.

The greatest value of critical path scheduling is that it plots the path that determines the progression of the project and very clearly indicates those activities which, if delayed, will delay the start or completion of other required tasks.

There is no flexibility in the time duration of the tasks that fall along the *critical path*. The activities outside the critical path can vary in the time period over which they're performed, up to the point at which they impact an activity that does fall on the critical path.

The Wall Schedule One of the most effective ways of working out either a bar graph schedule or a CPM diagram is to use a technique known as *wall scheduling*. Starting with a large blank wall and a stack of 3″ x 5″ index cards, the project manager arranges cards across the top of the wall. Each card represents a work week. Each task is identified and represented by two cards, one designating the beginning of the task and one indicating its completion. The cards are pinned to the wall

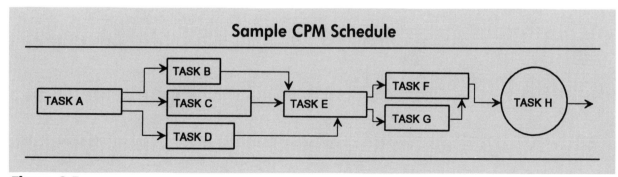

Figure 3.5

in the sequence that is appropriate for each task's start and finish. Usually each task is additionally identified by a letter or color designation indicating which member of the team is primarily responsible for it. The cards are shifted through a trial and error process until it becomes clear that they are in proper and workable order.

Wall scheduling has many distinct advantages. Among them are:

- Being a participatory process, it is based on consensus — since participants have a stake in it, they are more likely to meet its goals and objectives.
- It is easy to communicate.
- If it can remain in place, it is flexible and easy to update.
- It is a good way to start other scheduling types. A wall schedule can be easily converted to a bar graph or critical path schedule because it incorporates features of both.

Once a wall schedule is completed it illustrates where the potential bottlenecks might occur and what staffing problems might arise. Although the development of the schedule is undertaken by the project manager, it must involve the members of the team and ideally the client also. In this way everyone becomes aware of the role they are expected to play and how their performance affects all other aspects of the project.

When the wall chart is completed and everyone agrees with it, it can can be photographed and the prints distributed to all concerned or it can be simply reproduced on paper and translated to a simple bar graph or CPM diagram.

Choosing a Method of Scheduling In summary, the method of scheduling is not terribly important as long as it meets the project's objectives. Trying to schedule a large project based solely on a chart of target dates would probably be inadequate; likewise, trying to develop a critical path schedule for a one-week project would be overzealous.

If your office relies on computers for many applications, there are computer programs that address many of the factors you encounter in scheduling. If there are so many identified significant tasks that it becomes difficult to manage manually, computer applications should be considered for schedules that can be changed and updated very easily.

Although for discussion purposes we are dividing scheduling and fee budgeting into separate topics, they go hand in hand and must be undertaken simultaneously. Since they affect each other, trying to construct a schedule without considering its budget impact, and vice versa, is poor business practice.

FEE BUDGETING

Before embarking on a discussion of budgeting methods we must define certain terms and concepts. The following is an attempt to bring some important terms into focus.

Profit

Profit is the money that the project generates to reward the partners or shareholders of the firm and keep the design firm growing. It should always be subtracted first for budgeting purposes; the revenue that profit represents should be set aside initially and remain untouched. If this isn't done, profit is generally treated as the excess that remains after other costs are subtracted from total revenue. When this happens, no one is likely to monitor the process to see that it is accounted for until the end of the project, when it's too late to make adjustments to protect the planned-for profit. Obviously, profit targets are a management decision but it is evident that healthy firms usually plan for profit in the range of 10% to 20% of total compensation.

Consultant Fees

Consultants' fees represent a fixed obligation and must be treated as such. Outside of the fact that they are negotiable, there is no way to establish a rule of thumb about what impact they may have on the total budget. For small projects there may be no consultants required, while for large jobs consulting fees may comprise as much as 30% of the total budget.

After profit and consulting fees (if any) are set aside and subtracted from anticipated revenues, the remainder represents the amount available for production and includes direct labor expense and overhead.

Direct Labor Expense

Direct labor expense is the firm's total payroll burden including salaries and the cost of benefits, which includes vacation time, sick leave, bonuses, insurance, payroll taxes, and other employee benefits.

Overhead

Overhead is the aggregate of all costs of doing business that are not directly related to specific projects. Many inexperienced design professionals are astounded to discover that overhead is often two to three times more than that expended for direct labor that can actually be attributed to any particular project. What they often fail to realize is that overhead includes a great many factors that are often taken for granted. Consider that the cost of doing business includes the following administrative expenses:

- Office rent and maintenance
- Travel and entertainment expenses
- Utilities, including telephone costs
- Staff training and attendance at seminars
- Cost of supplies and equipment
- Depreciation of fixed assets
- Business development expenses
- Legal and accounting fees
- Liability insurance
- Professional dues
- Books and subscriptions
- Printing and reproduction
- Charitable contributions
- State and local taxes

While many of these costs can't be readily controlled, most firms can minimize their impact by undertaking steps to reduce or eliminate excess costs for those items that are controllable. Also, if you can negotiate design contracts that shift some of these items to reimbursable expenses, more of the fee that's generated becomes available for meeting production costs.

Calculating Overhead Costs The assignment of overhead factors can be done in a number of ways. The following discussion focuses on the development of a numerical factor related to direct labor costs, which should become a fairly reliable predictor of overhead costs related to current work.

Suppose that for a given period a design firm worked on a single project exclusively. In that instance it is easy to see that all costs incurred during that period, both direct and indirect, must be supported by the revenue (fees collected) from that project alone.

On the other hand, suppose that during a particular period a firm undertook a number of projects that were so similar in size and complexity that their direct costs were identical. The division of indirect costs in the form of overhead would logically be an equal division of those costs over the number of projects undertaken. In other words, if there were ten jobs, 10% of the firm's indirect costs should be apportioned to each so that the revenue from all projects covered general overhead.

The examples cited above are relatively elementary and readily illustrate the principles relating to the distribution of overhead. The problem is that neither scenario really describes how any firm normally functions. Firms are typically engaged in producing projects of varying sizes, differing scopes, and many levels of complexity—all at the same time. Those projects are produced over varying lengths of time. While several jobs may take place concurrently, no measurable time period is ever likely to coincide with milestone marks for all projects. For this reason, some convenient method of measuring how indirect costs (again, principally overhead) must be prorated over all projects is needed, so that each project bears a portion of those costs based on its share relative to all other projects.

To calculate the appropriation of costs that are not directly project-related, assume that there is a direct proportional relationship between known costs that can be tracked (i.e., direct labor charges billed to a project) and unknown costs (i.e., general overhead expenses). With that assumption, calculate the design firm's overhead costs for a specific period for which accurate figures are available (usually a calendar year). Then calculate the total revenue generated for the same period and subtract from that figure an amount that represents the profit that the firm expects to realize. Presuming that the firm is solvent and did realize a profit, overhead costs plus direct costs plus the profit target equals total revenue. Expressed as a simple equation:

$$\text{Direct Costs } + \text{ Indirect Costs } + \text{ Profit } = \text{ Revenue, or}$$

$$\text{Revenue } - \text{ Profit } = \text{ Direct Costs } + \text{ Indirect Costs}$$

Since both direct costs and indirect costs for a specific representative period are known, you can now establish a simple ratio that reflects the proportional relationship between them. For example, suppose a design firm earned $500,000 in fees during a particular year and it desired a 20% profit. Also assume that overhead costs for the firm during this period amounted to $200,000. Direct costs for producing the work amounted to another $200,000. The figures, then, look like this:

$$\text{Revenue } - \text{ Profit } = \text{ Direct Costs } + \text{ Indirect Costs}$$

$$\$500,000 - 100,00 = 200,000 + 200,000$$

This equation illustrates some important points. First, the ratio of direct costs to indirect costs is 1:1. Second, to produce the total revenue, including profit, and to pay for general overhead, you must multiply the total payroll burden (salaries plus the cost of benefits) by a factor of 2.5. This factor is the hypothetical firm's *multiplier*. This important number is used in two ways. First, if you can accurately estimate the direct cost (labor) for producing a project, that cost times 2.5 represents the fee that must be realized. Also, if the firm undertakes projects that are billed on an hourly basis, this number can be used to generate *billing rates*. So if a designer who costs the firm $15 per hour in salary and benefits works on the project, the client will be charged $37.50 for every hour the designer works on the project. This should pay for the project's fair share of the firm's direct and indirect costs and produce a profit.

The foregoing example is purely hypothetical — the factors developed for an actual design firm may be quite different. Each firm must use its own data to develop the ratios, multiplier, and billing rates that reflect how it functions. This caution also applies to the establishment of a profit target. This is purely a management decision. Some offices seem to exist on very low profit margins while others strive for greater profits to distribute to the firm's owners and employees and to create larger reserves for investment in new equipment.

Since some offices have a much heavier overhead burden than others, multipliers developed for different offices may vary considerably. As a very rough rule of thumb, overhead costs tend to range from two to four times direct labor costs. Offices with much lower factors have either learned how to operate very efficiently on limited resources or have higher than normal personnel compensation. Those with considerably higher factors should probably look for ways to better control overhead costs.

In summary, no guideline can adequately cover all facets of budgeting for all firms and all projects, but the breakdown for many projects might look something like that shown in Figure 3.6.

BUDGETING OR PREPARING THE BUDGET

The Unit Cost Budget

The simplest form of budgeting is known as the *unit cost* budget. The unit cost budget is derived from previous comparable projects for which carefully maintained records show accurate production costs. Firms that engage in many similar projects, particularly if they are for the same client, use this method quite successfully. If, for example, you are designing several branch offices for a single client where the program and scope of services are identical, or nearly so, the production budget for each project should be roughly the same. The budget for the first job, however, will probably be somewhat higher because it will require solving problems that may be common for all subsequent projects.

Sample Budget Breakdown		
	Small Project	**Large Project**
Profit	20%	15%
Consulting Fees	–	20%
Direct Labor	30%	25%
Overhead	50%	40%

Figure 3.6

Additive and Subtractive Budget Methods

There are essentially two ways to prepare a project budget without having a prior budget for reference: by an additive method or by a subtractive method. In the *additive* method, one simply identifies each task and estimates the cost to complete it. To this total are added the estimated cost of general overhead related to the project and the profit to be generated. The resulting figures then establish the project budget, provided it is not out of line with the office's expected total compensation. If it is, then adjust service factors by finding ways to reduce expenses, or accept a lower profit margin.

The essential steps are as follows:

1. Start with the task list and estimate the number of hours required to complete all tasks.

2. Multiply the projected number of hours by the *weighted salary average* of those employed on the project. The weighted salary average equals the payroll costs of those working on the project, adjusted to reflect the time each is expected to contribute to the project. For example, if three people will work on the project and one person paid $10 per hour will do 50% of the work, one person paid $12 per hour will do 30% of the work, and the third person paid $14 per hour will be responsible for the remaining 20%, multiply the respective hourly rates by the estimated percentages and total all three. In this example, the weighted salary average would work out to $11.40 per hour. The total number of estimated hours multiplied by this average yields the direct labor expense.

3. To arrive at the fee required to support the project, add to the direct labor expense the desired profit, plus estimated consultants' fees (if not billed to the client directly), plus non-reimbursable expenses, plus overhead. (Note that reimbursable expenses can be ignored since they are considered outside of the basic compensation.)

The required fee computed above must be equal to or less than the anticipated gross fee. If it is not, go back and see where factors can be modified. The direct labor expense is the most likely candidate for adjustment; the only way to adjust that cost is to adjust the hours required without sacrificing the quality of the job. Also re-examine nonreimbursable expenses that might be assigned to overhead.

The *subtractive* method works in reverse. First the profit target and anticipated overhead are subtracted from the projected total compensation. The remainder becomes the project budget for production costs, which is further divided into estimated shares for individual tasks. This becomes the project budget, presuming that the amount remaining is sufficient to cover the required scope of services.

Subtractive budgeting involves the following steps:

1. Subtract from the total compensation the desired profit, the estimated consultants' fees, the anticipated non-reimbursable expenses, and the cost of overhead. This yields the amount available for direct labor expense.

2. Divide the amount available for direct labor by the weighted salary average for those engaged in producing the project to find the hours available to do the work.

The available time must be sufficient to perform the required tasks. If it is not, some adjustment must be made. Usually that adjustment is to divide the amount available for direct labor by the estimated time to arrive at a new weighted salary average, then try to assemble a team that reflects that figure.

Try to budget using both methods, because they tend to reinforce each other. Some project managers have greater confidence in a particular approach — that method should become the primary one, provided the means to monitor the project on that basis is available.

PLANNING AROUND AVAILABLE STAFF

In addition to scheduling and budgeting techniques, one must have the ability to coordinate the project requirements according to the availability of staff to execute the work. This is particularly true in larger firms that employ individuals with specific experience and skills that may be required for a particular project. These people tend to be in great demand and may not be available when needed or for the length of time required to complete specific assignments. Therefore, it makes sense to engage in some long-range planning around available staff levels to arrive at commitments from specific people needed to satisfy your work plan. This, of course, means that you may have to adjust your schedule and budget accordingly.

SUMMARY

The methods of scheduling and budgeting that we have discussed are all designed to produce a work plan that accurately enumerates the tasks to be performed and assigns realistic durations and costs to those tasks. An experienced project manager considers all applicable factors to arrive at a practical and effective work plan, including the time that must be invested in project management activities to direct and monitor the project.

An important thing to remember is that one phase of a project cannot be shortchanged in terms of time or effort. Doing so will undoubtedly generate a handsome profit for that particular phase, but that profit is an illusion. It will invariably be translated into a loss on subsequent phases. If insufficient attention is paid to design development, the contract documents phase is sure to suffer, as additional time must be expended to overcome the shortcomings of the development phase. When the logical progression of the project is neglected, a dear price can be inevitably paid.

Beginning a trip without a road map, an idea of how long it will take, and how much it will cost is almost certain to result in a journey that doesn't live up to your expectations unless you enjoy surprises and can absorb unexpected expenses. In much the same way, projects that start haphazardly invariably end up over time, over budget, and poorly executed. Most often the client is dissatisfied and the design professional is undercompensated. Projects go awry for a variety of reasons—failure to effectively plan them is surely at the top of the list. While it may be impossible to guard against all potential pitfalls, the best place to start is with careful and comprehensive planning.

CHAPTER 4

DIRECTING AND CONTROLLING THE PROJECT

Effective project managers must deal with two distinct activities. One is the challenge of leading and motivating project personnel. Another is the mechanics of administering the project, or what we tend to think of as "paperwork." There are many competent managers who master the administrative tasks and there are some who have strong leadership ability, but those who combine both skills are rare indeed. The ideal manager is one who learns to compensate for personal weaknesses by involving others who possess the strengths that he or she lacks. In this way the manager creates a team that can achieve collectively what they could not accomplish individually. This approach assumes that the project manager has the confidence to guide and the maturity to accept the contributions of others without feeling that they are a threat to his or her authority.

Mastering the administrative chores of scheduling, budgeting, and record keeping, and reducing them to routine functions, buys freedom to concentrate on more creative tasks. The project manager who gets bogged down in paperwork forfeits the opportunity to exercise leadership skills that encourage superior work.

THE DAY TO DAY WORK FLOW

The project manager must be a leader who effectively communicates to the team the objectives established in the project planning phase. It is imperative that team members understand their role, what is expected of them, and how their efforts contribute to the overall success of the project. The methods the project manager employs can vary and might be altered from project to project depending on the scope and complexity of each project.

In Chapter 3 we recognized that virtually everything related to project management revolves around creating task lists and assigning realistic costs and time to the performance of those tasks. Since costs are inevitably tied to time in some way, it is essential that time is accurately recorded so the specific project can be monitored to meet objectives, and so the records that are generated can be used for future planning.

Monitoring and Recording Time

Beyond the fact that a good project manager has a feel for the project's status at all times, monitoring time expended against time remaining is one of the primary means of ensuring that the project will be successful.

Time recording is typically a function of payroll procedures — employees are required to account for their time by completing time sheets for each pay period. The office payroll clerk, however, is interested only in verifying that each full-time employee accounts for a forty-hour week. How that time was spent (or misspent) is of secondary importance and is considered only when the time is directly billed to a client. It is the project manager's responsibility to have access to and analyze that information and measure the progress of the work.

Time sheets must be designed to generate information that accurately assigns time to each project by name and number and provides the means to code or assign the time to a specific phase or activity.

Using Project Numbers for Time Sheets The assignment of project numbers is largely determined by each firm's requirements for recording and filing. A small firm may use a two- or three-digit number that is assigned on some basis that identifies projects for filing and recording purposes. Many larger offices use a five-digit number — the first two digits represent the year in which the project is initiated and the following numbers indicate the type of project and its sequential number within the base year. For example, the third digit may identify the project type by using a numerical code. Some firms may insert a letter code, but this practice is rapidly disappearing because numbers are more compatible with computer applications.

Below is a sample code list for project *type*. While this list may be appropriate for one firm, most would be well advised to generate one that corresponds to the particular client base of their own practice.

0 – Research project
1 – Feasibility study
2 – Commercial project
3 – Mercantile project
4 – Institutional project
5 – Public work project
6 – Residential project
7 – Consulting work undertaken with another firm
8 – Furniture and equipment selection only
9 – Graphic design or another specialty service

Using this system, the final two digits would be assigned in numerical sequence for each project that is undertaken either overall within the firm or within each identified project type. Therefore, if the first project undertaken by this firm in 1995 were the design of professional office space, it would carry the base project number 95201.

In addition to assigning a base number to each project, many firms add a one- or two-digit suffix to indicate the current *status* of the project as it moves through various phases. The suffix changes throughout the life of the project and might be designated as follows:

.00 – Marketing or advance work to secure the commission
.01 – Predesign or programming phase
.02 – Schematics phase
.03 – Design development phase
.04 – Contract documents phase
.05 – Bidding or negotiation phase
.06 – Construction administration phase
.07 – Additional services related to the base contract
.08 – Additional services outside the contract scope
.09 – Post-occupancy services

Returning to the example cited above, when the project advances to the design development phase, it will be recorded as 95201.03. When it moves into the contract documents phase, the suffix will change to .04. Since a project will normally be in an established phase at any point, all personnel recording time to the project should be using the same number. While phases might overlap from time to time, particularly when additional services occur, the suffix system is flexible enough to allow the project manager to track the progress of the project.

While the ideal project moves forward through each phase in sequence, sometimes it is necessary to backtrack and perform additional work that logically should have been completed in an earlier phase. Depending on how your client agreement addresses this issue, the time is either recorded to the earlier phase or transferred to the current one. In some cases, it is difficult to "re-open" a previously completed phase – thus the only option is to absorb the time in the current phase. When this can be done without unduly upsetting the project schedule or budget, most offices take this approach. However, when such work constitutes a major impact on the project, it may really be an additional service to be recorded and billed as such. Again, your agreement should be structured in a way that resolves this issue.

A project numbering system similar to the one described here seems to work well for many firms but, again, individual offices should tailor such a system to match their own needs and in the process might generate an entirely different arrangement that better reflects their scope of practice. Note that numerical systems are particularly easy to apply to a computer system that is able to sort and retrieve vital information. Also, the two-digit suffix allows the identification of more than ten project phases if this should be necessary or desirable.

Once a project numbering system is established, the recording of time charged to the project should be greatly simplified. In addition to identifying the project and its proper phase, you might expand the recording process to isolate specific tasks so that those activities can be closely monitored. Often this is done by entering the information in a separate column on time sheets. To standardize such notations, offices typically assign letter codes to be entered in that column. If you choose to take this approach, it is wise to limit such codes to *significant* tasks. Activities that consume a minimum of time are rarely meaningful and can be lumped with similar activities, since keeping track of small amounts of time has little value, particularly if it is non-recurring.

Accurate results and useful data are gained only if each employee combines the activities in the same way. Each office would be well advised to establish some standards for recording time by employees, including examples of what tasks can be lumped together. Records of time expended are of limited value unless there is consistency of interpretation among all employees and for all projects.

In addition to project-related task codes, time sheets must record vacation time, sick leave, general overhead tasks, and other units of time expended that cannot be charged to specific projects.

Figure 4.1 illustrates a sample time sheet that employs the principles discussed. Time should be recorded to the nearest half-hour, which we regard as the smallest unit that yields useful information. While it's possible that one might be able to account for smaller segments of time, doing so is not likely to be very meaningful and tends to over-complicate the recording process. It also makes it difficult for the project manager to monitor progress. Although people who work on multiple projects each day might find it useful to keep track of their time in quarter-hour increments for daily tallies, weekly time reports used for billing purposes should round totals for each project to the nearest half-hour.

PROJECT DOCUMENTS AND PAPERWORK

Even the smallest project generates hundreds, if not thousands, of pieces of information. This information provides a record of project objectives and decisions, and establishes a chronology of the job's progress. Although many design professionals find the task of organizing documents and information pertaining to the project to be an onerous one, it is important. It is virtually impossible to manage a project successfully and profitably without setting up a usable record-keeping system.

The design process is rarely simple or direct. It evolves through the interaction of people, problems, and ideas. The final design is the result of problem solving and decision making, and the totality of the design

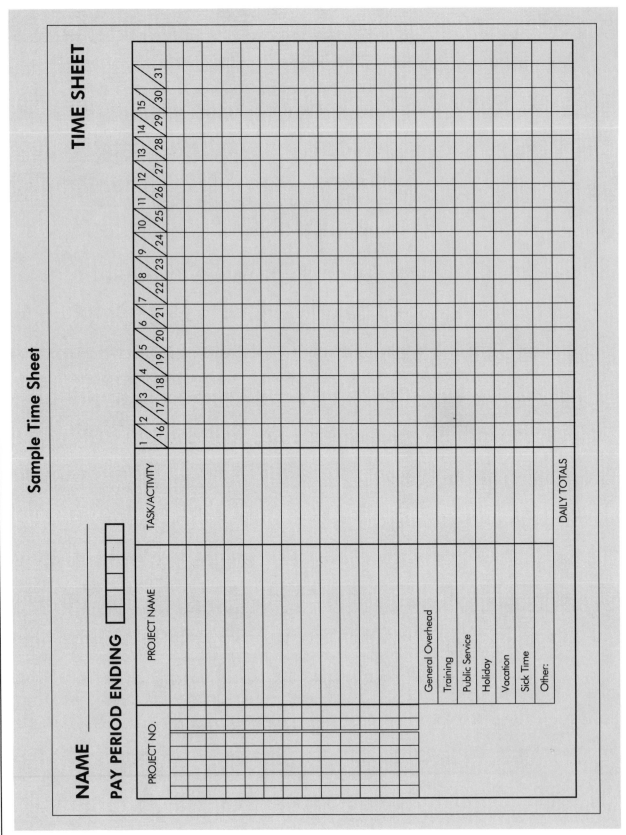

Figure 4.1

is understood only by those who participated in the process leading to it. For this reason, maintaining records that are readily retrievable is very important.

Types of Project Documents

Two types of documents are created during the design process:

- Permanent records, which must be maintained for the duration of the project and beyond.
- Documents that deal with specific issues, which can be discarded when decisions relative to those issues are reached.

The "permanent" documents are usually contract-related and should be securely filed upon receipt. The documents that deal with smaller, specific issues may be handled in a more informal way. Many project managers elect to keep these specific-issue documents close at hand for day-to-day review. The manager might use an expandable file jacket, with or without dividers, that is kept in a central location and is available to all people working on the project. This file might include catalog cuts, specification data, rough sketches, progress prints, memos, and other material that has a short life span. To be truly usable, however, the project manager should purge this file, at regular intervals, of all material that has served its intended purpose and is no longer of value.

In addition to these files, the project manager should maintain a simple chronological log. This log can be kept in a spiral-bound notebook that lists dates along with information culled from correspondence, meeting minutes, and telephone logs. The log might also include a record of the receipt of documents that might be filed elsewhere.

Periodic Progress Reports Typically, most documents are generated by the project manager—the most valuable of these are periodic progress reports created for the client's review. These reports usually coincide with the project billing cycle and the precise phase of the project necessary for approval before the next phase can begin. The progress report may be organized in any convenient form, but it should be brief. Its purpose is to give a quick summary of the status of the project without dwelling on minor issues. The client may not read meeting minutes or other communications but will rely on the progress report as a primary source of information about the project. With this in mind, the progress report should address the following points:

Status. The report should include the percentage of completion, in terms of schedule and fee budget. It may be sufficient to simply state, for example, that the project has progressed to the point where the contract documents are 50% complete and how this point corresponds to the allotted time. If the amount of fee expended is not in line with the payment schedule set forth in the professional service agreement, and if the project is not on schedule, explain what steps will be taken to get the project back on track.

Decisions Made. The report should provide a summary of major decisions that have been made in the interval since the previous report. This part of the report can be culled from meeting minutes and correspondence. Also, if you keep a telephone log that records the date and subject of telephone calls, this record indicates decisions that have been made in this manner.

Further Information Required. The report should include a reminder of what decisions remain to be made and what approvals are required before the project can proceed. List specific dates when these items are to be completed if any of them are critical in meeting established milestones. It is important to point out what impact any delays might have on continued progress.

Work to be Completed. The report should list briefly what work will be completed during the ensuing period. Show how the sequence of this activity dovetails with the established schedule and budget. Establish a schedule of meetings that may have to take place before this work can be completed. This is also the place to inform the client of any conditions that may require extra services, so that the client may respond to items promptly in order to minimize any additional work.

Estimate Update. If the agreement requires you to furnish any periodic updated estimates, you should attach them here. Even if you're not required to do so, you should at least re-state cost objectives and make any appropriate comments about how any recent decisions may have a cost impact. Remember, most clients do not equate their decisions with any damage to the project budget and, to be sure, many minor decisions have a relatively small impact, but together they may seriously impair cost objectives. The earlier the client is forewarned, the more receptive he or she will be toward taking steps to bring potential costs back under control. Of course, the earlier such steps are taken, the easier it is to get the project back on track.

Meeting Minutes Another important record-keeping tool is minutes of all meetings held (team meetings will be discussed later in this chapter). Since no one else is likely to do it or to grasp the full import of topics discussed, the project manager should prepare minutes of every project meeting. Almost all important decisions affecting the project are made at meetings and should be filed chronologically in your permanent file. In addition, for items contained in minutes that relate to specific issues, file copies in your day-to-day working file. Meeting minutes typically contain the following elements:

Number. Presuming that each meeting is part of a series of meetings, they should be numbered consecutively. Some people prefer to number meetings in a way that indicates the phase of the project. For example, the designation 3-4 might indicate the fourth meeting held during the design development phase.

Date. The date is essential on all written communication and notes. Without it, it is impossible to establish the chronology of decisions made.

Location. In many cases, the location of the meeting is insignificant and has no impact on the purpose of the meeting or what was discussed. However, it may be important in jogging participants' recollections about a specific meeting. Certainly if construction issues were discussed, it may be important to know if the meeting was held at the job site, where specific conditions were observed, or at some other location. In the second instance, any conclusions reached may be subject to review after participants are able to see the condition first-hand without having to rely on someone's description.

Participants. Without knowing who attended the meeting, it is impossible to know whether the conclusions reached were supported by those who had authority to make decisions.

Purpose of Meeting. All meetings have or should have a reason for being. State it if for no other reason than it gives you an opportunity to evaluate how well the meeting focused on the issues it was meant to address. If it fell short in any way, you will have immediate feedback on unresolved issues that should be included in a follow-up meeting.

Items Discussed and Conclusions Reached. This section is the body of the minutes. The minutes should state each item that came up for discussion, describe how it was resolved, and record who is responsible for taking action relative to its resolution. This does not imply that every item must come to a conclusion. Sometimes that's not possible — more information will be needed and the item will have to be carried forward to a future meeting for final resolution. Since this is a frequent occurrence, it is usually helpful to separate meeting minutes and agendas into categories such as "old business" and "new business" to make it easier to track specific items.

Record in the minutes what documents were presented at the meeting, including drawings, specifications, material selections, and similar items. Occasionally the meeting may be used as a convenient way to convey those materials and they may not be addressed at the meeting itself. Don't fail to record them, however, since the minutes establish the chronology of their transmittal relative to other issues.

Statement of Confirmation. It is customary to include a closing statement that says essentially that the minutes represent the writer's understanding and that corrections are solicited. Some writers like to set a time limit for such responses but that action seems somewhat counterproductive. After all, if someone discovers a discrepancy at some point beyond the deadline, should the error be allowed to stand? Of course not!

If a participant points out an error in the minutes, one of several actions should be taken. If an error of fact that affects all parties comes to light, the project manager may revise the minutes and reissue them in their entirety as a new record. If the discrepancy is not crucial, it may simply be rectified at the next meeting and noted in the minutes for that meeting. If it's a minor point but one that influences certain participants, it may be appropriate to simply notify the affected parties by telephone or brief memo.

Distribution. List the individuals who are to receive copies of the minutes. Normally the list will include all attendees, plus people who did not attend but need to act on some aspect of the minutes. Explain your distribution policy to your client, who may suggest others who should get copies. By listing these people, the party who types the minutes automatically knows who to send them to. The recipient list will also serve as a check for names that may be inadvertently omitted from future minutes and can at least question their exclusion. This simple list helps to maintain the internal control that is always important to a project.

Filing Paperwork

Paper breeds like rabbits. A single sheet of paper can generate a dozen more, and each piece of paper further represents the consumption of time. For each document you create, someone else must read it and most likely respond to it—thus a chain reaction is underway. Before you know it, you can be overwhelmed with paper.

The use of computers to electronically transfer information quickly and easily contributes greatly to reducing paper flow. When there is no immediate or future need for some bit of information in hard copy form, you can save yourself time and energy by communicating through e-mail.

Filing paperwork is a universal problem. At some point every office devises its own filing system, convinced that the act of doing so solves the problem for all time. Why, then, does it seem that at any given time most firms are in the process of reorganizing their system? How you deal with the paper that represents essential record keeping may not only play a part in the success of your project but may also determine how well you manage future ones. With this is mind, let's consider how you might set up a filing system.

From time to time, some offices actually come up with a system that works reasonably well. Having examined some, we find that the best systems seem to have several things in common:

- They are simple and easy to understand. After all, everyone involved in a project will have some occasion to use it. If the system is very complex, someone will invariably mistakenly misfile something important. Nothing, of course, is totally failure-proof.

- They are flexible. They can accommodate projects of every scope and character. For small projects it is entirely possible that two or three file folders may contain all pertinent information. For a large project that is active over an extended period, fifteen or twenty three-ring binders might be appropriate. The important thing to remember is that the rationale behind each extreme should be identical.

- They tend to group items by subject matter, not by what type of document is being filed. If you are searching for the history and pertinent decisions relative to a certain activity, you cannot be concerned if the information appears in a letter, a memo, a field report, project meeting minutes, or even a transmittal. You'll want all of the relevant data in one location.

Filing by Subject If you adopt the idea of filing by subject matter, you should begin to discipline yourself to generate documents that deal with a single topic. Initially this may seem difficult, but with some practice most people are able to organize their memos and correspondence to do just that. The difficulty usually comes in dealing with incoming documents. You can, of course, ask contractors to confine various documents to a single subject to facilitate response, and they will generally try to cooperate. You cannot insist that clients adopt the same procedure, although many clients will do it voluntarily once they understand why it's good practice.

It is inevitable that some items will need to be filed in several locations. Other than the fact that the bulk of the file may be increased slightly, it's better to have a few duplicates that are retrievable than a single copy that's stashed in an obscure location.

Using CSI Divisions. The major division for filing is, of course, the project name and number. From there it's convenient to use the CSI MasterFormat breakdown of divisions and sections (subdivisions) to create groups of files. CSI assigns Division 0 to documents largely related to bidding documents as the location for contracts and general administrative procedures. For most projects a single folder for each of the 16 MasterFormat divisions may be sufficient. For large projects it might be desirable to further subdivide this file into smaller segments, such as Proposals, Client Agreement, Client Correspondence, Consultants' Agreements, Schedules, Estimates, Bids, Contractor

Correspondence, and so forth. The balance of the project file is then divided into the pre-established CSI format. Just as the 16 divisions of work are always the same for every project specification, the filing system should mirror this arrangement. *Chapter 10: Specifications* covers the CSI MasterFormat divisions in more detail.

Some projects will require a number of subdivisions. Other subdivisions will remain unused. Although our specifications might include both wood and metal doors, for example, we would normally choose to file all information pertaining to doors under the one broad category (CSI Division 8 — Doors and Windows). Into this single file would go all data relating to doors, including product data, correspondence, and submittals. In this way everyone who needs to use the file can find what they're looking for without having to remember that a decision was made about doors during a project progress meeting, or discussed in a letter to the client. This is important because, over the life of the job, a number of people may be responsible for maintaining the file. If the system is this simple, there is little danger that the file will be misused — everyone who requires access to the file should understand the arrangement and have no difficulty in locating information.

Filing Transmittal Letters A transmittal letter is a preprinted cover letter with blank spaces to be filled in that identify the item being conveyed and how it is being sent. It may also include space to indicate its purpose if it isn't clear from the nature of the item. See Figure 4.2 for an example of a transmittal letter.

The filing of transmittal letters is largely a waste of time. Most of them simply document that some paperwork was sent to someone, for a stated purpose, at a specific time. Neither incoming nor outgoing transmittals normally have a useful life beyond their immediate use. People who slavishly file them defend the practice by suggesting that in case of a dispute (and design professionals are becoming increasingly aware of potential liability) it is important to establish the chronology of specific transmittals. We can hardly conceive of the merits of a case turning on such evidence, but if this is a concern of yours, file them or at least set up a simple transmittal log that records the pertinent details of these documents.

Square and Level Design Associates

123 Main St., Suite 111, Bricktown, WA 12345

Letter of Transmittal

_____

To: Date:

                                                       Re:

_____

We are sending by way of _____

_____ Enclosed   _____ Prints   _____ Correspondence   _____ Specifications
_____ Under separate cover _____ Reproducibles   _____ Bid Documents   _____ Other: _____

Copies	Drawing No.	Date	Description

_____

Remarks:

_____

Transmitted by: **cc:**

Figure 4.2

In some cases, a transmittal letter records a selection, confirms something, or otherwise documents a decision. When it serves that function you should, of course, file it. That circumstance may be an important item in the overall history of the project.

COMMUNICATION

While written records and your filing of them constitute a significant portion of the communications relating to the project, equally important is the communication that must occur among members of the project team.

Team Meetings

Some project managers choose to hold weekly team meetings. This is a particularly successful technique when the team is comprised of more than three or four members and is virtually mandatory for large teams where not all members interact on a daily basis. This method presents the opportunity to review and measure current progress, set new objectives for the coming week, and give each team member a better understanding of how his or her work relates to the efforts of the group.

Team meetings are generally somewhat informal but they must be structured with an agenda so that no time is wasted rehashing issues that have already been decided. Meetings should be action-oriented. Every issue should come to a conclusion and each person should leave the meeting with a clear understanding of his or her contribution to the conclusion. This doesn't mean that every problem must be resolved, but when a problem is raised there must be a course of action outlined that will lead to its resolution.

In a small office where team members work side by side on a daily basis, team meetings are not always necessary. The project manager must, however, take the time to interact with all team members on a regular basis to see that everyone has clear direction and has access to vital information and resources. Any time information is not shared, someone is certain to proceed on false assumptions that may adversely affect the entire effort.

Identifying and Describing Tasks

The project manager must identify the tasks that must be completed and in what form the completed work must appear. It does little good to assign a task if the person to whom the task is assigned doesn't have a clear picture of what the result of his or her efforts should look like.

Work Effort Each team member should also have an understanding of the magnitude of effort required to complete each task he or she is responsible for. If this isn't clear, the team member may take a week to work on a minor item that could have been completed in less than a day. Junior staff in particular tend to spend a great deal of time working on things they understand well by overdrawing and over-dimensioning insignificant details. In addition to jeopardizing the schedule and budget, this activity takes time away from more important tasks yet to be completed.

It's always helpful to have examples from prior work to illustrate what is desired. When the project manager assigns the task of drawing door details to a team member, door details from a previous project can provide a clear picture of what the task entails. Without them, the team member may spend an inordinate amount of time drawing repetitive elements that can be more easily conveyed.

Budget In addition to knowing what level of effort is required for each task, each team member must know the budget to be expended in completing it. If the activity is underbudgeted, the team member has an opportunity to use ingenuity to simplify the task so that it consumes less time. For example, if the task is to detail casework, he or she may find ways to standardize casework types so that fewer details are required to document the work.

Schedule When a team member is assigned a task, he or she must know when it needs to be completed. If it isn't finished at a designated time, he or she must also understand how the schedule is impacted. This is particularly true if one individual is responsible for multiple tasks and must manage work time by establishing priorities. If the team member doesn't have a stated deadline for each task, he or she may concentrate on work that could be delayed while neglecting something else that is more critical.

Team Strengths and Weaknesses In assigning tasks, the project manager should be aware of the strengths and weaknesses of the team members. It is not effective to assign routine tasks to experienced people or to assign difficult tasks to inexperienced personnel. This is not to say that those without comprehensive experience should always draw the assignments that tend to be drudgery. The effective project manager will look for ways to challenge them with tasks from which they will gain experience.

Delegation Perhaps the mark of a superior project manager is the ability to delegate important tasks. The project manager who reserves ownership of all decisions of importance alienates team members who are anxious to contribute their own ideas. Along with delegating meaningful tasks, corresponding accountability must be delegated. A team member who knows that initiatives will be met with resistance and that decisions are likely to be overruled will not readily accept responsibility and will not learn and grow in the process. This is a difficult concept for many project managers to accept because it requires allowing others to make mistakes that might have been avoided. Just remember that we all make mistakes and it is through this process that we learn. Denying others the opportunity of experience may have some limited short-term benefits but it gradually erodes morale and leads to a breakdown in the team effort.

SUMMARY

Project control is maintained through accurate records; the project manager's obligation to monitor those records is the only significant way to keep the project on track in regard to schedule and budget. While implementing good record-keeping practices for a current project is essential, those records may also be invaluable for future projects. Therefore, at the completion of every job allot time to carefully go through your file and pull out those items that have no lasting value. Try to reduce your project file to those "permanent" documents that have legal implications and must be maintained as well as those that provide information that can be profitably used in future work.

Although careful monitoring is essential, it should not become the primary goal of the project manager's efforts. The manager must also remember to communicate to the team the objectives established in the planning process. A team that does not have a stake in the process cannot effectively work toward a successful resolution of the project.

Leadership is founded on personal motivation, a passion for doing the work, and the effort required to communicate effectively. The project manager must have a clear vision of how the team should function and must be able to communicate how tasks are to be accomplished by individuals. The ability to clearly express objectives and expectations is fundamental and includes the ability to listen and to openly deal with difficult issues.

In conclusion, it is important to remember:

- Effective project management involves managing both administrative aspects of the project and the available human resources.

- Control is maintained through accurate records. Every significant task and event must be recorded in ways that allow monitoring of time and budget.

- Leadership is dependent on communication. Project participants must be aware of their roles in the overall process so that they can understand how their contributions dovetail into all other aspects of the project. If this is accomplished, the team will move forward toward well-defined goals in which each member has a stake.

The project manager who recognizes these principles and makes an effort to master the skills required to administer the project while leading and motivating the team will be rewarded with an outstanding project.

CHAPTER 5

WORKING WITH THE CLIENT

We have discussed the importance of monitoring the design project by recording work time, reporting progress, and organizing paperwork. Just as crucial to the success of the project, however, is the relationship between the client and the design professional. This relationship is so important that it alone can mean the difference between success and failure of the project. Like any other relationship, it hinges upon whether or not expectations are met. Expectations, however, are often elusive — it is a highly sensitive person who is aware of his or her own expectations, let alone able to communicate them clearly to someone else. Therefore, you may need to help your client to communicate his or her expectations in a way that is useful to you as you design the project.

Building a good client relationship begins with communication. Beyond using certain techniques to establish and nurture that relationship, the designer must focus on two things. First, to fulfill clients' expectations, you must understand their wants and needs in ways that can be translated into physical space. Second, you must involve clients in the process by keeping them continuously informed so that they understand how they can best participate in the project.

In general, all clients have certain expectations for their projects. They are:

- That the project will be completed within budget.
- That the project will be completed on time.
- That the project will fulfill its intended function.

- That the project will satisfy the client's sense of taste and aesthetics, and that it will be appropriate to support his or her self-image or that of the company.
- That the project will represent a good value in that it will enable the client's organization to operate in a pleasing environment and be functionally efficient.

All of these expectations should be addressed as you work closely with the client to establish goals for the project, to create the mechanics for conveying information, and to obtain the necessary approvals so that the project can move forward.

Most clients value accessibility, quick response to problems, and the ability to manage their projects in terms of cost and time. They may not value design or innovation simply because they may not recognize it. This doesn't mean that you can't design innovatively — just that you must do it in ways that address the client's values first.

The basic flaw in any discussion of client relationships is that it assumes dealings between reasonable people who are pledged to pursue common objectives. That isn't always the case. Your client may be incompetent, inconsiderate, or arrogant, but your role is to be supportive and respectful. The project manager who must deal with a difficult client has two problems. The project manager must first arrive at a way to work with the client and, second, find techniques to keep team members committed to the project. Projects that endure many changes and false starts as a difficult client tries the patience of the project manager and the project team can have a devastating effect on the team. Morale suffers and some team members may disregard the schedule and budget, knowing that further setbacks will render their efforts obsolete. When faced with a difficult client, you must be diligent in finding ways to cultivate the client's trust and feelings of self-worth. You must make it clear that you won't make promises that you can't keep and that any deadlines you accept are predicated on the client meeting decision obligations in a timely manner. Your client may not understand that position but if you follow that approach without exception and continue to conduct business in a thoroughly professional manner, you are likely to be rewarded with the client's respect and loyalty.

THE INITIAL CLIENT MEETING

The initial or "kickoff" meeting is held as soon as possible after the agreement is executed and is perhaps the most important meeting you will ever have with your client. Let the client set the tone at this meeting, and you will quickly learn how he or she expects your relationship to develop. If the client is "all business," you should respond in the same manner. If the client shows any inclination to establish a personal relationship, you should be prepared to spend time exploring common interests and getting to know each other. Later, make notes about your conversation. Record the client's likes, dislikes, interests, and any other data that will help you cultivate a personal relationship. Beyond establishing rapport, review the scope of your contract, establish communication and billing procedures, and initiate a discussion of how the project will proceed, what things can go wrong, and how setbacks may be handled. It may not be productive to discuss *specific* potential setbacks but it is important to let the client know that you'll be available to work through any problems that arise.

It is also important to convey the concept that the process involves teamwork and that the client is the most important member of the team because he or she sets the parameters (principally schedule and budget) under which the project is executed. While you as the designer play a significant role, you cannot make fundamental decisions without the client's involvement. Stress that the client must commit a designated portion of time to participate in decision making, and that every step requires careful consideration.

Make sure that the client understands that some time on the part of his or her staff will also be required. Point out that these people must set aside scheduled time to work on various aspects of the project and that this time may take a higher priority than some of their regular assignments. You might warn your client that it is not uncommon for key people in an organization to have to commit a major portion of their time to the project. Consider that someone from the client's staff will have to coordinate the collection of information requested and meet with department managers to see that their space and manpower requirements are projected. You may also encounter supervisors who will insist that they need more space than has been allocated, which leads to internal disputes between departments that must be resolved.

At the initial meeting you should also emphasize that the project will proceed in distinct phases and that you will require prompt decisions at each phase. Be sure to point out that these decisions will be requested when they become relevant to the progress of the project so that your client isn't overwhelmed with details at the outset. Discuss how the client's decision-making process must be sensitive to the project's schedule. Point out that there are times when specific decisions affect progress—if these decisions are not made promptly, the entire project may be adversely impacted.

Don't forget to tell the client that you also will perform in accordance with an established schedule. This is important to your client, since his or her financial planning is based on the forecasting of future events. For this reason, you must provide estimates and other cost information at the time when your client needs them for planning and budgeting purposes. Your failure to provide cost projections at specific intervals may cause the project to be delayed while the costs must be approved to be included in budget allocations.

At the same time, to avoid conflict you must learn what your client's schedule limitations are. Not only should you avoid conflicts, but you should seek to support the client's schedule. Find out what role the organization's board of directors play, when they meet, and how much time they need to act. Recognize, and discuss with the client, how planning can bring to light many factors that affect business planning. For example, issues of space planning may bring up the need for additional personnel or an investment in new equipment to support new directions in which the firm decides to move. These issues influence business planning; a schedule that fails to be sensitive to basic business issues does not serve the client's best interests.

Identifying the Client's Responsible Parties

During the initial meeting, the client should gain some understanding of the design process and how he or she can contribute to its success or failure. In general you will find that most clients are represented by two responsible parties: the *decision maker* and the *facilitator*.

The decision maker is usually the chief executive—while major decisions must be cleared through the decision maker, he or she will probably not have the time to review minor ones and will rarely show any interest in those aspects of the project that have little or no impact on the overall result. In addition, since the decision maker will be occupied with so many other responsibilities, he or she will probably not be readily available to the design professional. For that reason, a subordinate (the facilitator) will probably be designated to handle the day-to-day responsibilities of the project. For some reason, many decision makers like to act as if they are totally in charge and fail to inform the designer about how the project will be managed. The facilitator's job title may be almost anything; therefore, it is often difficult to find out not only who the facilitator is but also what authority he or she has, particularly when the role isn't immediately revealed or defined.

Recognizing these factors, the designer must initiate a discussion of what the line of authority will be and what responsibilities each person in the line will have. The best arrangement is one in which the facilitator is authorized to make most decisions without fear of being overruled by a higher authority. When issues arise that the facilitator is uncomfortable with or is not empowered to deal with, he or she should be able to call upon the decision maker to set up a procedure *involving the project manager* to address the issue promptly.

Always try to define the roles of the responsible parties. In an ideal arrangement, the facilitator should:

- Arrange enough appropriate time to spend on the project.
- Be attentive to detail and enjoy problem-solving responsibility.
- Be accessible to the decision maker, and be someone whom the decision maker respects as being able to deal with most issues.
- Have the clearly-defined authority to act.

The decision maker should:

- Attend presentations. This is vitally important. Presentations to the decision maker should never be made second-hand through an intermediary. When this is done, the emphasis is invariably skewed by the presenter's biases.
- Coordinate his or her schedule with key approval and decision dates.
- Involve and consult with affected parties and key personnel and get their input *before* a decision is reached. Sometimes the

decision maker is not aware of the needs of people in the organization; making decisions that adversely affect them may undermine the success of the project. Also, if the decision maker chooses to delegate decisions to a key personnel group, the decision maker should be prepared to support the group's consensus.

- Allow decisions delegated to the facilitator or others to remain unchanged, if possible.
- Be willing to take responsibility for unpopular decisions.
- Have faith in the design professional. While the decision maker may meet occasionally with his or her counterpart from the design firm, that opportunity should not be used to challenge the designer's or project manager's authority.

CULTIVATING THE CLIENT–DESIGNER RELATIONSHIP

Assuming that the first meeting has established rapport and laid the groundwork for a successful working relationship, it is important to devise ways to cultivate the client–designer relationship. The most important thing to do is *stay in touch*. One of the most effective techniques for maintaining client contact is to establish a scheduled telephone contact each week. For example, tell your client that you will call him or her every Monday morning at 10:00 a.m. (or some mutually convenient time), then do it religiously. Under this arrangement, the client will expect your call, include it in his or her schedule, and be prepared to discuss substantive matters related to the project. Before you place your call, take a few minutes to jot down the subjects you need to discuss. In this way you can cover all important matters at one time without having to bother your client with a series of unrelated, unscheduled, and potentially disruptive calls. There will be some times when there is nothing of importance to discuss. Make the call anyway just to keep in touch and reassure the client that the project is progressing. This technique has an added bonus: When it becomes necessary for you to call at some other time, the client will immediately recognize that you have a crucial matter to discuss.

Obtaining Information from the Client

After the basic working relationship is securely established and the client is aware of what he or she needs to know about the process, you should begin to gather the information you need in order to proceed with the design. The first step is to arrange a series of working sessions with the client and the key people in the organization to arrive at a program for the project. As with any endeavor, it is important to assemble some raw materials and tools before attacking the project directly. If you have prepared the client properly, he or she will understand the importance of this activity. Although many clients want to leap ahead to discuss specific design ideas and solutions, try to maintain your focus on collecting information. Figure 5.1 shows a checklist designed to elicit specific information.

Organizational Charts and Personnel Lists One of the first pieces of information you should seek is an organizational chart of the client's organization. A good organizational chart is invaluable to the designer. From it you can see the relationship between specific individuals and job functions as well as how various departments relate to each other. Organizational charts are particularly valuable because they show in a simple, graphic representation how the organization functions. They tend to show relative status from group to group and offer a clue about the status of a certain individual compared with someone in another group. If a client presents an organizational chart, however, don't simply accept it at face value. Go over it carefully with the client to ensure that it truly indicates the way the organization functions. Sometimes organizational charts depict an ideal organization that doesn't really exist. Even if it is accurate, it may be outdated.

If no organizational chart exists, you should work with the client to develop one. Doing this will help you to understand how the organization functions and often will provide insight for the client as well. Use the client's personnel list as a starting point. Personnel lists tend to be regularly updated, and individual titles are often more descriptive of job functions than those that show up on organizational charts. Be cautious about how you interpret titles. In one organization an individual with a given title might occupy a very significant decision-making position while in another, a person with a similar title may function in a limited supervisory role with very little or no input into corporate policy decisions.

Even if the client does present you with a good organizational chart, the personnel list may be a very useful tool for checking. It usually is more

Sample Pre-Programming Checklist to Elicit Client Information

To aid in the development of a successful Master Facility Plan approach to your project, certain tools are required by the programming team. Please review the following list and provide us with as many as possible at the earliest opportunity:

Current Organizational Charts

Floor Plans

Floor plans of the entire existing facility showing current conditions. Furniture plans are typically best suited for our purposes, as lines of demarcation between groups can be easily identified. It may become important to know the current amount of space per department as a comparison to what is requested.

Personnel Roster

The roster should show each employee's name and job title/function. It should be organized by department if possible. If you do not have such a document, we will assist you in creating one.
The roster should also include current approved vacancies as well as any plans to fill those vacancies.

Growth Projections

You must decide:
Will each departmental representative forecast the manpower projections for his or her department?
Will one person be responsible for all manpower predictions?
The target years of the project. Will the forecast be by calendar year or fiscal year?
How many years into the future do you wish to forecast?

Company Amenities

You must decide what company-wide amenities will be provided for the entire facility.
Will there be lunch room or cafeteria, day care, health facility, etc?

Company Policies

Inform us of any formal written or informal policies that must be followed:
Are there office and work station guidelines?
Is there a smoking policy? Should we provide dedicated smoking areas?
Will dedicated conference, copy, and other support rooms be provided by departmental request, or combined and shared by entire facility?

Figure 5.1

condensed, accounts for everyone, and includes phone numbers, which makes it useful for direct communication. Also, it usually guarantees that everyone's name is spelled correctly. In this regard it is an essential tool for preparing a signage program if this is part of your scope of work.

Organizational charts and personnel lists will help you to understand the physical requirements of various departments. For example, some departments may require different types of work stations to accommodate their functions. The accounting department may need more physical privacy in the form of fully enclosed work stations, more computer hardware, and storage for records and computer printouts. The marketing department, on the other hand, may require a greater degree of openness, to foster internal communication and to accommodate meetings with clients.

Long Range Plans of the Organization The next bit of information that must be elicited is an idea of the organization's long range plans. Most organizations do not remain static for long periods. By understanding how the organization may grow, you can begin to design spaces for eventual expansion. If you know how things might change functionally, you can design certain spaces for flexibility. For example, if the company thinks that it may start manufacturing a new product line, a new operations staff may have to be accommodated. In that event, you might begin to consider how space may be changed from a general use to a more specific one with differing physical requirements. In addition to expansion, you must also consider functions that may shrink. From time to time, certain functions outlive their usefulness and may be entirely discontinued. Finally, it is not unknown for some departments to be decentralized even to the point where they are moved to another location.

The organization's long range plans should also address technological advances. Just as typical offices today scarcely resemble those of just a few years ago, it is likely that future advances will be just as dramatic. Advanced audio-visual requirements and concepts of teleconferencing, which are currently on the cutting edge of technology, are likely to become commonplace in the near future. You should also conduct some research into what advanced technologies are already present in the client's industry. Knowing how the client's competitors function puts you in the position of being able to explore ways to help your client compete in his or her market.

Functional Requirements of the Organization Once you have a clear picture of how the organization functions, you can begin to collect data on specific functional requirements. There are hundreds of ways in which the physical environment either supports or stifles the way people interact in the workplace. The way support personnel work with other people in the office is particularly important. For example, consider the executive-to-secretary relationship. Most executives want their secretaries located in such a way that they can make eye and voice contact without leaving their desks, and secretaries want to be able to see whether the boss is in without leaving their work stations. In many instances, one secretary supports two or more executives. In that case, it is unimportant how the executives themselves interact. It's how they each interact with the secretary that ultimately affects the spatial layout.

Another functional consideration concerns how two different departments relate to each other. For example, management and marketing typically must be adjacent to each other both because there is often an overlap in functions and because they tend to meet frequently. Of course, there are certain areas that should not be close to each other, such as public spaces and those which require some degree of confidentiality.

There are also more prosaic functional requirements that must be addressed. For example, providing kitchen facilities near conference areas, and photocopying facilities adjacent to work functions that tend to be paper-intensive, are two relationships that are universal.

Existing Policies and Standards of the Organization After you have assembled basic information relating to functional requirements, you must integrate this data with the client's existing policies and standards. Policies may include regulations about smoking and coffee breaks. While these may not play an important role in the design process, provisions to accommodate these policies must be incorporated into the final design. Any designated smoking areas will have to be located in such a manner that smokers may use them without unduly interrupting their (or others') work routine. Also, consider whether it's desirable to include a number of dispersed coffee stations or, in a central location, coin-operated machines for coffee and other beverages and snacks.

Also important to the designer are company standards, particularly those that relate to offices and work stations. Some clients have very rigid standards, from the size of individual work stations and the furniture that is provided, to appropriate desk accessories for the level and function of each employee. Other clients may have no such standards.

In the absence of standards, it is wise to explore with the client the benefits of adopting some. Standards are useful for a number of reasons. First, they tend to help the designer to deal with spaces more cohesively. Once it is decided that people of a certain rank will have offices or work stations of a specific size that will accommodate specific types and quality of furnishings, it becomes easier for the designer to do the basic space planning. Also, if people tend to move within the organization on a regular basis, disruption is minimized since only the person moves, not all the furniture and office accoutrements. Besides saving wear and tear during the moving process, it becomes easier to maintain an accurate inventory of furniture and equipment. Finally, the imposition of standards tends to unify the personality of the company.

You should be able to help your client to determine how standardized he or she wants the organization to become. For some organizations, very rigid standards are desirable. Banks, for example, usually require that all employees occupy spaces that denote their status in the organization and may want each officer of a particular rank to have identical spaces and furnishings designed to establish a specific identity. On the other hand, professional offices that are organized on a collaborative basis, where each partner or principal serves an individual group of clients, may see a need for more individuality and personalization of work spaces. In that instance, every person above a certain rank may be given an allowance from which to choose furnishings and equipment that reflect and support his or her own working style.

The Client's Personal Tastes and Preferences In addition to company standards, you will need to consider the client's personal tastes and preferences. Try to understand the client's feelings in this area. A client may readily tell you what appeals to him, but more often than not he will not be able to give you clear direction. Here is where you as the designer must initiate the discussion by showing the client photographs or, better yet, by taking the client through a variety of spaces that differ in style and character to observe his or her reaction to each space. Try to provide examples of both contemporary and traditional spaces; areas that are essentially open and areas that are closed; spaces that are light and airy and those that are somber; and offices where hard surfaces are predominant as well as those that are essentially soft. Ask what the client likes and why. From this exercise you should be able to see not only what the client's preferences really are but also what aspects of design he or she perceives as inappropriate.

There is a large body of research that addresses the psychology of color. In addition to obtaining your client's stated color preferences, you should be aware of how color choices contribute to the overall impression of spaces. Try to elicit not only color preferences but also specific shades within a color choice by having the client show you examples.

Finally, try to draw out the client's preferences concerning patterns. The client may not be able to communicate such preferences clearly, but it may become apparent through the discussion about style and color. Your client may like highly patterned materials or have a preference for plain surfaces.

Organizing Information Obtained from the Client

As you collect various pieces of information from your client, you must sort and organize it in a way that helps you to develop a clear picture of the client's operation as it currently exists, as well as how it may grow and evolve in the future. Some clients will already have this information organized in a usable form; for others, you may have to dig deeper by interviewing key personnel and developing questionnaires to elicit clear data.

Once this information is arranged into a program, you will need to review it with the client to verify the information and resolve any conflicts that may have been uncovered.

SUMMARY

As you organize the data discussed throughout this chapter, you will begin to develop an understanding of what your client expects to achieve. You as the designer have an obligation to meet your client's goals; therefore it is essential that you help your client to effectively communicate these goals. At the same time, the project must respect the budget and must be completed on time. The design must solve problems, address functional requirements, and be appropriate for the client's perceived status.

While your relationship with the client depends largely on your own interpersonal skills (and the client's), if you can observe the guidelines listed below, you should be successful in dealing with most clients.

- Cultivate a personal relationship with your client. You don't have to become "best friends" with every client, but nurturing and maintaining a supportive relationship helps when problems inevitably arise. This is just as important as providing superior professional service.

- Listen to your client and have empathy for his or her concerns. Respond to the content of the client's message and the level of his or her emotional involvement. Listen for complaints and try to resolve them.

- Anticipate problems and decide how you are going to deal with them before they happen. Whenever possible, help your client solve problems that aren't directly related to design. Go out of your way to be helpful. Even if your fee suffers in the process, the good will generated will often repay you in the form of future projects.

- Don't hide or try to minimize problems. Admit your mistakes. Don't avoid your client when things go wrong.

- Keep in touch with your client on a regular and consistent basis. Establish an ongoing pattern of communication and maintain it even when the project is dormant or going through a period when no direct client involvement is necessary.

- Always tell your client the truth, even if it makes you look bad, and never make promises you can't keep.

- Help your client make decisions. Don't make decisions *for* your client, but provide all the information he or she needs to make them. That doesn't mean that your client should make every decision. As a paid professional, you should be prepared to make decisions that are within your area of expertise. Recognize when the client is asking you to make a decision and be prepared to make it.

- Don't change personnel assigned to the project unless it's absolutely necessary. The client may feel abandoned if someone he or she is comfortable with is suddenly no longer available. However, don't hesitate to change personnel if it's apparent that a conflict exists.

- Take responsibility for routine tasks. Prepare meeting minutes and set up meetings with approving authorities.

- Be punctual for meetings; issue meeting minutes and promised reports promptly.

- Make your client's representatives look good in front of their superiors. Prior to meetings with the ultimate decision makers, have all problems with the facilitator resolved. Don't ambush your counterpart who represents the owner. After all, the owner has entrusted this individual with the project.

CHAPTER 6

SURVEY OF EXISTING CONDITIONS

Since many interior projects deal with existing space, it is vitally important that existing conditions are accurately verified. The first step in this verification is to obtain an accurate set of drawings of the existing space. In new construction, the architect's drawings should reflect the conditions and provide the basis for establishing the interior drawings. For older buildings, original drawings often do not exist or if they do, subsequent renovations may have rendered them almost useless. If existing drawings are available, you should immediately make some field measurements to spot-check their accuracy. In verifying existing drawings, use the same points of reference for dimensions as those drawings do, whenever possible. If there are no discrepancies you may be able to use the drawings with confidence, further verifying only conditions that may be critical to your design.

If drawings are not available, or your spot check turns up discrepancies, you will need to make measured drawings. This process may consume anywhere from a day or two to several weeks, depending on the size, scope, and complexity of your project. The key is simple systematic preparation; the following discussion should get you started in that direction.

DRAWING A FLOOR PLAN

First, draw a rough floor plan as close to scale as possible. It doesn't have to be a "hardline" drawing; a good freehand drawing should be sufficient. You can make the drawing from quick sketches you make as you walk through the space. You can keep your sketches roughly to scale or in proportion by pacing off lengths as you go. Sometimes it helps to draw on graph paper. Also, existing modular elements are ideal sources of estimated measurement. By counting floor and ceiling tiles of known dimensions, you will arrive at roughly accurate measurements for preparing your preliminary floor plan. Translate your sketches into a floor plan, then add some of the major dimension lines to be verified. In this way, all you'll need to do in the field is actually record the figured dimensions; by doing so you'll guard against overlooking some critical dimensions. Sometimes you may also need elevation sketches, such as when measuring window elements and certain wall features.

MEASURING THE SPACE

Now you're ready to measure the space. You should have a 50-foot or longer metal tape measure and a 6-foot folding carpenter's rule (preferably one with a six-inch sliding extension on one end); you'll also need at least one other person to hold the "dummy" end of the tape. Start at a convenient point and begin taking measurements around the space, progressing in one direction until you arrive back at the beginning point.

Many designers attempt to measure in the same way dimensions are indicated on drawings by measuring each element in a string of separate dimensions. When you take measurements in this manner, you must move the tape for each measurement. Every time you move the tape, you invite error. In the end, minor discrepancies in individual measurements compound themselves over the entire string and the overall dimension becomes less than precise. Also, if an individual element is measured inaccurately, the overall dimension is similarly affected.

As with most procedures, there is an easy and accurate way to measure existing conditions. The easier and more precise method of recording dimensions is to pick a fixed point, secure the end of the tape measure at that location, and record all measurements relative to that point. In this way, even if specific measurements are misread or misrecorded, subsequent measurements and the overall dimension remain accurate. This method is similar to the way a land surveyor works. The surveyor sets up a transit at a known location, called a *benchmark*, and then records the distance and elevations of subsequent points relative to the benchmark. The transit stays at a stationary point rather than being constantly moved. If you measure a space using the same principles, the possible cumulative error of subsequent movement is avoided.

Figure 6.1 illustrates both the "traditional" measuring method and the method recommended above. We can't say that one method is incorrect and the other is correct, for if done carefully both methods should yield the same result. However, the recommended method is not only easier but is certain to maintain a degree of precision that the first method sacrifices.

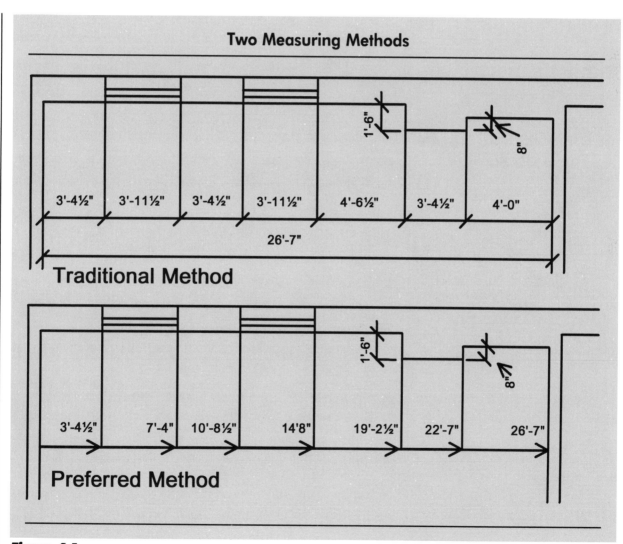

Figure 6.1

When measuring, consistency is important, particularly when several staff members may be working on the same project. Once you adopt a convention, you should observe it for all conditions. For example, if you are measuring to a wall with a wainscot that projects forward from the wall surface above, it makes no appreciable difference if you measure to the face of the wainscot or to the face of the wall above. Just do it the same way every time the condition occurs, note how you did it, and make certain that anyone who takes subsequent measurements observes the same parameters. If you don't, you're likely to generate several sets of measurements with slight variations that you'll have difficulty in reconciling. When measuring door openings, measure the clear door width and not the width of the frames. If the width of the frame is important for aligning adjacent construction, you can measure it separately. Also, be consistent in noting dimensions in feet and inches or in inches only. Finally, when measuring along a wall surface, always measure from left to right. If you measure from right to left, the tape will be upside down and easily misread.

IDENTIFYING ITEMS TO BE REMOVED

Don't neglect to locate and describe items that will ultimately be removed to accommodate new work. They will have to be delineated on a demolition plan and clearly locating them is important in describing the extent of their removal.

DETERMINING SQUARE AND LEVEL

It's also important to pay attention to how true the existing construction is. Construction is rarely completely square and plumb; assuming that it is may create some unwelcome surprises. This may be particularly important when measuring window openings, for example. If window blinds are meant to fit within a window recess, the recess must be square so that clearances around the blind are equal. If this or some similar condition exists, use a carpenter's level and square to check it. You should also measure the window recess in several locations. Measure near the top and the bottom and at the approximate mid-point. If they differ, the smallest measurement will govern the width of the window covering.

It is more difficult to determine how level the floor is. A standard length of metal wall angle that's used in suspended ceiling systems is rigid enough when laid on the floor to show where there are significant depressions and high points. If the floor is noticeably out of level, you may want to have the owner engage a surveyor to check it with a transit.

RECORDING OVERHEAD OBSTRUCTIONS

In addition to verifying the location of elements in a plan, it is important to record overhead obstructions. You cannot design ceiling coffers or coves, or even locate recessed lighting fixtures, until you have a clear picture of where existing beams, ducts, pipes, and conduits are located, along with their respective heights above the finished floor. The conflicts may not be discovered until their resolution will be difficult and costly. Depending on the complexity of the overhead obstructions and your proposed ceiling design, this may be a simple procedure or a very time-consuming one. If exact locations are critical, you will want to approach this task in a very meticulous way.

Perhaps the best way to start is to use an outline plan of the space. While walking through the space, plot approximate locations of all overhead work and make a note of anything that appears to be a possible source of conflict. Transfer your notes and approximate locations to an accurate scale plan, then measure the locations of all possible obstructions. Because measuring the location of overhead elements is sometimes difficult and might require two people standing on a pair of ladders, you might want to consider a simple technique that transforms the measurements to the floor plans. Drop a plumb bob (a weighted string will do nicely) from the overhead point and mark its location on the floor, then measure from that point to the nearest wall, column, or other fixed point. Remember, just because a point appears to run parallel to a wall, it may not. And if location is critical, it's essential that you check it at several points.

Measuring the height of possible obstructions above the floor is relatively easy. You will need to create what old-time carpenters call a *story pole*. Get an eight-foot length of wood lattice at your local lumberyard. Verify its length. (Just because it's sold as an eight-foot length doesn't guarantee that it's precisely 96 inches long.) If it's slightly longer or shorter, you'll have to account for discrepancies in your measurements. Holding it upright under the possible obstruction, measure the distance from its top to the bottom of the obstruction with a yardstick or your folding rule. This dimension plus eight feet equals its height above the floor. Pay attention to such things as pipe fittings and duct flanges. It accomplishes little to establish the height of the bottom of a duct if the duct is supported on hangers that extend several inches below that point. Also, valves in piping and damper controls in ductwork may need to be located so that ceiling access may be provided at those points to facilitate maintenance and adjustment. Don't forget, too, that electrical junction boxes concealed above the ceiling must be accessible to comply with the National Electric Code. These provisions, of course, will be easily met if you are using a suspended acoustic panel ceiling system. If you're using a hard surface ceiling material, however, you will have to provide access panels — so locating these elements becomes very important.

PHOTOGRAPHING THE SPACE

Take photographs of every feature that could be difficult to convey in drawing form. As a general rule, take about twice as many photos as you think will actually be required to record the space. In all probability, most of them will be of limited value, but it's a sure bet that some of the ones you originally thought would be of little importance will turn out to depict an important element that otherwise would have been overlooked. When in doubt, take a picture. It really may be worth a thousand words (or dollars!).

Don't just snap pictures at random. Plan each one to show something that's worth recording and mark on your floor plan sketch where you were standing when you took the photograph, the direction you were facing, and the numerical sequence of the photo. A list of simple descriptions (room name, type of equipment, etc.) of what you are photographing can also be very helpful later. When the photos are developed, transfer the numerical sequence and descriptions to the prints. This way they are usable by someone else and can be identified at a later date when the space is not as fresh in your memory. Rather than trying to manage stacks of loose prints that invariably get misplaced, it is a good idea to store your photos in plastic sheet protectors designed to fit in a three ring binder.

In general, take pictures from a position that is perpendicular to the object you wish to show. In that way, it's shown in true elevation undistorted by perspective. You might have another person stand next to it holding a six-foot rule or some other object of measurable height. You can then enlarge the photo to a true scale on a photocopier. Copiers that are adjustable in increments of one-half percent are particularly useful for this purpose. As a simple example, suppose the six-foot rule on your photo measures one inch. By copying the photo at 150%, you enlarge the measurement to 1-1/2″ and reproduce the photo as an accurate elevation at a scale of 1/4″ equals one foot. Of course, it would be pure luck to produce photos that convert this easily, so you'll have to use some simple proportional equations to adjust the copier enlargement ratios to achieve a usable result. You can't rely on this technique for extreme accuracy, but questions involving clearances as small as two or three inches can usually be satisfactorily resolved.

Attempting to employ newer technology, some design professionals have begun to use video cameras to provide a record of conditions within a space. While this technique may create a good way for those who have not actually seen the space to visualize it, it has little value as a continuing source of reference. Holding a photograph in one's hands and being able to examine it remains much more valuable than the fleeting image on a television screen.

RECORDING MECHANICAL AND ELECTRICAL SYSTEMS

Beyond measuring the space, there are many other items that must be observed and recorded. Most of these are elements of the mechanical and electrical systems. If your design is to include new plumbing fixtures, for example, you must locate existing plumbing stacks at chases or "wet" columns. New plumbing must fall adjacent to these areas or close enough that horizontal runs of waste and vent lines can be tied into them. The location of existing plumbing fixtures usually clearly indicates the course of piping; you can often identify hidden pipes as they are usually exposed above partitions and column surrounds. The finish may only extend to a point above the ceiling and the exposed piping becomes visible above that point.

The items that must be verified in surveying existing conditions are so extensive that any attempt to discuss every potential item could never be complete. Figure 6.2 is a checklist that illustrates a range of issues that must be addressed. Adopt it and modify it as may be required to make it responsive to your own needs for a specific project.

Project Space Survey Checklist

Project Name:	Project No.
Survey completed by	Date

General Data: (Answer all questions. Use N/A if question does not apply.)

Building owner or leasing agent

Address

Contact person	Phone

Consultants: (Check those applicable and list names, addresses, and phone numbers on a separate sheet.)

_____ Architectural	_____ Lighting design	_____ Audio-visual
_____ Structural	_____ Asbestos abatement	_____ Security
_____ HVAC	_____ Graphics/signage	_____ Kitchen/food service
_____ Plumbing	_____ Acoustics	_____ Other (describe)
_____ Electrical		

Are existing drawings available?	Yes	No
If so, have they been checked for accuracy?	Yes	No
Are there building standard conditions that must be matched or maintained?	Yes	No
Is there a workletter that limits improvements to leased space?	Yes	No
If so, attach to this survey.		
Does the building management have standard conditions regarding the work of contractors that must be incorporated into the project manual?	Yes	No
If so, attach copy.		
Who awards contracts?	Bldg. Mgmt.	Tenant
Other (describe).		

Codes and Regulations:

List applicable codes.

Does space currently comply?	Yes	No

If no, describe conditions that must be corrected.

List applicable provisions of ADA accessibility guidelines.

Figure 6.2

Is an occupancy permit required?	Yes	No
What approvals are required?	State/Local Officials	Fire Marshal
Other (describe).		
Does intended use conform to zoning requirements?	Yes	No
If no, describe variances required and process to obtain.		

Physical and Structural Conditions:

Floor Construction. (List materials and description. Indicate thresholds or transitions.)		
Will there be any heavy loads such as concentrated file areas or fixed equipment such as vaults or commercial food service equipment that may require structural engineering analysis?	Yes	No
If yes, describe.		
Wall/partition construction. (List materials and description.)		
Is finish material at exterior walls to remain?	Yes	No
If yes, describe.		
Will there be any requirement to cut openings in existing structural components?	Yes	No
If yes, describe.		
Are there noticeable structural defects such as floors not level, walls out of plumb, major cracks, etc.?	Yes	No
If so, describe.		
Size and material of studs.		
Thickness of plaster, drywall, or other finish.		
Size and type of windows.		
Are windows operable?	Yes	No
If so, note clearances to be maintained.		
Interior material and color of sash.		

Figure 6.2 (continued)

Can they be painted?	Yes	No
Height of sill above floor.		
Material and color.		
Is there a building standard window treatment?	Yes	No
If so, describe.		
Does building management supply?	Yes	No
What is ceiling height?		
Material and construction.		
Must it be maintained or matched?	Yes	No
If yes, describe.		
Existing doors and hardware (describe).		
Must these be maintained or matched?	Yes	No
If yes, provide specifications.		
Must hardware be masterkeyed to building system?	Yes	No
Baseboard height and material.		
Maintain or match?	Yes	No
Other trim (describe).		
Maintain or match?	Yes	No
Are there any existing materials or items to be salvaged for reuse?	Yes	No
If yes, describe.		
Finishes in building core and public spaces (describe).		
Are these to remain?	Yes	No
If not, how are new finishes to be coordinated?		

Mechanical:

Describe HVAC system. (Locate convectors, supply diffusers, return grilles, other terminal devices, thermostats, etc. and note sizes.)

Figure 6.2 (continued)

Are new plumbing fixtures required?	Yes	No
If so, can location of existing chases and wet columns be located?	Yes	No
Can ceiling cavity under floor be opened to run new piping?	Yes	No
(Locate standpipes, fire hose cabinets, sprinklers, and other plumbing specialties.)		

Electrical:

Type of cable/wire distribution system. (floor, ceilings, etc.)

Types of outlets and characteristics.

Height of outlets above floor.

Are there building standard light fixtures that must be used?	Yes	No
If so, describe.		
(Locate electrical and telephone panels, fire alarms, smoke detectors, emergency lights, lighted exit signs, door bells, card access doors, and other electrical specialties.)		
Does the building owner mandate the use of specific mechanical or electrical contractors with whom there is a maintenance agreement?	Yes	No
If yes, is the choice of new equipment and fixtures limited?	Yes	No
If yes, give particulars.		

Additional Comments: (List below any pertinent data not covered by this form.)

Figure 6.2 (continued)

CHAPTER 7

CONSTRUCTION BUDGETING AND ESTIMATING

Any discussion of cost budgets must focus on what items are included and what is excluded. Owners tend to look at the bottom line figure and lump together all expenses, including fees and incidental expenses. The design professional typically separates costs and considers construction cost separately.

Most designers would probably argue that the most important event in a project is the moment at which he or she conceives the essential character of the design. While we can't dispute the significance of this magical moment, it may rank second to the preparation of the initial budget. How you handle this one event may very well determine the success or failure of the entire design effort. There is an unwritten law stating that the first figure that is discussed will become the budget that is cast in stone. No one who hears the figure, or sees it scribbled on a scrap of paper, will ever forget it. Even if the project scope and design change significantly, it will remain the yardstick by which the project will be measured. Therefore, it's to your advantage to control budget preparation.

To exercise some control over the budgeting aspects of a project, and to keep the project on track, it's important to understand construction costs and to be able to analyze the factors that influence costs and construction schedules. In your initial discussions with the owner, he or she is likely to ask two questions: "How much will it cost?" and then, "When will it be finished?" If the client is comfortable with the first answer, that figure usually becomes the project budget. If the second answer seems reasonable, that deadline will be the basis for the project schedule. Understanding the importance of this scenario, the designer must develop the ability to deal effectively with costs and schedules. Unfortunately, there is no substitute for judgment gained through experience.

It's also important for the owner to realize that there is a difference between a designer's estimate and a contractor's bid quotation, since the designer has no control over actual costs. Too often design professionals become enmeshed in professional liability claims when an owner has budgeted in accordance with the designer's estimate, only to find that it was inadequate. The owner may then argue that he or she properly relied on the professional's expert evaluation.

A designer's inability to monitor project costs may have other serious implications. Some widely-used agreement forms obligate the designer to modify the Contract Documents to comply with any agreed-upon fixed cost limit when that fixed cost is exceeded by the lowest bonafide bid. What this means is that you may find yourself making extensive revisions at your own expense if you can't discipline yourself into designing within a stated budget. And you can't do that if you don't have some basic cost estimating savvy. Add to this the increased risk of a professional liability claim and it becomes clear that this isn't a topic the designer can ignore.

THE ESTIMATE

Since the term "estimate" is subject to misunderstanding—many owners interpret the design professional's estimate as some sort of guarantee—most design firms are careful about how they use the term. The most common way to avoid misunderstanding is to simply not label anything as an estimate, calling it instead an "Opinion of Probable Construction Cost" or some similar title. This may not successfully avoid legal pitfalls, but at least it begins to convey the idea that there is some room for variation.

Estimating (for the purpose of brevity, we'll continue to use the term) is not only important in helping to establish project budgets but the skill must be utilized to monitor costs and work throughout the project. It's amazing how quickly even the simplest project can veer out of control when no one thinks to monitor costs and potential costs. Only when you have a clear understanding of the nuances of a design and how they influence cost can you really begin to design with confidence.

Designers tend to be optimistic in estimating. They have a natural desire to over-promise in terms of both cost and time factors, simply because they become so enamored of their own work that they can't believe that it won't be translated into reality. Good cost monitoring is the mark of the mature professional; if you are an inexperienced designer, just remember that it's unlikely that a design professional was ever sued for preparing estimates that were too high (although that may be embarrassing) or forecasting construction schedules that were too long.

Estimate Variations

Estimating is an art, not a science. Most inexperienced designers have difficulty understanding this distinction and slavishly apply whatever unit prices they've collected along with accurately calculated quantities, expecting to arrive at an unassailable concluding figure. Sorry, but it's just not that way. Look at the bid tabulations for some recent projects that you know about. You will probably find that the variation between high and low bids is about 10% of the total cost. Where there may be some "courtesy" bids in the mix, a range of 20% would not be unusual. All of this indicates that there can be legitimate disagreement about the "correct" price. And keep in mind that this range applies to bids based on what are presumably complete documents. Knowing this, you should be able to see that all you're doing is making an informed forecast at best. The more you know about the conditions, the better your forecast. For example, if you were to predict the winning time in a 100-yard dash, you might arrive at an estimate of about 10 seconds. Under most circumstances, that would be a very good estimate. But, how good do you think it is if we told you that the race was to be run on a muddy uphill course by middle-aged competitors?

What are some of the common factors that may alter prices and affect your estimate? Some are listed below.

- Location is always a factor. In metropolitan areas, traffic congestion may be a problem in scheduling timely delivery of material. Conversely, a location far removed from common material sources may incur extra delivery charges.

- If the schedule is too tight, extensive overtime might be required to complete the project.
- Local bidding climates change from time to time. Where there is a great deal of construction, contractors tend to be less competitive by increasing their anticipated profits.
- Weather is not usually a factor in interior construction, but if your project is in a new building under construction that is not fully enclosed at the time your project is to start, or access is blocked by weather conditions, the resulting delay may have a heavy impact on your project costs.
- If your project is a very small one, ordinary cost figures will not usually apply.

There are no hard and fast rules about adjusting your estimate to cover these factors, but you should be sensitive to these potential problems and make some effort to address them.

Estimate Types

There are four types of estimates. They vary in the amount of time it takes to prepare them and the probability of their being accurate. The first two types are used primarily in the early stages of the project only. When the project takes on quantifiable form, more sophisticated types must be employed.

Order of Magnitude Estimates

An *order of magnitude* estimate is a ballpark estimate that is arrived at quickly, based on scanty information, and is intended to indicate only a rough range of probable cost. While it has considerable shortcomings, an owner may see an order of magnitude estimate and think it is a meticulously prepared analysis of real costs. With that in mind, be very careful about how this type of estimate gets used.

The advantage of the order of magnitude estimate lies in its ability to quickly assess the scope of the proposed work and relate it to the actual cost of a known project. To do this, the designer must have a background that includes dealing with cost analysis and an understanding of the ramifications of various conditions that may affect costs.

If you have good cost figures for a comparable project, you already have the basis for an order of magnitude estimate. In this instance, your estimate may consume only a few minutes of your time, and if your experience is such that you can quickly evaluate the factors involved and know that the projects being compared are truly comparable, you should have a valuable measurement. Of course, this is often difficult to do, and if your understanding is in error in any way, your estimate may be virtually worthless. For this reason, the prudent estimator always adds a large contingency factor, as much as 20%.

Square Foot Estimates The second type of estimate is the *square foot* estimate. It is similar to the order of magnitude estimate and almost as notorious in its inaccuracy. The square foot estimate requires a knowledge of costs from a comparable project, but it can be more effectively applied even when there is some disparity in the size of the projects. If the level of quality is essentially the same and the time separation has not been a period of wide cost fluctuations or inflation, costs per square foot ought to be very similar. Increased size increases economy because many fixed project costs tend to remain nearly identical— so the unit price for a smaller project will probably be slightly higher. Again, it takes some experience to be able to confidently evaluate these factors.

Designers are often quick to latch on to overall square foot or cubic foot figures and make broad assumptions about applying them. A designer might say something like "The ABC job cost so much per square foot and we're doing basically the same thing on the XYZ project. Since our budget is the same, we should be all right." But wait a minute! Perhaps the ABC project was located adjacent to a loading dock and the XYZ job is on the tenth floor of a building on a congested one-way street. How might material handling influence costs? What if access to the freight elevator is restricted to off-peak hours? Are construction schedules the same? What if the job must be done without disrupting adjacent occupied space? There are literally hundreds of factors, including the state of the local economy, that can affect the cost of the project. Unless you can control these variables or accurately assess their influence on costs, broad square foot figures are likely to be very misleading.

The square foot estimate is often completed in less than an hour. While it's usually a bit more reliable than the order of magnitude estimate, a contingency factor of about 15% is still warranted.

Components Estimates Instead of relying on an inconclusive square foot figure, the *components* estimate breaks the project into its significant components and tries to analyze the probable cost for each of them. The best way to begin this type of estimate is to compile actual costs from previous projects as they are reflected on the contractor's bid breakdown, commonly known as a schedule of values. You can immediately see that this estimate is more definitive than the previous two because it begins to tailor the estimate to specific items that actually appear on the new project.

By developing a separate cost for various elements in a project, you automatically exclude unusual items that may skew a square foot estimate. Also, by focusing on components, you are able to recognize potential "trade-offs." Instead of guessing how an upgraded product in one area will affect the projected square foot cost, you can plug in the probable cost in place of the deleted item and immediately have a feeling for how the total may be affected. This gives you a menu from which to pick and choose. By looking at the relative cost of components, you can select the mix that gives the proverbial "biggest bang for the buck."

Putting together a components estimate will probably consume several days even for a relatively small project, but the increased time spent usually presents large dividends. It is much more accurate than the other types discussed; the contingency factor might be reduced to about 10%.

Unit Price Estimates The *unit price* estimate is the method used by contractors to arrive at their bids. It's an exhaustive and time-consuming process and one that a design office would seldom undertake. Besides being very time consuming, it can be prepared only when the documents are at a stage of virtual completion. For that reason, it can't serve as a checkpoint during the production process. In the second place, it requires tracking down a great many separate prices, something most design professionals show little interest in doing. We feel, however, that every designer should go through the process at least once. Doing so will help the designer become aware of and appreciate the multitude of cost factors that don't ordinarily come to mind. Several factors related to the preparation of a unit price estimate are discussed in the following sections.

The Procedure. To perform a unit price estimate, the best way to start is to list every item that will go into the project. Use or devise a form that provides columns for material cost, labor cost, overhead and profit for the installing contractor if the item is normally a subcontracted one, and the total cost. (See *Chapter 8: The Construction Contract* for a discussion of contracting procedures.) After you've established a workable format for recording data, you are ready to begin. See Figure 7.1 for an example of a form that can be used for preparing an estimate.

Go through the drawings and specifications and make a list of items that aren't covered in sufficient detail or require decisions or clarifications. Lacking those items need not delay the estimate preparation unless they're major, but they will have to be accounted for before the estimate can be completed.

Then prepare a thorough takeoff. Measure and quantify everything that shows up in the documents as well as things that may not be indicated graphically. For example, toilet accessories may not be graphically indicated since they may be covered more adequately in the specifications, but since you know that they exist, you must account for them. Enter the items on your form and be sure to record the units. Try to calculate in units for which pricing is normally expressed. Figuring carpet in square feet when prices are usually quoted in square yards requires additional conversion. If you inadvertently fail to make the conversion, your estimate for that item will be in error by a factor of nine.

Most estimators like to use colored pencils to mark off items that have been measured. When that technique is used, the estimator can tell at a glance what has been done and what may have been overlooked. With a little experience you will begin to have an idea of what measurements can serve for more than one item. For example, if your project has extensive millwork trim, the lineal measurement for all running trim (base, chair rail, picture mold, and crown) may be identical. The only difference might be the interruption at door openings. But

Means Quantity Sheet

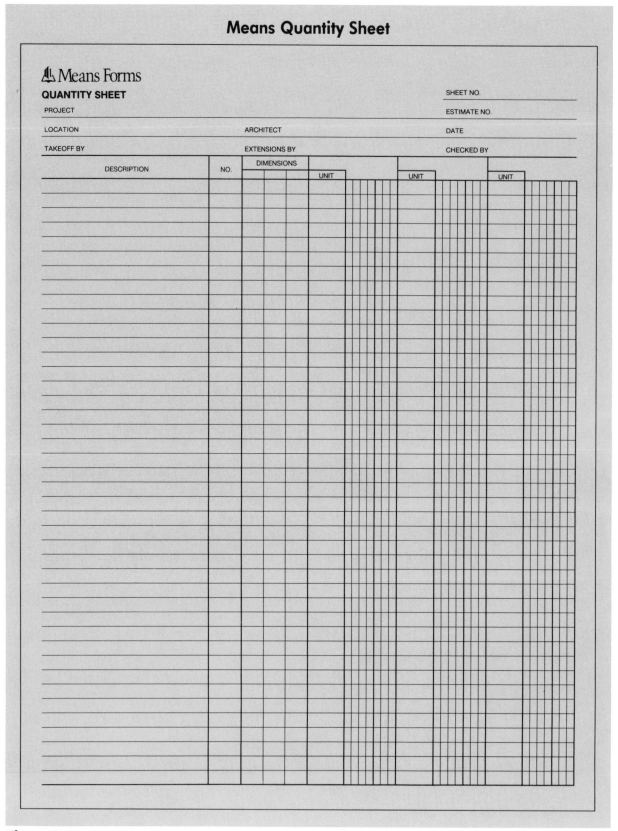

Figure 7.1

then, we would not subtract that quantity anyway. The few extra feet of material would be more than offset by the labor intensive activity of cutting and fitting.

Be creative in anticipating things that may not show up on the drawings. You know that every toilet room will have certain accessories. Account for them even though they might not appear graphically. Build the project in your mind. Anticipate every operation that must take place.

After you have established quantities and appropriate units, the difficult part (or fun part, depending on how you look at it) begins. Locate prices for every item and task you have identified. Assign a value to *everything*. Even if you have no reliable cost figure for a particular item, any value — even if it's a pure guess — is better than nothing at all. In reality, high and low guesses tend to offset each other.

Cost Information Sources. Where do prices come from? The most reliable sources are listed in order below:

1. A direct quotation from a contractor who is interested in actually performing the work.

2. A recent project for comparable work.

3. A project that wasn't entirely comparable but could be reasonably modified to reflect the change in conditions.

4. The option most often relied upon in most design offices is a price taken from a published cost index (see the *Recommended Readings* at the end of this book for some resources).

5. An educated guess — not a very good alternative, but better than nothing.

In any one estimate it is likely that you will use all of the sources described above.

You will find that most contractors will be willing, if not anxious, to provide you with cost information. If you give them specific enough information to work with, they'll respond with accurate pricing that truly reflects material and labor conditions in your specific area. After all, it's really in their interest to be cooperative. As a design professional you are in a position to see that they are given consideration in the selection of a contractor in a negotiated contract arrangement or, at the very least, added to the bidders list. Call them and give them as much information as you can. Don't ask them to calculate things you can do for yourself. If you establish a good rapport with local contractors, you will be able to assemble a great deal of accurate price information quickly and easily.

Suppliers, of course, are another source of cost information; they are more than willing to provide prices for the products they distribute. Remember, however, that they are not always objective and can give you accurate data only on material costs. Accept their guesses about installation costs and their analysis of the costs of competing products with some question.

Previous projects for which you have good cost information are an excellent source for a current estimate, but make sure that the items you are pricing are really identical. If you ascertain any minor differences, you may be able to adjust costs to reflect them. For example, if the installation cost for a particular product is known, you may safely use that figure even if the new product you're intending to use carries an increased material cost.

While the use of published cost indices helps to fill in the voids where accurate local cost figures cannot be easily obtained, they should not be relied upon to the exclusion of better pricing information. Most experienced estimators prefer to use such sources as a quick check against costs that are generated by other channels and not as a sole cost authority. They should not be used as a substitute for informed judgment and analysis of specific applications. Too many designers use unit costs from handy references and apply them directly without adjusting them as the cost indices invariably instruct. Costs may vary from one locality to another by as much as 40–50%. Also, prices fluctuate in roughly the same way as the general economy, so modifications must be made to compensate for the time lag between the time a price is generated and the actual time frame for your project's construction.

Additional Cost Items. The line item costs you generate don't tell the whole story. You must also consider waste. If your design requires extensive cutting of stock materials in a way that produces a significant amount of waste, you must account not only for the increased quantity of material but also for increased labor to make the installation. Also, if your design uses small quantities of a material and the contractor is forced to purchase the product in a larger quantity than is actually required, you must include the cost of the larger quantity.

You also need to flag items that are normally subcontracted and add overhead and profit for the installing contractor. This amount can vary from about 15% for major and extensive subcontracts to 20–25% for small subcontracts performed by specialty contractors. To the subtotal for all work, you must add an amount for what we usually call General Conditions. This includes the cost of bonds, insurance, taxes, permit and inspection fees, and similar project-related costs. This amount typically ranges from 6% to 10%. The contractor, of course, will have to add his or her own figure for overhead and profit. Overhead includes the cost of construction equipment, project supervision, temporary facilities and utilities, disposable supplies, and home office expenses related to the project. These expenses can vary widely from one contractor to another but allowing an additional 10% is common. The allocation of profit is a management decision and usually falls between 7% and 15%. You'll have to assess market conditions and decide for yourself just how "hungry" bidders are apt to be.

Rounding Off Numbers. Working with odd quantities is cumbersome — rounding off to a more workable number tends to compensate for waste without having to actually account for it. Likewise, you would never present to a client an estimate of $263,437. An estimate of $275,000 is every bit as valid and, in reality, expressing it as a range of $250,000–300,000 is probably just as accurate. Many design professionals prefer to do just that, if for no other reason than it reinforces the fact that the estimate is not a guarantee of actual cost and cannot be so without fully accepted final specifications.

As you extend each line item you will be faced with the problem of having to round off. Some estimators round off all three-digit figures to the next higher $10, all four-digit figures to the next higher $100, and so on. The guidelines you adopt for rounding figures should be used consistently. There are some estimators who do not round off individual line items, claiming that to do so invites errors. They point out that:

- It is rare to make an error in transcribing an uneven figure.

- In transcribing rounded-off figures, it can be easy to write $100 or $10,000 instead of $1000.
- When using a calculator to add a column of rounded-off figures, you might hit one too many — or too few — zeros without realizing it.

There is no "correct" or preferred way to deal with rounding off — but whichever method you adopt should be followed consistently.

Computer-Based Estimating Programs The preparation of a unit cost estimate may take a week or more to complete. You might speed up some of the process by using a computer as a "numbers crunching" tool if you can effectively set up the takeoff and pricing information you've generated within a database program. Remember, however, that to have continuing value the data you produce will have to be regularly and systematically updated. Some design professionals purchase computer-based estimating programs with the idea that these programs are the ultimate tool for setting up and producing valid estimates. These programs undoubtedly range from excellent to worthless but they all have some drawbacks. They can only retrieve stored data — if that information is in error, the result will have no value. Perhaps the greatest advantage to such programs is that if they are comprehensive, they will create a convenient checklist. A single line item can be corrected, updated, or changed and be immediately reflected in the total.

A computer will do whatever it is capable of with lightning speed but it will not unroll a set of drawings, read a project manual, do a takeoff, consider special project conditions, or perform a calculation for which it has no data entry or stored information.

Contingency Factors The question of a contingency factor with a unit cost estimate should become a non-issue. If you have been careful to prepare an estimate that is reasonably conservative in the calculation of quantities and costs, it should fall within a normal bid spread without adding any contingency. While it is in your interest to be conservative, the bidders must engage in some judicious risk-taking. That's the only way they have of successfully competing.

Estimating Construction Time

The problem of estimating construction time is extremely difficult. There are simply too many unknown (and sometimes unknowable) factors to consider. One simple item that cannot be obtained at the time it is needed can influence hundreds of other items and set a project back by weeks. Scheduling is not necessarily related to project size, either in quantity of space or cost. We've all seen million dollar projects that are completed in a month or two, while a ten thousand dollar job can languish for twice as long. With that in mind, here are some rules of thumb for projects of medium complexity with average quality for materials and finishes:

- Small projects ($100,000 and under) tend to take an average of 3 to 4 months for construction.
- Projects up to one million dollars average 4 to 5 months to construct.
- Projects costing from $1,000,000 to 2,000,000 generally require 7 to 8 months for construction.

The best way to attack a time estimate is to start with a checklist of tasks to be completed. Since every project has different requirements — the typical project might include literally hundreds of tasks to be accomplished — it's impossible to prepare a checklist that would serve all projects. It must be done individually for each project. The list should normally start with demolition, followed by floor leveling (if required), partition layout, mechanical and electrical rough in, wallboard installation, and so on, leading to the final tasks such as carpet installation, painting touch-up, and other miscellaneous finishing activities leading up to the owner's move-in.

Recognize that virtually every operation is performed by a specific group of craftspeople, usually called "trades." Some trades may work together simultaneously while others cannot even begin until the work of another is complete. A general contractor will advise you on the logical sequence of work for a particular project. Different regions have different criteria resulting from weather, codes, and inspection requirements. Once you have a checklist, develop a list of products required, noting any that may not be readily available "off the shelf." Check those for long lead items and note how their delay might affect other work. With these potential delays in mind, establish a probable duration for every task. Old project records can be an invaluable aid here. Finally, establish a logical sequence in which the tasks might be accomplished. At this time it should be apparent that some tasks must precede others. Some cannot begin until others are completed; still others can overlap or be performed in parallel.

Once you have a rudimentary feel for how the project will proceed, lay out the tasks on a simple time line. This activity should establish a probable project duration; from it, you can develop a bar-chart schedule that should give a reasonably accurate overview. If scheduling is a crucial factor, it is also a good idea to plot the critical path through the tasks. The critical path simply indicates which tasks, if delayed, extend the total project duration. This process will sometimes reveal that the inclusion of certain long lead items in the project comes at a juncture when other activities absorb the extra time without affecting the overall schedule.

SUMMARY

This chapter has examined construction cost issues and related scheduling concerns that influence all phases of every project. It is presented in this sequence primarily because it addresses the preparation of the initial budget, which often becomes the overriding determinant for all subsequent activities.

Monitoring probable costs is an ongoing process that the project manager cannot afford to ignore. At every juncture, as additional information becomes available, the project manager must update cost estimates to maintain control. If this isn't done, costly excursions in trial and error condoned in the name of design tend to creep into the process almost unnoticed. When this is allowed to happen, the project costs get quickly out of control and painful major surgery is required to salvage the project.

Once you've mastered the techniques of estimating both cost and schedule and understand how many different considerations become interwoven in the process, the other tasks that make up project management ought to be more easily handled.

CHAPTER 8

THE CONSTRUCTION CONTRACT

Virtually all construction is performed under contract. Occasionally an owner (the client) will maintain a staff that is capable of executing small projects, but this is relatively rare and, even when it does apply, the effect on the designer is usually minor. Your documents may be somewhat less formal, and the instruments designed to support and clarify the agreement between owner and contractor may be omitted. On other occasions, your client may be a contractor. In this situation, your documents may be tailored to permit the Owner/Builder to more easily subcontract specific portions of the work. In this chapter, we will discuss the most common approach—the classic construction contract in which the owner and the contractor are separate entities—as well as the documents (other than the drawings and specifications) that form the Contract Documents, which set the parameters of the contract. Drawings and specifications will be discussed in later chapters. A simple illustration of the elements of the Contract Documents appears in Figure 8.1.

Examples of the Contract Documents described in this chapter will be illustrated with the Sample Project in Chapter 15.

WHAT IS A CONSTRUCTION CONTRACT?

A contract is an agreement between two parties to exchange something of value within a stated time period. If the value of the contract is substantial, as virtually all construction contracts are, it is usually put in writing to avoid any misunderstanding. If the value is negligible, the contract may be a verbal agreement. Although there is an old gag line that says, "A verbal contract isn't worth the paper it's written on," verbal agreements are binding and so common that each of us is likely to make one on any given day. If you admire a friend's possession and offer to purchase it from her for a stated sum and she agrees to sell it, you have made a contract. What she agrees to sell and what you agree to pay constitutes value — what the law calls "consideration" — and the time for performance is understood by both parties as being in the present.

To reach an agreement, one party has to make an offer and the other party must accept. Negotiation involves making offers and counter-offers until there is acceptance and an agreement is struck. Sometimes two parties to a contract do not deal with each other on a one-to-one or face-to-face basis. One or the other engages a consultant or specialist to establish the criteria and compose the offer required for the other party to make an offer. An example of this is when an owner proposes to contract with a general contractor to construct or remodel a building for the owner's company. The owner will engage an architect and/or designer to design the details for the building or remodeling. The designer functions as the intermediary who creates and establishes the criteria (that is, the design) on which offers will be based. Bidders are invited to submit offers (bids) in response to the established criteria. If the owner

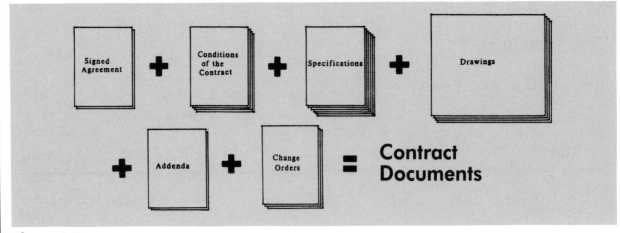

Figure 8.1

receives an offer that serves the owner's interests, the owner accepts it and a contract is forged.

Although the design forms the basis of the construction contract, the designer is not a party to the contract. The designer is engaged by the owner under a separate contract of defined scope of services (see *Chapter 2: Contract Negotiation*). The designer functions as the owner's representative, but the agreement is between the owner and the contractor. Although the designer may have been given wide latitude in the preparation of the Contract Documents, once the contract is executed the designer may not change it in any way without the mutual agreement of the parties to the contract. Designers often regard the design as their personal property and frequently do not understand this basic concept. They feel that they should be free to make changes for whatever reasons they feel are valid. In instances where extra costs are not involved, tacit agreement or lack of objection by the parties may allow the designer to function in this manner, but it is always a risky course of action.

Only if you comprehend the principles stated above, and understand the tremendous responsibility you undertake in framing the contract, can you proceed with the preparation of documents. There are methods that have stood the test of time in meeting and solving problems. That doesn't mean that there aren't alternatives, but it does mean that if you disregard some fundamental concepts, you could create problems for everyone. Our discussion will attempt to focus on methods for dealing with common problems and leave you with more time for creative efforts—which is why you became a designer in the first place.

TYPES OF CONTRACTS

The vast majority of construction projects are executed under a single lump sum contract. Although the lump sum contract is the form you will most likely deal with on a consistent basis, you should realize that there are other types of contract structures that you may need to address from time to time.

The Single Lump Sum Contract

Under a *single lump sum contract,* the contract is awarded to a "general contractor." The general contractor may perform all of the work of the project using workers or tradespeople who are his or her employees.

At the opposite end of the spectrum is the large general contractor who subcontracts the various elements of the project to others who specialize in certain trades or specialties needed to complete the project. Both of these scenarios are extremes. A middle road is most common: The general contractor executes some of the work with his or her own employees and subcontracts only those portions that can be done more effectively by others. In any case, the subcontractors do not become a party to the agreement between the owner and the contractor. Therefore, the owner has no direct relationship with them, and you as the owner's representative cannot deal with them directly. All communication must go through the owner to the general contractor.

The relationships in a typical lump sum contract are illustrated in the flow chart in Figure 8.2.

The Negotiated Contract

Sometimes a *negotiated contract* is employed. There is no official bidding involved in the negotiated contract except as the selected contractor sees fit to request of various subcontractors. The contractor is selected on the basis of his or her credentials and enters into negotiations with the owner to arrive at a contract sum.

In some instances, the contractor is engaged very early in the project and has input into some of the design decisions by providing cost parameters in a process that is commonly known as *value engineering*. If this technique is utilized properly, it can benefit everyone involved by setting viable alternatives for reaching design decisions, ensuring that the budget is not exceeded, and, in most instances, saving time, resulting in earlier completion. In addition, the documents may be more effectively prepared by concentrating on aspects that better serve the particular contractor.

The preparation of Contract Documents for a negotiated contract is essentially the same as for a single lump sum contract.

The Segregated Contract

In a *segregated contract,* there are a number of separate prime contractors—one for each major portion of the work. Each separate contractor may have his or her own subcontractors. Under this arrangement, there is no single entity responsible for the total scope of

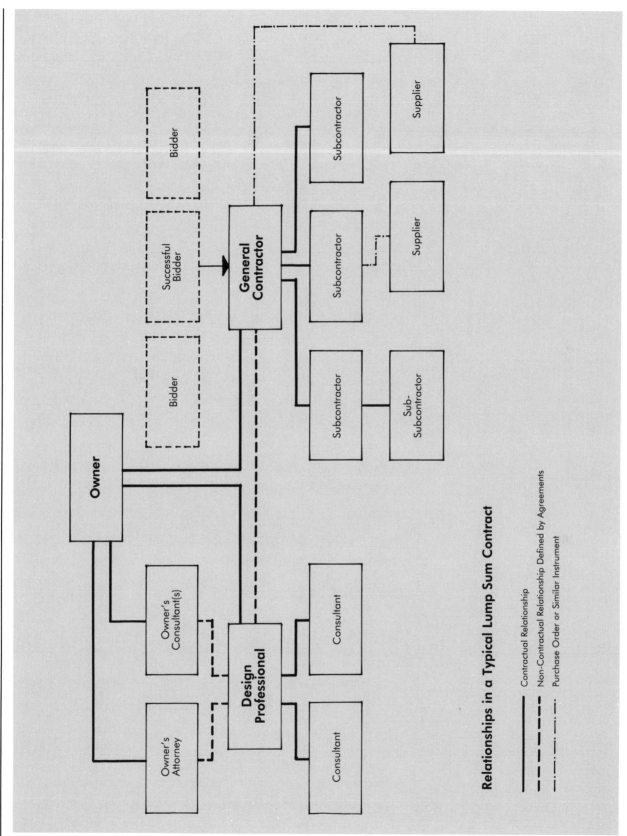

Relationships in a Typical Lump Sum Contract

——————— Contractual Relationship

– – – – – – – Non-Contractual Relationship Defined by Agreements

–·–··–··– Purchase Order or Similar Instrument

Figure 8.2

the work—the task of coordinating the work of a number of contractors rests with the owner, who often relies on the design professional to act as coordinator. In addition, the designer must prepare documents in such a way that multiple contracts may be awarded.

Considering the extra work and the increased risk of conflicts, why would one ever use such an arrangement? Two reasons:

- The owner may feel that by eliminating the general contractor's role and the overhead and profit charged for coordinating the work of subcontractors, he or she will save money. Unless the owner is sophisticated and adept in construction and experienced in handling projects of similar scope, the savings, if any, are likely to be so minimal that they aren't worth the extended effort.

- Some jurisdictions have laws that require segregated contracts for publicly-funded projects. These statutes are grounded in the same basic premise as stated above—that there will be substantial savings to taxpayers by limiting the general contractor's overhead and profit while creating more competition in bidding. Again, the savings are likely to be illusory but the practice will probably continue because large specialty contractors tend to lobby for this method, which gives them a greater degree of autonomy.

There are instances where segregated contracts work well, but most design professionals who have experience with them are reluctant to advise a client to pursue this route.

The Cost Plus Contract

In a *cost plus contract,* the selected contractor agrees to complete the work of the project for whatever amount it costs him or her *plus* a fixed fee or a percentage of the cost to cover overhead and profit. On one hand, this is an equitable arrangement. The contractor cannot lose money and the owner is assured of getting exactly what he or she pays for. On the other hand, in this arrangement the contractor has no real incentive to save money for the owner.

When a cost plus fee contract is used, the fixed fee arrangement usually works better than a percentage basis. A percentage of cost is open-ended, and even the most scrupulous and conscientious contractor may be under suspicion of inflating costs. In addition, if something goes wrong on the project, the relationship between the owner and the contractor is likely to deteriorate rapidly.

A typical twist to the cost plus contract is the inclusion of what is called an "upset price" or an "amount not to be exceeded." This arrangement places some constraints on the contractor and, coupled with a well-defined system of accounting for costs, can work well. The guaranteed maximum cost structure, however, works only when the Contract Documents are carefully prepared and fully complete. Otherwise, there is a built-in potential for dispute arising from the contractor's claim that work incompletely or improperly done falls outside the scope of the project as understood when he or she agreed to the upset price.

One of the more creative ways of dealing with the inherent dilemmas of the cost plus arrangement is to set up a procedure whereby the contractor is encouraged to suggest means of saving costs and then share in the resulting savings. For example, if the contractor proposes to furnish an alternative, but fully acceptable, material for a stipulated saving, his or her fee would be increased by some prearranged percentage of that saving. Again, an accurate method of cost accounting and verification, along with complete and well-prepared documents, is essential.

The Construction Manager Contract

Yet another type of contract is a somewhat hybrid form called a *construction manager contract*. It is typically not a contract at all; it's a commitment by an individual or firm to administer what is usually a segregated contract. This individual is simply the broker-contractor in a different role.

The term "construction manager" is used so indiscriminately that it's difficult to pin down the meaning unless one knows the specific conditions of the project. The construction manager, in whatever form, most often comes into play on large architectural and engineering projects; you are not likely to encounter a construction manager unless you are working on a project that is part of a larger-scale project.

Review of Contract Types

When considering the types of construction contracts, remember that you as the designer are not a party to the contract, but it is your work that frames and defines it. It's an awesome responsibility and one that shouldn't be undertaken until you have a clear understanding of the role of the Contract Documents and of the relevance of the separate instruments on specific contract types.

Another important consideration is that, to be able to advise your client, you must understand the salient points of various contract types. See Figure 8.3 for a summary of the contract types we have discussed. While each type has certain advantages that may neatly dovetail with the conditions of a specific project, it is the "tried and true" single lump sum contract resulting from competitive bidding that is usually the most satisfactory arrangement for the widest variety of circumstances.

In any event, the primary item that produces an equitable contract that protects the interests of all and results in a superior project is a set of carefully prepared, thoroughly professional Contract Documents, which include the Agreement and the Conditions of the Contract.

THE AGREEMENT

The *Agreement* is a relatively simple document that legally binds the owner and the contractor. It must fulfill five fundamental tasks:

1. Identify the agreeing parties
2. Identify the work to be performed by the contractor
3. Set forth the terms of payment for the work (what the law calls *consideration*)
4. State the time for performance
5. Be sealed with the signatures of the parties

The signed agreement, commonly referred to as the "contract," is actually just one element of several that make up the contract. The other elements include the Conditions of the Contract, the Drawings, and the Specifications. These three elements, along with the Agreement plus any modifications in the form of addenda (incorporated before the agreement is signed) or change orders (incorporated after the agreement is signed), make up the contract. The individual elements are collectively known as the *Contract Documents*. The basic qualities of a valid contract are listed in Figure 8.4.

The concepts related to Contract Documents are fundamental to the entire process, but to many design professionals trained in aesthetics, they seem like pretty dull stuff. Understand, however, that you cannot bring anything but the smallest project to a successful conclusion

Summary of Contract Types

Single Lump Sum	Contractor is prime party responsible for the construction of the project. Executes some work with own employees; subcontracts more specialized work in separate agreements. No direct relationship between owner and subcontractors.
Negotiated	Contractor is selected and then negotiates with owner to arrive at contract sum.
Segregated	Several contractors are engaged, each of which accomplishes a major portion or stage of the work. Owner must coordinate work of contractors.
Cost Plus	Contractor completes work for cost plus a fixed fee or percentage of the total for overhead and profit. "Upset price" places limits on contractor's profit.
Construction Manager	Individual contractor or firm is hired to administer what is usually a segregated contract. Construction manager provides continuous management of the project.

Figure 8.3

without a thorough grounding in the principles that govern all construction projects embodied in the agreement and its accompanying conditions.

Forms of Agreement

There are a number of preprinted agreement forms available for use. Most design professionals prefer those developed by the American Institute of Architects (AIA). If you are using the AIA preprinted General Conditions (discussed later in this chapter), it is almost imperative that you use one of the companion documents because they are designed to work together. Since the Agreement and the General Conditions together form a complete document, mixing documents of different origin invariably creates conflicts. Some governmental agencies require the use of their own forms coupled with their own version of the

Qualities of a Valid Contract	
Legal	Content-Enforceable
	Form
	Language
I.D.	Correct Names
	Addresses
	Signature
	(Seal)
Offer (Bid)	Responsive
	Correct Sum
	Signature/Seal
Acceptance	By Responsible Party
	Correct Signature/Seal
	Correct Sum
	Exhibits/Attachments
Technical Competence	Professionally Prepared
	Complete
	Legally Reviewed
	Properly Issued/Bid

From *The Building Professional's Guide to Contract Documents* (R.S. Means, 1990).

Figure 8.4

general conditions. These are usually satisfactory when used strictly for the type and scope of projects they were intended to address but you should review them carefully, particularly for provisions that have an impact on your services and responsibilities.

Every owner thinks that his or her project is unique. Of course it is, but not all projects are so different that they warrant the drafting of a unique agreement. If an owner, or owner's attorney, entertains such notions, you are well advised to dissuade them if at all possible. Agreements that are different and unfamiliar are usually met with resistance by the contractor, and rightly so. After all, if the contractor is familiar with standard agreement forms, he or she automatically knows the ground rules for administering the contract. Presented with another document, the contractor is likely to wonder what potential traps are set within its clauses. Likewise, discourage an unsophisticated owner from assuming that he or she can undertake a construction project under the terms of a purchase order. As we have stated, a purchase order may be adequate for buying office supplies but it is clearly inadequate for dealing with the complex issues of construction.

The AIA Standard Form of Agreement for Construction

Services AIA Document A101 "Standard Form of Agreement Between Owner and Contractor where the Basis of Payment is a Stipulated Sum" is perhaps the most common and familiar agreement form in use. It neatly dovetails with AIA Document A201 "General Conditions." Together they form a comprehensive document that addresses the needs of virtually all construction projects. These documents are shown with the Sample Project in Chapter 15.

The cover page of A101 establishes the date of the agreement, identifies the parties to the agreement, identifies the project, and names the architect (or design professional). The essential terms of the agreement begin on page 2. **Article 1** simply defines the contract documents and **Article 2** defines the scope of work. Specific items of work that will be performed outside the scope of the contract should be enumerated here. For example, if the installation of some equipment, such as the owner's computer system, is to be done under a separate contract, this fact should be so stated.

Article 3 should be reviewed with care because it establishes the time for performance, an essential element of the agreement. The date of commencement is usually the date of the agreement itself or a date established in a Notice to Proceed, which is often issued concurrently with the agreement but, in some cases, may be delayed for a variety of reasons (such as the need to wait until specific approvals are received). Article 2 also establishes the date of substantial completion and provides for liquidated damages for failure to complete the project on time if this provision is applicable. (This provision is discussed later in this chapter in the section "Contract Time.")

Article 4 states the contract sum and identifies any accepted alternates that are included in the contract. If the decision on alternates is delayed beyond the execution of the agreement, a schedule of such alternates should be inserted along with the period of time the prices for those alternates will remain valid. Paragraph 4.3 identifies any unit prices or allowances that are defined in the contract documents.

Progress payments are covered in **Article 5.** Normally the contractor submits an Application for Payment each month for work completed within the calendar month, but other periods or stages of payment may be agreed upon and inserted in Article 5. Usually the contractor is instructed to submit an Application within five to seven days following the payment period for the designer's review and approval. The owner agrees to make payment within the following five to seven days. Obviously, all of these are variables and can be written to reflect actual circumstances that may apply.

Paragraph 5.6.1 sets retainage, which is usually 10%. The contractor is not paid in full for work completed; instead, a certain amount is set aside to protect the owner and is released as part of the final payment. Retainage also applies to stored materials; this percentage is entered in Paragraph 5.6.2. Upon substantial completion, the contractor is normally paid all but the accrued retainage, plus an amount sufficient to pay for any uncompleted work should he or she fail to fully complete the work.

Under some contracts, particularly for large projects, the percentage of the retainage is reduced as the work moves satisfactorily toward completion. This can take several forms. Typically, when the project reaches a point where it is estimated to be 50% complete, subsequent invoices are paid in full and the retainage accrued to that point remains a fixed amount. This means that if the original retainage was 10%, it would apply only to the first 50% of the project. At the completion of the project, a total of 5% of the contract sum would be withheld. If reduction or other limitations on retainage are agreed upon, those terms should be inserted under Paragraph 5.8.

Article 6 sets forth conditions for the final payment; space is provided for the insertion of special requirements if it is desirable to include them. Sometimes final payment is delayed pending receipt of specific approvals or permits; those requirements are detailed here.

Article 7, "Miscellaneous Provisions," allows the insertion of interest due on any unpaid approved payments.

Article 8 invokes the terms of the General Conditions relative to termination or suspension of the project.

Article 9 enumerates the contract documents, including documents contained in the project manual, the specifications, the drawings, and any addenda. All elements may be enumerated and listed in detail, although it is common practice to simply identify them and describe them as exhibits attached to the agreement. Bidding documents, including such instruments as Instructions to Bidders and the bid itself, are not automatically part of the contract documents (bidding documents will be covered in Chapter 9). If, however, it is desirable to include them, they can be enumerated and inserted under Paragraph 9.1.7. Most professionals never do this since the salient points covered in these documents are effectively supplanted by the agreement itself. There are some, however, who like to incorporate these instruments, reasoning that in the case of a dispute, they help to establish the chronology of the project, which may be essential in establishing certain points and intent.

The last page of the form provides space for the parties to sign the agreement. This form, when properly filled out and executed, fulfills the five fundamental tasks set forth earlier in this section.

Review the agreement form and the conditions of the contract included for the Sample Project in Chapter 15. Pay particular attention to how they support each other and together form the heart of the Contract Documents. Once you understand the role of these documents, you should be able to see how important they are to the success of a project and why they must be so carefully coordinated.

CONDITIONS OF THE CONTRACT

The *Conditions of the Contract* are part and parcel of the agreement itself. Their provisions may be thought of as the "fine print" of the agreement. In fact, some standard agreement forms incorporate the provisions within the agreement form itself. The Conditions of the Contract usually appear as a separate document, mainly because their requirements govern all work under the contract and are needed for reference by many people who are not privy to the other terms of the agreement. This is particularly important for privately funded work where the owner may have valid reasons for keeping some aspects of the agreement confidential.

The Conditions of the Contract are usually comprised of two separate documents – the General Conditions and the Supplementary Conditions. Since the General Conditions usually appear as a preprinted document, the Supplementary Conditions are used to expand their terms and modify them to suit the requirements of a specific project. Since the Supplementary Conditions are used only to modify the General Conditions, they are part of the General Conditions and cannot stand alone.

General Conditions

The General Conditions define the rights, responsibilities, and relationship of the parties to the agreement. They also deal with the rights and responsibilities of third parties, such as the design professional. In short, they define the basic rules under which the construction is to be undertaken, including a wide variety of contract administration activities.

Preprinted General Conditions are published by the American Institute of Architects (AIA), the National Society of Professional Engineers (NSPE), and the American Society of Civil Engineers (ASCE). These documents are widely used for private work. Some governmental agencies have their own forms, which may be mandated for use on public work. Even some large corporations employ their own documents, which are sometimes called "General Provisions" or "Standard Terms and Conditions." AIA Document A201, "General Conditions of the Contract for Construction," traces its lineage back over 100 years; this alone makes it a valuable document. It has been revised and "fine tuned" many times in its history and has established many legal precedents. It is familiar to virtually everyone engaged in the construction industry and its use ensures that all basic contractual-legal provisions are thoroughly covered in a way that protects all parties. Another advantage of Document A201 is that it is part of a family of documents, with each companion document supporting the other documents in a logical and cohesive fashion.

The problem with government versions and those drafted by corporation attorneys is that they have often been pieced together by individuals who may be well versed in the law but have little knowledge of construction. They sometimes include a hodge-podge of unrelated and conflicting information couched in esoteric legal terminology. They also tend to be unbalanced, protecting the interests of the owner at everyone else's expense. All of this produces confusion and leads to a high incidence of litigation. From time to time you may have a client who insists on using his or her own version of the General Conditions. When this happens, you have no recourse other than to take extra care in understanding how its use may influence construction administration, plan accordingly, and perhaps check with your own legal counsel.

Supplementary Conditions

Construction projects, regardless of size and scope, have a great degree of similarity. It is for this reason that a preprinted standard form can address the issues most common to all projects. At the same time, we must recognize that no two projects are ever identical — each has unique aspects that must be covered in ways that no standard form could ever achieve. Also, the General Conditions include provisions that apply to the vast number of projects but may be irrelevant to a specific one. This is why the Supplementary Conditions must be prepared for each project — to tailor the General Conditions to the specifics of that project.

The Supplementary Conditions are intended to accomplish the following:

- Modify the General Conditions to suit particular requirements, such as specific amounts of insurance coverage.
- Delete material from the General Conditions that may be inapplicable to a particular project. The owner, for example, may wish to delete all references to arbitration of disputes, preferring to leave open other avenues for dispute resolution.
- Insert additional provisions, such as a requirement for the payment of predetermined prevailing wage rates or the inclusion of equal employment opportunity requirements.

Supplementary Conditions modify the contractual conditions of the agreement and have broad legal implications that should be reviewed by the owner and his or her legal counsel. On the other hand, administrative and procedural requirements for contract administration, those items typically characterized as "housekeeping" chores, are inherently part of the specifications and should be included in Division 1 — General Requirements. Initially this distinction may be a bit confusing, but as you become familiar with the standard General Conditions and how they apply, you will begin to understand the unique roles that the various documents are meant to play.

We have used AIA Document A201 for the Sample Project in Chapter 15, along with specially prepared Supplementary Conditions. You may use this as a guide along with the excellent AIA publication entitled "Guide for Supplementary Conditions" (AIA Document A511), which walks through the General Conditions article by article, giving suggested wording for modifications that most often occur.

Since Supplementary Conditions are unique to each project, it would be unwise to attempt to prepare a boilerplate document intended to be used for all your projects, no matter how similar they may be. You will find, however, that after preparing this document for a number of projects, common phrasing of substantial portions may appropriately reappear in several projects.

Besides specific examples you may find in the Sample Project or other sources, some of the more common General Conditions clauses amended by the Supplementary Conditions are:

- Article 4, Administration of the Contract, assumes that the design professional with responsibility for contract administration is an architect. If you are *not* an architect, you will want to modify this article and all other references from "architect" to "design professional" (or other appropriate title).

- Paragraph 4.5 requires that arbitration under Construction Industry Arbitration Rules of the American Arbitration Association be used to resolve all construction disputes. Most design professionals endorse this procedure and recognize its effectiveness but on occasion you may find an owner, or his or her attorney, who is uncomfortable with surrendering the right to pursue other legal options.

- Paragraphs 9.3 and 9.4 set forth requirements concerning applications for and certificates for payment. Some owners may have other procedures mandated by internal accounting practices that require certain modifications here.

- Article 11 discusses provisions for bonds and insurance in very general terms and must be expanded for every project to address the specific project requirements.

Review of Conditions of the Contract

It is important to understand that Conditions of the Contract establish the basic "rules of the game" and are an essential element of the Contract Documents. The Conditions are usually comprised of preprinted General Conditions (to which the Construction Specifications Institute assigns the organizational number 00700) and project-specific Supplementary Conditions (CSI 00800), which modify or expand the provisions of the General Conditions.

Again, it is always wise to use standard General Conditions because they are tailored to construction practices, have stood the test of time, and are well known and understood by design professionals and contractors.

CONTRACT TIME

The contract time, an essential element of the contract, is set forth in the Agreement. Despite its inclusion there, it is difficult to enforce. When the construction of a project exceeds the time limit — an all-too-common situation — it is technically a breach of the contract. However, if no damages are suffered by the owner, the breach is avoided or remedied by extending the contract time by change order. When the contractor flagrantly neglects the work and fails to complete the project on time, the owner has limited recourse. The owner can, with proper notice, terminate the contract and discharge the contractor. The owner may then invoke the provisions of a performance bond, if one has been provided, or engage another contractor to complete the project. Any costs incurred can be charged against the original contract by withholding payments due. If those costs exceed the outstanding amount, the owner may have no recourse other than to sue for damages. In any event, any termination action is likely to result in protracted legal proceedings. For this reason, every avenue short of legal action should be pursued first.

Commencement and Completion Dates

The commencement date and the completion date should be carefully covered. The bid form often extracts a pledge to begin work immediately upon execution of the agreement. If the time between the opening of bids and the signing of the agreement is an extended period and the time for completion is expressed as a specific date, the contractor is placed at a significant disadvantage. Most design professionals prefer to handle this problem by calling for work to start on a specific date identified in a "Notice to Proceed," and to be substantially completed in a specific number of calendar days thereafter. The Notice to Proceed is not issued until the agreement is signed.

If the execution of the agreement is delayed for any reason and there is some question about the urgency of starting work or placing orders for long-lead items, the owner should consider issuing a "Letter of Intent." This instrument simply acknowledges that the owner intends to enter into a contract and provides for payment for work performed in advance of that event. The contractor is then protected if something prevents the execution of the agreement.

Liquidated Damage Clause When the nature of a project is such that the owner will suffer losses if completion is delayed beyond the time limits established in the agreement, he or she may be able to recover damages from the contractor. These damages may include loss of revenue, payment of rent for other premises, and similar provable situations. The owner has no recourse if the only loss is inconvenience or disappointment at not being able to occupy the new project.

If no provision is provided to protect the owner, he or she would be forced to pursue legal action, which would undoubtedly consume a great deal of time and additional expense. To avoid having to prove losses and engage in a lawsuit, a liquidated damage clause may be included in the agreement. When properly used, it is fully enforceable. It would normally take a form similar to the following:

> *"For each calendar day during which the Work is not completed following the agreed upon completion date, the Contractor agrees to pay the Owner as liquidated damages the sum of $ _____ , which is reasonably estimated to cover the losses incurred by the Owner by reason of the failure of the Contractor to complete the Work."*

The owner's lawyer should be consulted in drafting such a clause to ensure that it fully complies with the law of jurisdiction. You may also have to include some incantations about "time being of the essence of the contract" and "a material consideration thereof."

Many owners are quick to latch on to the idea of a liquidated damage clause and view it as leverage in controlling the project completion date. They begin to think of it as a way of penalizing the contractor for missing a deadline. It cannot be used in this way. The losses suffered by the owner must be real; any amount of damages must be related to those losses. The contractor cannot be held liable for the owner's minor inconveniences or impatience. If the amount is excessive, it will be seen by the courts as a penalty and will not be enforced.

Liquidated damage clauses also tend to produce some other undesirable conditions. In the first place, bidding is often adversely influenced. Cautious bidders who recognize that they may not be able to meet the completion date simply inflate their bids to cover the cost of any damages that may be assessed. If they are able to complete the project on time, their profit is simply increased. In either case, the owner can only lose. Secondly, the contractor is encouraged to speculate and may also be tempted to use shortcuts to execute the work, resulting in problems that may not be immediately discernable. "Rush jobs" often lead to latent defects.

Penalty/Bonus Clause If you cannot make a case for liquidated damages and the owner insists on penalizing the contractor for late completion, the courts have consistently held that a penalty may be invoked—but only if a compensating bonus is also offered. In this case, the date of substantial completion is set and the contractor is charged a stated sum for every day the project remains incomplete after that date—and a corresponding sum is paid to the contractor for every day the project is completed before that date. A penalty/bonus clause might be stated as follows:

> *"For each calendar day during which the Work is not completed following the agreed upon completion date, the Contractor agrees to pay the Owner the sum of $ _____ , in consideration of which the Owner agrees to pay the Contractor the sum of $ _____ for each calendar day in advance of the agreed upon completion date that the Work is completed."*

Again, appropriate legal advice should be sought in drafting such a clause. A penalty/bonus clause is rarely used. Most owners are reluctant to commit to spending an additional sum for early completion. As you might suspect, when an owner is faced with this alternative, absolute deadlines become less important.

Substantial Completion Remember that the operative date in the case of liquidated damages or a penalty/bonus clause is the date of "substantial completion." Substantial completion is defined in the General Conditions as the point at which the owner has beneficial use of the project, being able to occupy it and conduct business normally. It does not mean 100% completion, nor does it include the resolution of minor problems—items that might normally be included on a punch list.

Review of Contract Time

While liquidated damage and penalty/bonus clauses appear from time to time, they invariably cause problems, not the least of which is the adversarial relationship that is immediately produced. Proceed with caution in this area.

Probably the easiest way to deal with the issue of contract time is to stress its importance. Some advise that in completing the Owner-Contractor Agreement form, the provisions establishing the completion date should be amplified by a clause that states that the time for completion is an "essential condition" of the contract and that "time is of the essence." Making the effort to include language of this type establishes its importance and tends to make this contract provision more enforceable.

LIENS

A *lien* is an instrument that gives an unpaid contractor or material supplier a security interest in the real estate to which labor or materials have been furnished. The law recognizes that the real estate has been enhanced and that any party who contributed to the increased value should be paid accordingly. There is no way to discuss liens in detail because laws relating to them are created by each state and each state's statutes are unique. We will attempt to present a broad overview but caution the reader not to generalize from this discussion. You must seek appropriate legal counsel regarding specific lien laws in effect in your jurisdiction.

In addition to the agreement itself and the protection that's afforded under payment bonds (discussed later in this chapter), it's advisable to include, either within the agreement or in a separate document attached to the agreement, some method of dealing with potential liens. What the owner really wants to do is to gain protection in case the contractor fails to meet his or her obligations and the owner is forced to satisfy a lien, in effect paying for something twice. Although the owner has protection under a payment bond (if it has been required), there are instances, depending on governing state laws, where he or she may have exposure to liens.

The concept of liens, when you consider it, is an extraordinary remedy. They convey an interest in another's property without that person's voluntary consent and often without that person having done anything to cause the situation. For example, an owner may have paid a contractor in full only to find that he or she is required to satisfy liens filed by subcontractors and suppliers who were not paid in turn. For that reason, the law typically requires stringent compliance with the applicable statute to obtain a valid lien. There are usually very strict limitations for giving notice and filing with the court or jurisdiction. If these requirements are met, a valid lien can be converted to cash through foreclosure and sale in much the same manner as a mortgage default.

Liens are normally identified as *mechanic's liens,* which have to do with an unpaid entity having furnished labor for a project, and *materialmen's liens,* which relate to unpaid suppliers whose materials are incorporated into the project. Although they arise from different circumstances, we essentially treat them interchangeably.

Under most statutes, there are mechanics for precluding the filing of liens. These methods have the same net result: those who are furnishing labor or material for the property simply agree to waive their rights. Sometimes this is accomplished by a document called a "Waiver of Lien Rights," "Stipulation Against Liens," or some other title, while at other times it is necessary to register the agreement as a no-lien agreement with an appropriate office of the courts. In either case, the executed document has the standing of a public record and all parties are put on notice that they have relinquished their rights to file a lien against the property. In most cases, the contractor is required to include the same document in all subcontracts, attach it to purchase orders, and provide verification of having done so to the owner. The applicability of any of the foregoing procedures must be verified with governing statutes. Again, legal requirements vary so widely that it is dangerous to draw any conclusions or make any assumptions based on this brief discussion. What may be appropriate in one state may be wholly inappropriate in another.

When a job goes sour there is often not enough equity in the real estate to satisfy all liens. Although laws vary, they generally establish some precedence for payment, which is usually tied to some chronological order. For example, the entity that started and completed his or her work early in the project has greater standing than those whose contributions occurred near completion. If this is the situation in your jurisdiction, it might be wise to monitor the contractor's payments to subcontractors and suppliers early in the project. Problems that arise then generally indicate that more serious problems will be encountered later on. If you have some evidence that liens may be filed, you would be well advised to exercise your authority under the General Conditions that give you the power to withhold certification on the contractor's progress payments in amounts that may be necessary to protect the owner.

As a further precaution, it is sometimes desirable to require the general contractor to furnish a "Contractor's Affidavit of Payment of Debts and Claims" or a "Release of Liens" form signed by all subcontractors and suppliers to establish the absence of claims before final payment is made.

The design professional should be aware of the pitfalls surrounding liens and should, together with the owner and the owner's legal counsel, be prepared to structure and execute the agreement in ways that provide effective protection for the owner's interests.

ALTERNATES, ALLOWANCES, AND UNIT PRICES

Alternates, allowances, and unit prices are three devices that enable the owner and designer to forestall making decisions in regard to items that may represent unknown conditions at the time the Contract Documents are prepared. The contract requirements can then be adjusted when more knowledgeable decisions are made. These three devices have certain similarities but there are basic differences between them.

An *alternate* is a defined unit of work, specified by the design professional, on which each bidder places a monetary value at the time of bidding. The unit of work can then be added to or deleted from the contract requirements before the agreement is executed, although it is possible to defer acceptance or rejection of an alternate until after construction is under way if both parties agree to do so.

An *allowance* is a cash amount identified in the Contract Documents to cover an item that is not specified in detail. The amount of the allowance is determined by the design professional; each bidder includes that amount in his or her bid. Decisions relative to its application are made during construction.

Unit prices are cash values for defined units of work, the extent of which are unknown at the time of bidding. The values are established by the bidder and stated in his or her bid. Unit price adjustments to the contract sum are made during construction as the quantity of the work they address becomes measurable.

The following discussion covers each of the three devices in greater detail.

Alternates

Alternates are frequently used to adjust the contract sum in the event that the low bid exceeds the owner's budget. Alternates can expand the scope of the contract (add) or reduce the scope (deduct). An alternate may also substitute one material for another; this is perhaps the most common type of alternate.

Alternates are often used when budget constraints dictate exploring ways to save money. For example, suppose you have designed a space where you have made extensive use of fabric wallcoverings and there is some question as to whether or not available funds are sufficient to permit this level of finish. You may decide that painted surfaces, although less desirable, may be acceptable, particularly if the saving is of a necessary magnitude. Therefore, you can specify painting as an *alternate* to fabric wallcovering.

An alternate may also change the physical scope of the project. You may use an alternate to simply add or delete all work in a given area.

The procedure favored by most design professionals is to prepare the Contract Documents to describe the work in its minimum acceptable scope and include alternates for additional items that are desirable but may not be affordable. In this way, the viability of the project is immediately established by the base bid alone. Then, if additional funds are available, alternates that increase the quality of the project may be added up to the limit of the budget. Using this method, all items listed are "add" alternates that increase the contract sum.

Some designers approach the process in the opposite way. They design what they regard as the desired result and then adjust the cost, if required, by subtracting items that may be desirable but not totally necessary if they can't be absorbed within the budget. Conventional wisdom, however, holds that bidders tend to quote "deduct" alternates as actual estimated prices without reducing overhead and profit figures. Therefore, it may be much more difficult to bring an over-budget project into line than to approach it from the other direction.

It is important to use one method or the other. If both add *and* deduct alternates are used, the process becomes confused and it's difficult to make a direct comparison of bids. Alternates not only should be kept to an absolute minimum, but they should be calculated to produce a real difference. If an alternate adjusts the cost by only $100 on a $1,000,000 project, it serves no purpose and imposes a complexity on the bidding process that is totally unwarranted.

To be as fair as possible, alternates should be listed in the sequence of their priority and, if possible, accepted in that order. Under no circumstances should alternates be considered in a manner that would favor one bidder over another. For example, if add alternates are used, one should not reject an alternate solely because it would cause a favored bidder's price to become lower than a less desirable bidder's. The manipulation of alternates to the advantage of one bidder or the disadvantage of another is unethical and subverts the whole process.

Also guard against establishing an alternate that is in any way dependent on acceptance or rejection of another alternate. Consider, for example, the confusion that might be created if one alternate calls for changing the carpet in a space to a hard-surfaced flooring material, while another alternate adds an undercarpet flat cabling system. This not only distorts the bidding process, it also almost always results in a change order that negates any potential cost saving.

Allowances

Allowances are useful when a selection cannot be made at the time the Contract Documents are prepared. Such allowances constitute an acceptable specifying method. For example, hardware requirements may not be known, or the owner or designer may wish to delay hardware selection. In this case, the designer would include a stated allowance for hardware in the Contract Documents and all bidders would include that sum in their bids. When the hardware is selected, the contract sum would be adjusted in accordance with actual costs. If the selected hardware costs more than the allowance, the owner pays the difference. If it costs less, the owner is paid a credit for the saving.

The standard General Conditions define an allowance as the actual cost of the material delivered to the job site. All other costs, including installation, are normally included in the bidder's stipulated sum.

For this reason, the products covered by an allowance should be quantified so that the bidder has some basis on which to estimate installation costs. If this is unclear, you should modify the General Conditions by employing a clause in the Supplementary Conditions that expands the scope of the allowance to also include installation costs.

Contingency Allowances A contingency allowance is used when the owner recognizes that it is almost inevitable that there will be a few afterthoughts or unforeseen conditions requiring extra work. To cover the cost of such items, the owner instructs the contractor to set aside, within the contract sum, a stipulated amount that will be drawn upon as needed. This may seem unnecessary, but often the client is hamstrung by financing arrangements or by internal control systems that make getting necessary approvals for increased costs very difficult. By using a contingency allowance, the client can tap a source of funding that already exists without having to go through more formal procedures. Also, since extras are paid for by the contingency allowance, the change order process is avoided — money for changes can be processed through a line item in the normal application for payment.

Any contingency allowance should be clearly defined, including installation costs where applicable. This is only fair to the contractor, who cannot be expected to estimate delivery, storage, handling, installation, and other related costs for unknown items.

Unit Prices

Unit prices are best applied when the work to be accomplished can be adequately defined but the scope of that work cannot be ascertained at the time the Contract Documents are prepared. In interior work, unit prices have rather limited application but are often used when extensive renovation might uncover a condition that cannot be quantified in advance. For instance, suppose the work calls for the removal of existing wallcovering, to be replaced by new wallcovering. What might happen if it becomes impossible to remove the existing finish without damaging the substrate? Perhaps the underlying wall surface will have to receive a lining paper or even a skim coat of veneer plaster to create an acceptable substrate for the new wallcovering. If the specifier has any reason to suspect that this condition might exist, he or she can specify whatever is considered to be the requisite remedy and then call for a unit price quotation for that work on a square foot or square yard basis. Then, if certain areas don't require the specified work, the quantity of the omitted work is measured and the contract sum is adjusted by a deletion using the predetermined unit price.

The opposite approach might also be used. In this instance, the specifier would again detail the appropriate remedy and call for a unit price that will be applied only if the work is necessary and added to the contract cost. In either case it is important for the specifier to be very clear about whether or not the specified work is to be included in the base bid, and to set forth how measurements are to be taken and quantities established and verified.

The number of unit price quotations should be kept to a minimum and should never be used in determining the low bid.

Some owners want unit prices included for items about which they are undecided, intending to use the figures generated as a basis for decision and then use the prices to adjust the contract by change order. There is nothing inherently wrong with this method, but it's simple courtesy to tell bidders how the prices may be used. Bidders may have a legitimate reason for quoting a unit price at one rate to represent quantities added to the contract and another rate to reduce the work of the contract. If you're undecided, give bidders the option of quoting unit prices in whatever manner is most comfortable for them.

Unit prices are commonly found in commercial development. Developers often call for unit prices on major components that are common to most projects. Accepted unit prices then become known as "building standard" and are included in tenant workletter allowances. Tenants then know the unit cost for items should they desire either to add more units than provided for within the standard lease or to delete "standard" items and add others that may be more desirable.

Unit prices are often used on public work, but allowances are rarely permitted and the use of alternates is almost always discouraged. If they are permitted, their use is usually severely restricted. When alternates are used, public policy often requires that there be no order for consideration—alternates may be accepted or rejected on whatever basis the owner decides is in the public's interest. For this reason, it is essential to take extra care in seeing that one alternate is in no way dependent on another.

Review of Alternates, Allowances, and Unit Prices

The use of alternates, allowances, and unit prices gives the owner some advantages in allocating available funds in the best interest of the project. They should be employed sparingly and in good faith. Don't make bidders jump through hoops to help you make simple decisions, and don't use these tools in a manner that manipulates bids or discriminates between bidders.

It is also important to understand that alternates, allowances, and unit prices serve very useful and specific purposes and should not be used as a strategy to delay making decisions that can be made at the time of document production. Pertinent decisions should be made before issuing documents whenever possible to avoid the use of these devices. Besides the additional administrative effort imposed on all parties, these devices tend to undermine the bidding process and create confusion if not clearly drawn. It is also important to consider well ahead of time how the ultimate decision may affect other elements of the project. Making as many decisions as possible before the contract documents are issued will reduce the incidence of change orders required as a result of a later decision's unforeseen impact. The main thing to remember about alternates, allowances, and unit prices is that each addresses variables in its own way; and because variables by their very nature tend to complicate bidding and contract procedures, they should be employed sparingly.

BONDS AND CONSTRUCTION INSURANCE

An owner who commits a sizeable sum of money to a project wants some protection for the investment. The safeguards that ordinarily offer such protection are *bonds* and *insurance*.

Bid Bonds

An owner wants some assurance that the low bidder will honor his or her bid by furnishing any required Performance and Payment Bonds (defined later in this chapter), and by executing an agreement in the prescribed form for the amount of the bid. The owner requires the bidder to furnish proof that he or she is financially capable of performing the work by submitting a *bid bond* or *bid security*. Without documentation that guarantees the bidder's capability to honor a bid, the owner would incur the additional expense associated with awarding the contract to the next higher bidder and might even have to re-bid the project. In either case, increased costs and delays are likely.

By posting a bond, the low bidder is obligated to honor his or her bid or forfeit an amount equal to the difference between the bid and the next higher bid. If the low bidder realizes that he or she has seriously underbid the job and withdraws, the bidder sacrifices the security deposit on the basis that he or she would lose more than the deposit if the work was executed. Since the difference between the low bid and the next lowest bid is usually a relatively small amount, the amount of the security deposit that becomes the maximum sum that must be forfeited is usually set at 5% or 10% of the bid amount. This security is in the form of a bid bond, in which a secure entity with demonstrable assets called a *surety* assumes that obligation on behalf of the bidder, or some other negotiable instrument such as a certified check or government bonds.

A bid bond carries with it the surety's obligation to underwrite Performance and Payment bonds. Because the surety is assured of that business if his or her client is the successful bidder, the surety furnishes the bid bond at little or no cost. If those bonds are not required, it is more common for the bid security to be in another form.

Contractors generally prefer that the amount of the bid security be stated as a specific lump sum. The reason for this is if the bidder is submitting a certified or cashier's check, bank draft, money order, or some similar negotiable instrument as bid security, the bidder cannot acquire the draft check or money order before arriving at the total bid amount and the percentage amount for the instrument. In the bidding process, this usually occurs at the last possible moment.

Some form of bid security may keep unqualified bidders from submitting a purely speculative price and then deciding whether it's in their interest to honor it when they discover how they stand relative to other bonafide bids. In fact, it is almost never forfeited. The chances of winning the Irish Sweepstakes are probably greater than encountering the forfeit of a bid security. A bidder who surrenders his deposit places himself in an untenable position. How many times do you suspect this bidder will be asked to bid on other projects? In reality, he would literally be putting himself out of business. Most contractors, therefore, may request the opportunity to withdraw their bids at no penalty (and preferably with no publicity) if they find themselves in this position. If this course is denied, every contractor who values his or her reputation will grin and bear it by signing the agreement.

On publicly-funded projects, the authorities who administer the contract may not have the power to allow a bidder to withdraw a bid without penalty. Private owners do have this ability, and many design professionals will recommend that they exercise it when necessary. Why? Because signing an agreement with a contractor who is then bound by an inadequate bid is certain to create a situation that everyone will regret. The contractor whose financial situation creates problems throughout his or her entire organization may not deal fairly with anyone. Subcontractors will be squeezed and the contractor will spend every waking minute trying to find loopholes in the documents that will allow shortcuts or claims for extra work. It will not make for a pleasant job. Owners who have been through a situation like this will probably be the first to advise that a seriously low bidder be allowed to withdraw the bid or, if it makes a cleaner situation, the owner should simply reject the bid.

In certain cases where the bidder can prove that he or she made a typographical error or some other error for which he or she was not fully responsible, there is legal precedence for allowing withdrawal of the bid. This is an area where the courts may intervene; the decision is not yours or the owner's to make. The only prudent advice we can give is to proceed with great caution until there is clear and competent direction from the owner's legal counsel.

Since the bid security affects only the potential low bidder and becomes null and void once the contract is awarded, it is not only pointless but can work a hardship on other bidders if the security is not promptly returned. It is accepted practice to retain only the bid security of the two lowest bidders until an agreement is executed. For bidders who are out of consideration, it is customary to return their deposits within a day or two of the bid opening.

Performance and Payment Bonds

Surety bonds in the form of Performance and Payment Bonds assure the owner that the project will be completed in accordance with the Contract Documents, including payment of all obligations. Performance and Payment Bonds are instruments in which one party, called the Surety, agrees to answer to another party (the owner), in this case called the Obligee, for any failure of a third party (the contractor), called the Principal. It may sound confusing, but the idea is quite simple. If the contractor defaults by failing to perform the work of the contract, the Surety will step in and fulfill those obligations at no expense to the owner. The Surety is usually a corporation, like an insurance company, which is in business to underwrite bonds. The Surety extends credit to the contractor by lending its integrity and financial worth to the venture in return for the payment of a premium. The contractor must be able to qualify financially for these bonds.

The contractor may default on a contract for a variety of reasons. Sometimes the default is not related to the contract in question, but arises from inadequate bids or other circumstances on past or current contracts. One unsuccessful venture may very well topple other projects like a house of cards. Performance Bonds provide protection for the owner against loss resulting from the failure of others to perform. They are written for a specified sum of money, usually the full contract amount, for which the surety is liable. This is called the "penal sum." Theoretically, the contractor could be liable for damages that are virtually unlimited, but the surety's obligation cannot exceed the penal sum.

Banks don't lend money to customers who may be unable to repay their loans. Likewise, a bonding company would not write a bond for a contractor who might default on a contract. They back only "sure things." The contractor must, in essence, prove to the bonding company that he or she has the resources to fulfill all obligations and imposes little or no risk. Contractor defaults on contracts covered by bonds are so rare as to be almost nonexistent.

The Performance Bond ensures that the work of the project will be completed. The labor and material Payment Bond protects the owner from liens or suits arising from the contractor's failure to meet obligations to subcontractors or suppliers. At one time it was common for a single bond to be written for both performance and payment aspects. This combination bond, however, is a very unwieldy instrument in actual practice. Although both bonds ultimately protect the owner, the Payment Bond primarily protects the interests of those who may furnish labor or material in connection with the project. Therefore, in a default situation under a combination bond there is a built-in conflict. Since the owner's claims would take precedence, the settling of claims by other parties might drag on for an interminable period while priority issues are sorted out and resolved. For this reason, the dual bond system has found almost universal acceptance.

Bond premiums are set by the bonding company in each instance, according to how they assess their risk. Just as ordinary life insurance premiums are determined by actuarial tables, the relative financial stability of the contractor dictates both premium and the maximum penal sum for which the contractor may qualify. In general, bond premiums average about 1% of the contract amount. Contractors with a limited "track record" might pay more; those with a more substantial record of performance might expect to pay slightly less. Contractors who have once failed to complete a contract may become unbondable.

Bonding companies are regulated by the states and must be licensed to do business in the state where they are offering to write bonds. Major bonding companies are well known and do business nationally through a network of local agents. You will readily recognize their names, so investigate carefully a bond that is underwritten by a surety you've never heard of. Don't hesitate to require documentation to support the standing of a bonding company.

Questioning Bond Requirements Since the owner pays for bonds, albeit indirectly, it is sometimes advisable to waive the requirement for furnishing them—particularly on small jobs or on jobs where the selected contractor's financial responsibility is beyond reproach. To require a "blue chip" contractor to post bonds on a minor project imposes an expense to the owner that may be better applied otherwise. The procedure for handling this is most often accomplished by making the bond premiums a separate cost item on the bid form. When the low bidder is known, the owner can weigh the pros and cons of requiring bonds. We have used this approach in the documents for the Sample Project in Chapter 15.

The idea of partial bonding is frequently advanced. The theory is that any default, if it occurs, is likely to happen after the project is well underway and at least a portion of the work has been completed. Therefore, instead of requiring bonds for 100% of the contract price, the penal sum is reduced to some lesser percentage of the total. The fallacy of this approach is that it doesn't produce a lesser bond premium. Bonding companies tend to perceive no reduction in exposure even though their maximum liability may be reduced.

Another question that is often raised is whether requiring bonds of the general contractor is advisable when his or her subcontractors will be bonded. Why not simply require that the owner be named as a co-beneficiary of those bonds? Proponents of this idea refer to the usual practice of separate bonds as "double bonding." This approach has been used with apparent success, but until there is sufficient evidence that everyone's interests are adequately protected, we are reluctant to endorse it as an effective method.

Deciding whether to require bonds is a lot like deciding how to acquire a family pet. You can buy a mutt of uncertain parentage — that adorable puppy might grow up to be a lovable companion or a monster. Or you can purchase a pedigreed pooch with papers that attest to the dog's ancestry, virtually ensuring that you'll get no surprises as your pet matures. In other words, dispensing with bonds might spawn a nightmare, while the mere fact that the contractor is bondable is likely to ensure that there will be no surprises. In either case, you pay a premium for peace of mind. The decision comes down to one question: Is it worth it?

Insurance

Requirements for the contractor's insurance must be covered under the Supplementary Conditions. There are certain types of insurance that are covered by statutory provisions, such as workers' compensation insurance, which cannot be modified. Other types of insurance may vary according to location and the type of project. All are designed to ultimately protect the owner and can be written for a variety of limits and coverages. The owner and his or her lawyer and insurance counselor should make these determinations, not the designer. The owner should be asked to furnish this information very early in the project.

Many surmise that insurance coverage should bear some relationship to the project cost, but this conclusion is not accurate. Taken to extremes, it would follow that a very large project would require a blockbuster policy, while a very small one would require little or no coverage. Think about it. Exposure for both projects, particularly if there is loss of life, may be very similar.

As a designer, your responsibility in dealing with insurance is to make certain that the requirements are fully spelled out and that certificates of required insurance are furnished to the owner. These certificates should show that the policies they describe are in force and make provisions for notifying the owner in advance of any cancellation.

Review of Bonds and Insurance

While the design professional must understand the purpose of bonds and insurance and be prepared to discuss their salient points with a client, it is the client, with the advice of appropriate risk management professionals, who must decide what protection is desirable.

SUMMARY

In this chapter we have covered a very broad range of topics concerning what a contract is, the common forms of construction contracts, and the written document (the Agreement) that is commonly but erroneously called "the contract"—including a number of other documents that are, or can be, incorporated into the contract.

There's no question that the various elements can be a bit confusing until you grasp the total concept of what the contract includes. The contract is comprised of the following five elements:

- The Agreement
- Conditions of the Contract
- Specifications (covered in Chapter 10)
- Drawings (covered in Chapter 12)

- Modifications to any of the above through addenda or change orders

Collectively, these five elements are the Contract Documents. Separately, no single element constitutes a contract. Nothing else is a contract — not the contractor's bid; not designer sketches; not renderings or colorboards; not correspondence — only the documents that make up the Contract Documents. All of these documents are shown in the sample project manual in Chapter 15.

CHAPTER 9

THE BIDDING DOCUMENTS

I n Chapter 8 we discussed construction contracts and the principal documents that define them, including the Agreement and the Conditions of the Contract. The Conditions are comprised of the General Conditions and the Supplementary Conditions, plus any number of other documents – including bonds; insurance requirements; instruments that limit the owner's exposure to liens; and other provisions – that may be required by the owner, public policy, or governing statutes.

In addition to the Agreement and Conditions of the Contract, the Contract Documents include the Drawings and Specifications, plus any modifications to any of the other elements. Specifications establish the quality and level of workmanship of the *specific products* on which the contract is based. Drawings graphically establish the physical relationship of the *product types* on which the contract is based. Specifications are covered in Chapter 10. Drawings will be discussed more fully in Chapter 12.

The *bidding documents* include both the Contract Documents and the bidding requirements. The *bidding requirements* are the procedures established by the client and designer for contractors' submissions of bids. Once bids are received, the bidding requirements become null and void – so, although the bidding documents include the Contract Documents, the Contract Documents do not include the bidding documents.

The bidding requirements normally include an Invitation to Bid (which is often called "Advertisement for Bids" or "Request for Proposals"), Instructions to Bidders, and the Bid Form. The bidding requirements may also include any number of additional documents that bidders must attach to their bids for them to be considered.

A simple illustration of what is included in the bidding documents appears in Figure 9.1.

THE INVITATION TO BID

If you were going to throw a party, you might send out written invitations. If you were planning a very informal gathering, however, you might just telephone a few friends to extend the invitation. The Invitation to Bid on a construction project follows the same basic principle. If your project is public, and any potential bidder may participate, your invitation will probably have to be published among the legal notices in general circulation newspapers. In this case, your client will probably have very specific requirements about the form and wording that must be used to comply with governing statutes. If the project is private, your client may want to restrict bidding to a few pre-selected bidders. In this instance the invitation may be extended informally in a brief note or even a telephone call. Any method that generates a response from the selected bidders is appropriate. If your project were to be completed under a negotiated contract, a formal Invitation to Bid would be pointless.

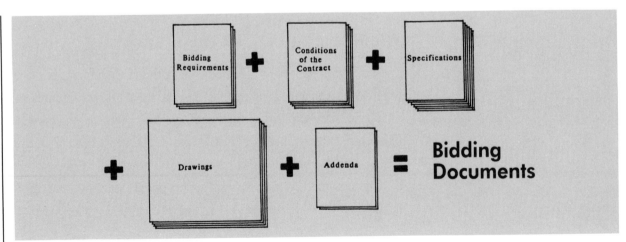

Figure 9.1

Before determining the form of the actual invitation to bid, two important questions need to be considered: How long should the bidding period be? and When should bids be opened?

Determining the Length of the Bidding Period

Impatient owners often want to shorten the bidding period. When they do so, they shortchange themselves. Prudent bidders faced with unrealistic deadlines tend to overestimate by a margin designed to cover their uncertainties about items for which they've been unable to generate accurate costs. To gain full advantage of competitive bidding, it's essential for both the owner and the designer to understand contractors' problems and procedures. After obtaining documents, bidders need time to do several things:

- Familiarize themselves with the project
- Study the documents
- Determine types and quantities of materials required
- Estimate labor costs
- Obtain prices and lead times from suppliers and subcontractors

Anything that impedes this process jeopardizes your opportunity to receive valid bids.

How much time is enough? The answer to that question is affected by the scope and complexity of the project. For very small projects involving the coordination of just one or two trades, a week may suffice. For larger, complex projects, bidding periods of up to six weeks may be warranted. For most jobs, three to four weeks should be allowed.

The bidding process is akin to taking a test. Think about the last test you took. How did you approach it? You probably first skimmed through the entire test to get a feel for what information was being tested. Then you may have answered all the easy questions, reserving time to tackle the more difficult ones. Perhaps as you worked through the exam, some items that initially seemed vague were clarified. If you were forced to guess at any answers, you probably did that as time was running out. A bidder puts a bid together in much the same way. Is it any wonder that a barrage of questions from bidders always comes at the eleventh hour? Many designers see this as proof that bidders don't look at the documents until the last few days before the bid opening — therefore, bidding periods could be shortened. But most questions are posed by bidders at the time when their interest and energy are focused on the project, and when questions on availability are brought to their attention by suppliers and sub-bidders. Of course, there are some bidders who try to put together a bid at the last moment, but the majority of competent bidders approach the task in an organized and systematic way that fully utilizes all the available time. Give them time to do their job.

Determining the Bid Opening Date

The overall project schedule determines the narrow time frame during which bids must be received for the project to stay on schedule. After arriving at a workable time frame, you must set the actual bid date. Try to avoid conflicts with other bid openings by checking with local builders' organizations, public agencies, and other design firms. This isn't always possible in large metropolitan areas or where there is a large pool of potential bidders. In these cases you're unlikely to find any date when there are no conflicts.

The process of assembling a bid is hectic; most bidders will need at least one business day to put together sub-bids, secure a bid bond or other security if required, and check and double-check the bid form and supporting documents. Therefore, avoid scheduling bid openings on Mondays, and never schedule an opening on the day after a holiday. The time of day is somewhat less important, but afternoons between 2:00 and 4:00 are usually preferable.

The Invitation Form

Typically, a simple one-page invitation states that the owner wishes to receive proposals from qualified contractors in response to the requirements of the Contract Documents. The invitation is prepared and inserted in the front of the project manual, which is the bound volume that contains all documents except the drawings (see *Chapter 11: Project Manual Production*). In most cases the invitation is merely a formality—by the time the bidder reads it, he or she already has the documents in hand, having learned about the project through some other means. Knowing this, there are many who will argue that the invitation is superfluous and should be dispensed with. In the sample project manual in Chapter 15, we have included one as an illustrative example.

If you use an invitation and the form is not dictated by law or your client's own policies, it should include, at minimum, the information listed in Figure 9.2.

Rejection of Bids We have stated that the invitation should include a basis for bid rejection. The wording that is most often used is: "The Owner reserves the right to reject any and all bids without explanation and to waive any bidding informalities." This gives the owner a bit of leeway in dealing with unusual circumstances. It gives the owner the opportunity to disqualify a bidder who, for whatever reason, suddenly becomes less than desirable during the bidding period — and the opportunity to bail out a competent and otherwise desirable bidder who fails to observe some rule that, on second thought, doesn't seem so important. There have been numerous debates over the difference between a "formality" and an "informality" in the bidding. Generally, anything that can easily be remedied and is fair to other bidders is an informality. Anything that gives a particular bidder a competitive advantage is regarded as a formality that will not be waived. For example, a typographical error in dating the bid would be an informality, but the insertion of a qualification by a bidder would be a formality that would cause rejection.

Clauses such as this one are so rarely invoked that it's not worth extensive discussion. It's wise to include one in case you need it, though; simply resolve any problems as they occur after consultation with the owner's attorney.

An invitation to bid is not always needed, but when it is necessary there are certain pieces of information that it should include. Figure 9.2 has identified those pieces of information. Now we will address the Instructions to Bidders that accompany the Invitation to Bid.

INSTRUCTIONS TO BIDDERS

The Instructions to Bidders are accurately described by their title. In the simplest form, the Instructions tell each bidder precisely how to submit a bid and the requirements for its acceptance. The Instructions should accomplish the following:

- Define the components of the bidding documents.

Invitation to Bid Requirements

Identification	Provide the name and address of the project along with a description, and identify the owner. Keep the description brief. Potential bidders need only enough information to decide whether or not they're interested in the project. If it sounds like something worth pursuing, they'll examine the other documents for further clarification.
Date, time, and location of bid opening	Tell bidders whether the opening will be public or private.
Type of bid(s) required	Stipulate whether you require a single lump sum bid for a general contract or you are soliciting segregated bids.
Document acquisition	Inform bidders how they may review and obtain documents; what deposits, if any, are required; and how many sets may be obtained.
Bid guarantee requirements	State whether a bid bond or other type of security is required. (Bid bonds are covered in Chapter 8.)
Bond requirements	Tell bidders whether they will have to furnish Performance and Payment Bonds if they are successful in bidding the job. (Performance and Payment Bonds are also discussed in Chapter 8.)
Liquidated damages	State whether a liquidated damage clause is required. (Covered in Chapter 8.)
Prequalification requirements	State any qualification conditions that must be satisfied to establish eligibility to bid. Also identify any legal requirements, such as an approved Equal Employment Opportunity program, that must be satisifed.
Basis for bid rejection	It is a time-honored procedure for the owner to reserve the right to reject any and all bids and to waive certain requirements when it's in the owner's interest to do so.
Time of bid validity	Tell bidders how long bids must be available for consideration.

Figure 9.2

- Require the bidder to examine the documents and to acknowledge that in submitting a bid, the bidder intends to enter into an agreement that binds him or her to their requirements.
- Require the bidder to report any omissions or discrepancies to the designer and to be bound by any modifications or clarifications made subsequently by addenda.
- State the methods of proposing substitutions.
- Explain how bidding documents may be obtained and returned.
- Describe how the bid form must be completed and what attachments are required.
- State how the contract will be awarded and what post-bid information or documents must be submitted prior to the execution of the contract.
- Identify the form of the contract to be executed.

Several professional organizations publish standard preprinted Instructions to Bidders; while these documents are comprehensive, they cannot be specific for any project. For this reason, if you elect to use a standard form, you'll be required to write Supplementary Instructions to Bidders to cover items that are not adequately covered in the standard form.

SAMPLE FORMS

If you plan to use a special contract form or one with which bidders may not be familiar, you should insert a copy of that form along with the other bidding requirements so that each bidder may become acquainted with it. If you don't, the successful bidder may refuse to execute an agreement that contains provisions of which he or she was unaware.

Likewise, if you require the posting of bonds or other documents such as certification of insurance coverage in a prescribed form, you should include sample copies. Bidders should, as a matter of simple courtesy if nothing else, be made aware of all provisions in the documents they may have to submit to enter into a contract if their bid is accepted.

BID FORMS

In our discussion of contracts in Chapter 8, we said that in soliciting bids we really request that bidders submit offers. By accepting an offer, the owner is initiating a contract. Since each offer should be in response to the requirements of the Contract Documents, it is important that all offers (bids) are in a form that permits them to be compared. If we were to allow each bidder to frame his or her own offer, each would undoubtedly draft it to contain exclusions and proposed substitutions. This would create a series of offers that may not even resemble each other. The lowest bid might either exclude work that was clearly a part of the Contract Documents or include substitutions that may not be acceptable. Once this bid is modified to conform to actual contract requirements, it may no longer be the lowest bid. To eliminate confusion, draft the offer for each bidder in a consistent form, within which the bid price itself is the only variable. When alternates or other allowable modifications are included, there will be additional variables, but the form should still be standardized to permit direct comparison.

Some clients, particularly public agencies and large corporations, have their own bid forms that have become sanctified through long use—these you will have to use without modification. Normally, however, you will develop your own form. The significant items that you should cover in the bid form are listed in Figure 9.3.

As long as the items in Figure 9.3 are covered, there is no real prescribed order that the document must take. Usually it is written in the form of a business letter with each point covered in a numbered list. We've included a sample form in the project manual in Chapter 15. It addresses the points discussed here—if you can modify it to reflect your own project's circumstances, it should serve you well.

Bid Attachments

For most small projects, and particularly for privately funded ones, the bid form itself, along with the bid security if it's required, is all that bidders need to submit for consideration. You can, of course, require that other documents be submitted—and for public projects those other documents may be extensive. Most design professionals and certainly all contractors prefer to keep the bid preparation process as simple as possible by eliminating extraneous and unnecessary bid attachments. All of these supplements are, however, perfectly legal and you can ask bidders to tell you anything about themselves as long as what you're asking is not in itself discriminatory. If you've made the revelation of certain information a consideration of the bid and provided a clear

Bid Form Requirements

Address and date	The bid should be addressed to the owner and dated.
Identification of project	The bid should describe the project being bid as specifically as possible. If it doesn't, there is nothing to prevent a bidder from claiming exclusions.
Bidder's representations	Bidders should be required to state that they have received and examined the proposed Contract Documents, including any addenda, and that they have visited the site and correlated their observations with the requirements of the documents. Also include statements that acknowledge the intent to be bound by particular requirements that you wish to call attention to.
Bid amount	Provide space for bidders to insert the proposed contract sum, which is usually written out in words as well as numbers in basically the same way a check is written.
Other amounts	Provide space for bidders to insert sums for alternates to be added to or deducted from the contract sum. Be careful here. These amounts should be stated in such a way that they are individual additions or deductions, not cumulative totals. Also provide space for unit prices or other sums that may be used to modify the contract sum.
Receipt of addenda	Provide space for bidders to acknowledge that they have received issued addenda. If you don't, bidders could subsequently claim that they never received a particular addendum that may have significant requirements.
Acknowledgement of attachments	If other bid supplements such as bid security, non-collusive affidavit, subcontractor listing, bid breakdowns or statement of qualifications are required, provide space for bidders to state that they are, in fact, attached to the bid.
Execution	Provide space for bidders to sign the bid and to identify the individual who is authorized to sign it. Also provide space for a corporate seal (if applicable) and identification of principals related to the bidder.

Figure 9.3

justification for need, bidders may privately grumble about it, but they will usually comply and submit a bid.

All attachments are designed to validate the bid in one way or another and may include such instruments as a non-collusive affidavit, where the bidder testifies that he or she has not conspired to rig the bidding process or submit a sham bid. Other documents that are commonly included are described in the following sections.

Statement of Bidder's Qualifications A statement of bidder's qualifications may be useful on public work, where there is open bidding, but should not be used on private work where bidding is by invitation. If you must, pre-qualify bidders before extending the invitation to bid.

List of Subcontractors To reveal the identity of subcontractors, bidding documents often require the bidder to provide a list of his or her proposed subcontractors as a supplement to the bid. There are pros and cons to this requirement. The General Conditions give the owner the right to approve all subcontractors engaged for the project. Although it seldom happens, the owner has the option of rejecting a particular subcontractor and paying the general contractor the difference between that subcontractor's quote and the price charged by the replacement subcontractor. Bidders do not like to provide a list of subcontractors for a number of reasons, some of which are objective and warrant consideration and others which are self-serving and can be detrimental to the project. Weigh the pros and cons carefully before you decide which course to follow.

One reason why bidders don't like to provide a subcontractor list is because, in the pressure of putting a bid together, the line-up of subs can change literally by the hour. Sub-bids are usually assembled in the form of telephone quotations; it's not uncommon for several competing subs to make repeated calls to the general contractor who is preparing the bid to modify their quotes. It's also not unusual for a general contractor to use a figure lower than the lowest quote he or she has in hand, knowing that if he or she is the low bidder, perhaps that number can be negotiated even lower with the leverage of actually having the job. In that case, the contractor really isn't sure who the subs will be. Also, if there are alternates involved, subcontractors may change according to the specific alternates that may be accepted. A change in the scope of a subcontract resulting from an alternate may change the relative prices of several potential subcontractors. For these reasons, the bidder may simply not know at the time of bid submission which combination of subcontractors he or she may actually use if awarded the contract. Unless there is some overriding reason to pin bidders down at this point, there is little to be gained by including this requirement.

One reason often cited for requiring a subcontractor listing is that it prevents the general contractor from a practice known as "bid shopping," where the successful bidder plays potential subcontractors against each other to reduce fixed costs and increase profit. While there are some unscrupulous contractors who are notorious for employing this gambit, it's unlikely that requiring the contractor to list subs will effectively curtail this practice. You'll know the identity of the subs who are being squeezed. No one endorses bid shopping or any of the other less-than-ethical practices that are often used in the wheeling and dealing between general contractors and subcontractors, but recognize that you are powerless to materially affect the process. If you include a subcontractor listing you might provide space for the bidder to list up to three potential subcontractors for each major component. This gives the owner some insight into the relative qualifications of the subs proposed by each bidder while giving the bidder some latitude in assembling his or her team once all factors are known.

Bid Breakdown Again, there are few advantages and many disadvantages to a bid breakdown. Asking the bidder to furnish a detailed bid breakdown with a bid rarely serves any purpose. First of all, the bidder may not have totally accurate figures for all items of work—it's a rare bid that doesn't contain some items for which the bidder is carrying an educated guess with his or her fingers crossed. The bidder may have a number of indeterminate sub-bids, some of which may be hunches about what the bidder expects to be able to "buy" once the contract is in hand. To get a truly accurate breakdown, you can wait until the successful bidder furnishes the Schedule of Values, which establishes an accurate breakdown, prior to the submission of the first Application for Payment. If you require the bidder to furnish the same information with the bid, you are likely to get a rather distorted version. If the bidder suspects, as is usually the case, that the owner intends to use such information as a tool for negotiating changes, the bidder will simply devise a game to foil that plan — perhaps overvaluing items for which no meaningful changes can be made and undervaluing items that might be deleted from the scope of work. For example, the bidder may see that you cannot alter the requirements for painting in any significant way so he or she will inflate the cost. But the same bidder may suspect that you or the owner may attempt to decrease costs by omitting window treatment from the contract. For this reason, the bidder will understate that cost and gladly agree to its deletion. Don't put bidders in the position of using this kind of subterfuge.

Substitutions for Specified Products In the interest of keeping costs contained, bidders are sometimes asked to propose substitutions for specified products when those substitutions will result in cost savings. In these cases, a separate form entitled "Proposed Substitutions — Bidder's Initiative" is included. On it, bidders list the specified product, the products they propose to substitute, and the amount by which the bid will be reduced if the substitution is accepted.

While this device challenges bidders to help control costs, it can make it difficult to compare bids. Most designers prefer the more traditional method of qualifying proposed substitutions from all sources and notifying all bidders by addendum in advance so that any potential savings are reflected in all bids.

Miscellaneous Statutory Disclosures These documents include equal employment opportunity programs, minority business enterprise utilization plans, and other items too numerous to mention. If you're working for a public client, they'll provide you with the proper forms to be included.

Controlling Subcontractor Selection by Bidders

For some projects it may be desirable, or even essential, to control the selection of a particular contractor for some portion of the work. For example, if your design makes extensive use of special millwork that must be superlatively executed to be successful, you will want to influence how that particular subcontract will be awarded. There are several ways to do this:

- Name specific acceptable contractors in the *quality assurance* article of the appropriate trade section of the specifications with the restriction that no others will be acceptable unless specifically approved by the design professional prior to the submission of bids.

- Preselect the contractor for the critical trade and require all bidders to compile their bids using *only* the quote of that subcontractor. In this instance, this stipulation should be clearly set forth in the Supplementary Conditions, covered in an appropriate section in Division 1 of the specifications, and cross-referenced in the affected trade section.

- Persuade the owner to let a *separate contract* for the critical trade by direct negotiation with the preferred contractor or by limiting bidding negotiation for this work to only those contractors who have been prequalified and determined to be capable of executing that work at the desired level of quality. Under this approach, that contractor becomes a separate prime contractor and the contractor for all other work has no obligation to coordinate his or her work. That becomes the responsibility of the owner.

Bid Attachments: Yes or No?

It is advisable to keep the bid preparation process as straightforward as possible by keeping attachments to a minimum. In conclusion, don't hesitate to ask for supplements and attachments to the bid if they're necessary for evaluating the bid, but don't require them unless there's a good reason for doing so.

SUMMARY

We have discussed the mechanics of soliciting and securing bids for a project, stressing that the bidding requirements are intended to serve *only* that function. It's important to remember that bidding requirements, unless specifically referenced in the Agreement, are *not* Contract Documents. Therefore, they must not include anything that relates to the contract itself. Any provision that you intend the contractor to be bound by in executing the work must be part of the Contract Documents and not stated among the bidding requirements.

CHAPTER 10

SPECIFICATIONS

The specifications establish the quality and level of workmanship of the products on which the Contract is based.

- Specifications may be *proprietary,* calling out specific products by name.
- Specifications may be *descriptive,* relating pertinent features of a selected material.
- Specifications may describe *performance* by calling for certain attributes that are suitable for obtaining the desired result.
- Specifications may use *reference standards* to establish minimum levels of quality and/or workmanship.

The specifications are written by the design firm executing the project. Most often it is the project manager who undertakes this task, although he or she may delegate it or portions of it to another team member. In large offices it is not uncommon to find a specification writer whose primary responsibility is to write specifications for all projects. The major advantage to this arrangement is that the spec writer typically researches products and is therefore better equipped to aid in the selection of specific products required for a project.

In most metropolitan areas there are specifications consultants who work in much the same manner as consulting engineers. Some offices engage a spec consultant to prepare specifications for all projects while others call them in as required to supplement their own in-house capabilities.

SPECIFICATION TYPES

Each specification type has certain advantages and disadvantages. Although most specifiers try to use one type consistently, there is nothing wrong with employing several types on a single project. In fact, because some products and applications lend themselves to a particular specification type, it's usually unwise to try to manipulate them into another type just for the sake of consistency.

Proprietary or Closed Specifications

Proprietary or *closed* specifications are probably the easiest to write and the type favored by most designers. The specifier identifies the selected product by name, including manufacturer's model number, color or finish selection, and other proprietary characteristics. Installation instructions are usually the manufacturer's recommendations repeated in whole or in part in the project specification. Manufacturers' representatives are usually very cooperative in supplying information; many will even volunteer to actually write the specification, since such specifications promote their products to the exclusion of others.

Another advantage to using proprietary specifications is that we as designers are likely to be familiar with most products on a proprietary basis. When we think of particular products, we immediately gravitate toward those we know the most about. For example, the Formica representative may have done a good job convincing us of the merits of Formica plastic laminate products; the Armstrong salesperson may have been generous in supplying us with up-to-date samples of resilient flooring materials. Is it any wonder then that we might look to those sources for specification information? Manufacturers' representatives are generally very knowledgeable not only about their own products but also about competitors' products. Even though their primary interest is in stimulating sales of their own materials, they also often protect the designer from making serious errors in selecting materials that are inappropriate for the intended application.

Designers generally find the following additional advantages to writing proprietary specifications:

- The designer retains full control over all components and materials that are incorporated in the project. This is particularly important when portions of the design have been based on aesthetic characteristics of a particular material or item of equipment.

- The owner may express a preference for specific products based on previous experience with them. If the owner has several similar facilities, he or she may wish to standardize materials for ease of maintenance, replacement, reconfiguration, storage, or a variety of other reasons.

- The designer is able to prepare detail drawings based on the selected product and is able to rely on exact dimensions and other physical characteristics.

- Bidding procedures are generally simplified because of narrower competition, and bidders save time by not having to do extensive price analysis.

- No drawing revision or field coordination is required to accommodate products with physical characteristics that are different from those on which the drawings are based.

- The specifications are typically shorter and more easily enforced since the product supplied is either the one called for and is therefore accepted, or it isn't and is therefore rejected.

Proprietary specifications, however, do have certain drawbacks. The disadvantages include the following:

- Competition is virtually eliminated. When a particular supplier knows that his or her product is the only acceptable one for the project, it's unlikely that the price will be competitive with similar products that are excluded and the owner may not get the best value for his or her money.

- If a bidder is unfamiliar with the selected product, he or she may overestimate the cost of installation. Bidders may also be reluctant to guarantee installation of a material with which they have no previous experience.

- The selected product may not be available from sources with whom the bidder normally does business and therefore may not be available at favorable terms.

- The designer may unwittingly assume liability for the failure of the selected product if it doesn't perform as expected.

Another disadvantage is that the use of proprietary specifications is normally prohibited on publicly-funded projects. Most public agencies operate under laws that require open bidding; in this case restrictive specifications may be used only under unusual circumstances. Most design professionals and public employees who administer design contracts are under the impression that proprietary specifications can never be used, but such regulations are routinely waived when it's in the interest of the project to do so. Perhaps the best illustration of this is when a project requires the matching of existing work. It would be sheer folly to enforce regulations prohibiting sole source specifications if it meant that the carpet had to change in the middle of a corridor or that new hardware couldn't be keyed to an existing masterkey system.

We have described the proprietary specification in its rudimentary form. Proprietary specs may also be used to create "open" specifications by naming additional similar products that meet the same criteria or by adding an "or equal" clause. In this case, competition is enhanced and most disadvantages of a "closed" or restrictive specification are removed. The real trick here lies in determining what products are truly equal and fulfill the designer's intent. A number of questions must be answered:

- Is the product equal in appearance and design? If not, is this a determining factor?
- Is the product appropriate for the intended use?
- Does the product function in the same way or will it require modifications to other work in order to incorporate it into the project?
- Is the product competitively priced? If not, is there any validity in including it, since competition is effectively removed?
- Is the product equal in durability? If not, does it still meet requirements?
- Is the product available with the same warranty and reliable service as the primary product?

Since no two products are likely to be identical, the designer must spend time evaluating and weighing a number of factors. This can be a very time-consuming activity but there are no shortcuts. Simply naming several products that appear to be similar is not sufficient.

If you opt for naming one or more products as a standard of quality and then adding the term "or equal" or "or approved equal," you may assume another responsibility. You must be very clear about the procedure to be followed by a bidder or the successful contractor in proposing substitutions. You must also be very clear about how you will make a determination that the proposed substitution is acceptable. If you fail to do this you may be inundated with proposed substitutions requiring hasty consideration, possibly losing control over your own project.

Descriptive Specifications

In *descriptive* specifications, the desired product and its installation is described in minute detail without actually naming the particular product. While descriptive specifications may be used successfully in some cases, they should not be used as a subterfuge for proprietary specifications. If the specs actually limit acceptable products to the one described, nothing is accomplished. In some cases, the specifier might launch into a lengthy and tedious description concluding with a phrase that states "...and shall be model number 123 as manufactured by the XYZ Company." If that's what you really want, why not say so?

Be wary of manufacturers' representatives who offer to prepare descriptive specifications for your use. The descriptive specifications that they typically produce may appear to be nonproprietary but they are almost invariably loaded with requirements that are exclusive to their own products and cannot be easily supplied by their competitors. You may even find patented manufacturing processes described along with other properties that are clearly not standard within the applicable industry.

Other disadvantages of descriptive specifications include the following:

- A great deal of research is usually required to reduce the content of the specs to those attributes that are truly essential and can be met by a reasonable number of potential suppliers.
- Descriptive specifications are almost always too long and often too obscure to be easily referred to and enforced. Bidders tend to regard them as an elaborate guessing game, wondering just what the specifier had in mind.

- Descriptive specifications place the burden of performance on the designer. If what you so carefully describe fails to meet the project requirements, your liability is substantially increased.

Fortunately, descriptive specifications have largely fallen into disfavor. They rarely achieve a result that cannot be obtained by using another more straightforward approach.

Performance Specifications

Performance specifications have a somewhat limited application, particularly for interior projects, but for some instances they are ideal. Performance specs simply establish the end result without attempting to dictate how it is to be achieved. In cases where you can formulate the criteria for accomplishing a goal and do not care how the contractor achieves it, a performance specification may be the best choice. In renovation work, for example, you may be primarily interested in matching or obtaining a result consistent with an existing condition. If you attempt to achieve that result by telling the contractor how to do it, you assume the responsibility for meeting that objective. If you simply establish the criteria for the end result, you will have given the contractor the opportunity to use some creativity and to select materials and methods he or she has confidence in.

This may sound like the designer is shirking responsibility and transferring liability to others, but most contractors readily accept the challenge because their experience on previous projects often gives them insight into a range of successful solutions unknown to the designer. Some bidders also see performance specifications as a way to get a competitive advantage if they are particularly skilled in the techniques required to produce the intended result. Thus they may bid with more confidence.

The major drawback to using performance specifications is that you must be certain that the desired result can actually be achieved. Attempting to obtain a result that is virtually impossible may lead to disputes, delays, and excessive costs. It is best to consult with manufacturers, suppliers, and potential bidders to make sure that what you intend to achieve is possible. Otherwise, you may be embarking on a risky course of action.

Reference Standard Specifications

Reference standard specifications, including Federal Specifications, describe accepted criteria for the manufacture and installation of a wide variety of materials. While entire specification sections may be effectively reduced to the invocation of a reference standard, it is actually more common to include them in other specification types by appropriate reference. For example, most designers are familiar with the standards set forth by the Tile Council of America for ceramic tile installations. Tile contractors are also familiar with those requirements. If you have an interior wall with a gypsum wallboard surface to which you intend to install ceramic tile using an organic adhesive, you may effectively cover its installation by incorporating the requirements of TCA Standard W242 without having to spell out those requirements in greater detail.

The major drawback in relying on reference standards is that most design offices find it nearly impossible to maintain a comprehensive library of current applicable standards. Using an obsolete standard or referring to a standard without being well versed in its requirements can be dangerous. You may come to find that you have included stipulations that do not apply to your particular project or that additional provisions have been adopted that conflict with your intent.

Another disadvantage is that many reference standards cover only minimum levels of performance and may not serve your interests if you desire a higher quality of installation. Also, some standards cover several grades and types of materials. Unless you call for a specific grade or type, you may be at the mercy of a contractor who will be obligated only to furnish products that comply with the lowest level included.

The principal advantage that reference standards offer is that the designer is saved the effort of writing extensive text to describe performance characteristics that are widely accepted in the applicable industry or trade.

If you elect to use reference standards, and in many cases you should, it is imperative that you do the following:

- Make certain that you have a complete copy of the standard, that it is the current edition, and that it applies to your intended use.

- Become familiar with both the scope and content of the standard and know how to apply and enforce it.
- Examine the standard for conflicts with other project requirements and resolve those conflicts so that ambiguities do not result.

Cash Allowance Specifications

Cash allowance specifications are used when certain products can be selected during the course of construction, when more time can be devoted to their selection. In some instances an owner may wish to delay the choice of some finish materials until he or she can better visualize the completed space. Hardware, decorative light fixtures, carpet, and manufactured casework are examples of items that are often included under allowances.

So that such items are accounted for at the time of bidding, a certain amount of money is set aside within the contract to cover these purchases. It's essential that a reasonable cost be determined so that an adequate amount is reserved. Obviously, if you or the owner ultimately choose more expensive products, the contractor is due an "extra" for the excess cost. Conversely, if you choose less expensive products, the owner is due a "credit."

Judiciously employed cash allowances can be used to great advantage. However, when they are used to avoid making timely decisions they can become a nightmare. For example, failure to make a prompt decision about one product may delay the installation of other related products.

If you decide to use cash allowances, ensure that they are clearly stated. Does the allowance cover the purchase price of the material only, or does it also include installation? Does it cover storage or delivery charges? Does it include the contractor's overhead and profit? How are costs charged against the allowance to be verified?

Two or three cash allowances on a single project might be manageable. More than two or three are likely to lead to chaos resulting from last-minute decisions and delays.

Specifications for the Sample Project

In the hypothetical specifications we have included for illustration of the sample project in Chapter 15, we have tried to use some examples of all the specification types discussed here. You will find, however, that most sections contain proprietary statements modified to permit open bidding. Most specifiers are comfortable with this form. For your own specifications you may prefer to use a different approach. The choice is yours.

SPECIFICATION ORGANIZATION

Specifications have always been the stepchild of the design professions. In an earlier era they simply did not exist as a separate document. Only when construction materials and techniques became so extensive that requirements could not be fully documented by drawing notes did they begin to appear as independent instruments intended to amplify the drawings.

The History of Specifications

In the aftermath of World War II, the explosion of new materials and methods made it necessary for architects, engineers, and interior designers to address ever-increasing complexities by developing methods to accurately specify the products they were incorporating in their designs. While specifications had existed in some form for decades, for all practical purposes specifications as we know them today date from the building boom of the late 1940s and early '50s.

The major problem specification preparation faced in the immediate post-war era was that of reproduction. Modern copy machines had not yet been invented. To produce multiple copies of typewritten specifications, design offices were restricted by the limitations of available reproduction methods. Many professionals had specification pages typed on tracing paper, usually with a carbon backup where a carbon paper sheet was reversed from its normal position to offset on the back of the original to create a denser image, then simply printed on available blueprint or diazo machines just as the drawings were printed. Others resorted to spirit duplication or mimeograph, which were not especially well suited to the relatively short runs required for the typical project specification. All of these methods were cumbersome and required a fragile master or stencil that was inherently messy and difficult to change in any way once it was prepared. For this reason, many offices developed standardized specifications for frequently-used materials and methods. They prepared project specifications by assembling stock sections of pre-written and pre-printed specifications to be supplemented by new material only when it was required for the specific project. As you may imagine, the specifications were kept very general so they could be used on the widest range of projects. They also had a very inhibiting effect on design. The designer was hesitant to employ new products or techniques that were outside the scope of the stock specifications he or she had to work with. The evolution of computerized spec preparation is discussed further in *Chapter 11: Project Manual Production.*

Organization was another problem. How should specifications be written in some logical order? Individual sections or divisions had to be put in some sequence that made them usable. Most often the specifier tried to arrange specification sections in the chronological order in which the individual trades appeared on the job. For a typical interior project, carpentry was likely to be among the first sections, while carpeting was among the last items to be covered. One well-known architectural specification handbook organized specifications into six major categories: site work, structural, masonry, weather protection, metal work, and finishing. There were also some attempts to arrange topics in alphabetical order. One might begin by specifying aluminum railings and conclude with zinc chromate primer. Consider the contractors' estimators and job superintendents who had to use these documents. Would they find wood doors under D for door or W for wood? And if they did find them, where might they unearth the specification for door frames?

Needless to say, confusion was commonplace. No two offices were likely to adopt the same system; if similarities did exist it was probably because personnel moved from one office to another and imposed organizational standards with which they had some experience. In certain isolated geographic localities, certain formats began to reappear with some regularity simply because of this crossover between firms, but as distance increased so did basic organization disparities.

The Development of CSI MasterFormat

In the early 1960s, the Construction Specifications Institute (CSI) advanced the idea that all construction specifications could be grouped into 16 broad families of related items. The concept had immediate appeal, if not universal acceptance. Many specifiers wanted a larger framework requiring further subdivision and some suggested drawing the dividing lines at different points, but no such counter proposals offered any substantial benefit. Consequently, the original CSI 16-division format survived intact and it is the one that virtually all design professionals in the country employ today. The CSI MasterFormat divisions are as follows:

Division 1 – General Requirements
Division 2 – Site Work
Division 3 – Concrete
Division 4 – Masonry
Division 5 – Metals
Division 6 – Wood and Plastics
Division 7 – Thermal and Moisture Protection
Division 8 – Doors and Windows
Division 9 – Finishes
Division 10 – Specialties
Division 11 – Equipment
Division 12 – Furnishings
Division 13 – Special Construction
Division 14 – Conveying Systems
Division 15 – Mechanical
Division 16 – Electrical

These are fixed and unchanging subject groupings. Assembled within each are related sections, which denote basic units of work describing particular products and their installation. Initially most specifiers adopted the division format and rearranged their specification sections accordingly, often creating an alpha-numeric arrangement. For example, under finishes, a section specifying gypsum wallboard might have been designated as Section 9A, followed by Section 9B Acoustic Tile, Section 9C Resilient Flooring, Section 9D Tile Work, and so on. While this practice represented a dramatic improvement, the CSI format goes much further. It identifies each section by a five-digit number, with the first two digits distinguishing the relevant unit of work. This method took longer to be embraced by the design professions but is now almost universally utilized. While there are permanently assigned numbers for sections, there is some flexibility available for creating new numbers for individual applications or combining several brief related sections on a small project into one section of broader scope.

See Figure 10.1 for a complete list of CSI MasterFormat divisions and sections.

A section, much like a chapter in a textbook, provides information on one subject. The sections that are included in Division 1 deal primarily with procedural matters or what might be called the "housekeeping" aspects of the project. The sections that fall in the remaining 15 divisions are technical sections that describe a unit of work in the form of written instructions to the contractor. These are often called "trade sections" and indeed most specifiers try to segregate units of work to be performed by a single trade into an individual section. The term "trade," however, may be misleading since the work of many sections requires the participation of two or more separate trades. In any case, it is common to confine the work of each section to what may presumably be the province of a single subcontract. In this way, the general contractor can reserve whatever portion of the work he or she elects to do and divide other portions among various subcontractors, each of whom performs the work described by one or more specification sections. Do not forget, however, that it is the privilege of the general contractor to distribute or combine the various technical sections in any manner he or she chooses. The fact that you have included varying requirements in a single section does not obligate the contractor to assign the entire section to a single subcontractor.

In some instances the specifier may be required to prepare specification sections so that the scope of each section can be awarded as a separate contract or subcontract. This is especially applicable when your client is a developer functioning strictly as a broker who lets out for bid a series of contracts that are easily defined by the requirements of one or more entire sections. When specifications are prepared any other way, contract administration becomes very difficult. If the work of a section requires the services of more than one contractor or subcontractor, there is always the danger that both (or neither) will include certain items that fall in the overlapped area. Therefore, it's likely that the owner will

BIDDING REQUIREMENTS, CONTRACT FORMS, AND CONDITIONS OF THE CONTRACT

00010 PRE-BID INFORMATION
00100 INSTRUCTIONS TO BIDDERS
00200 INFORMATION AVAILABLE TO BIDDERS
00300 BID FORMS
00400 SUPPLEMENTS TO BID FORMS
00500 AGREEMENT FORMS
00600 BONDS AND CERTIFICATES
00700 GENERAL CONDITIONS
00800 SUPPLEMENTARY CONDITIONS
00900 ADDENDA

Note: The items listed above are not specification sections and are referred to as "Documents" rather than "Sections" in the Master List of Section Titles, Numbers, and Broadscope Section Explanations.

SPECIFICATIONS

DIVISION 1 -- GENERAL REQUIREMENTS

01010 SUMMARY OF WORK
01020 ALLOWANCES
01025 MEASUREMENT AND PAYMENT
01030 ALTERNATES/ALTERNATIVES
01035 MODIFICATION PROCEDURES
01040 COORDINATION
01050 FIELD ENGINEERING
01060 REGULATORY REQUIREMENTS
01070 IDENTIFICATION SYSTEMS
01090 REFERENCES
01100 SPECIAL PROJECT PROCEDURES
01200 PROJECT MEETINGS
01300 SUBMITTALS
01400 QUALITY CONTROL
01500 CONSTRUCTION FACILITIES AND TEMPORARY CONTROLS
01600 MATERIAL AND EQUIPMENT
01650 FACILITY STARTUP/COMMISSIONING
01700 CONTRACT CLOSEOUT
01800 MAINTENANCE

DIVISION 2 -- SITEWORK

02010 SUBSURFACE INVESTIGATION
02050 DEMOLITION
02100 SITE PREPARATION
02140 DEWATERING
02150 SHORING AND UNDERPINNING
02160 EXCAVATION SUPPORT SYSTEMS
02170 COFFERDAMS
02200 EARTHWORK
02300 TUNNELING
02350 PILES AND CAISSONS
02450 RAILROAD WORK
02480 MARINE WORK
02500 PAVING AND SURFACING
02600 UTILITY PIPING MATERIALS
02660 WATER DISTRIBUTION
02680 FUEL AND STEAM DISTRIBUTION
02700 SEWERAGE AND DRAINAGE
02760 RESTORATION OF UNDERGROUND PIPE
02770 PONDS AND RESERVOIRS
02780 POWER AND COMMUNICATIONS
02800 SITE IMPROVEMENTS
02900 LANDSCAPING

DIVISION 3 -- CONCRETE

03100 CONCRETE FORMWORK
03200 CONCRETE REINFORCEMENT
03250 CONCRETE ACCESSORIES
03300 CAST-IN-PLACE CONCRETE
03370 CONCRETE CURING
03400 PRECAST CONCRETE
03500 CEMENTITIOUS DECKS AND TOPPINGS
03600 GROUT
03700 CONCRETE RESTORATION AND CLEANING
03800 MASS CONCRETE

DIVISION 4 -- MASONRY

04100 MORTAR AND MASONRY GROUT
04150 MASONRY ACCESSORIES
04200 UNIT MASONRY
04400 STONE
04500 MASONRY RESTORATION AND CLEANING
04550 REFRACTORIES
04600 CORROSION RESISTANT MASONRY
04700 SIMULATED MASONRY

DIVISION 5 -- METALS

05010 METAL MATERIALS
05030 METAL COATINGS
05050 METAL FASTENING
05100 STRUCTURAL METAL FRAMING
05200 METAL JOISTS
05300 METAL DECKING
05400 COLD FORMED METAL FRAMING
05500 METAL FABRICATIONS
05580 SHEET METAL FABRICATIONS
05700 ORNAMENTAL METAL
05800 EXPANSION CONTROL
05900 HYDRAULIC STRUCTURES

DIVISION 6 -- WOOD AND PLASTICS

06050 FASTENERS AND ADHESIVES
06100 ROUGH CARPENTRY
06130 HEAVY TIMBER CONSTRUCTION
06150 WOOD AND METAL SYSTEMS
06170 PREFABRICATED STRUCTURAL WOOD
06200 FINISH CARPENTRY
06300 WOOD TREATMENT
06400 ARCHITECTURAL WOODWORK
06650 SOLID POLYMER FABRICATIONS
06500 STRUCTURAL PLASTICS
06600 PLASTIC FABRICATIONS

DIVISION 7 -- THERMAL AND MOISTURE PROTECTION

07100 WATERPROOFING
07150 DAMPPROOFING
07180 WATER REPELLENTS
07190 VAPOR RETARDERS
07195 AIR BARRIERS
07200 INSULATION
07240 EXTERIOR INSULATION AND FINISH SYSTEMS
07250 FIREPROOFING
07270 FIRESTOPPING
07300 SHINGLES AND ROOFING TILES
07400 MANUFACTURED ROOFING AND SIDING
07480 EXTERIOR WALL ASSEMBLIES
07500 MEMBRANE ROOFING
07570 TRAFFIC COATINGS
07600 FLASHING AND SHEET METAL
07700 ROOF SPECIALTIES AND ACCESSORIES
07800 SKYLIGHTS
07900 JOINT SEALERS

Figure 10.1

DIVISION 8 -- DOORS AND WINDOWS

08100 METAL DOORS AND FRAMES
08200 WOOD AND PLASTIC DOORS
08250 DOOR OPENING ASSEMBLIES
08300 SPECIAL DOORS
08400 ENTRANCES AND STOREFRONTS
08500 METAL WINDOWS
08600 WOOD AND PLASTIC WINDOWS
08650 SPECIAL WINDOWS
08700 HARDWARE
08800 GLAZING
08900 GLAZED CURTAIN WALLS

DIVISION 9 -- FINISHES

09100 METAL SUPPORT SYSTEMS
09200 LATH AND PLASTER
09250 GYPSUM BOARD
09300 TILE
09400 TERRAZZO
09450 STONE FACING
09500 ACOUSTICAL TREATMENT
09540 SPECIAL WALL SURFACES
09545 SPECIAL CEILING SURFACES
09550 WOOD FLOORING
09600 STONE FLOORING
09630 UNIT MASONRY FLOORING
09650 RESILIENT FLOORING
09680 CARPET
09700 SPECIAL FLOORING
09780 FLOOR TREATMENT
09800 SPECIAL COATINGS
09900 PAINTING
09950 WALL COVERINGS

DIVISION 10 -- SPECIALTIES

10100 VISUAL DISPLAY BOARDS
10150 COMPARTMENTS AND CUBICLES
10200 LOUVERS AND VENTS
10240 GRILLES AND SCREENS
10250 SERVICE WALL SYSTEMS
10260 WALL AND CORNER GUARDS
10270 ACCESS FLOORING
10290 PEST CONTROL
10300 FIREPLACES AND STOVES
10340 MANUFACTURED EXTERIOR SPECIALTIES
10350 FLAGPOLES
10400 IDENTIFYING DEVICES
10450 PEDESTRIAN CONTROL DEVICES
10500 LOCKERS
10520 FIRE PROTECTION SPECIALTIES
10530 PROTECTIVE COVERS
10550 POSTAL SPECIALTIES
10600 PARTITIONS
10650 OPERABLE PARTITIONS
10670 STORAGE SHELVING
10700 EXTERIOR PROTECTION DEVICES FOR OPENINGS
10750 TELEPHONE SPECIALTIES
10800 TOILET AND BATH ACCESSORIES
10880 SCALES
10900 WARDROBE AND CLOSED SPECIALTIES

DIVISION 11 -- EQUIPMENT

11010 MAINTENANCE EQUIPMENT
11020 SECURITY AND VAULT EQUIPMENT
11030 TELLER AND SERVICE EQUIPMENT
11040 ECCLESIASTICAL EQUIPMENT
11050 LIBRARY EQUIPMENT
11060 THEATER AND STAGE EQUIPMENT
11070 INSTRUMENTAL EQUIPMENT
11080 REGISTRATION EQUIPMENT
11100 MERCANTILE EQUIPMENT
11090 CHECKROOM EQUIPMENT
11110 COMMERCIAL LAUNDRY AND DRY CLEANING EQUIPMENT
11120 VENDING EQUIPMENT
11130 AUDIO-VISUAL EQUIPMENT
11140 VEHICLE SERVICE EQUIPMENT
11150 PARKING CONTROL EQUIPMENT
11160 LOADING DOCK EQUIPMENT
11170 SOLID WASTE HANDLING EQUIPMENT
11190 DETENTION EQUIPMENT
11200 WATER SUPPLY AND TREATMENT EQUIPMENT
11280 HYDRAULIC GATES AND VALVES
11300 FLUID WASTE TREATMENT AND DISPOSAL EQUIPMENT
11400 FOOD SERVICE EQUIPMENT
11450 RESIDENTIAL EQUIPMENT
11460 UNIT KITCHENS
11470 DARKROOM EQUIPMENT
11480 ATHLETIC, RECREATIONAL, AND THERAPEUTIC EQUIPMENT
11500 INDUSTRIAL AND PROCESS EQUIPMENT
11600 LABORATORY EQUIPMENT
11650 PLANETARIUM EQUIPMENT
11660 OBSERVATORY EQUIPMENT
11680 OFFICE EQUIPMENT
11700 MEDICAL EQUIPMENT
11780 MORTUARY EQUIPMENT
11850 NAVIGATION EQUIPMENT
11870 AGRICULTURAL EQUIPMENT

DIVISION 12 -- FURNISHINGS

12050 FABRICS
12100 ARTWORK
12300 MANUFACTURED CASEWORK
12500 WINDOW TREATMENT
12600 FURNITURE AND ACCESSORIES
12670 RUGS AND MATS
12700 MULTIPLE SEATING
12800 INTERIOR PLANTS AND PLANTERS

Figure 10.1 (continued)

DIVISION 13 -- SPECIAL CONSTRUCTION

13010 AIR SUPPORTED STRUCTURES
13020 INTEGRATED ASSEMBLIES
13030 SPECIAL PURPOSE ROOMS
13080 SOUND, VIBRATION, AND SEISMIC CONTROL
13090 RADIATION PROTECTION
13100 NUCLEAR REACTORS
13120 PRE-ENGINEERED STRUCTURES
13150 AQUATIC FACILITIES
13175 ICE RINKS
13180 SITE CONSTRUCTED INCINERATORS
13185 KENNELS AND ANIMAL SHELTERS
13200 LIQUID AND GAS STORAGE TANKS
13220 FILTER UNDERDRAINS AND MEDIA
13230 DIGESTER COVERS AND APPURTENANCES
13240 OXYGENATION SYSTEMS
13260 SLUDGE CONDITIONING SYSTEMS
13300 UTILITY CONTROL SYSTEMS
13400 INDUSTRIAL AND PROCESS CONTROL SYSTEMS
13500 RECORDING INSTRUMENTATION
13550 TRANSPORTATION CONTROL INSTRUMENTATION
13600 SOLAR ENERGY SYSTEMS
13700 WIND ENERGY SYSTEMS
13750 COGENERATION SYSTEMS
13800 BUILDING AUTOMATION SYSTEMS
13900 FIRE SUPPRESSION AND SUPERVISORY SYSTEMS
13950 SPECIAL SECURITY CONSTRUCTION

DIVISION 14 -- CONVEYING SYSTEMS

14100 DUMBWAITERS
14200 ELEVATORS
14300 ESCALATORS AND MOVING WALKS
14400 LIFTS
14500 MATERIAL HANDLING SYSTEMS
14600 HOISTS AND CRANES
14700 TURNTABLES
14800 SCAFFOLDING
14900 TRANSPORTATION SYSTEMS

DIVISION 15 --MECHANICAL

15050 BASIC MECHANICAL MATERIALS AND METHODS
15250 MECHANICAL INSULATION
15300 FIRE PROTECTION
15400 PLUMBING
15500 HEATING, VENTILATING, AND AIR CONDITIONING
15550 HEAT GENERATION
15650 REFRIGERATION
15750 HEAT TRANSFER
15850 AIR HANDLING
15880 AIR DISTRIBUTION
15950 CONTROLS
15990 TESTING, ADJUSTING, AND BALANCING

DIVISION 16 -- ELECTRICAL

16050 BASIC ELECTRICAL MATERIALS AND METHODS
16200 POWER GENERATION - BUILT-UP SYSTEMS
16300 MEDIUM VOLTAGE DISTRIBUTION
16400 SERVICE AND DISTRIBUTION
16500 LIGHTING
16600 SPECIAL SYSTEMS
16700 COMMUNICATIONS
16850 ELECTRIC RESISTANCE HEATING
16900 CONTROLS
16950 TESTING

Reprinted from the Construction Specifications Institute (CSI) and Construction Specifications Canada (CSC), MasterFormat (1988 edition), with permission of CSI.

Figure 10.1 (continued)

pay for some things twice and will pay additional for other items that both contractors claim to have overlooked in their price quotations.

How much information should be included in a section? How long should a section be? While some specifiers have preconceived ideas about what constitutes the proper length and breadth of a specification, it should be fairly obvious that there can be considerable variations, any of which may be appropriate for a particular project.

You may hear the terms "broadscope" and "narrowscope" applied to sections. A *broadscope* section encompasses an entire family of work, while a *narrowscope* section includes only a small stand-alone segment of the overall subject. For example, a small project may generate a section titled "Carpentry" that might easily include rough framing, finish carpentry and millwork, and even casework. This would be a broadscope section. Conversely, a larger project might be better served by covering each aspect in its own narrowscope section, particularly if each of the items is extensive enough that it might conceivably become the province of a separate subcontract. Broadscope and narrowscope sections can be used on the same project. You may have simple requirements for resilient flooring where several types might be conveniently combined in one section, but you may have a plethora of specialized woodwork that would warrant the writing of several sections. In general, you will probably begin to gravitate toward narrowscope sections because once you've written an effective section, it is likely to be usable with little or no editing on subsequent projects.

The Three-Part Organization of Sections

Now that you've assimilated the basic format and have an understanding of how sections fit into divisions, let's look briefly at the internal organization of sections. There are three basic issues that must be addressed in the typical technical section:

Part 1: General — Those procedures that relate to the specific subject, such as what samples or shop drawings may be required or how the products should be handled.

Part 2: Products — The materials or items of equipment themselves.

Part 3: Execution — The methods and quality of the application or installation of those products.

This is the classic three-part section format. Once you have become accustomed to using this format, you will see that every bit of information you need to cover falls very neatly into its own pigeonhole that is consistent throughout each section. Besides conforming to construction industry standards, this arrangement achieves several other important benefits:

- It assists you in your writing because it automatically provides a checklist that prompts you to organize pertinent data.
- It reduces the chance for inadvertent omissions and conflicts within the section.
- It assists the user in locating the data he or she needs without having to read through the entire section to ferret out buried information.

Before this concept came into existence, most spec writers, having created some reasonably logical section distinction, went on to specify each product it encompassed and everything pertaining to it under a single heading. For example, if the specifier were dealing with resilient flooring, he or she might call out the selected vinyl composition tile followed by requirements for samples and details for installation. Having exhausted that subject, the specifier would then proceed to sheet flooring and subsequently to resilient base, each time treating the subject with exhaustive detail and often repeating the same or similar information. With this arrangement, a materials supplier would be forced to search through the entire section to locate the pertinent products on which to base a price quotation. At the same time the installing contractor would be undertaking a search to extrapolate the requirements under each heading that related to submission procedures and installation. The three-part format overcomes these problems with simplicity. Each tidbit of information automatically falls into its own niche and virtually nothing is allowed to escape attention.

These parts, again, are fixed and unchanging. They occur in each section throughout the specification. In some instances, one part may not be needed for a particular section. For example, if the owner is to furnish certain materials or items of equipment to the contractor for installation only, Part 2 of the appropriate section might be omitted or noted as inapplicable. In rare instances, you might specify some products in one section and call for them to be installed in another section, especially if those materials are part of a larger assembly. Accordingly, you might dispense with a single part in one or more of the affected sections. These are unique applications and while they do not occur with great frequency, you should be aware that they do exist and are handled by inserting a statement saying that the part doesn't apply to that specific section. If we omit Part 2, however, we don't renumber Part 3.

As you might suspect, there is a preferred arrangement of articles that fall within each part. Although the framework is established, there is great latitude in their use. Additional headings may be inserted if the topic is particularly germaine or unique to the specific project. Article titles are numbered in consecutive numerical order, but since headings vary from section to section, identical titles in different sections will not necessarily have the same number.

Part 1 Articles The article titles ordinarily assigned to Part 1 — General are as listed in their usual sequence in Figure 10.2. Each title includes a brief description of the subjects they might include.

The first article under Part 1, usually titled "Summary," is where most writers insert a potpourri of items. Unfortunately, many of the things that end up here are carry-overs from earlier spec writing practices. The category is often abused and includes things that detract from good specification procedures. Under this or a similar heading, the writer often invokes the provisions of the General Conditions, Supplementary Conditions, and the sections under Division 1, stating that they apply to the section at hand. It's an old custom and not likely to be abandoned any time soon by its proponents. But does it serve any purpose? The named documents apply to all work under the contract, whether we say so or not. Repeating it doesn't make those provisions more enforceable. What about documents that aren't cited? Aren't the drawings, the agreement itself, bond requirements, and a multitude of other instruments also applicable? Of course they are, not to mention addenda or change orders. This practice stems from the notion that since an individual section might be the basis for a separate subcontract, the designer should warn unsuspecting subcontractors that they must meet additional requirements of other documents that aren't spelled out in the technical section. While this intent may be admirable, the obligation for full compliance and division of the work belongs to the general contractor. Provisions of this sort really intrude on the general contractor's area of responsibility. If the contractor doesn't advise subs that other documents apply to their work, there is little the designer can, or should, do to save their skins.

Many writers then move on to describe the scope of the section's text. Often this takes the form of a statement something like "Provide all labor, materials, and equipment to satisfactorily complete work as

Part 1 — General	
Summary	A brief description of what the section includes, what it ordinarily might be expected to include but excludes, what is specified elsewhere that has a direct bearing on the work of the section, and any applicable allowances or alternates.
References	Citation of any applicable reference standards.
Definitions	Definitions of any terminology that might be unique. (Don't include items that have established and recognized meanings.)
Submittals	Requirements such as shop drawings; samples; product data; test reports; compliance certificates; manufacturer's instructions; record documents; operation and maintenance manuals; and warranties and guarantees.
Quality Assurance	Special qualifications for the manufacturer, supplier, or installer, along with any certifications required.
Product Handling	Description of any special provisions for delivery, storage, and handling of the included products.
Project Conditions	Any environmental conditions to be maintained, along with existing conditions or required field measurements.
Schedule	Special schedules or sequence of construction.
Maintenance	Any requirements for continuing maintenance or adjustments, along with extra (attic) stock of materials to be furnished to the owner for repairs.

Figure 10.2

indicated on the Drawings or reasonably inferable therefrom and/or as specified herein, including but not limited to the following:" The writer then proceeds to an extensive listing of everything that pertains to the section topic. Again, what does this really accomplish? The listing can never be complete enough to enable the estimator to rely on it for completing a takeoff. The hedging of the language itself is an admission that the specs may be incomplete. If that's the case, it's sufficient reason to eliminate the practice altogether. More and more specifiers are beginning to feel the same way; the trend is clearly toward omitting elaborate scope descriptions under the Summary.

Our preference is to use a brief general listing of major items and to use the Summary heading to clarify anything unusual. We might, for example, want to point out what would customarily be included in a particular section but for reasons of organization or clarity is specified elsewhere. We might also identify any products that are specified within the section to be installed under the work of another section, or vice versa. Or we might point out that the section includes the handling or installation of materials or equipment that are not furnished as a part of the contract. Other than those unique situations, we never use language that attempts to quantify or compile items of work. Besides the potential for conflict with the drawings, the inadvertent omission of an item might lead to a claim that the contractor has no obligation to provide it since it was not identified as being part of his or her scope.

The balance of Part 1 includes brief statements under the other available headings that might apply. Obviously, not all topics will pertain to every section. Don't fall into the trap of thinking that because there exists a convenient place for every subject, you must use it. When in doubt, it's usually better to eliminate a heading rather than invent a contrived requirement just to occupy the space. Your efforts will not be judged on the basis of how much you are able to write but on how pertinent what you do write is to the topic. Verbosity will not be rewarded.

Part 2: A Shopping List Part 2—Products includes everything necessary to specify the type and quality of materials. It should normally be the easiest part to write, since it's usually very clear what should be included and what belongs elsewhere. If it isn't something tangible or directly related to something that is, it's probably out of place.

You might think of Part 2 as the shopping list of materials and equipment required to complete the work of the section.

For many of the primary products you will need to call out secondary or incidental products that are necessary for their installation. For example, in a resilient flooring section, in addition to the tile or sheet goods you specify, you will have to select the proper adhesives. You may also need to specify tapered reducer strips or other accessories. If floor preparation is part of the requirements of this section, as it usually is, you must state what leveling or patching compounds will be used.

There is always the chance that you'll forget some minor item. You may elect to cover that eventuality by including an additional paragraph that charges the contractor with providing all products required to produce the intended result even if specific ones are not mentioned. In that event, reserve the right to reject such products in the event that they are inappropriate or contrary to your intentions. This practice runs counter to much of our basic philosophy but it rarely comes into play and we've never had a contractor take exception to it. As you gain more experience and have a clearer understanding of how complete your product listing is, you should resort to this type of device with less frequency.

Some of the typical article titles used in Part 2, along with brief descriptions, are listed in Figure 10.3.

Part 3: Applications of Products Part 3 — Execution is often the largest part of a typical technical section in terms of sheer verbiage. Many sections will involve only one or two products but the procedures required for their installation may be very extensive. Although this part may be quite lengthy, it's usually relatively simple to write because Part 2 has already given you its content. Part 3 is merely a detailing of the application of each product listed in the previous part.

All of the on-the-job steps that have to be taken are set forth, beginning with examination of substrates and job conditions that affect the execution.

Part 3 Articles. Articles commonly used in Part 3 are listed in Figure 10.4.

Spec writers tend to be of two minds about the amount of detail to be included in Part 3. Some like to write a very detailed description of the execution process, which is often a reiteration of the instructions prepared by the product manufacturer. There are several dangers inherent in this approach. If you are not writing a proprietary specification, how do you really know which specific product will be supplied? And, of the several possible acceptable products that may be selected for use, it is unlikely that each potential manufacturer will call for identical installation procedures. Also recognize that manufacturers typically hide self-serving requirements within their instructions – since you depend on their printed material to prepare your own specification, you may inadvertently repeat provisions that contradict your intent. Therefore, you may insert the requirements of one manufacturer only to find that they are inappropriate when applied to the products of a competing manufacturer.

We recommend a second approach. If you are writing a *proprietary specification,* refer to the specified manufacturer's installation instructions

Part 2 – Products

Manufacturers	List acceptable manufacturers or open the specifications to competition.
Materials	An item-by-item list of the specific products on which the contract is based.
Equipment	Same as "Materials," but used for items that are typically manufactured units or components as opposed to materials.
Accessories	Secondary products directly related to those specified under preceding headings.
Mixes	Proportioning of components. (Rarely applies to interior projects.)
Fabrication	Requirements for shop fabrication and finishing.

Figure 10.3

as the standard. It is redundant to repeat it verbatim and even more dangerous to try to edit it. If you're writing an *open specification*, require that the selected manufacturer's instructions be part of the submittal data and upon approval become an integral part of the project requirements.

There are, of course, some instances where these methods aren't effective, but in the vast majority of cases you should find that they work well and produce a clear, concise, and easily understood specification. After all, that's what it's all about.

Creativity and the CSI Format

If this is your introduction to specification organization in accordance with CSI format, you may feel that the form is too rigid and confining. Many designers initially feel that the predetermined arrangement somehow suffocates their creativity. But the way you specify is important

Part 3 – Execution	
Examination	Verification of conditions that influence execution and methods to be employed.
Preparation	Steps that must be taken before specific installation may commence.
Erection/Installation/ Application	Any special techniques that must be employed, interface with other work in place, and tolerances required for acceptable work.
Field Quality Control	Any tests or inspections required to prior acceptance.
Cleaning	Any special cleaning or protection of completed work that may be required. (Don't, however, repeat general cleaning, which is covered under Division 1.)
Demonstration	Used if proper operation and maintenance of equipment must be demonstrated to owner's personnel.

Figure 10.4

in determining how effectively you are able to communicate. Using a recognized and accepted format eliminates confusion and allows you to convey your intentions without difficulty. This frees your imagination to concentrate on *what* you specify, which after all is the true measure of your ability as a designer.

SPECIFICATION LANGUAGE

Architects and engineers, who have traditionally accounted for the overwhelming volume of construction specifications, tend to come from backgrounds that have experienced the evolution of specifications. With this orientation, many cling to old notions that the specs, being part of a legally binding set of documents, must borrow terms and phraseology from the legal profession. All too often this affliction produces language that is repetitive and indefinite—the stilted, legal-sounding jargon may create work for lawyers who will be only too happy to argue its precise meaning in court. Unless you want your words to be subjected to this kind of scrutiny, you are well advised to avoid anything that looks like it could have originated within three blocks of a law office. Fortunately, this style of writing is beginning to die out because it is not only cumbersome but also often creates ambiguities that get in the way of clear understanding.

The real purpose of specifications is communication. Your intent is to give the contractor clear, concise, and comprehensive instructions. Anything that obstructs or interferes with that goal is of no value. Just as you wouldn't give someone directions from New York to Philadelphia by way of Detroit with stopovers in Cleveland and Pittsburgh, your specs shouldn't follow similar circuitous routes. Your words should be understandable to those who have to read them. Vague or ambiguous language is always open to interpretation and may be interpreted in a way that is quite different from your intent. A good specification is one that contains the fewest words required to describe the particular item, procedure, or result without any room for misunderstanding.

Writing Readable Specifications

Recognize that your specifications are directed to a reader: the contractor. The contractor, who may be an individual or some collective entity, encompasses the estimator, project superintendent, trade foremen, suppliers, and individual installers or mechanics. Each individual who reads your specs is a real person, not some imaginary being to be referred to in the third person. Phrases that begin "The Contractor shall..." are antiquated, overused, and accomplish nothing. If you were giving directions to a friend, you wouldn't dream of prefacing every statement with similar hackneyed verbiage. Make the *material* or *method* the subject of all sentences, not the word "contractor." Each sentence will be shorter and the key words will be right up front where they'll contribute to easy reference. Consider the following example:

> *Poor:* The Contractor shall prepare all surfaces which are to be painted.

> *Better:* Prepare surfaces scheduled to receive paint.

Use simple declarative statements in imperative mood. Remember, these are instructions that you want someone to follow. Don't use indefinite terms such as "to be" or "should be" as in the example above.

Use standard and accepted abbreviations. For example, everyone knows what "sq. yd." means so there is no point in spelling it out. While this may not be appropriate style for an academic essay, it's ideal here. If you were writing a recipe, which is really very similar to a specification, you could easily lose your reader in a morass of spelled out measurements.

Use numerals instead of writing out numbers. They are more familiar and more quickly grasped by your reader. To write out "eighteen gauge" when you can simply write "18 ga." is a waste of time and space. It is also unnecessary to write out a number followed by the numeral in parenthesis, as in "eighteen (18) gauge." Your job is difficult enough. You don't have to needlessly complicate the process and confuse the issue at the same time.

Finally, never, ever, use "etc." This implies that there are more items or further instructions. If you don't know what they are, how can you expect the contractor to make a determination? And while we're on the subject of making the contractor guess, don't insert phrases such as "to the satisfaction of the Designer" or "as directed by the Designer." Tell the contractor what will satisfy you by stating minimum tolerances or performance requirements—and if you're going to give directions, give them now!

Some other common maxims to follow are:

- Don't use "and/or." It's really one or the other.

- Don't use "any" when you mean "all." "Touch up *all* imperfections" is much more definite than "Touch up any imperfections." In fact, "Touch up imperfections" is even better.

- Use "both," not "either," when you don't intend to present a choice. If you say, "Install signs on either side of columns," it could be construed as giving the contractor the option of choosing which side.

- Don't use "said" as an adjective, as in "Install said products." This requires reference to antecedents that may not be readily apparent.

- Don't use "same" as a pronoun, as in, "If work does not conform to tolerances, remove same." Instead, say, "Remove work that does not conform to tolerances," or simply, "Remove non-conforming work." There's the action up front again, right where it belongs.

- Capitalize for clarity. Besides normal rules for capitalization, you should always capitalize the parties to the contract, including Owner and Contractor, and all of the components of the Contract Documents such as Agreement, General Conditions of the Contract, Drawings, and Specifications. Capitalize other words when doing so contributes to communication.

Using the "Residuary Legatee" In most projects, several classes or qualities of the same basic material are often used. Whenever possible, their locations should be clearly indicated on the drawings. In rare instances it becomes difficult to do so and some clarification must be made in the specifications. When we do this, we use a principle that roughly approximates that which the law, when applied to bequests, recognizes as the "residuary legatee." For example, say a man wishes to leave his estate to his wife except for several minor bequests. His will would first list the minor bequests and then state, "The residue of my property I bequeath to my wife." She is the "residuary legatee." Applying this principle to specifications, we would first list the material that forms the exception to the general rule. Usually it is the one that occurs in the fewest locations or in the smallest quantity. We would then state that the remaining material applies to all other locations and conditions. The material then becomes, in a sense, the "residuary legatee." When specifying wallboard we might call for water-resistant gypsum wallboard to be used in kitchens and toilet rooms, fire-rated gypsum wallboard to be used where fire-rated assemblies are indicated or required, and that regular gypsum wallboard is to be used in all other locations.

Spec Language Disasters Before we conclude our discussion of specification language, we'd like to share several real horrors we've culled from actual project specifications. These monuments to obfuscation include:

> "In the case of overlapping or conflicting requirements, the most stringent (generally) language written directly into the contract documents clearly indicates that a less stringent requirement is acceptable." (We're not sure that this *clearly indicates* anything. If it does, we're not sure that we endorse it.)

> "Where optional requirements are specified in a parallel manner, option is intended to be the Contractor's unless otherwise indicated." (We don't know what a *parallel manner* is, but we do understand that since specifications are instructions to the contractor, when an option is presented, it has to be the contractor's.)

> "Actual work must comply within specified tolerances or may exceed minimums within reasonable limits." (We think this tells the contractor that the specifier is not too keen on superior performance. If the contractor does a really terrific job, it might be found unreasonable. Presumably, then, the work would be rejected.)

SUMMARY

Perhaps the best advice, besides the admonition to adopt a writing style that prizes brevity, is the old adage, "Say what you mean and mean what you say." Do list all the requirements that are important to the project, but don't include anything that's not required or that you don't intend to enforce. Specifications padded with unnecessary stipulations only tell the contractor that you aren't really sure about how the work should be done. Everyone respects professionalism; it is the mark of the professional to reduce the process to that which is truly essential through the use of precise, concrete, descriptive language.

Be brief and use clear, unencumbered language. Eliminate superfluous words and you'll eliminate most of the problems and pitfalls associated with poorly drafted documents. Reduce your writing to pure kernels of information and you will have succeeded. Isn't that what creativity is all about?

CHAPTER 11

PROJECT MANUAL PRODUCTION

The *project manual* is the bound volume containing the bidding requirements, the Conditions of the Contract, and the specifications. These documents are always bound in the manual in the order stated. Since the bidding requirements and Conditions appear first, they are often referred to as the "front end" documents. They are also sometimes called "boilerplate" documents because some of them are preprinted and rarely change substantially from project to project, except for minor tailoring to match specific project circumstances.

The term "project manual" has been in existence for approximately 30 years and is the term recognized by all segments of the construction industry. Because specifications usually make up the bulk of the volume, you may hear people refer to it as the "specs" or the "spec book" — but once you understand the unique role each separate group of documents plays, you will see why these terms are inaccurate and misleading.

EVOLUTION OF THE PROJECT MANUAL

In an earlier era (and in some small offices today), text for all project documents, particularly technical spec sections, were hand-typed for each project. Recognizing the labor-intensive aspect of this activity, many offices created some form of master specification. In its simplest form this master specification consisted of carefully maintained, typed originals that were recopied for each new project. Sometimes there were blank spaces in the text for insertion of project-specific language to create new originals for each project. Occasionally the master specification was photocopied and edited by a careful cut-and-paste method, and some newly-typed insertions, to produce new pages. Depending on the sophistication and completeness of the master, this method served its purpose with minimal effort even though, by current standards, the results were rather spotty.

The use of automatic typewriters, then computers with word-processing software, has completed the evolution of "customized" master specifications. Most offices now use this equipment to allow an existing master to be edited on an individual word, sentence, or paragraph basis. Renumbering and page formatting can usually be done at the same time. With this flexibility, the old office masters or commercially available masters are electronically stored and easily shaped and supplemented before a hard copy is produced for making multiple copies. Both the AIA and CSI, along with some private software producers, offer prepared programs of master specifications that can be tailored to specific project needs. These programs have many advantages and are well worth the investment for offices with extensive production requirements. Because these prepared specifications typically encompass the entire range of construction, architectural firms use them more frequently than interior design offices do unless the specific program offers an "interiors version" that eliminates sections not normally used by interior designers.

When we discussed the evolution of specification organization in Chapter 10, we mentioned that the lack of effective means of reproduction hindered systematic development of contemporary specification standards. That impediment disappeared in the early 1960s with the advent of the electrostatic copier. Almost overnight, copy machines became readily available and quickly became the method of choice for specification reproduction. An unlimited number of copies could be produced and the typed originals, unlike masters for most other methods, could be easily modified—particularly if the originals were prepared on word-processing equipment where type style, format, and size are easily controlled on the masters. As copier technology has continued to advance, the ability to create two-sided copies and collate pages in a single operation makes this reproduction method so quick, easy, and cost effective that other methods are rarely even considered.

Because of the limitations of earlier technologies, project manuals were traditionally printed on one side of each sheet so that, when bound, all left-hand pages were blank. This practice continues to be used by some offices but the availability of two-sided copiers, coupled with a desire to reduce the bulk of the manual and to save paper resources, has altered this approach so that book-style project manuals, with two sides of the page printed, have become the norm. The preference is to start each new document or technical section on a right-hand page. This does produce some blank pages but it also fosters consistency: all right-hand pages are uniformly odd-numbered and left-hand pages are even-numbered. Most book publishers follow the same system for pagination.

PROJECT MANUAL CONTENTS

The project manual is compiled by assembling the documents in a predetermined sequence. The first page is the *cover* (described in more detail later in this chapter), which includes the name of the project and the name of the design firm. Some firms follow the cover with a page called the *project directory,* which lists the names and addresses of consultants and may also include names and telephone numbers of specific contact people. This directory is followed by the *table of contents,* which lists each document included in the project manual.

After the table of contents it is customary to insert a copy of the Invitation to Bid, followed by the other bidding requirements discussed in Chapter 9. The bid form is inserted next, followed by the various documents, if any, that are required to be attached to the bid. Public clients typically have very specific requirements for these attachments and will provide you with standard forms to be inserted, such as a *Non-Collusive Affidavit,* which requires the bidder to testify that he or she is not submitting a sham bid or bidding in collusion with another bidder. The next element is the Conditions of the Contract, which includes a copy of the Form of Agreement, sample copies of other forms that are required in the execution of the contract, the General Conditions, and the Supplementary Conditions. If there are any other statutory provisions required by your client, such as Equal Employment

Opportunity statements, they should be inserted next. These should be followed by a *Prevailing Wage Rate Determination* if the laws governing your project mandate that prevailing wage rates as determined by the state or federal Department of Labor be paid to all workers on the project.

The final element that makes up the project manual is the specifications.

Figure 11.1 lists the various documents that might be included in the project manual and indicates their frequency of use depending on the project type. This table also shows the preferred sequence of their arrangement. You might come across a document that is not listed here, but an understanding of the purpose of the document should indicate where it might appropriately be inserted.

PROJECT MANUAL PAGE FORMAT

For many bidding and contract forms, page format is established by the preprinted forms that are used. For specification sections, however, there are a variety of choices. The first thing you will have to decide is how you want the page to look. Some specifiers prefer an indented style, in which a hierarchy of information is established and elements of descending importance are successively indented from the left-hand margin. Others find a block style to be more readable. In general, simple formats tend to look cleaner and be more easily modified but there is really only one rule: *Be consistent.*

The way you lay out the pages of your specifications is largely a matter of personal taste along with considerations dictated by the equipment you're using to produce the work. If you're doing work for government or military projects, you may have to set up specs according to some standard format. Some large private clients may also have standard page layouts that you will have to use. When confronted with this requirement, there is little you can do but conform. Unfortunately, standardized page formats adopted by most bureaucratic agencies force you to put a great deal of text on each page, resulting in skimpy margins and little or no white space to separate changes of subject. Project manuals that are prepared in this manner quickly lull the reader into a state of somnolence and destroy all efforts at good communication.

From time to time, different page formats have been promulgated by varying sources. None have been widely adopted.

Elements of the Project Manual

Item or Document (in preferred sequence)	Public Projects — Always Included	Public Projects — Usually Included	Public Projects — Optional	Private (Bid) Projects — Always Included	Private (Bid) Projects — Usually Included	Private (Bid) Projects — Optional	Notes
Cover Sheet	●			●			(1)
Project Directory			●			●	
Table of Contents	●			●			
Invitation to Bid	●				●		(2)
Bidding Requirements:							
Instructions to Bidders	●			●			
Supplementary Instructions to Bidders			●			●	(3)
Information Available to Bidders	●			●			
Bid Form		●			●		(4)
Form of Bid Bond		●				●	(5)
List of Subcontractors		●				●	(6)
Substitution Listing		●				●	(7)
Statement of Bidder's Qualifications		●				●	(8)
Non-Collusive Affidavit		●				●	(9)
Schedule of Values			●			●	(10)
Contract Provisions and Conditions:							
Form of Agreement	●					●	(11)
Form of Performance Bond	●					●	(12)
Form of Payment Bond	●					●	(12)
Certificate of Insurance	●					●	(13)
Non-Lien Agreement or Stipulation Against Liens	●					●	
General Conditions	●			●			
Supplementary Conditions	●			●			
Miscellaneous Statutory Provisions	●					●	(14)
Prevailing Wage Rate Determination	●					●	
List of Drawings		●				●	(15)
Specifications:							
Divisions 1 through 16	●			●			

Notes:

(1) Sometimes used to identify owner, design professional, and consultants, along with appropriate contact people.

(2) Sometimes called by other names. Often omitted on private work where invited bidders are solicited by other means.

(3) Used only when preprinted Instructions to Bidders must be modified.

(4) Discloses existence of as-built drawings, work performed under other contracts (such as asbestos abatement), etc., and how such information may be reviewed. "Optional" if such information does not exist. If it does, it should be included.

(5) For very minor projects, bidders may be permitted to submit their bids on their own letterheads. This is not recommended, since bidders may insert exclusions that essentially modify the contract documents.

(6) Not required if bid bond or other security is not required. Also, form may be omitted if owner will accept surety's standard form.

(7) A bid attachment mandated by some owners. Disadvantages are discussed in Chapter 9: The Bidding Documents.

(8) Required by some owners. Can be detrimental to the bidding process when it makes it difficult to compare bids.

(9) Often required to be submitted in advance to establish eligibility to bid.

(10) Required as a contract condition, but has questionable value as a bid attachment.

(11) Often included by reference only.

(12) Not required if bonds are not required. Form may be omited if owner will accept surety's standard form.

(13) Insurance company's standard certificates are usually acceptable.

(14) May include mandatory equal opportunity provisions, provisions for utilization of minority business enterprises, and other requirements of public agencies.

(15) Sometimes inserted after table of contents.

Figure 11.1

The specifications for the sample project in Chapter 15 show the authors' preference for page format. We like generous margins and space between separate topics. We use all uppercase part titles. For other titles, we use upper- and lower-case type, which is generally considered more readable. We underline subtitles, which aids in locating specific provisions. Because the text under many subtitles consists of only one or two short paragraphs — or even a single sentence — we dispense with a number or letter designation for each clause. This eliminates a profusion of 1's and 2's or A's and B's, which can become annoying in their redundancy. We think that readers can easily discern and locate five or six separate clauses under a subtitle without having to see the numbers. When we use a heading that might normally precede an excessive number of separate clauses, we simply insert some additional subtitles.

We like to use a header on each page that identifies the project by name. Some designers would suggest that this is wasteful of space and unnecessary. However, bidders, particularly subcontractors, may be working on as many as a dozen projects simultaneously, often using separate specification sections removed from the bound copies of their respective project manuals. Just keeping track of which section corresponds to which job can be difficult. Giving the reader a bit of guidance in that respect simply helps in the communication process — the better we communicate, the better we serve our clients and their interests.

Where does the page number go? There are, of course, a variety of preferences. Some designers like to set the page number at the bottom center of each page because it is consistent for all pages, whether the project manual is one-sided or two-sided. Others prefer the top of the page, on the outside margin. This requires that all odd-numbered pages be numbered on the right and even-numbered pages be numbered on the left. Otherwise, some numbers will end up on the bound edge of two-sided copies and may be difficult to easily locate. Obviously, if your word processing program allows you to move numbers easily, their location is of less importance since they can be changed with little effort.

There are those who date each page of the project manual as they would date each sheet of the drawings. Most specifiers feel it is sufficient to date only the cover page of the project manual.

Some specifiers print project numbers or file numbers on each page, primarily as a means of future manual or electronic retrieval. Remember, though, that this information is useless to the bidder and if it unduly intrudes on the text, basic communication suffers.

Since page format is principally a matter of personal taste, adopt a layout that reflects your own design sense. Generous margins create white space, which results in visual appeal. While there's no correct arrangement of white space, a page in which text is uncrowded not only looks better but is generally easier to read. Keep some space between sections without isolating headings. It's a good way of visually organizing the page and informing the reader about what is important and where parts begin and end.

Some specifiers like to separate portions of the project manual by printing various sections on different colored paper. There have even been some proposals for doing so as a universal standard. None of these proposals has met with more than very limited acceptance. Those who do promote this idea usually suggest that, at minimum, the bidding requirements, Division 1, and Divisions 15 and 16 be printed on distinctive colored stock. These particular elements are selected because the bidding requirements and Division 1 require frequent reference and because the work of the mechanical and electrical divisions is virtually always comprised of major subcontracts. Others go so far as to suggest that each of the separate elements of the project manual have a pre-assigned color, creating a volume that is a veritable rainbow of hues, so that color coding will aid in locating specific provisions more easily. Although we have experimented with such ideas, we find no significant value in adopting them. The reproduction process becomes unnecessarily burdened. If, however, the notion appeals to you or is commonly employed in your area, you might adopt it for your own work.

Project Manual Covers and Binding

Once the pages of the project manual are collated mechanically or manually, the question of covers and binding method must be addressed. Most offices use covers of heavy paper designed to protect the pages and distinguish the manual from similar documents. Sometimes the covers for each individual project are printed or duplicated on a copier or laser printer that accepts heavyweight stock. In this instance, the cover for each project might have a distinctive design and color. We've seen some very elaborate covers, complete with four-color reproductions of project renderings. More often, pre-printed standard covers are designed so that project names and other designations can be added. This type often employs a die cut window that allows titles on a separate title sheet to show through, although some firms prefer to type pertinent information on adhesive-backed labels that are affixed to the printed covers.

Plastic spiral binding is the binding method of choice for the vast majority of offices. The equipment and supplies required for this method are readily available and within the means of most offices who elect to do the binding in-house. Most small print shops have the capacity to perform this task for firms that prefer to have binding done by outside sources. The principal advantages of this method are that, when opened, the pages lie flat, and removing individual pages or sections is accomplished without much difficulty. Some firms still use a variety of other methods, including brass fasteners, screw-type binding posts, and even loose-leaf binders, but these approaches offer few advantages and are fast disappearing.

There are a few firms that prefer that the bidders not separate and remove sections from the manual. For this reason, they choose more permanent commercial binding methods. This is their way of ensuring that all potential subcontractors are exposed to all pertinent documents. While we understand the motive, we aren't convinced that the idea has overriding merit.

SUMMARY

The thrust of this chapter has been to establish the contents of the project manual and the order in which the documents appear. Sequence is important because those who must use the manual are familiar with the established organization and might overlook essential provisions if they are misplaced.

The project manual for a small project for a private client might contain only a handful of essential documents, while one for a publicly-funded project might include dozens of bid attachment documents and specific forms to be included with the agreement. While the latter might produce a weighty volume, the task of assembling it is not as formidable as one might suspect. The design professional is responsible only for properly incorporating the prescribed forms, not for generating them.

CHAPTER 12

THE DRAWINGS

The drawings graphically define the physical relationships of the product types on which the contract is based. What does this mean? It means that the drawings depict aspects of the project that can best be described by graphic means. That in itself excludes items that relate to quality or workmanship. Those items fall within the province of the specifications and should not be repeated on the drawings.

It is possible that the drawings for a project could be so incomplete that it would be nearly impossible to bid or build it. Actually, the opposite is more likely to be true. The poorest sets of documents are typically those that are overdrawn and filled with redundant and, often, conflicting drawings. Repetitive drawings full of misleading and contradictory information are frequently more confusing than a lack of information.

The real trick, of course, is to know when a drawing contributes to understanding and when it simply takes up space. Perhaps this problem can be addressed by asking the question: Does this drawing show something that cannot be ascertained from the floor plan itself? If the answer is yes, then the drawing has value and should be included.

Drawings may be *diagrammatic,* using symbols to indicate relationships (some of which may be hidden in the completed project). Plans, sections, and details are diagrammatic drawings. They use graphic symbols to depict materials, the surfaces of which are the only aspects perceived in the finished work.

Drawings may be *pictorial*, depicting relationships of products as they would actually appear. Elevations are pictorial. Although they do not indicate depth, the relationship of various elements is indicated in two dimensions.

Drawings may use information in *tabular* form to indicate relationships or parts in a total assembly that cannot be easily indicated graphically. Finish schedules and door schedules are two primary examples. Each indicates physical relationships by graphically locating specific items.

In any plan drawing, it is important to use standard drawing conventions. Do not invent your own unique methods of indication. Creativity is important in the design, but not in the method of communicating it. Drawings are a means of communication; to achieve this goal the sender must speak the same language as the receiver.

The complete set of drawings plays a specific part in the total Contract Documents package. Together with the specifications they describe the scope of the project. While drawings and specifications work together, any areas of repetition or overlap increase the likelihood for conflicts, ambiguity, and error. Once you understand and accept the role that drawings play, you must begin to address the specific methods by which they are organized.

THE CONDOC METHOD: AN INTRODUCTION

In the traditional method of formatting drawings, both graphics information and the notes that identify graphic elements are randomly placed. Dimension lines and leader lines often cross and obscure each other. Some notes are repeated several times at different locations on the same drawing, involving much time-consuming lettering. In short, information is sometimes difficult to find and there is considerable visual clutter.

At the time you are reading this, you may have already leafed through the sample project manual in Chapter 15 and glanced at the illustrative drawings. Unless you've already been exposed to the methodology employed in their preparation, the drawings may look a bit unusual. The multitude of notes and material identifications are missing from the graphics, replaced by some cryptic numbers with alphabetical suffixes that seem to be keyed to a consolidated list of notes. Although you may never have used a similar drawing system, if you are open to new ideas you should immediately recognize that the basic format offers a substantial benefit in terms of readability. The method we've used is dubbed "ConDoc" and is the result of the collaboration of two architects, James N. Freehof and Onkal K. (Duke) Guzey, both of whom did considerable research in the methods of organizing architectural drawings. The AIA sponsors the adoption of this organizational system, which, if properly applied, produces drawings that are clear and consistent.

The basic elements of ConDoc have been established, but it continues to grow and develop as users respond with new refinements. We believe that ConDoc will ultimately do for drawings what the CSI MasterFormat has done for specifications.

The ConDoc method organizes drawings by major discipline with a preassigned numbering sequence, divides the drawing sheet into identifiable modules for the incorporation of graphics, and then links the graphics to the specifications through keynotes. The normal arrangement is to use a wide strip at the right-hand edge of the drawing sheet to accommodate the keynotes and the title block.

The Title Block

Before discussing keynote preparation, let's look at the information that is included in the title block. While there are no hard and fast rules about what has to be included, the following information should be included, at minimum:

- The name and address of the project and the owner's name and address, if it is different from the project's.
- The design firm's name, address, and telephone number, along with space for the professional registration seal if required or applicable.
- The names and addresses of any consultants engaged for the project.
- The drawing number and the date of the drawing (usually the date when it's issued).

In addition to the above items, it is customary to provide space for listing the project number. This is a number that is established internally for filing and control purposes, however, so if it's omitted no one but the designer will ever notice. Also, it's common practice to include spaces for initials of those who prepare, check, and approve the drawing, but we've seen so many drawings issued with those spaces left blank that we wonder if the practice really serves any purpose — unless what you really want to do is have a readily identifiable individual on which to pin errors. It's also common and useful to have some space reserved for the recording of any revisions to the drawing. Many drawings are revised over the course of a project to reflect changes. What was modified, and when, is an essential record to maintain. Space for the sheet title and scale of the drawing are also usually provided, which may be redundant since the same information is repeated on the graphic elements themselves. We like to use a sheet title for easy reference when thumbing through a set of drawings, but we usually omit repeating the scale particularly when the sheet contains more than one graphic element at differing scales.

Numbering Drawings For many years it has been standard practice to number drawing sheets with a letter prefix indicating the specific discipline it addresses. Architectural and interior design drawings are commonly numbered A-1, A-2, A-3, and so on. Mechanical drawings usually use H (for heating, ventilating, and air conditioning) and P (for plumbing) prefixes, while electrical drawings use E in their numbering sequence. Other disciplines, when they apply, use other appropriate designations. ConDoc adopts this procedure and expands it by the addition of a three-digit number. The first digit designates the type of drawing; the following two digits indicate the drawing number from 00 to 99, which means that there could be 100 drawings related to each prefix.

The currently-assigned first digits, designating the type of drawing, are shown in Figure 12.1.

At present, 7-series through 9-series drawings have not been assigned. As ConDoc is more widely implemented and evolves through use, perhaps the previously-assigned numbers will change slightly and the number of drawing groups will expand. If you've followed this explanation, you should see that a drawing numbered A403 would be the third sheet of a group of drawings relating to ceiling construction.

You would know this automatically, without ever having seen the drawing itself; you would thus find it much easier to locate particular information.

For interior work, only three or four of the drawing groups listed in Figure 12.1 would normally apply. As the methodology advances and is adapted to the requirements of contemporary practice, there will probably be some further adjustments and fine tuning of the numbering system. This is not to suggest that individual designers should take the liberty of devising their own numbering system to be superimposed over what already exists. The real beauty of the whole process, like

Figure 12.1

Drawing Designation Numbers

0. General Information	This category might include a drawing index, a location map, a symbol legend, schedules, and a list of abbreviations.
1. Plans	Various plans required and any details relating directly to the plans.
2. Exterior Elevations and Transverse Sections	Drawings that rarely relate to interior design projects.
3. Vertical Circulation	Typically, stair sections and details along with drawings relating to elevator shafts. Again, rarely related to interior projects except for ADA issues.
4. Reflected Ceiling Plans	Include all details relating to ceiling construction.
5. Exterior Envelope Details	Interior designers can virtually forget about this series, which shows the construction of exterior walls and roofs.
6. Interior Detailed Plans, Elevations, and Details	The series that should encompass the work for interior designers.

MasterFormat, is that a national standard is being adopted. Until it is widely understood, applied, and thoroughly tested, any variations are likely to detract from its further development.

Another distinct advantage to the numbering system is that it allows a new sheet to be inserted at a logical point within an existing set. Also, a sheet that becomes obsolete for some reason can be pulled out without disrupting the numbering system, and subsequent sheets needn't be renumbered.

Graphic Modules

The balance of the drawing sheet is divided into a grid with the coordinates defined by numbers on the x-axis and letters on the y-axis, the way a standard road map is divided. The modules do not have to be square but should be nearly so. Depending on the sheet size, the grid modules should generally be three or four inches square. There are some proposals to standardize the grid size at a smaller module, but at present we see no advantage in doing so. A specific graphic itself is then identified by the grid coordinates of its lower left-hand corner. A key indicated on a plan drawing as C4/A602 tells the user that a detail of the indicated condition appears at grid coordinates C4 on the second drawing sheet of the 6-series drawing group.

The graphic module has its own internal organization. Each module has its own title block, which gives the grid coordinate number, the graphic title and scale, and any cross reference to other drawings. This usually takes up about one inch across the bottom of the module. A margin of approximately one inch around the remainder of the module is used for dimension lines and indication of column lines and center lines of pertinent features. The center of the module remains free for the graphic itself and its keynote symbols. This simple organization ensures that all drawings on a sheet and all drawings within a set are consistent.

Material Keynotes

Besides creating orderly and consistent drawings, ConDoc proceeds to another level of standardization that links the drawings to the project specifications. This is done by replacing lengthy lettered notes calling out materials with *keynotes* consisting of two parts: a prefix of the five-digit specification section where the indicated material is specified, plus a letter chosen by the designer to indicate material more specifically. Fire-resistive gypsum wallboard might be assigned the keynote of 09250.B. The prefix 09250 is the preassigned specification section number for gypsum wallboard under the CSI coding system, and the B suffix is the designer's own designation for fire-resistive type. If you look only at the amount of lettering saved, you can see that the 09250.B note contains only seven characters including the period, while lettering out the entire material designation uses 28 characters unless abbreviations are used. Multiply that savings by the number of times that note might appear on a set of drawings, and you can begin to appreciate both the time savings and the reduction of clutter that are natural by-products.

In addition to material keynotes, there may be a need to use some general notes that are not material-specific. These are numbered consecutively. Some prefer to call them out as "Note 1" and so forth. Our own preference is to place the number in a square in much the same fashion as a revision number is placed in a triangle or delta symbol (Δ).

To effectively adopt the ConDoc keynote system, you will need to develop a master list of keynotes. Probably the best way is to review old sets of drawings to compile a list of commonly used notes. If they were appropriate on previous projects, they will probably continue to occur with some frequency on future projects. You will undoubtedly discover a multitude of notes that describe one product in a number of different ways. Here's your opportunity to standardize these notes into one standard keynote. We've often seen sets of drawings where the product called "gypsum wallboard" in the specifications was noted on various drawings as "drywall," "gyp. board," "gypsum drywall," and several other variations. Think of the confusion saved when a specific material is called out in one consistent fashion in both the drawings and the specifications.

Once your master list is prepared, only selected people should be able to modify it. If too many people have the authority to make modifications, your list will be in a constant state of flux and unnecessary and redundant notes may begin to appear. For each project, then, a project-specific list of keynotes will be compiled from the master list.

Drafters can then note drawings by using the standard project keynotes. If situations arise in which there is not an appropriate keynote for the condition, it should be brought to the attention of the project manager. He or she will then go back to the master list. If the desired note is not found there, a new note should be adopted and added to both the project keynote list and the master.

Advantages of the ConDoc Method

Once you've had experience with the ConDoc methodology, we think you'll recognize the following advantages:

- Drawings are clear, consistent, and conform to a standard that is rapidly being adopted on a broad scale.

- Drawings and specifications are positively linked, resulting in fewer inconsistencies.

- The designer is forced to make technical decisions during drawing production, allowing the specifications to develop along with the drawings.

- Drawings are less cluttered and therefore more readable. The pertinent information contained in the keynotes is organized in one location where it's easily referred to.

- Little time is spent composing drawings. The ConDoc format automatically creates a framework in which the drawings are easily composed.

- There is little chance that information will be repeated unnecessarily. When something is changed, it is changed once—in the keynote. There is no need to scour the drawings looking for obsolete notes, and no need to worry that you may have missed one.

- Contractors and material suppliers realize the system's benefits. They can tell at a glance, from the keynotes on each drawing sheet, whether specific information they might need is indicated on the particular sheet.

Just as specifications have become easier to prepare and use through the widespread adoption of the CSI format, drawings prepared using ConDoc methodology—which includes the CSI format—will undoubtedly become clearer and more easily used.

Having espoused a method for preparing drawings in general terms, we will now discuss specific drawing groups.

PLAN DRAWINGS

A plan drawing is any drawing that slices horizontally through the space and depicts the elements that lie below the point where the cut is made.

The Floor Plan

The most important drawing for any project is the *floor plan*. It is the generator of all other drawings and provides the most fundamental information. Virtually all building trades find a major portion of their information on this drawing. It must be well developed before most of the other drawings can even be started. Because of its importance, the floor plan will consume more production time than any other drawing in the set; in many instances, the time spent on the floor plan alone will equal the time spent on all the other drawings combined.

Once the floor plan is drawn in its basic form, it will be used to create duplicate plans for the indication of finishes, ceiling construction, mechanical work, electrical work, and any other discipline that may require a plan drawing for delineation. When extensive demolition work is required, a separate plan to clearly call out the scope of that work will be needed.

Because of its importance and the fact that so many other drawings are derived directly from it, it is of paramount importance that the floor plan be accurately made. While other drawings can tolerate some degree of inaccuracy without compromising their usefulness, the floor plan cannot afford to be treated in a similar manner. Since the floor plan will be the place where virtually all significant changes will be recorded in the development of the documents, it is essential that it remain as error-free as possible. Otherwise, errors tend to multiply as changes are made.

Let's look at the type of information that must be conveyed by the floor plan. Since it will be used to lay out the work, it must show the location of all partitions noting their types, and the location of doors, windows, built-in equipment, and recesses required to accommodate items that may be partially or fully concealed in the finished space.

It must clearly show any changes in the floor plane itself, such as patterns, changes in materials, and changes in elevation including ramps, curbs, steps, elevated bases or platforms, mat recesses, and similar items.

When the design is particularly complex and the information that is required on the floor plan becomes difficult to indicate clearly, separate drawings at a larger scale may be required for portions of the plan. For example, toilet rooms, where a significant amount of information must be shown within a confined space, are often drawn at a larger scale (see the "Enlarged or Detailed Plans" section later in this chapter). Also, if separate finish plans are being prepared, information relative to floor finishes and patterns is more appropriately conveyed there.

Dimensioning All items for which location is important must be clearly located by dimensions tied to fixed and unchanging features. Column centerlines and the surfaces of existing walls, partitions, and pilasters are typical points with a known location. Start your dimensioning at one of these points and ensure that all subsequent dimensions relate to them. A particular item can only be located relative to something that is already in place, so be careful not to dimension something relative to a feature that doesn't exist at the time the information is needed. For instance, don't locate a partition that's related to the surface of some built-in casework. That relationship may be important to you, but in the normal sequence of construction the casework will be one of the last things to be installed. Dimension only those items for which the location is critical for laying out the work. If the location of an item can vary slightly without causing problems, pinning down its location, particularly if doing so might conflict with something else that really matters, has little value. If two features are to line up with each other, call out the dimension for the one that is controlling and note the other as aligning with it. If something is to be subdivided into a number of equal parts or spaces, it is acceptable to indicate the divisions and to dimension them as "equal." Trying to work out exact equal dimensions, particularly where field conditions may exhibit some variation in the overall unit, is unnecessary and often wasted effort.

Unless it is absolutely unavoidable, do not repeat dimensions, either on the same drawing or on more than one drawing. The reason is simple. If that dimension ever changes, it can be changed in one place without having to search out other references to it.

When dimensioning the location of partitions there are several schools of thought about how to do it. Adopt the system that best serves your needs and use it consistently. The principal methods are:

- Dimension to the centerlines of partitions and ignore their ultimate thickness. This is perhaps the easiest method and results in fewer dimensions of small increments, but requires additional dimensions to indicate partition thicknesses.

- Dimension to the finished face of the partition. Designers frequently prefer this method — furniture layout is easier when one knows the finished dimensions required to accommodate specific pieces. The only drawback to this system is that it may complicate field layout, particularly if the finished construction on opposite sides of the partition is unequal in thickness. The contractor must carefully allow for those thicknesses when laying out the location of framing members.

- Dimension to the "rough" face of the underlying framing system. Contractors tend to prefer this system since it is the framing system's location that must be determined first and ease of establishing it is of primary importance. With this system, the contractor transfers the marked dimensions to the floor surface, snaps chalk lines, and sets the runner track to receive metal studs (or the sole plate in the case where wood studs are used) neatly on the chalk lines. While this method is advantageous from a construction standpoint, finish material thicknesses must be subtracted to arrive at clear finished dimensions for the layout of furniture.

Whichever method you choose should be followed consistently and clearly explained and noted on the drawings. If you're forced to change methods for some reason, clearly call out where and how that non-typical condition exists. Otherwise, confusion will invariably result.

Try to limit dimensions to the largest increment possible. Small fractions are difficult to deal with and construction does not proceed with the degree of precision that one might expect. Although lasers as measuring devices are increasingly used in construction, the steel tape measure and the carpenter's folding rule still determine most measurements. Even under the best of circumstances, these devices can be read accurately only to the nearest 1/8″. Dimensioning to smaller increments only increases the chance of error. Design professionals would be well advised to create large dimensions to the nearest quarter-inch and to reserve 1/8″ increments, if they must be used, for such measurements as material thicknesses.

Keying the Floor Plan to Other Drawings

Since the floor plan is the generator of virtually all other drawings, it is important to orient the user to the relationships among the various drawings from the plan itself. This is done by a system of "keying" or "targeting." A *key* is a standard symbol used to locate the related drawing. Two examples are shown in Figure 12.2. In most instances the key designates the drawing on which more information is located.

Some designers adopt very elaborate keying systems, but any simple indication that conveys essential references is usually preferable. The ConDoc system and the methods employed in the drawings for the sample project in Chapter 15 of this book illustrate an efficient system. Use keys to locate partition types and sections, details, interior elevations, door designations, enlarged plans, and similar data that are more fully developed elsewhere.

Enlarged or Detailed Plans

Enlarged or *detailed plans* are often required to delineate small spaces or those where a concentration of items requires close tolerances that cannot be accurately located on smaller-scale plans. Toilet rooms, kitchens, areas with built-in casework, areas to receive complex floor patterns, and small spaces for mechanical or electrical equipment are typically enlarged for this purpose. To avoid conflicts you should not repeat the same information at both scales. The level of detail indicated on the smaller-scale plan should be confined to essential elements only, leaving the detail plan to show features in greater detail. For example, if you are enlarging a toilet room plan to show locations of accessories and perhaps a complex tile pattern for the floor, show only the plumbing fixtures and other major components on the small plan. Trying to duplicate other features only obscures the plan and leads to conflicts between the two drawings. Reference to the enlarged plan is made on the base floor plan by a note or by drawing an outline around the area and keying it to the detailed plan.

Reflected Ceiling Plans

Projects that have major design configurations or elements that occur within or near the ceiling plane usually require a *reflected ceiling plan,* so called because it is drawn as though one were looking at the ceiling in a mirror on the floor. It can be used to locate soffits, lights, mechanical grilles and diffusers, coves, drapery tracks and pockets, sprinkler heads, smoke alarms, speakers, access openings to mechanical or electrical equipment, patterns of finish materials, or other changes in material or level at the ceiling. Since it is really a horizontal section cut just below

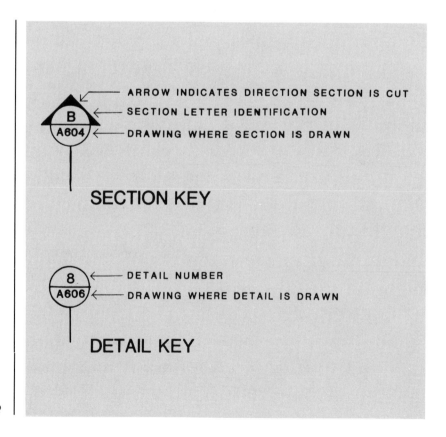

Figure 12.2

the ceiling itself, elements such as doors and their swing paths, which are normally shown in plan, are omitted, as are the door openings themselves unless they extend to the ceiling. As with floor plans, reflected ceiling plans must be keyed to related drawings.

Finish Plans

Another drawing that is rooted in the floor plan is the *finish plan*. A finish plan is simply a floor plan devoid of extraneous information; it is annotated by a keying system to denote floor and wall finishes. It is particularly useful when a number of different finishes are incorporated in a single space and it is important to show their limits. It is generally not used for simple projects where a schedule or other simple device can delineate finishes. The finish plan, too, must be keyed to related drawings that may be required to illustrate finish details or to indicate finish limits where finishes change at points that are not major intersections. For example, say the fascia of a soffit is finished differently from the adjoining wall, or opposite sides of a door and its frame are to receive different finishes. In these instances, separate details or elevations may be required.

Furniture Plans

The *furniture plan* shows the location of furniture and equipment. In most cases furniture is supplied and installed under a separate contract (see *Chapter 14: Furniture*), but if furniture placement is critical with respect to elements to be built under the general contract, it should be included within the drawing set for the contractor's reference and coordination. In this instance, it is simply labeled as "Not in Contract, For Reference Only."

Mechanical and Electrical Plans

Mechanical and *electrical plans* are required unless their information can be shown on the base floor plan. If engineering consultants are engaged for the project, these drawings are their responsibility — however, their drawings are developed directly from the designer's floor plan. Mechanical and electrical plans commonly include a plumbing plan; an HVAC (heating, ventilating, and air conditioning) plan; a fire protection plan (showing where a sprinkler system is to be installed); a power plan that also shows communications and data wiring; and a lighting plan.

Sometimes the work for mechanical and electrical trades is done under a *design-build* contract, meaning that the design professional sets the essential parameters for the functioning of the systems and the respective subcontractors engineer and construct the systems. Under this scenario, the designer furnishes drawings that indicate only the desired locations and characteristics of exposed components. The installing contractors then prepare what are essentially shop drawings, which are submitted for review and approval. In either case, mechanical and electrical drawings are essentially diagrammatic in nature and rarely establish exact locations. For that reason, if a ceiling diffuser must be in a precise location because it relates to a design element, or if lighting fixtures must be placed in a particular fixed pattern, you may have to supplement these drawings with either specific dimensions or details that set forth those requirements. This is necessary, for example, in the location of electrical receptacles. The electrical engineer may indicate a sufficient number of receptacles to comply with program and code requirements but neglect to consider their exact placement as they relate to furniture arrangement.

PLAN DRAWING CHECKLIST

At this point, it should be obvious that the floor plan determines the content of virtually every other drawing. That's why it's so important that the floor plan is developed carefully and in such a way that it can be easily cross-referenced to the other drawings. Since the amount and type of data that must be shown on plan drawings is so extensive, it is wise to approach the task in a systematic fashion. Figure 12.3 is a checklist that attempts to do that. You might adopt it, or develop your own checklist that responds to the needs of your project.

ELEVATIONS, SECTIONS, AND DETAILS

As we've seen from the previous section, the plan drawings tend to show the most critical information, but they alone cannot fully depict all of the project requirements. They must be supplemented with elevations, sections, and details.

Elevations

Elevations are the most pictorial of all drawings since they show vertical surfaces as they would actually appear in the completed project.

Plan Drawing Checklist

Floor Plans

Dimensions	Fully coordinated, locating partitions, openings, shafts, and chases with all dimensions tied to column centerlines or other fixed points. Avoid closing dimension strings when not necessary.
	Room names and numbers coordinated with Finish Schedule or Finish Plan.
Walls	Keyed to partition types with fire walls and area separations indicated. Low walls distinguished from full-height partitions.
Demolition	Existing work to remain or to be removed unless indicated on Demolition Plan.
Floor information	Elevations, changes in material, depressed or raised areas, mat recesses, access flooring, ramps, and flooring patterns if not shown on larger scale pattern.
Doors	Door swings and door marks referring to Door Schedule.
References to other details	Section cut lines, large scale plans, interior elevations, and miscellaneous plan details.
Architectural woodwork	Location and outline of cabinets, countertops, shelving, and other millwork keyed to appropriate details and large scale plans.
Specialties	Location of directories, fire extinguishers and cabinets, operable partitions, lockers, and other similar items.
Equipment	Location of built-in furniture, library stacks, display cases, vending machines, and other fixed equipment.
Furnishings	Location of fixed artwork, manufactured casework, fixed seating, and similar items. Coordinate with Furniture Plan.
Plumbing	Fixture locations, floor drains, drinking fountains, service sinks, and toilet partitions. Coordinate with Plumbing Plan.
Electrical	Location of outlets critical to casework and furniture installation. Coordinate with Electrical Power Plan.

Figure 12.3

Plan Drawing Checklist

Reflected Ceiling Plans

Ceiling information	Indicate ceiling changes in plane and material, location of skylights and other major elements that have a direct relationship with Floor Plan elements.
	Indicate suspended acoustic ceiling grids, access panels, drapery and blind pockets, trim around columns, and similar items.
	Indicate coves, soffits, and similar items keyed to appropriate details.
Electrical	Location of light fixtures coordinated with Electrical Lighting Plan.
Plumbing	Location of sprinklers coordinated with Fire Protection Plan.
HVAC	Location of ceiling diffusers coordinated with HVAC Plan. Check clearance of structure and ductwork.

Figure 12.3 (continued)

Elevations typically do not use graphic symbols, nor do they show work that will be ultimately concealed.

Elevations should be relatively simple, straightforward drawings, but some designers try to make them do strange things. One of the more common techniques is to try to combine all four elevations of a single space into one drawing called a "wraparound" or "unfolded" elevation. While this has some creativity associated with it and isn't too confusing for a simple rectilinear room, it becomes a veritable brain teaser when the space has recesses or projections into it. If this technique intrigues you, save it for schematic presentation drawings. Don't use it on working drawings where clear communication is the goal.

Interior elevations have a particular purpose — to show elements that cannot be indicated on other types of drawings. Too often, designers fill up sheets with interior elevations that contribute little to documenting the project requirements. An elevation that shows a blank wall containing only a door is not very valuable. The door and its configuration are located in plan and described in the door schedule; and any notes calling out wall materials merely duplicate the finish schedule.

Elevation drawings generally show two things:

- The heights of items that cannot be shown elsewhere.
- The limits of two or more materials, typically those that have a horizontal juncture and thus cannot be delineated in plan.

Sections

Section drawings cut through the construction vertically in the same way a plan cuts through construction horizontally. For that reason, sections employ graphic symbols. Much of what they indicate is concealed in the finished work. Section drawings are particularly useful in depicting offsets or changes in the vertical plane. For example, moldings or reveals that have depth would appear only as lines in an elevation, but their profile would be delineated in a section.

Vertical Dimensions

Since both elevations and sections show vertical elements, it is important that they indicate vertical dimensions just as plans indicate horizontal ones. Plans should indicate horizontal dimensions, while elevations and sections should indicate vertical dimensions without repeating horizontal ones. As with plans, all dimensions should be tied to and from fixed and unchanging points and should set the tops of pertinent elements.

Details

One of the masters of modern architecture, Ludwig Mies van der Rohe, once said, "God is in the details." Most thoughtful design professionals couldn't agree more.

A detail is a section (either horizontal or vertical) cut at a point that shows the manner in which several materials come together and relate to each other. A detail is drawn at a scale that is much larger than other drawings to show actual thicknesses and close tolerances that cannot be shown on more general or smaller drawings.

Remember, any time you create a condition for which you do not provide a detail, you give the field mechanics the option of deciding how to execute it. Usually, their decision will be technically sound and appropriate from a functional viewpoint, but the risk is that their decisions are very likely to be less sensitive from an aesthetic viewpoint than the design professional's solution would be. This is not intended to make a case for detailing absolutely everything. Young designers, in particular, should be reminded that not every condition should be a "showstopper." Some conditions should be executed in the most simple, straightforward manner possible. In fact, most experienced designers understand that a project devoid of a multitude of "fussy" details tends to highlight the few really important details that set the project apart from more mundane efforts.

What details must be drawn? This is always a difficult question to answer and must be carefully considered for every project. Inexperienced designers frequently over-detail the parts of the project that they clearly understand and gloss over the parts with which they have less familiarity.

We cannot list details that will be required for every project, nor can we make rules that establish even typical ones. The basic parameters for using details follow.

- **Any type of joint where two materials meet** is a good candidate for a detail. Consider how the ceiling plane meets the wall. If this juncture is articulated with a recess, a drapery pocket, a molding, or some other special condition, you must show the contractor just what finished condition must be obtained; that can be done only with a detail. On the other hand, if the juncture is one where the materials meet in a simple right-angled inside corner, drawing the condition adds nothing to the contractor's understanding. The contractor needs to know the height of the finished ceiling—this information can be adequately conveyed on a schedule or a dimension that is shown on an elevation or section.

- **Any point where a material changes planes** is usually illustrated by a detail even if it's just a simple drawing that shows the finished profile. For example, if wood trim turns a corner, you will need to show whether the transition is intended to be a miter or a simple butt joint.

- **Any condition where a manufactured item is to be installed in or on field-built surfaces** is usually shown in a detail. Recessed items might include fire extinguisher cabinets, projection screens, various toilet accessories, and miscellaneous mechanical and electrical items. In these cases, it is often important to show how transitions at junctures with surrounding construction are to be made. In some cases, surface-mounted items may be treated in the same manner as recessed ones, but more often it is sufficient to call out mounting heights and centerlines. Virtually all manufactured items can be drawn in outline and identified by notation with only their connection to other construction detailed. Too often, drafters draw ready-made products as if the contractor were to actually manufacture them, by showing extrusions and hardware items including screw and bolt threads. The result is beautiful drawings that serve no real purpose. Remember that the purpose of drawings is to communicate and that they are not an end in themselves; they are only the means to an end. That end is the constructed project.

- **Any conditions related to the expansion and contraction of materials exposed to changing temperature and humidity conditions** are usually illustrated by a detail. This requires an understanding of the physical properties of the materials one is using. The prudent designer recognizes the potential occurrence of these problems and designs for them by creating joints with reveals or other features that permit movement of the material in a way that masks dimensional changes in the material. While differential movement may be quite small and insignificant over a limited area, large expanses of the same material may cause the cumulative effects of the expansion to cause problems that may domino and create damage elsewhere.

Let's look briefly at conditions that must normally be detailed. Custom-designed casework must be carefully detailed and dimensioned. Some design professionals take this to extremes, attempting to prepare what are, in reality, shop drawings. Shop drawings are the cabinetmaker's drawings that indicate how the casework will be built. They show details of construction and joinery that are matched to their expertise and the equipment they have available. If you attempt to do the same thing in the contract documents, you may create problems by indicating conditions that are contrary to contemporary shop practices. It is sufficient for you to show the casework in its basic form, clearly setting forth profiles, finishes, and dimensions, and leave other aspects to the cabinetmaker.

Detailing Millwork Generally, millwork sections such as moldings and door frames must be detailed. However, if they are stock manufactured items that are to be applied in a conventional manner, you can simply call them out and note their locations without actually drawing them. If you are using standard metal door frames, nothing is gained by drawing them in minute detail unless they join with another material in an unusual manner. Then it is appropriate to draw them in profile to illustrate the desired treatment at the juncture. Recognize that a door frame has both sides (jambs) and a top (head), but most of the time these elements are identical. If you must draw a detail of the jamb condition, it is usually sufficient to merely note that the head condition is similar.

For most interior work, door sill details are superfluous. Occasionally you may have a flooring transition that occurs at a door — the relationship of that change to the door frame, particularly if a threshold or saddle is required, is an important consideration. If the transition is a simple one, however, the requirements may be covered with a note. Most designers make it a practice to join the two materials at a point where the joint will be concealed by the door when it is in a closed position. Creating a drawing that indicates this is unnecessary; the condition can be covered with a note on the drawings or within the specifications under "Execution" in the appropriate sections.

Detailing Hidden Construction Hidden aspects of construction rarely need to be shown in detail. Excessive detailing is often used for soffits, furred spaces, and similar items. Most of the time actual job conditions are different enough from what the drafter assumed that the construction is improvised to suit working conditions. What is really required is a simple drawing, devoid of unnecessary detail, that clearly indicates the desired result. The contractor will use whatever means are available to produce that result.

Detail Checklist

As you may imagine, drawing is not the problem — it's knowing *what* to draw. Some of that knowledge comes from experience, but mostly it's a matter of analyzing the project requirements with an eye toward understanding what needs to be communicated and then choosing the most direct ways of communicating essential information.

No list of details would apply to every project or even a majority of projects. The following list, however, categorizes some typical conditions for which details may be required:

- Changes in floor plane, such as steps or platforms.
- Changes in ceiling plane, such as soffits and coves.
- Changes in wall plane, such as built-in niches and recessed items.
- Custom built casework, counters, and furniture.
- Millwork and trim, including door and window frames, bases, chair rails, picture molds, and crown molds.
- Doors and windows, if custom made.
- Corners, particularly if the corner is a transition point between two materials.
- Any transition point between two materials.
- Partition types (details must show how they're constructed).

- Built-in items such as recessed projection screens, fire extinguisher cabinets, and pocket doors.
- Any point at which a material changes in color or finish to create a pattern.
- Any instance in which other drawings are at a scale that is not sufficient to clearly indicate the scope of work.

Having established what drawings are needed to fully describe the project requirements, it is time to consider how those drawings can be effectively produced. The following section covers principal production techniques along with a system designed to produce clear, concise, and comprehensive drawings that coordinate with the specifications.

DRAWING PRODUCTION

The term *drawing* may be a bit misleading, since production will increasingly rely less on original drafting and more on assembling prepared graphics that may not be drawings as such. This section covers everything from pencil drawings on tracing paper to computer generated automated drafting (CADD) and everything in between. If you're an old hand at using a variety of systems drafting methods, you might pick up a few new tricks here. If you're still producing drawings the way you did 10 or 15 years ago, hold on to your hat — you're sure to learn many new methods that can cut your production time drastically.

Saving Production Time

Why is reducing production time important from a project management viewpoint? Suppose your firm's ordinary profit target is 10% of gross fee. If your total fee for a project is $50,000, the expected cost of producing design development and construction drawings might consume up to $30,000 in direct costs. If you can save 20% in production costs, that figure is reduced to $24,000. Going back to our original assumption, the budgeted profit would have been $5,000. Coupled with the $6,000 savings in production, the total profit on the project would more than double. And that's just from an easily obtainable 20% improvement in production costs.

Some may take issue with this simplistic accounting; but whether the assumptions are accurate is really immaterial. The point is that small savings in actual production costs can result in significantly higher profits. That recognition alone is enough to recommend any methodology that holds promise for savings.

Remember, however, that saving time is rewarding only if you are working under a value-based agreement. Refer back to *Chapter 2: Contract Negotiation* if this proposition is unclear.

The Evolution of Drawing Production Methods For decades, design professionals have been producing drawings in much the same fashion. It starts with a drafting board equipped with a parallel horizontal ruling device, triangles, scales, and a pencil (or other drawing instrument). The drawing is done directly on tracing paper and copies are made by blueprinting or diazo printing. It is a time-consuming, labor-intensive process, but one that often must be mastered before a designer can move on to more advanced techniques.

The long recognized problem with drafting is that so much of it is repetitive. For this reason, design professionals have concentrated on devising methods of reusing previously drawn items without having to actually redraw them.

At one time virtually every design office had a drawer full of rubber stamps containing repetitive drawing elements. Because the alignment of these elements on the finished drawing was always a difficult chore, the most effective stamps were actually not rubber but clear soft plastic images mounted on clear lucite blocks. In this way one could see through the stamp and with just a bit of care could achieve perfect registration, assuming that one could accept the almost inevitable smearing of the stamp pad ink.

The next major advance was the appearance of clear appliqués that could be applied directly to the drawing. The use of adhesive-backed films pre-printed with repetitive data first appeared nearly 40 years ago. Initially they were used mainly for drawing title blocks, but quick-thinking design professionals soon realized that virtually any item that was used repetitively could be treated the same way. The development of standard office copiers and corresponding films that could be processed with them caused this technique to be widely used.

Appliqué drafting involves a wide variety of products, including dry transfer type (the kind you burnish through a carrier sheet), various types of "stickyback" sheets, shading films, and press-on tapes. Although some designers have had great success using these products — they are still widely used — they tend to have several drawbacks that have led many to abandon their use. The disadvantages to using appliqués are:

- Most appliqués are difficult to position precisely.
- Once applied, the appliqués are difficult to modify or change in any way.
- Many types of appliqués are almost impossible to remove if it becomes necessary to do so.
- Some appliqué products will not withstand the heat generated by diazo printing machines and will blister and break up in the process.
- Virtually all appliqué films, being less transparent than the tracing to which they are applied, leave a "ghost" when printed. This may also be caused by the fact that the adhesive employed is resistant to the ultra-violet light of the diazo machine. Some people have chosen to resolve this problem by creating graphics on clear acetate, commonly known as "slicks," and taping the slick to the tracing. Of course, they still have to contend with the unsightly ghosting of the tape itself.

This background discussion is intended only to give some perspective about continuing efforts to resolve the issue of using graphics that may reappear on every project, and indeed may even repeat many times on a single project, without going through the laborious process of redrawing the item each time it appears. This is not to suggest that you adopt some of the earlier efforts to deal with the problem. Some of these techniques do have continuing application, but most of them are relatively crude compared to more recently developed methods.

Advances in Drawing Production Technology

Overlay Drafting. The first major advancement in production technology began to emerge in the 1970s. It is known as *overlay drafting.* You may also know it as *registration* or *pin bar* drafting. Overlay drafting recognizes that many of the drawings that make up the set of project drawings are prepared over the same base. That is, virtually every plan drawing for a specific floor or area, regardless of its purpose or discipline, starts with the same drawing. Why then should it be redrawn over and over? That's nothing more than a colossal waste of time.

For years, design professionals have been drawing duplicate backgrounds called "blanks" or "dummies." Some have tried to eliminate the duplication by using sepia transparencies, but the results have never really been satisfactory. With the emergence of modern reprographic equipment and cameras along with polyester drafting film (which you may know by the trade name Mylar), many new possibilities were opened. Overlay drafting is simply a separation technique whereby information common to a number of drawings is drawn once on a *base* sheet and graphic details relating to a particular discipline are drawn on *overlay* sheets. The two or more sheets are then combined to produce a finished master sheet, from which prints are made. In this process, a single base sheet might be used to produce many separate finished sheets.

It is important to understand that everything drawn on base sheets will appear everywhere that the base sheet is used. What is drawn on the overlay sheet is unique and will be shown only once. Therefore, don't think of a composite drawing as one with a single base sheet (although that may be so) and multiple overlays. Think of it as a single overlay with one or more base sheets. For example, a printed sheet with title block and borders may be a base sheet because it will appear throughout the set or it may be the overlay sheet because of unique data that will be added. The same graphics cannot appear on two sheets since any slight misalignment in the printing process will create a double image.

The advantages of overlay drafting include the following:

- The base sheet is drawn only once. Changes to the base plan are made once rather than many times on a number of separate sheets.
- Drawing checking is easier. Since overlay sheets work over the same base and are in registration with each other, simply laying one overlay on top of another reveals areas of possible conflict.

While the advantages are significant, overlay drafting does have some disadvantages. The principal ones are:

- Overlay drafting is not a total system. It is ideal for plan drawings but has little or no application for other types of drawings.

- Polyester drafting film must be used. Ordinary vellums are not translucent enough or dimensionally stable enough to maintain registration.

- Reproduction methods are more sophisticated than those that can be undertaken in-house for all but the very largest firms. The service of a good reprographics shop is required for camera work and the photo reproduction of the overlays. Checkprints can be made by the diazo process by running the base sheet and overlays through the machine together, but it's nearly impossible to maintain proper registration in this manner. A flat bed *contact* or *vacuum frame* can be used to make a diazo sepia exposure by keeping the layers in true alignment and contact, but high quality work requires the use of a process camera to combine the separate layers photographically.

- Drawing in ink is almost mandatory. Pencil lines simply burn out in the process. Some advocates do claim that ink drafting, once mastered, is just as fast as pencil drawing, but there is enough resistance by many drafters, coupled with the difficulty of making corrections, to make this requirement a disadvantage.

- The use of pin bars (the devices that keep sheets in registration) and the need to pre-punch sheets for this purpose requires additional equipment and serves as an impediment. Pin bars are, however, readily available and your repro shop will probably pre-punch your sheets for you.

If you decide to use overlay drafting, you will need to pre-plan your job very carefully. Your base sheets will have to be developed to the point where they contain only the background reference data that must appear on all drawings. Since not all drafters can use the same base sheet simultaneously, you will want as many duplicates as you'll need to be produced photographically. As each drafter or consultant receives a base sheet, he or she will attach it to the pin bar on the drafting table, align a sheet of polyester film over it, and begin to create the overlay graphics.

You will need to plan an indexing system for the order of drawings to control the overlay process and indicate the sequence of overlays to be used in the reproduction process. This is usually done by creating identification numbers that are written on each sheet outside the trim margins of the drawing. Perhaps a code such as B-1, B-2 for base sheets and 0-1, 0-2 for individual overlays is the simplest method of identification. Then, when the sheets are sent to the repro shop for assembly you can indicate that drawing sheet number A-201 is comprised of base sheets B-1 and B-4 plus overlay sheet 0-3, or whatever sequence is appropriate. Figure 12.4 diagrams the basic assembly. Note that although the title block is shown on an overlay sheet it could occur on a base sheet.

Because the overlay system separates information in layers and because the overlays are held in close registration, it is easy to introduce color into the reproduction process through offset printing. In this way the base sheet(s) can be printed in black or gray ink and unique data on the overlay can be printed in another color. Because it is difficult to handle large sheets in the printing process, this technique is more commonly used when the drawings are reduced to half size. If you are interested in exploring this method, pay extremely careful attention to the scale of the originals. Lettering, line weight, and poché must be sufficient to retain clarity after reduction. While colored prints are infrequently used, it is more common to encounter single-color half-size prints since many people prefer the convenience of a smaller drawing package, particularly when the project is a large and complex one.

Composite Drafting. *Composite drafting* probably has the broadest application of all the methods discussed here. You may know this technique as "scissors drafting" or "cut and paste drafting." Composite drafting is based on the concept that virtually anything can be assembled in the manner of a patchwork quilt, and photographically or electrostatically reproduced to create a new original. This means you can use details from previous projects, manaufacturers' details, typewritten notes, and even photographs (more about photodrafting later) to produce a finished drawing sheet—often in hours, instead of the days or weeks that a comparable drawing using conventional drafting techniques might take.

With the emergence of large document copiers that can produce copies 36 inches wide by virtually any length on bond paper, vellum, or

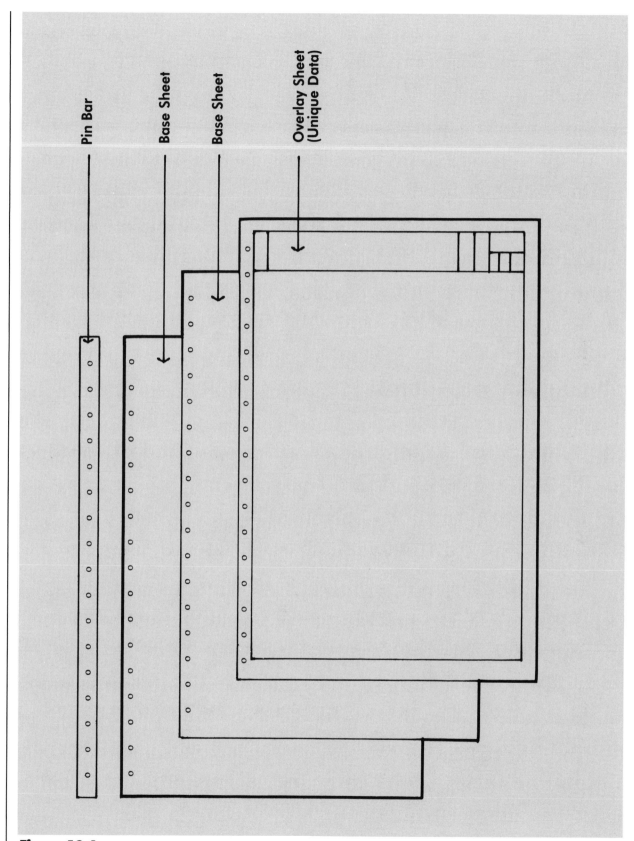

Figure 12.4

polyester, almost unlimited possibilities abound. Nearly every project contains numerous details that are similar to those used on previous jobs. It's easy to assemble entire sheets from previously drawn graphics (sometimes with just a few simple revisions) by attaching them to a base sheet carrier and having the resulting collage copied onto vellum or polyester film.

As you can see, the source of usable graphics is virtually unlimited. Many design professionals are reluctant to reuse manufacturers' details on their own working drawing sheets because they reflect a different drawing style and thus detract from the uniform appearance of the sheet. Aside from the fact that we all subscribe to the idea that the real purpose of the drawings is to convey information, the reality that a particular graphic looks out of place does constitute an affront to our aesthetic senses. The adoption of the ConDoc methodology, however, goes a long way toward resolving this dilemma. Once all of the drawing's original printed dimensions and material notations are removed in a copying, cropping, and retouching process, all that remains is the basic graphic. When new keynotes and dimensions conforming to ConDoc procedures are added to the graphic, its basic appearance will be so similar to the other graphic elements that any differences will not be apparent.

Since every graphic is a candidate for reuse, keep a file of all details that you develop. To use this method, you should try to develop details only to the point where they show information that might be common to other conditions. Suppose, for example, that you are drawing a wood door frame detail. Before you note that it is to be executed in a specific wood species that might render it inappropriate for another project, stop, copy, and file the detail for future use. Then complete the detail as required for the specific project. It's a good idea to also file the completed detail to serve as an example of how the reference detail can be appropriately adapted. Be careful about naming your detail file. Call these details (and think of them as) "sample" or "reference" details and note that they are to be adapted as required to meet specific project conditions. If you label them as "master" or "standard" details, inexperienced drafters are likely to copy them without regard to their applicability, thinking that they should not be altered.

One of the beauties of composite drafting is that the electrostatic copying process accepts originals without regard to their origin. Some originals do copy better than others, so do a little experimenting to find the most effective techniques. If you have difficulty visualizing how drawings from a variety of sources will combine on the finished sheet, you might prepare a test sheet. Simply take a sample of every type of graphic you might ever want to reproduce and assemble them on a carrier sheet. Use pencil drawings, ink drawings, blueline prints, photographs, drawings and pictures from catalogs and magazines, CADD plots, typewritten copy, and any other source you can think of. Use the graphics both in their original form and in enlarged and reduced copies. Have your reprographics shop make a full-size copy on vellum so you can see how well each type of original will reproduce. While this exercise will indicate the copier's capabilities, most people find that the best results are obtained when all graphic elements that make up a single sheet are reproduced on a standard office copier before being pasted up on the carrier sheet. In this way it is easier to obtain more uniform image intensity by regulating the copier exposure for each individual graphic. Even light pencil drawings, provided they're crisp and without wide variations in line weight, reproduce in such a way that they're indiscernible from ink originals or drawings that have been taken from other sources.

There are some common misunderstandings about the term *paste-up*. Many people have visions of having to secure every graphic with rubber cement, spray adhesive, or some other type of permanent mounting. Of course you may do that if you wish, but it's not really necessary. Simply align the individual graphics and tape down the corners with ordinary cellophane tape (the removable matt surface type is preferable). If you use the removable type, you can easily reposition elements if the need arises; once they have served their purpose, the graphics can be completely removed and the carrier sheet can be used again for another drawing. Try to secure elements well enough so they lie flat. If the edges curl, you may get an outline on the final print. Don't worry if this happens now and then; an electric eraser will easily remove stray marks.

Besides the ease and convenience of composite drafting, several people can work on the same sheet at the same time and each of them can be working in different media.

Screened Intermediates. One of the advantages of modern reprographics is the ability to make screened intermediates (that is, solid images that are printed as closely-spaced dots) over which additional drawing information is placed in solid lines. Then the background prints as a subdued image, subordinate to the added data. This can add immeasurably to the clarity of certain drawings, since specific information can be emphasized while maintaining its relationship to other elements without those elements obscuring it in any way.

Ordinarily this process involves expensive camera work, but you can use a few tricks to obtain nearly identical results with a copy machine and a bit of ingenuity. Use a sheet of acetate film large enough to fill the image exposure surface of your copier (usually 11″ x 17″). Buy some adhesive-backed shading film with closely spaced *white* dots and transfer it to the entire surface of your acetate sheet. Then simply copy the drawing that you want "screened" through this assembly. The copier print will come out looking very much like an expensive photographically-screened print. You may then add new data directly on the copy and paste it up on your carrier sheet to be re-copied as a new original. If the drawing you want screened is larger than the maximum size print your copier will make, copy it in sections and splice the sections together.

CADD. Computer-aided design and drafting (CADD) has had a major impact on drawing production and promises to be the major influence for the foreseeable future. It has been embraced by firms that are capable of absorbing the capital outlay for both hardware and software as well as the cost of training staff. Because systems are constantly changing and hardware costs are continuing to decline, even very small firms may find it profitable to invest in a system.

Design professionals have a love/hate relationship with computers in general and CADD in particular. CADD proponents tend to get so caught up in its almost unlimited potential that they fail to recognize some of its inherent weaknesses as they apply to actual practice. Resistors, on the other hand, are too quick to dwell on CADD's drawbacks without conceding that, when appropriately employed, it can do truly amazing things to save time and labor.

Perhaps resistance to CADD is better understood when one considers that graphic communication is at the heart of all training for the design professions. Designers stimulate creativity by drawing. They use sketches to explore thoughts and ideas that in many cases represent a very personal and sensitive language. A computer begins to intrude on the dialogue a designer sets up with his or her sketch pad. A CADD drawing is created by a series of electronic impulses that are carefully manipulated and controlled. It does not possess a life of its own and does not lend itself to exploring a thought; its realization is grounded in decisions already made.

Despite its limitations, CADD is a marvelous tool. It easily produces accurate drawings of repetitive elements, automatically stores and copies those elements, recreates mirror images, calculates dimensions and areas, updates keynotes, and concurrently develops schedules. Every project manager who has carefully tracked production time has usually found that the time spent making changes and corrections nearly equals the original drafting time. It's here that CADD really shines; wholesale changes can be made in the blink of an eye.

CADD realizes the benefits of overlay drafting as drawings are put together in layers in much the same way that bases and overlays are assembled. It also uses many of the principles of composite drafting as it easily manipulates stored graphics, moving and repositioning drawings with ease.

Because in most offices the CADD-literate people are not those who make design and production decisions, internal communication can be a problem. The back and forth process of designers preparing rough sketches for CADD input, checking the plotted result, and making corrections may take as much effort as that required for more traditional methods. The real advances with CADD are realized when the people operating the system are, in fact, the generators of the drawings.

One of the major selling points of CADD has been its touted ability to reduce errors, but this is not necessarily so. Of course, errors are eliminated from largely repetitive work because once something is done correctly, any repetitions are automatically correct. However, the opposite is just as true and CADD may actually mask errors that jump right out in manual drafting because the drawing looks so finished and precise that the checker is lulled into overlooking items that might otherwise be apparent.

Some of the other disadvantages of CADD include the following:

- Most plotters are painfully slow. As a result, plots are made very sparingly and instead of working with current information, most people are working from last week's plots. Also, the project manager often has a difficult time knowing the status of the project because producing a set of checkprints may be difficult.

- CADD contributes to overdrawing. Because it draws so quickly and efficiently and the generation of extraneous lines is so automatic, we are prone to simply accept over-rendered graphics, not because they contribute to understanding but because they may enhance the appearance of the drawing. We don't immediately recognize that more important information is often sacrificed or obscured.

Despite a few drawbacks, CADD will come into even more widespread use as its sophistication increases and its cost decreases. Coupled with the fact that draftsmanship is a dying art and its practitioners command ever-increasing salaries, there is little wonder that CADD usage promises to grow in geometric proportions.

Having discussed some overall approaches for drawing production, let's turn our attention to several specific techniques that can be utilized within the basic systems described.

Freehand Drafting Sketches and simple diagrams are the designer's means of communication — not only with others but with him- or herself. Design professionals are literally the only occupational group that has at the core of its educational process the mastering of visual communication skills. For years experienced production people have used these skills by drawing freehand details and then passing them along to junior drafters to "hardline" directly on the drawing sheets. More often than not, some aspects suffered in the translation and the completed graphics simply lacked the clarity of the sketches. Why not find a way to utilize the freehand drawings themselves?

Experienced senior designers who are accustomed to drawing accurate freehand details will adapt to doing finished details in this manner with ease and will endorse the concept enthusiastically. Others will never master the technique and will strongly oppose its use. Some, if forced to draw freehand details, may surreptitiously tool-draft the graphic and then trace it. That, of course, defeats the whole purpose and makes double work. It may be best to confine those designers' work to aspects of production with which they are most comfortable and not expect them to do any freehand work.

Although floor plans and other small-scale drawings are not normally suited to freehand drafting, large-scale details are ideally suited for this treatment. Most experienced drafters are comfortable working directly on inexpensive white or canary sketching tissue, often called "flimsy" or "bumwad." While this paper is somewhat fragile, it is sufficient for this purpose and accepts both pencil and ink very well. Many designers work directly over a graph paper underlayment that helps to keep freehand lines straight and aids in scaling without having to constantly use a scale itself. Soft pencil is commonly used but sure-handed drafters often work directly in felt-tipped pens, using a fine point one for secondary lines and an ordinary medium bold marker for emphasized line work.

An advantage of freehand drafting is the fact that you're normally forced to work at larger than usual scales; thus detail problems that aren't apparent at a smaller scale become instantly clearer. Elements that seem to be coordinated in small-scale drawings are suddenly exposed as having clearance or alignment problems.

You should experiment with the reduction process so that you have a clear understanding of how a freehand original reproduces at a smaller size. From these experiments you will be able to determine how to modify your techniques to realize the most desirable results. For example, any lettering or figured dimensions will have to be considerably larger on the original to be readable when reduced. Many designers avoid this problem by omitting all lettering from the original graphics, preferring to add the lettering to the finished reduced graphic. This is a particularly good method when a drawing sheet is comprised of a number of graphics drawn at varying sizes. By leaving the lettering to be done directly on the sheet when all individual drawings are at their ultimate size, the overall appearance is enhanced by the uniformity of the numbers and letters.

Even a mediocre typist can type about twenty times faster than the most proficient drafter can hand-letter the same information. Since everyone recognizes this fact, why not type as much data as possible directly on the drawings? The obvious answer is that most drawing sheets won't fit in a typewriter and even in an open carriage typewriter (such machines do exist), the handling of large drawing sheets would be extremely cumbersome. Remember, though, that using the techniques of appliqué drafting and composite drafting, typed material can be treated just as details are. That is, original material can exist in any size and be easily transported to the drawings. You will see that the drawings for the sample project in Chapter 15 use this technique for assembling schedules and keynotes, which are ideal components to employ this simple technique.

Photodrafting Photodrafting is an underused technique that more design professionals should take time to explore. It's really a very simple concept. Instead of conveying all drawing information with orthographic drawings, photographs combined with keynotes communicate essential information. We've all heard that "a picture is worth a thousand words" and, particularly in the case of renovation work, it may be the best possible way of explaining how existing conditions are meant to be treated. If you have a section of paneling that you wish to remove or replace, for example, why not take a picture of it and include it within the contract drawings along with specific notes about what exactly is to be done? The photographs can be combined on standard drawing sheets along with other detail drawings and notes. Sometimes photos are used primarily to supplement drawings, but often they can be stand-alone graphics in place of drawings.

If you think photodrafting is an expensive reprographics procedure requiring a large process camera and the making of halftones, you are thinking of the mechanics of a high-quality technique that is still valid but unnecessary for most work. With the arrival of office copiers with enlargement capabilities and large document copiers that can produce full-size drawing sheets, a whole new opportunity for photodrafting has evolved. Entire small projects have been completely drawn with photodrafting quickly, easily, and at far less cost than traditional methods.

Here's how it's done. First, take the photographs you need. Modern cameras are so easy to use that anyone who can sight through the viewfinder and hold the camera still should be able to produce usable photos. They don't have to be beautiful compositions; snapshot quality pictures that show the essential elements are sufficient. Just make sure that they're taken under lighting sufficient to produce sharp images with good contrast. Enlarge the photos to any size you need on a plain paper copier. You may have to make adjustments to the copier's exposure controls to produce optimum contrast, but a bit of practice should enable you to get clear and well defined black and white images on white bond paper. These, of course, may be cropped or trimmed to eliminate unwanted background or inapplicable elements. You can even "retouch" these photographs with pencil, felt-tipped pen, or liquid correction fluid. Treat these photos as you would any other graphic element used in composite drafting.

Planning Drawing Production

Now that we've given attention to various systems of drawing production and techniques that may be used to implement them, we must return to the fundamental issue of planning and laying out a set of drawings for a specific project. The first step is normally to compile a list of the drawings that one expects to generate. Having previously developed schematic and design development documents, you should have a clear idea of the number and types of drawings that will be required. For even the smallest project you'll need a floor plan, a finish schedule, and some selected details, at the very minimum. Beyond that, the size and complexity of the project will dictate the amount and type of information that will be required to document the contract requirements.

Cartoons or Mini-Mockups For anything but the smallest project, you would be wise to plan each drawing sheet in advance. This is done by sketching the layout of each sheet anticipated to obtain a rough set of small scale layouts called "cartoons" or "mini-mockups," which become working drawings for the working drawings. This process is invaluable. Among its advantages are:

- Every person working on the project knows exactly what goes on each sheet so there is no duplication.
- The mockups enable the project manager to do better time and cost estimates for production.
- The mockups help keep the project on schedule. The status of the final drawings, when compared with the cartoons, becomes more apparent.
- Clients can more readily see the scope of the work.

Remember, the reason for doing the mockups or cartoons is to plan the required project drawings — excessive refinement and overdrawing doesn't add to the process. For example, if you use a standard door schedule format, you know how much space it will consume. Just block out that space on the cartoon. There is no reason for a drafter to laboriously reproduce it in miniature. For most drawings, draw the rough outlines only and confine indications to the minimum amount required to convey the essential content of the drawing. One way to do many of the cartoons quickly, particularly those for plans, is to simply reduce your design development drawings to use as pasteups on your mini-mockup set.

Full-size Mockups Many firms have used the production of full-size drawing mockups very successfully. Recognizing that normal drafting procedures frequently require the drafter to block out rough drawings of the very graphics that will appear on the finished sheet before moving on to the final drawing, simply assemble the various study drawings on a mockup of the finished sheet. This technique gives a preview of the ultimate layout of the drawing set early, bringing critical issues into focus when problems can be resolved before they create a crisis under the pressure of a deadline. In this way many production decisions can be made quickly and changes can be effected before the finished drawings are finalized. Since problems tend to get resolved earlier, production gets expedited as the final days (or weeks) are devoted to execution without the usual delays associated with reconciling unanticipated conflicts at a time when even the smallest change can have a major impact. Although the ultimate drawings are less complete at any point than might be the norm, more information is worked out earlier in the process and is available to those who need it to proceed.

The emphasis in this process should be placed on getting a good representation of all necessary drawings assembled without undue regard for how "finished" it looks. After all, it's merely an intermediate exercise designed to create a road map for the final drawing. There are instances, however, where the mockup might be complete enough, and the graphic composition professional enough, that with just a little cleaning up, the mockup itself may be treated as a completed pasteup. If this happens too often, however, you're not using the technique to its fullest advantage since you are obviously moving directly into finished composite drafting.

If this idea appeals to you, you should recognize some of its pitfalls. The drafting of the finished drawings goes very quickly but is skewed toward the end of the time allotted for production, meaning that well into the production phase there is little to show that looks complete. This makes some clients nervous; even some project managers become impatient and subvert the whole process before its advantages can be enjoyed.

Drawing Production Summary

We have provided a broad overview of production methods and techniques. Try some of the methods we have discussed; and when you do, give them an adequate chance to work. With every method there is an initial period of trial and error until one masters its essential principles. Until you become comfortable with a technique, you are likely to experience some frustration and an inclination to revert back to the methods you have already mastered. All too often great time- and money-saving techniques have been discarded right on the brink of a significant breakthrough.

DRAWING AND CONTRACT DOCUMENT CHECKING

While the most extensive effort will be expended in checking drawings, the specifications and other instruments that make up the contract documents must be coordinated and checked also.

The purpose of all checking is not just to find errors, although that's important, but to eliminate conflicts. Simple errors are often discovered at a time when they can be rectified without having a damaging impact on the project. Conflicts, however, aren't always recognized as errors and tend to create problems that cause costly extra work to resolve.

It's important to understand that for even the smallest project, coordination can be an acute problem. It makes no sense to have a well-designed project that falls apart as a result of poor document coordination.

The Project Manual

We discussed production of the project manual in Chapter 11. All too often, the project manual is checked only for misspellings and punctuation errors. While this procedure has merit, a beautifully typed and duplicated project manual can be rife with technical errors, omissions, and conflicts.

Checking the project manual should begin with the front end documents. Compare the bidding and contract requirements with the project scope as defined by your agreement with the owner. Review the scope of the job and its limitations with the documents that have been produced. Ensure that the proper documents are included, that they are in the correct form, and that any modifications to preprinted standard documents are accurate. Checklists included with the sections of this book related to these documents should be a good starting point.

Check the project manual table of contents to see that all required specification sections have been written. Check each section to make sure that the proper format has been followed and that all three parts are included. Review Part 1 in each section for compliance with contract requirements and the sections included under Division 1. Coordinate Part 2 with the drawings to make certain that the products specified conform with the materials indicated on the drawings and that they are in the same context as they appear on the drawings. Some of the more common types of discrepancies that occur are the identification of a standard manufactured product in the specifications while the drawings call for a custom-made component. Another example is when the specifications offer the contractor a choice of several comparable products while the drawings indicate a specific proprietary one. Finally, check Part 3 to ascertain that the installation or application methods and procedures reflect the requirements of the products that have been specified.

Checking the Drawings

There are essentially three levels of drawing checking that are undertaken for a typical project. The first two occur for every job; the third applies to projects where the work of several different disciplines must be coordinated. The first type is nothing more than the day to day checking that each person on the project team must undertake to see that his or her work is accurate and consistent with the other work on the project, coupled with the project manager's daily review of the status of the drawings. Each team member must be alert to the fact that his or her work influences all other work on the project in some way and that he or she must constantly check for areas of potential conflict.

The second type of checking is more structured. At regular intervals, the project manager must undertake a formal checking of all drawings. The manager can do it or, whenever possible, have another experienced person do the checking. Someone who approaches the project "fresh" is more likely to spot errors than someone who is perhaps too familiar with the drawings to note obvious discrepancies. That person, also, is more likely to raise questions about items that are not clearly communicated.

If the project manager elects to do the checking, here's a simple trick that's sometimes helpful. It may sound strange but try it! Run the prints backward, that is, reverse reading. The reversed prints immediately look like a different job; many of the graphics that you have looked at a hundred times will be seen in a new light. Obviously, this technique makes it difficult to read notes and dimensions but the extra effort may yield dividends.

There is no standardized method of checking drawings, but most experienced checkers use a simple system similar to the one described below. It, or some variation thereof, should be very effective for most checkers.

First, make two sets of check prints and bind one that will become the master set. The other set of sheets should be loose, temporarily held together with spring clips. The reason for keeping this set unbound is because individual checked sheets can be easily distributed to team members who are directly responsible for making corrections.

Drawing checking requires a consistent notation system to be effective so that every person who uses the check print clearly understands the checking process at any point. Most checkers rely on some color coding system in which the color of each notation immediately conveys the status of the work. If there is anything approaching a universal standard, it is a system that uses three colors: red, yellow, and green — just like a traffic light and with some of the same connotations. This coding is readily understood by virtually everyone. A green mark indicates that the checker has reviewed the item and finds it correct. A red notation indicates that an appropriate correction must be made. Yellow is applied over red marks to signify that the drafter has made the correction. The checker then verifies that the correction is complete by shading it with green.

A brown pencil can be used by the checker on his or her first pass through the check prints. There's nothing sacred about brown; it could be any color other than red, yellow, or green. However, if you're using blueline prints, blue is not a good choice because it doesn't stand out well enough from the rest of the print to make it useful. The brown pencil pass is used merely to mark items that need closer checking, make notations about cross references, and pose questions to be answered. Brown pencil marks are always supplanted by a red or green marking.

On the second pass through the drawings a red pencil (or pen) and a light green broadtipped highlighting pen are generally used. Highlighting pens are preferred because they don't obscure the drawing elements. Remember, it's just as important to mark the things that are right (in green) as it is to find errors. If you don't, you'll find yourself wasting time by rechecking the same drawings over and over.

If the checker finds something that requires a detail, he or she sketches it right on the check print or does it on a separate sheet and tapes it directly on the print.

After all the markings are made on the master set, the checker carefully transfers them to the unbound set and distributes the sheets to the individuals who are to make the corrections. When a drafter makes a correction, he or she goes over the red mark with a yellow highlighting pen. When all corrections are made on an individual sheet, the sheet is returned to the checker, who verifies each yellow mark with a green one that signifies that the correction has been made and transfers the marking to the master set. The unbound sheet can then be discarded.

The problem that usually arises from checking incomplete drawings is that as the drawing progresses toward completion, it is checked again; at each subsequent checking procedure the previously-checked elements are checked again, along with new work. One way to save the time that might ordinarily be spent reviewing previously-checked work is to use a simple overlay system. Instead of making notations directly on a checkprint, clip a sheet of tracing paper over the print, holding it securely in place with small spring clips along the top edge near the corners of the sheet. Mark the corners of the sheet border on the tracing paper to serve as registration marks so that the sheet can be realigned if it slips during handling, label the sheet number on the tracing, and date it. Then proceed to use normal checking methods, working directly on the tracing paper overlay. Everyone involved in the process keeps the overlay intact so that it continues to function in the same way as a true checkprint. As graphics are added to the original, an updated print is made and the working overlay is transferred to it.

When checking dimensions, a calculator that computes in feet, inches, and fractions is almost indispensable. There are a number of such models that are readily available for a relatively modest cost, an investment that will pay for itself many times over.

Be sure to check dimensions to see that they are ultimately tied to a fixed point and not "floating" in space. Make sure that dimension strings are added correctly, and use a scale to verify that they are graphically correct. Since architectural scales are arranged with two scales on the same face, one reading from left to right and the other reading from right to left, it is easy for the drafter to misread a dimension when scaling, or transpose numbers when reading a scale upside down.

Coordination Checking *Coordination checking* entails comparing the general construction drawings with those prepared for mechanical, electrical, and other specialty work. The primary thrust of this check is to look for conflicts and interferences. The obvious place to start is with ceiling construction, where so many aspects of the work come together in a limited space. For this reason, it's important that all plan drawings are prepared at the same scale and oriented on the drawing sheets in the same direction so that the drawings for all disciplines can be overlaid. In this way, conflicts are easier to spot. For example, if you place the lighting plan over the reflected ceiling plan, the lighting fixtures on both drawings should coincide. While most checkers use the original drawings for this purpose, there is an even better way using prints. Since prints are opaque, or nearly so, this process does require a light table. The technique is very simple. Take a print of the reflected ceiling plan and color in all lighting fixtures with a *blue* highlighter pen. Then take a print of the lighting plan and color the fixtures with a *yellow* highlighter pen. Align both of the prints on your light table. All fixtures that coincide will appear *green* and any areas that remain either blue or yellow will indicate that a fixture is shown on one plan but not the other.

This process should be repeated for other elements, such as HVAC and fire protection devices. For example, color in ceiling diffusers on the HVAC plan in one color and the diffusers shown on the reflected ceiling plan in another color. The resulting combined color when the two plans are overlaid will indicate that the drawings coincide, while any areas of a single color will point up the fact that the item has been omitted from one of them. Then lay the HVAC plan over the lighting plan. In this instance you will be looking for the colored elements to be separated. If any coincide, a conflict is indicated that must be addressed.

In addition to checking the location of mechanical and electrical work against the reflected ceiling plan, be sure to check vertical clearances. First check the ceiling heights against the bottom elevation of major structural members. Then, check the actual depth of recessed lighting fixtures for clearance under beams and the path that ductwork and piping must take to avoid interference. If you're working with a new building, the structural drawings should provide the information you need. If not, you will have to go back to your space survey.

The light table technique also works well for items that are located on wall surfaces. For example, you can check the power plan against the furniture plan in the same manner to see that junction boxes, receptacles, and telephone and data outlets are correctly located relative to furniture panels and the fixed equipment they serve.

The Final Check The final checking that should be undertaken just prior to the issuance of the contract documents is a combination of the types of checking that we have described. Special emphasis in the final checking should also be given to such things as seeing that the title blocks are properly completed and that all sheets are numbered and dated, with seals (if required) affixed.

In virtually every project there are typical conditions that repeat many times. In some cases, because of some minor variation in controlling parameters, a condition that is similar to but not identical to the typical condition is created. When this happens, it's important that it has been specifically called out as such lest the field mechanics assume that it is a typical one and execute it that way. Check to see that this has been clearly communicated.

Drawing Checking Checklist

Checking can be a burdensome task but it's absolutely essential. An all-inclusive checklist might make it easy. Unfortunately, we must rely on experience; each person who approaches the task must be prepared to address unforeseen problems. Although there is no way to generate a truly complete list, the following checklist has been compiled to help you approach the procedure of drawing checking in a systematic manner:

- Does the general appearance of the drawing conform to office design and drafting standards?
- Is the drawing complete? Does it contain the necessary graphics in proper relation to one another?
- Are necessary dimensions shown? Do the dimensions agree, and are unnecessary and duplicate dimensions avoided? Are the dimensions arranged to avoid unnecessary field calculations?

- Is the drawing to scale?
- Does the drawing communicate economical and efficient construction methods?
- Are clearances adequate?
- Are all necessary graphic symbols indicated? Are there sufficient notes to clearly indicate what is required?
- If materials indicated are manufactured in stock or modular sizes, are those sizes clearly indicated?
- If the drawing has been revised, has information damaged by erasures been restored, and have all related drawings been revised to conform?
- Have floor covering patterns and changes in elevation and material been clearly indicated?
- If modular materials are used to create a pattern, does the pattern conform to the material module without excess cutting and joint variation?
- Is the door schedule complete and accurate? Are door swings, along with indications for thresholds or saddles, shown and referred to appropriate details?
- Are ceiling heights, along with soffits and coves, clearly shown?
- Are plumbing fixtures, floor drains, and stalls shown and referenced to details and large scale plans?
- Are items such as fire extinguisher cabinets, access panels, drinking fountains, telephone booths, folding partitions, corner guards, railings, chalkboards, and tackboards located and identified?
- Are casework elevations shown and referenced?
- Has floor loading capacity been checked to see that it will adequately support concentrated heavy equipment loads?
- Have ADA requirements for handicapped accessibility been met?
- Have code requirements for exits and fire separations been met?
- Do electrical drawings show exit lights and emergency lighting (if required)?
- Do fire protection drawings (if required) conform to code requirements for sprinkler head locations and spacing?

- Have sight lines been checked to see that coves are deep enough to conceal lighting fixtures?
- Are the terms and nomenclature used on the drawings consistent and identical from drawing to drawing and the specifications?
- Are there specification items that do not belong on the drawings? If so, are the items covered in the specifications?
- Is blocking indicated to support wall-hung elements? Are shelving and other horizontal elements adequately supported, and supported at close enough intervals, to limit deflection of the material to acceptable limits?
- Are vertical elements such as low partitions laterally braced?
- Do drawings reflect a desirable construction sequence? Do details show conditions where some portion of finish work must be in place before adjacent rough work can be completed?
- Does the finish schedule agree with other drawings and specified products?
- Is the scope clear? If some work is to be done under separate contracts or if some items are to be furnished by the owner, are the contractor's responsibilities relative to those items clearly indicated?

In addition to the foregoing, ensure that work that might normally involve two trades or two separate contractors is shown in such a way that both are aware of the work. For example, exhaust fans should be shown on the HVAC drawings, and the power and switching for them should appear on the electrical drawings. Although all work may ultimately be the general contractor's responsibility, you can't expect the electrical subcontractor to make an exhaustive search through all other drawings to ascertain what items may require power. When that happens, a dispute inevitably arises and although invoking the provisions of the contract may forestall an extra charge, those involved will be sure to look for other ways to exploit each and every minor discrepancy in the documents.

Putting together a good set of contract documents can be a monumental task. Don't stop short by failing to check them thoroughly and carefully. It's probably nobody's favorite pastime, but it's absolutely essential.

DOCUMENT DISTRIBUTION

In every project there comes a time to issue documents for bids. That raises some questions. How do bidders obtain bidding documents? From whom? Is there a charge or deposit required?

In some cases, owners have established policies. In most cases, however, the owner will look to you for guidance. Some offices prefer to issue documents from their own offices for all local projects. When the project is located at some distance, the documents are distributed by the owner, who presumably is local to the project. Other firms prefer that the owner always issue the bidding documents. Still others, particularly when there is a charge involved, designate the blueprinter who is handling reproduction, and have the bidders secure documents directly from that source. It probably doesn't make much difference which system you choose so long as the issuing party keeps a bid register to account for all sets of documents that are distributed. This is particularly important when it comes to issuing addenda. You can't send an addendum to a potential bidder unless you know who he or she is.

At a time when modern reproduction methods were not so prevalent, it was reasonably important that documents used by unsuccessful bidders be returned for construction use. The prohibitive cost and trouble of producing additional sets of documents made it worthwhile to salvage all existing sets. To accomplish this, it became standard practice to require a security deposit for the issued documents to be refunded upon their return in good condition within a reasonable time after the bid opening. This practice has continued and is so widely accepted that it's almost never challenged, but we question whether it has continuing validity. Among its drawbacks are the fact that handling deposit checks invariably becomes a headache for someone. In addition, bidders often don't return documents promptly; trying to retrieve them and to deal with the disposition of deposit checks is time-consuming and creates accounting nightmares. Defining "good condition" also becomes a problem. Because bidders need to be able to mark up drawings to do a thorough takeoff, it would be unreasonable to insist that documents be returned unmarked. If you'll accept some markings, how much is too much? How many red marks per sheet will be acceptable? What is the penalty for coffee stains? Not to mention the condition of the project manual. Do you really want to page through each returned copy to ascertain that no pages have been torn out?

Even if you can satisfactorily resolve these issues, how much have you really accomplished? What is the actual cost of producing clean new copies of the documents? If you give it some serious thought, you're likely to find that it's less than the real cost of dealing with document deposits. While we recognize that this position further burdens waste handling procedures in this throw-away society, we think that there are far better ways of conserving paper than trying to reuse a few dog-eared sets of bidding documents.

A public agency may have an established policy over which you will have no influence. For private work and for publicly-funded projects where you are accorded some input, you might consider the following procedures:

1. For public projects where the bidding process is open to all, issue documents in whatever quantity each bidder requires at an established cost (not refundable) to the bidder. The cost should be the approximate reproduction cost per set. Issue documents to potential subcontractors, suppliers, builders' association plan rooms, and other parties with a bona fide interest in the project on the same basis.

2. For private work, particularly where bidders are limited by invitation, issue an established number of document sets to bidders, subcontractors, and major suppliers at no cost. On small jobs (under $100,000), two sets per bidder ought to be sufficient. On larger projects the number of sets might be increased for general bidders. On all but the very largest projects, a single set for each potential subcontractor or supplier should suffice. If any party wants additional sets, he or she should be able to purchase them under an arrangement similar to the procedure described above.

With the universal availability of office copiers and the growing prevalence of large document copiers, many firms are looking at the advisability of issuing one set per bidder and giving a limited license to all holders to make whatever copies they require for bidding purposes, realizing that copies will probably be made anyway.

Invariably someone will object to the expense of providing free documents if that is part of the policy. Objectors may see reproduction costs as a substantial expense, but compared with fees and other project-related costs, such expenses are really a miniscule portion of the cost of producing a project. Coupled with the possibility that making the process convenient for the bidder might be reflected in lower bids, the idea might be a very cost-saving process indeed.

SUMMARY

We have explored the requisite project drawings along with techniques for producing and checking them, emphasizing careful planning and methods for saving production time without sacrificing the quality of the drawings. Remember that the drawings are one element of the Contract Documents and play a very specific role: They establish the physical relationships of the *product types* on which the contract is based. While it is nearly impossible to avoid drawing indications of specific products, particularly when they are integral to the overall design, those indications are the province of the specifications and should appear there and not on the drawings.

Together the drawings and the specifications form an interlocking instrument. The principal reason they should not repeat information is that the drawings cannot fully indicate all requirements. While you may call out a specific material on the drawings, you cannot indicate all requirements related to it. To show only the product itself is like giving someone a recipe that lists only ingredients without explaining preparation and cooking directions.

CHAPTER 13

CONTRACT ADMINISTRATION

When a professional agrees to perform services on behalf of a client, the professional assumes certain responsibilities that may incur liabilities. Contract administration and construction review spawn almost all liability claims. You cannot avoid liability but you can limit your exposure by understanding your role in the process. All successful commercial interior projects are the result of collaboration between the owner, the contractor, and the design professional. Anything that changes a cooperative relationship to an adversarial one has an unfavorable impact on the project. Deadlines are missed, cost overruns occur, and frequently all communication ends up taking place through lawyers.

The design professional has clearly defined responsibilities during the construction phase. The primary duties are to make periodic site visits to ascertain that the work is progressing in accordance with the contract documents, to conduct regular job meetings, and to prepare and process the documents required to facilitate the work. In addition, the designer must certify the contractor's applications for payment, resolve conflicts, issue change orders when appropriate, and conduct a final inspection.

Even the best contract documents cannot survive haphazard construction review and poor construction administration. Note that we use the term "review" rather than "inspection" or "supervision." Design professionals who undertake this phase of a project and identify their services by these seemingly innocent terms open themselves up to liabilities they never dreamed of. The courts have typically held that inspection and supervision imply responsibility for results — no designer can afford to shoulder the burden of that meaning. Construction performance is solely the responsibility of the contractor.

Review your contractual obligations in the area of construction review in your agreement with the owner. Be sure of what your responsibilities are and discuss this aspect of service with your client. All construction has certain risks and, although carefully prepared documents can begin to minimize those risks, the owner must be prepared to accept this hard reality. After all, it is the owner who stands to benefit most from a successful project — and thus is it the owner who must accept the consequences associated with the risks. You, the designer, have no room to pick up the cost of errors. The contractor's profit, considering his or her risk, is far too modest to absorb the cost of unanticipated problems. If everyone cooperates, most projects go relatively smoothly. If not, there's bound to be a rocky road ahead.

Communicate to both the owner and the contractor that you are obligated to be fair and objective in your decisions, and that you will not approve inferior work, but that you do intend to give the contractor a certain amount of latitude in performing his or her responsibilities under the contract. Then follow through. Although you are paid by the owner and are acting as the owner's agent or representative, it makes no sense to team up with the owner against the contractor. Everyone involved must be part of the same team.

SUBMITTAL REVIEW

The contractor is required by the General Conditions, and by particular requirements of the specifications, to submit data to the design professional indicating that products to be furnished meet the requirements of the contract documents. The following items fall into the category of *submittals:*

- *Shop drawings*, which are prepared specifically for the project by the contractor, a subcontractor, a supplier, or a manufacturer to illustrate how a particular product or assembly will be fabricated and incorporated into the project.
- *Product data*, which are manufacturers' printed brochures that illustrate and describe the physical properties of a product or item of equipment that will be used in the project.

- *Samples* of actual products selected for use, which serve as the standard of quality on which the subsequently installed materials will be judged. Samples include field samples and field-built mock-ups of assemblies constructed for approval.

- *Test reports*, which describe the tests performed on particular products to demonstrate their compliance with stated standards or code requirements.

The submittal review process is an important element in the design and construction process. This step translates the requirements of the contract documents into the materials and equipment that make up the finished project. For this reason, the design professional must take great care in managing the process.

Keep in mind that submittals can be a costly element in any project. All too often the specifier calls for the submission of shop drawings and samples of virtually everything specified without regard for their necessity. It's important to remember that these items are not free. Submittals are included somewhere in the contractor's computations for general project overhead. They cost the contractor money to prepare and they cost you money and time to review them. Although you will need to request submittals for components that must be carefully coordinated, you should determine the specific submittals that are required before you call for them on a broad scope.

In addition to identifying which submittals *are* required, you should have a clear understanding of which *are not* required for review. Sometimes a design professional will review an unnecessary submittal and give it an endorsement only to find that he or she has unwittingly assumed some liability for the appropriateness of a method or assembly that was the contractor's responsibility. For this reason, you might create a category on your review stamp to indicate that the submittal is not required or that it was not reviewed. (See Figure 13.1 for an example of a submittal review stamp.) Then when a contractor submits something inappropriate, you can simply return it without taking action. This category is also useful for those instances where the submittal is clearly deficient. It's your way of telling the contractor that you aren't willing to spend time looking at something that is totally inappropriate. For example, if your project calls for prefinished, solid-core red oak doors, you should simply refuse to look at a submittal for unfinished, hollow-core birch doors.

An appropriate section within Division 1 of your specifications should establish the mechanics for submittals. This section should accomplish the following:

- State that all submittals must come from the contractor.
- Establish the quantity and form that submittals must take.
- State how submittals will be processed.
- Establish the disposition of submittals after review.

If you have written a proprietary specification and do not intend to consider a substitution, requiring the contractor to submit a sample is

Figure 13.1

Sample Submittal Stamp

☐ **Approved**   Fabrication/installation may be
                                  undertaken.

☐ **Approved as noted**

☐ **Not Reviewed**   No action taken.

☐ **Revise and Resubmit**   Fabrication/installation may
                                  not be undertaken.

☐ **Rejected**

Submittal has been reviewed for general arrangement and design conformance only. Contractor shall be responsible for quantities and for verifying field dimensions and conditions. Approval does not relieve Contractor of full compliance with all provisions of the Contract Documents. In resubmitting, limit corrections to marked items.

Name of Design Firm

By _____   Date _____

of questionable value. You may want one for verification purposes, but realize that doing so places a premium on this coordination.

Field samples and mock-ups need to be reviewed promptly to allow lead time for ordering. If you have accurately described the desired result and established guidelines that define acceptable work, samples may be obtainable, particularly if there is a natural range of appearance inherent in the specified product or if units of the product must be obtained from different production runs or dye lots. You have every right to expect blending and even distribution of color and pattern within a surface area if the installing mechanics take reasonable care. You do not have the right to insist on extra work or extraordinary standards of workmanship unless, of course, you have established restrictive ground rules and tolerances in advance.

When you approve a mock-up, ensure that your stated approval is documented in writing. Stipulate that it is for design conformance only and does not direct or endorse the means to achieve it. That responsibility is the contractor's alone — you don't want to assume that liability. Also, since the approved sample or mock-up becomes the benchmark for judging subsequent work, make sure it will remain in place unaltered until the work it represents is completed.

Managing the Review Process

Other than submittals that must be reviewed by consultants, very few require more than several days to review and process. If you can reduce the turnaround time for submittal review to less than a week, you will go a long way toward maintaining good relations with the project contractor and keeping the project on schedule. Delay in processing submittals is the most common complaint contractors have about design professionals. Prompt action makes a very favorable impression and produces a cooperative atmosphere on any project that yields large dividends. The only time quick turnaround might be undesirable is when a particular submittal is part of a larger assembly or depends on another component. In that instance, it is wise to hold it until all related submittals are received and can be reviewed together to ascertain that their compatibility and interrelated aspects are truly resolved. Inform the contractor when the processing of a submittal is delayed for this reason.

Prompt action is not synonymous with haste. There is no substitute for a thorough and comprehensive review. Toward managing the process as efficiently as possible, consider the following recommendations:

- Create a log for required submittals. (See Figure 13.2 for an example.) Record the date of receipt of each item, create a tickler file to assure prompt follow-up, and establish a time by which the review process must be completed.
- If there is a problem that might prevent the submittal from being promptly reviewed, notify the contractor and explain why the delay is necessary.
- Route the submittal to the person who is best able to review it and hold him or her responsible for following through. The person who is assigned the task of checking shop drawings should not only be thoroughly familiar with the Contract Documents and the schedule, but must also have the skill both to verify that the design criteria have been met and to evaluate the submission in the context of other determining factors.

"Approving" Submittals

In the current atmosphere of increasing litigation, it is important to understand how the prudent professional must limit the submittal review to statements that are consistent with the scope of services. Figure 13.1 indicates the type of language that may appropriately be used on a submittal review stamp. While there may be no perfect stamp form, using wording such as that indicated or something similar should go a long way toward protecting your interests and that of the project.

Traditionally, most designers have used the term "approved" to denote that a submittal is appropriate. Since non-professionals tend to interpret such language as meaning "unqualified acceptance," some segments of the design profession have become reluctant to use the term. Those designers, with the support and perhaps even a nudge from their insurance carriers, have chosen to use such terms as "reviewed" or "no exceptions taken" when processing submittals. While all design professionals want to avoid the potential consequences of increased liability, hedging all bets by using such euphemisms seems less than truly professional. When a contractor seeks your approval of a product so that it can be ordered, he or she doesn't want to know that you've *reviewed*

Sample Submittal Log

Project:

Description of Submittal	Spec Section	Date Received	New Submittal	Resubmittal	Action				Reviewed By	Action By	Date Returned	Remarks
					Approved	Approved as Noted	Revise/Resubmit	Not Approved				

Figure 13.2

it. What does that really mean? The contractor wants to order and install the product with the assurance that once the item is in place, it won't be rejected as being non-conforming. Because of this, many firms continue to use "approved" but with careful attention to using supplementary language that clearly limits the meaning of the term, such as that shown on the stamp illustrated in Figure 13.1.

When modifications are required, terms such as "approved as noted" or "revise as noted" are typically used. If the submittal does not correspond to contract requirements, appropriate wording such as "rejected" or "revise and resubmit" is typically used. Again, selected terminology should be incorporated on a submittal review stamp that also places limits on your review. Such terminology should clarify that review is for general conformance and compliance with design intent only.

No action indicated by the designer alters the requirements of the contract documents. The contractor remains responsible for full compliance, including verifying all dimensions and conditions, establishing appropriate fabrication processes, employing proper construction techniques, and coordinating all work. Therefore, you should resist the impulse to modify any contract requirements through the submittal process. For example, suppose you had specified a premium-grade plastic laminate such as the type where the color runs throughout the thickness so that no backing shows when it's assembled to make outside corners. The contractor might submit chips of ordinary laminate material in an attempt to revise the requirements of the contract to his or her advantage. Likewise, you as the designer may not change the requirements by rejecting a product that conforms to the specifications and choosing an upgraded product because you feel that it may be more appropriate.

If the submittal review reveals conditions that should be revised to achieve a more favorable result, use a Change Order or other form to alter the contractor's obligations with respect to the contract documents. The submittal review itself will not effect such changes.

Pitfalls in the Submittal Review Process

Although it is a necessary step, there are certain drawbacks to the submittal review process:

- Today's construction techniques have become increasingly complex; the submittal review process contains many pitfalls in regard to professional liability. In fact, disputes over this aspect probably generate more claims against professionals than any other single source.
- When submittals are required, the contractor cannot order the materials they represent prior to the designer's review. Therefore, any delay in processing submittals jeopardizes the project schedule and exposes the designer to claims for extra costs.

CONSTRUCTION REVIEW

While all phases of every project are important, it's how you handle construction review that can "make" or "break" a job. Unfortunately, many design professionals do not assign time needed for a project until the finish materials are being applied. By then, if there are construction problems that haven't been addressed and satisfactorily resolved, it's too late to obtain the quality that may be important to the designer.

Site Visits

The frequency of site visits and project meetings is subject to professional judgment coupled with the scope of services enumerated in your agreement with the owner, the pace of the project, and travel distance to the project site. Large projects that are close at hand may require daily site visits and weekly project meetings. Smaller, more distant jobs might be served by bi-weekly visits coinciding with project meetings. Unless the owner is unwilling to pay for this level of service, most experienced design professionals agree that regular and frequent site visits establish good relations among all parties, help to forestall problems, and contribute to timely resolution of problems that do occur. Remember that construction never moves at a constant pace. Sometimes weeks go by with minimal observable progress; at other times work moves so rapidly that the complexion of the project changes almost daily. Site visits must, therefore, respond to the pace of the work and the changing need for critical review. It is imperative to communicate this to your client in advance.

In making site visits, you must always observe the lines of communication established in the contract. Confine substantive discussions to the contractor's project manager or field superintendent. Do not deal directly with subcontractors, instruct workers, or give directions to the contractor regarding means and methods that are the contractor's responsibility alone.

Job Meetings

The agenda for job meetings should be kept as simple as possible, ideally including just two topics: "old business" — progress since the previous meeting; and "new business" — activities scheduled for the following interval. Note that we did not include a discussion of problems. This is not because we expect the project to be problem-free but because the resolution of problems is best and most efficiently handled by the people involved outside of the meeting. When handled in this manner, prolonged discussion of problems does not waste the time of others who are not directly affected. Also, when problems are the result of someone's error, airing them at a project meeting embarrasses that individual and leads to a deterioration of relations. Pretty soon meetings involve much finger pointing and attendees become concerned with protecting their own flanks rather than the advancement of the project.

The number of attendees at job meetings should be kept to a minimum. Large groups tend to get into far-ranging discussions that delay decisions on essential matters. Often only the project manager and representatives of the owner and contractor are needed at the meeting. At various stages in the job, it may be wise to include principal subcontractors or others who have a direct interest in the project at that moment — but little is accomplished by requiring attendance by individuals whose contributions to the project aren't directly related to current progress or agenda items.

An effort should be made to see that job meeting attendees are the *same* people from meeting to meeting and that they are the individuals who are authorized to make decisions.

Although it is a chore that most people do not willingly undertake, you should write and distribute minutes of project meetings. It's commonly recognized that the individual who writes the minutes controls the interpretation of events, so unless it is excluded from your scope of service, you should undertake the responsibility. It is a time-consuming activity, however, and you should be adequately compensated for it, so be sure that you include it when negotiating your scope of services. Keep the minutes brief and to the point. Adopt a consistent format that not only records significant points but also assigns responsibility for proper follow-through.

Reviewing Contractor Billing

Under most contracts, the contractor bills monthly for work completed during the previous month less 10%, which is retained until final completion of the project. To do this the contractor submits an Application for Payment, which the project manager reviews and approves prior to submitting it to the owner for payment.

Prior to the first Application for Payment the contractor prepares a "Schedule of Values" for the design professional's approval. The Schedule of Values breaks down the contract sum into the values for all major components of the work, which the project manager uses to assess the progress of completed work and the validity of each monthly billing. If the Schedule of Values assigns a value of $10,000 to painting, for example, and the current billing includes $5,000 for painting, the designer is able to decide quickly if, in fact, 50% of the painting was completed within the preceding month. The design professional is not obliged to do an exhaustive analysis of the quantity of work completed, but merely ascertain that the claimed work is reasonable.

In reviewing the Schedule of Values the project manager should be alert to any effort by the contractor to "front load" the job. Front loading refers to the practice of overvaluing the work that will be completed early in the job and undervaluing work that will occur near completion. In this way the contractor will be overpaid at the beginning of work — the retainage generated may not be sufficient to cover subsequent operations if the contractor should default or fail to perform satisfactorily. The design professional is authorized to reject the submitted schedule if he or she feels this is being done and to require a more equitable distribution of values.

The contractor is permitted to bill for stored materials, either on-site or off-site. Since the contractor cannot completely control the scheduled delivery of products, materials often arrive before they can be properly installed. Because these materials represent an expense, the contractor is entitled to be paid for storing them. If there is adequate storage space at the project location that is clean and secure, materials may be delivered directly to the job. It is relatively easy to ascertain that the products are, in fact, stored when you see them as you visit the project. Before approving payment for products that are stored off-site, you should have evidence that the materials do exist, that they have been paid for, and that they are fully insured. It may create additional paperwork for both you and the contractor, but you must protect the owner's interests. Ask for appropriate supporting documentation before you approve payment.

Documenting Changes

On virtually every project, changes are made after the contract is executed. Some are only minor clarifications; others may be so extensive as to change the basic scope of the work. All changes must be documented. Those that affect the contract price or completion date must be documented by change order (discussed later in this chapter).

While the basis for this discussion assumes that changes ordinarily increase the contract sum or time, reductions are not precluded. Sometimes changes result in a credit or a decrease in contract time. The recap portion of the form reflects this condition.

In the design community there is a pervasive myth that contractors love change orders. This myth assumes that the contractor is motivated to increase his or her profit margin by inflating the cost of minor changes. While there may be a few contractors who have attempted to use change orders in this way, the vast majority of contractors dislike change orders as much as owners and design professionals do. In most cases, just processing the paperwork consumes more overhead costs than can ever be recouped.

The AIA has developed several forms that effectively record the necessary information related to changes. The following discussion refers to those documents. You are not obliged to use these particular documents but you should become familiar with their content so that if you devise your own procedures you can be sure that they conform to accepted practice.

Supplemental Instructions Occasionally minor changes are required that do not alter the contract price or time. If the change is necessary only to effect a clarification of the documents, to revise a previously selected color, or to change the location of an item, it is best covered by issuing a supplemental instruction. The AIA document devised for this purpose is the "Architect's Supplemental Instructions" (Document G710), shown in Figure 13.3. When you issue this form, or a similar one, it is understood that no change in the contract sum or contract time is warranted. If this is indeed the case, the contractor merely signs the document to signify acceptance. If, however, the contractor feels entitled to an additional amount of money to make the change, or needs additional time to do so, he or she has the option of so stating. If the modification requested is agreeable, the change must be covered by a change order. Otherwise, the executed supplemental instruction stands alone without further documentation.

Proposal Requests If it is recognized that a change will incur additional money or time, standard practice dictates issuance of a Proposal Request. A Proposal Request requires the contractor to respond with an itemized quotation for making the proposed change. AIA Document G709, shown in Figure 13.4, is designed to function in this way. Once there is agreement about any modifications required, a change order must be prepared to reflect the change.

Construction Change Directives From time to time a condition will arise that must be addressed immediately. For example, a door must be moved to alleviate a conflict with some other feature. In these instances it will be apparent to everyone involved that a change must occur to reconcile the conflict. When this happens, there is often insufficient time to proceed in a formal manner. To wait for the preparation of a proposal request and subsequent change order might delay progress on the job and might even increase the resulting cost of the change. In this situation, a Construction Change Directive (AIA Document G714) instructs the contractor to make the change, within certain guidelines, without waiting for the preparation of a change order. This form is shown in Figure 13.5. Once the final impact of the change can be assessed, provided it is in line with the parameters set forth in the document, it is converted to a change order.

Change Orders The change order itself is a document (AIA G701) that details changes to the contract along with adjustments to the

ARCHITECT'S
SUPPLEMENTAL INSTRUCTIONS

Owner	☐
Architect	☐
Consultant	☐
Contractor	☐
Field	☐
Other	☐

AIA DOCUMENT G710 (Instructions on reverse side)

PROJECT:
(name, address)

ARCHITECT'S SUPPLEMENTAL
INSTRUCTION NO:

OWNER:

DATE OF ISSUANCE:

TO:
(Contractor)

ARCHITECT:

CONTRACT FOR:

ARCHITECT'S PROJECT NO:

CONTRACT DATED:

The Work shall be carried out in accordance with the following supplemental instructions issued in accordance with the Contract Documents without change in Contract Sum or Contract Time. Proceeding with the Work in accordance with these instructions indicates your acknowledgement that there will be no change in the Contract Sum or Contract Time.

Description:

SAMPLE

Attachments: *(Here insert listing of documents that support description.)*

ISSUED BY:

Architect

AIA **CAUTION: You should sign an original AIA document which has this caution printed in red. An original assures that changes will not be obscured as may occur when documents are reproduced.**

Figure 13.3

Sample Proposal Request

PROPOSAL REQUEST

AIA Document G709

(Instructions on reverse side)

OWNER	☐
ARCHITECT	☐
CONSULTANT	☐
CONTRACTOR	☐
FIELD	☐
OTHER	☐

PROJECT:
(Name and address)

PROPOSAL REQUEST NO.:

DATE OF ISSUANCE:

CONTRACT FOR:

OWNER:
(Name and address)

CONTRACT DATED:

ARCHITECT'S PROJECT NO.:

TO CONTRACTOR:
(Name and address)

ARCHITECT:
(Name and address)

Please submit an itemized proposal for changes in the Contract Sum and Contract Time for proposed modifications to the Contract Documents described herein. Submit proposal within _____ days, or notify the Architect in writing of the date on which you anticipate submitting your proposal.

THIS IS NOT A CHANGE ORDER, A CONSTRUCTION CHANGE DIRECTIVE OR A DIRECTION TO PROCEED WITH THE WORK DESCRIBED IN THE PROPOSED MODIFICATIONS.

Description:
(Insert a written description of the Work.)

Attachments:
(List attached documents that support description.)

REQUESTED BY:

_____   _____
(Signature)   *(Printed name and title)*

Figure 13.4

Sample Construction Change Directive

CONSTRUCTION
CHANGE
DIRECTIVE

AIA DOCUMENT G714

(Instructions on reverse side. This document replaces AIA Document G713, Construction Change Authorization.)

OWNER	☐
ARCHITECT	☐
CONTRACTOR	☐
FIELD	☐
OTHER	☐

PROJECT:
(name, address)

TO CONTRACTOR:
(name, address)

DIRECTIVE NO:

DATE:

ARCHITECT'S PROJECT NO:

CONTRACT DATE:

CONTRACT FOR:

You are hereby directed to make the following change(s) in this Contract:

PROPOSED ADJUSTMENTS

1. The proposed basis of adjustment to the Contract Sum or Guaranteed Maximum Price is:

   ☐ Lump Sum (increase) (decrease) of $ _____

   ☐ Unit Price of $ _____ per _____

   ☐ as provided in Subparagraph 7.3.6 of AIA Document A201, 1987 edition.

   ☐ as follows:

2. The Contract Time is proposed to (be adjusted) (remain unchanged). The proposed adjustment, if any, is (an increase of _____ days) (a decrease of _____ days).

When signed by the Owner and Architect and received by the Contractor, this document becomes effective IMMEDIATELY as a Construction Change Directive (CCD), and the Contractor shall proceed with the change(s) described above.

Signature by the Contractor indicates the Contractor's agreement with the proposed adjustments in Contract Sum and Contract Time set forth in this Construction Change Directive.

ARCHITECT _____

OWNER _____

CONTRACTOR _____

Address _____

Address _____

Address _____

BY _____

BY _____

BY _____

DATE _____

DATE _____

DATE _____

Figure 13.5

contract sum, the contract time, or both. This document is shown in Figure 13.6. A change order is written authorization approving a change from the original drawings, specifications, or other contract documents, as well as a change in cost. With the proper signatures, a change order is considered a legal document. Change orders are numbered consecutively; each one recaps cumulative changes to the contract. To be valid, a change order must be issued by the design professional and signed by both the owner and the contractor because any change that is not acknowledged by the parties to the contract would have no validity.

Attachments With all of the foregoing documents, some additional attachments will be required. At the very least a contractor's price quotation for making the change will be required, even if the change itself can be adequately described. Often, additional graphic material in the form of a supplementary drawing or a revised drawing will be necessary to fully explain the proposed modification. Whenever possible, we try to use supplementary drawings prepared on 8-1/2″ x 11″ paper so that the form itself, along with supporting documentation, forms a manageable package. In every case it's important that any supplementary drawings are keyed to the documents they modify.

On rare occasions it is necessary to revise a previously issued drawing and to reissue it to describe the change. This process requires great skill. The revised portions must be clearly delineated so that the scope of the change is not misunderstood. In most instances we discourage the reissuance of previously prepared contract drawings, preferring to keep intact all documents that form a part of the original agreement. Drawings with multiple revisions have a tendency to produce confusion, particularly when the chronology of the changes themselves becomes unclear, and when changes are subsequently changed again. It is important, however, to ultimately record all changes on a master set of drawings for the owner's record. Chapter 12 covers drawing production in more detail.

Once the change, whatever its nature, is documented by change order, it becomes an integral part of the agreement between the owner and the contractor. When the contractor submits his or her next periodic

Sample Change Order

CHANGE ORDER

AIA DOCUMENT G701

OWNER ☐
ARCHITECT ☐
CONTRACTOR ☐
FIELD ☐
OTHER ☐

PROJECT:
(name, address)

TO CONTRACTOR:
(name, address)

CHANGE ORDER NUMBER:

DATE:

ARCHITECT'S PROJECT NO:

CONTRACT DATE:

CONTRACT FOR:

The Contract is changed as follows:

Not valid until signed by the Owner, Architect and Contractor.

The original (Contract Sum) (Guaranteed Maximum Price) was . . . . $

Net change by previously authorized Change Orders . . . . $

The (Contract Sum) (Guaranteed Maximum Price) prior to this Change Order was . . . . $

The (Contract Sum) (Guaranteed Maximum Price) will be (increased) (decreased)
  (unchanged) by this Change Order in the amount of . . . . $

The new (Contract Sum) (Guaranteed Maximum Price) including this Change Order will be . . $

The Contract Time will be (increased) (decreased) (unchanged) by   (   ) days.

The date of Substantial Completion as of the date of this Change Order therefore is

NOTE: This summary does not reflect changes in the Contract Sum, Contract Time or Guaranteed Maximum Price which have been authorized by
          Construction Change Directive.

ARCHITECT	CONTRACTOR	OWNER
Address	Address	Address
BY	BY	BY
DATE	DATE	DATE

AIA DOCUMENT G701 • CHANGE ORDER • 1987 EDITION • AIA® • ©1987 • THE
AMERICAN INSTITUTE OF ARCHITECTS, 1735 NEW YORK AVE., N.W., WASHINGTON, D.C. 20006

G701—1987

Figure 13.6

Application for Payment, the change is recorded in its appropriate location on the form and adjustments are made in any current payments due.

Other Types of Changes As you may remember from the discussion of allowances in Chapter 8, some changes may be charged against a contingency allowance. This doesn't obviate the need for a change order, however. It simply charges the amount to an existing reserve that's already included in the agreement.

A single change order may address more than a single change. Often it's desirable to lump together several similar changes on the same change order, particularly if the end result reduces paperwork. Most designers, however, prefer to segregate changes that are essentially different onto separate change orders. It's easier to remember that a particular change order deals with finish changes while another one effects electrical modifications. Mixing different disciplines on a single document tends to be confusing and undoubtedly complicates matters if a subsequent change deals with similar issues.

While some changes don't require immediate documentation, project managers who direct the process most effectively do not procrastinate in the preparation of change orders. Those who subscribe to the theory that modifications can be held until there are a sufficient number to lump together into one change frequently find themselves in a dispute. When changes are held in this manner, it becomes difficult for all parties to remember what change actually occurred and sometimes the very reason for it becomes blurred with the passage of time. Be wary of the contractor or owner who says, "Don't worry about it. It will all be reconciled in the final accounting." More often than not, a dispute will arise at the end of the project and you'll have the unpleasant task of trying to mediate the conflict. If there's going to be disagreement about any aspect of a change, it's far better to resolve it as it happens.

Again, document *all* changes. Trying to sort out changes after the fact is not only a headache but is also time consuming. Use the tools you have available to do it effectively. On occasion you may have a client who doesn't understand the process or one who wants to use his or her own devices to record changes. Resist vigorously if you must. Any procedure that differs too much from accepted practice is practically guaranteed to be difficult.

Avoiding the Problem of "Horsetrading"

There is a common practice in the construction industry known as "horsetrading," in which the contractor and the project manager alter the contract requirements "off the record" to their mutual advantage. This commonly occurs when the designer has failed to include an item that is essential to the project. To save personal embarrassment and spare the owner the cost of the resulting extra, the project manager makes a deal with the contractor to eliminate or reduce the requirements associated with an item of supposedly comparable value, in return for the contractor's including the omitted item at no charge. This activity is unethical and contrary to the principles of the agreement. Not being a party to the contract, the project manager has no authority to change the contract documents and the contractor cannot do it unilaterally. In this situation, the owner always loses and the contractor always wins, because it is the contractor who has some ability to control costs and will always trade the elimination of a significant item for the inclusion of an insignificant one.

The admonition to eschew "horsetrading" notwithstanding, it is important to recognize that the contractor needs some latitude in performing his or her end of the agreement. In every project there are conditions where the Contract Documents call for products or procedures that are clearly excessive. The contractor can suggest to the owner that those requirements may be reduced without compromising the quality of the project. Usually these are very small items that are too insignificant to cause an adjustment in the contract sum. For example, suppose that a floor-mounted door stop is specified for a particular door, but upon inspection it is obvious that it is really unnecessary and, in fact, its installation would result in an obstruction and perhaps a tripping hazard. With the owner's knowledge and approval, it can simply be eliminated with no suggestion that a credit is expected. More often than not, the contractor will provide a similar minor item at no cost. Purists may argue that this is horsetrading and should not be allowed, but most people experienced in the realities of construction feel that such informal swapping, when done with the full knowledge of all the parties to the contract, is both appropriate and ethical. It need not be covered by change orders or other formal documentation, although it would be appropriate to record it in project meeting minutes.

Final Inspection

Every design professional has a procedure for conducting a final inspection and preparing a punchlist. If the project has moved smoothly and communication between all parties has been good, the process should be very simple. The contractor will not request a final inspection until he or she is reasonably certain that the project is in good shape and that the punchlist will be relatively brief.

One of the keys to an effective inspection is to be well prepared in advance and approach the process in a systematic manner. At the very least, you should prepare a checklist form that lists every space and includes columns to check off major components of the work along with a generous "remarks" column to record specific comments that cannot be covered by a general category. One very effective way to approach the task is to make several prints of the floor plan, then cut out the plan of each separate room or space and mount it on a separate letter-size sheet. Make copies of each sheet, including a key for specific points that need to be addressed. Conduct your inspection by recording incomplete or defective items directly on each sheet, keyed to your prearranged comments with arrows pointing to specific locations.

At the conclusion of your inspection, issue several copies of your checklist to the contractor. The contractor can tape a copy concerning each individual room on the door leading to that space, telling everyone at a glance what items need to be remedied in that room. Each trade that is required to make corrections can mark off each correction that is made directly on that sheet. When all keys are marked off, all corrections will have been made and any reinspection will be done quickly and easily.

Project Closeout

The design professional's final responsibility under the construction phase is to administer close-out procedures. Review the contract for an itemization of these tasks. Normally the designer must issue a Certificate of Completion; assemble the required record documents; see that the contractor processes warranties and regulatory approvals; arrange for all required inspection certificates to be delivered to the owner; and approve final payment.

At this point the owner will probably have a party to celebrate the completion of the project. If you've done your job well, you'll probably be the guest of honor.

SUMMARY

In this chapter we have defined the responsibilities of the design professional throughout the construction phase. Although the primary responsibility for construction belongs to the contractor, the design professional must administer the contract on the owner's behalf. Keep in mind that successful projects are always the result of a collaborative effort and that how you perform your job directly affects the result.

CHAPTER 14

FURNITURE

Although the contract documents for construction establish the design and construction of the space itself, the owner can hardly occupy the space and function without furniture. While the general contractor's expertise is in construction, he or she rarely has experience in purchasing, delivering, and installing furniture. For this reason, provisions for furniture are normally included in a separate contract and are not part of the construction contract documents. This means that the interior designer must develop a separate package of documents so that furniture can be bid or negotiated as a separate contract. This package parallels the documents for construction and employs the same basic elements (bidding requirements, agreement, conditions of the contract, drawings, and specifications) as those for construction.

When the required furniture is made up entirely of moveable pieces that have virtually no impact on the construction process, the two contracts may exist independently. In many cases, however, it is important to refer to elements of the furniture contract within the construction contract documents. For example, when careful coordination of furniture location is essential, such as locating electrical connections to systems furniture or providing blocking to anchor permanently-installed components, the furniture plan is included within the construction drawing set and clearly marked "For Reference Only" since it is not a part of that contract.

The size, formality, and complexity of furniture contracts varies widely—there has been much less standardization of the documents used to establish the basis of this contract than there has been in the construction industry. This lack of standardization is mostly the result of the relative youth of the commercial furnishings industry.

The commercial furnishings industry started out as little more than the purchase and delivery of some desks and chairs, and maybe some window blinds. The owner chose between wood or metal, each offered in one color, and was on hand during delivery to point to where they should be placed. A handshake was the contract and the sales receipt the "specifications." Drawings were rarely necessary. A "builder" constructed the building, with or without the benefit of an architect. All the interior finishes were the same; it rarely occured to the owner that they should be different. There was no "interior designer." In comparison to the cost of the building, the cost of the furniture was very low. Delivering it required no great skill, and since lead time was often somewhat unpredictable, schedule slippages were tolerated. Lawsuits arose only if the owner didn't pay the vendor. In other words, the amount of money involved and the possibilities for misunderstanding, error, and accident were so limited that the risks were very low; thus protection was unnecessary. Who needed documents?

THE CHALLENGE OF PRODUCING STANDARD FURNITURE CONTRACT DOCUMENTS

The evolution of this transaction from one of such simplicity into the often highly complex practice it has become today happened in the blink of an eye compared to the centuries over which buildings have been designed and constructed. Choices of and demand for commercial interior furnishing products and related technologies have steadily multiplied, along with an ever-more specialized cast of supporting players. When the scope of interior furnishings work began to represent substantial financial loss when something went wrong, vendors, designers and owners began to create appropriate documentation to coordinate responsibilities among the parties involved and to ensure desired quality. It is now generally recognized that some standardized format, similar to that developed by the AIA and ASID for agreement forms and by CSI for construction specifications, would be of wide benefit. Several design professionals, attorneys, and professional interior design organizations have developed and published forms and procedures that are excellent guides; in addition, virtually all vendors have their own standard agreement forms stating the terms and conditions of the sale. Some of the available standard documents will be discussed later in this chapter. To date, however, no single preferred method has floated to the surface. The designer is faced with selecting among the available choices and/or developing his or her own method.

Sometimes the amount of new furniture involved in an interiors project is minimal in comparison to the interior construction. On the other hand, sometimes furniture represents the bulk of the work, requiring far more extensive documentation than the construction. Considerable refurbishing, reconfiguring, or relocation of existing furniture may be required. These services may be included in a contract with new furniture, as part of the general construction contract, or in a separate contract. Such widely varying scopes do not naturally lend themselves to standardization.

Because of this wide disparity in scope and complexity, no single format of documentation is likely to be appropriate for every project. The time spent editing a formal, preprinted agreement would be ridiculously out of proportion to the rest of the work for a small project requiring nothing but in-stock furniture. By the same token, a vendor's signed proposal and a few notes on a drawing would not be adequate for a project involving three floors of new systems furniture combined with existing furniture being relocated, along with seating and casegoods from ten different manufacturers, built-in files, art, plants, and accessories to be installed in six different phases coordinated with new interior construction.

Since there is no "standard" furniture contract, designers are free to tailor the contract documents to the requirements of the project as they see fit. (They must, of course, consider consumer protection laws such as the Uniform Commercial Code governing the sale of goods.) The flip side of this freedom, however, is the designer's responsibility to fully understand the basic elements of furniture contracts and in what forms they can or should appear in projects of various scopes. Only with this understanding can a designer conscientiously create appropriate documents and evaluate, on the owner's behalf, documents submitted by others.

Our effort here will not be focused on presenting yet another "form" for writing furniture specifications or purchasing agreements. Rather than add to the proliferation of non-standard methods of documentation, we have elected to draw parallels between the kinds of information that may typically be found in furniture contract documents and that which is set forth in standardized construction contract documents. The organizational concepts already developed and widely used by architects and contractors can be applied to furniture contract documents to achieve completeness and consistency, even among projects of widely varying scopes. Armed with an understanding of an organizational system that has withstood the test of the courts and thousands of construction projects, you can create documents that are as simple or as complex as they need to be, for any type or size of project. You can also use these concepts to evaluate and supplement documents that you are required by others to use with the confidence that you have covered the bases appropriately for each individual situation. Going through the same mental checklist of subject matter every time will help you avoid unnecessary and potentially conflicting repetition between documents, as well as equally costly omissions. You can take what works for you from many of the various forms and formats, fit them into the appropriate "slots," and produce consistent, professional documents every time.

BASIC ELEMENTS OF THE FURNITURE CONTRACT

The furniture contract can be thought of as a "mini" construction contract with the same purposes and elements as a construction contract. The furniture contract documents are generated simultaneously with and in coordination with the construction contract documents. It is worth emphasizing the importance of *coordinating* the content of the furniture and construction contract documents, since both overlaps and gaps between them can cost time and money.

Just as the construction contract is between the owner and the general contractor, the furniture contract is between the owner and the furniture vendor (sometimes referred to as the furniture "contractor"), who usually is a dealer but in some cases may also be the manufacturer of the product. Unless your design firm is also a furniture dealer, you as the designer are not a party to this contract—but in many projects you will play a major role in the development, negotiation, and execution of the contract documents. For the purposes of this discussion we will assume that the designer's role is that of specifier, not vendor. When an owner uses the services of a furniture dealer's design staff, it is usually with the intent of purchasing the merchandise through that vendor.

The Purpose of Furniture Contract Documents

Furniture contract documents exist for two reasons:

1. To communicate the goods and services the client wants to buy so that the desired results are achieved.

2. To protect all parties involved in the event of a dispute.

The designer must be able to evaluate how much documentation is required to communicate #1, and the extent of risk to which any party may be exposed in the event of default or dispute referred to in #2. For a simple one-office project, the owner does not need to pay $800 to a designer to edit a 20-page agreement to protect the owner against the risk of losing a $2,000 deposit in the event that the vendor goes bankrupt before his furniture is delivered. The owner's signature on a vendor's proposal forms a contract, which entitles the owner to make a claim—so $800 is a poor investment relative to the low risk involved. That same $800 is well spent, however, when used to set forth the responsibilities of all parties on a $500,000 order.

Parts of a Furniture Contract

The parts of a furniture contract are similar to the parts of a construction contract:

1. The Agreement
2. Conditions of the Contract
3. Specifications
4. Drawings
5. Modifications (addenda when issued before contract execution; change orders when issued after contract execution)

The organizational principles of construction contracts described earlier in the book can also be applied to the preparation of furniture contract documents. Select a form of agreement appropriate to the size and circumstances of the project and tailor the conditions of the contract as necessary, usually through some sort of supplement that describes any changes to the general conditions that apply to the specific project. Furnishings specifications should be developed using a system that acts as an automatic checklist, prompting attention to procedural and installation considerations as well as products (such as the system used in the CSI MasterFormat). Furniture plan drawings and detail drawings should be carefully coded to relate to the specifications; their effect on the content of the construction drawings should be clearly identified.

CHOOSING A FURNITURE VENDOR

In some cases, owners procure and install furniture through predetermined channels. In other cases, the owner may ask the designer to recommend a procedure. In either situation, it is important for you to be familiar with the ways in which furniture vendors may be chosen. In the former case, this knowledge allows you to navigate smoothly through the process, knowing all players' responsibilities. In the latter, it allows you to guide your client through the various choices to determine the best method for the specific project.

Development of the contract documents takes place after the design has been finalized, furniture and finish selections have been made, and the furniture plan and overall budget have been approved by the owner. However, the way in which furniture and furnishings will be purchased for a project should be discussed with a potential client even before you submit a proposal for providing interior design services. It can influence considerably both the design and the contract document phases of the project. You should be prepared to present the pros and cons of the various choices to assist your client in reaching a decision.

Direct Selection

Owners of privately-funded businesses typically choose commercial furniture vendors in one or a combination of three ways. The simplest is by *direct selection* of a vendor. This method is usually used for small purchases and for purchases that occur as a continuation of a previous project. The owner may have developed a comfortable relationship with a vendor and may therefore prefer to continue to purchase through this vendor, even for larger projects. This owner sees no reason to put others through the bidding process when he or she is already satisfied with the prices and service of a particular vendor.

Direct selection is the least time-consuming purchasing situation. Design documents can be simpler, since the owner and vendor most likely will have previously agreed upon terms and conditions. You should simply verify that they are applicable to the new project, or identify where changes are required. Bidding documents are not necessary at all. While drawings and specifications must be complete, less information may be required in the general and installation sections if the vendor is already thoroughly familiar with the owner's site and preferences and has provided the same products in the past.

This less formal documentation represents a savings in time that is evident both in the project schedule and in lower design fees. Those cost and time advantages could very well outweigh any savings in purchase price the owner might realize if a number of vendors were engaged in a competitive bidding situation. Most vendors will offer their best price when a designer who does a good bit of business in the area is involved and/or the client is a good candidate for repeat business. Vendors know they will be invited to participate again only if they gave good service for a reasonable price the last time. A materially lower price is likely to be offered only when there is a particularly "hungry" vendor invited to bid.

Competitive Bidding

In spite of the advantages of direct selection, competitive bidding remains the most common method for the selection of a furniture vendor or vendors for typical commercial interior projects. Competitive bidding in furniture follows the same principles as selecting a contractor for the interior construction. Many believe that a fair price can be offered and recognized only in the presence of competition, and perhaps rightly so. The incentive to outperform the other bidder nourishes excellence and inspires creativity. It is time consuming for all parties involved, but most owners emerge more confident that they will be getting their money's worth if they have the opportunity to "comparison shop" especially if the project involves items or services never purchased before.

Competitive bidding is an effective method for identifying a vendor with whom to start a potentially ongoing relationship, which may involve direct selection purchases in the future. In cases like this, the list of vendors invited to bid should be limited to those with whom the client would feel comfortable doing business on a long-term basis. Instead of waiting until the bidding documents are released before requesting bidder qualification statements, it may be wise to invite any unfamiliar vendors to make informal presentations to the client in the early stages of project development before the bid list is developed, especially so the owner and the vendor can meet each other. This requires a certain commitment of time on the part on the owner, and he or she should be willing to make a suitable investment of time.

Most of the detail associated with both furniture and construction documents evolved to support the competitive bidding process. The more products, services, procedures, requirements, and people that are involved with a project, the more ways there will be to interpret intent. A "tight" set of documents means that you have anticipated to an optimum degree where those questions of intent may be, and have provided the information before the questions can arise. Generally speaking, you will be able to evaluate just how successful you were by how close the bids are to each other in terms of dollar figures, and by how closely the bids resemble the amount you budgeted for the project. Disparate bids mean varying interpretations; high numbers mean such uncertainty in interpretation that bidders padded the bid to cover themselves. Your responsibility is to provide enough relevant information to get the best price for your client without eating up all the savings in design fees!

Again, the bidding for furniture vendors follows the same principles as that for contractors. Develop a standard bid form so vendors don't submit bids on proposal forms that may contain language that conflicts with the Agreement. Also use an invitation to bid form, instructions to bidders, and bidder qualification forms as necessary. While bidding is in process any changes or further clarification required must be distributed to all bidders in writing at the same time; this means no quick telephone answers to the one(s) who call with questions.

Bidding means considerable time and work for the competing vendors, which may or may not result in a return on that investment. They deserve absolute fairness in return for their time investment. The formality of construction industry bidding procedures ensures that fairness.

Furniture vendors deserve no less. Once the owner, advised by the designer, selects a vendor, the designer informs both the successful bidder and unsuccessful bidders of the outcome. Ideally, this takes place before the interior construction documents go out for bid, when furnishings contractors (vendors) are already known. It affords the opportunity to fine tune the scope of the interior construction contract. This information can be used either to control the cost of the project or to accommodate any particular requirements or limitations of the furnishings vendor(s).

Negotiation

The third way to choose a vendor for the purchase and/or installation of furniture is through *negotiation*. Most frequently this is done on the local dealer level but for large projects can also be done on the manufacturer level. One disadvantage of competitive bidding between dealers is that most dealers buy the specified product from the manufacturer at more or less the same price, with two exceptions:

- When a particular dealer qualifies for a higher discount off the price of a product from a certain manufacturer because he is a regional representative or "authorized dealer."

- When a dealer is not an authorized dealer of a certain manufacturer's product, he may actually arrange with a dealer of that product in another area to sell him the specified items so he can participate in the bidding for the entire furniture section. Unless he and the dealer he buys from have some sort of reciprocal arrangement for purchases at dealer cost, he will pay a higher price for the merchandise than if he had bought it directly from the manufacturer. Without this reciprocal arrangement, the other dealer will expect to make some profit on the transaction.

When quoting prices based on strictly proprietary specifications, unless one of these special situations exists, the only places where a vendor can reduce his price to come in "low" are in the profit he makes on the sale and on the cost of the service he provides to the client. Reducing profit is valid only for a large order. Just how and where the vendor reduces the cost of service to the client is a concern. A low bid that results in inadequate service is no bargain.

To address this concern, the designer prepares a package that falls somewhere between what would be done in a direct selection situation and in a complete bidding package — without bidding documents. A selected vendor would then be asked to submit a proposal showing the *vendor's cost* to purchase the products from the manufacturers and, in addition to that, percentages of that amount that the vendor would charge for overhead, profit, and the services required to fulfill the requirements of the contract documents. The owner is then free to accept the proposal or suggest modifications. The modifications may be in the form of direct reductions in percentage charges; changes to the terms, such as the amount of deposit required; changes in the level of service proposed; or some other creative arrangement. Proposals and modifications are discussed until agreement is reached and a contract price is established.

For very large orders or for corporations interested in establishing a long-term contract to buy products directly from a manufacturer (though not all manufacturers will sell direct) the negotiation process may begin before a local dealer becomes involved. To use systems furniture as a typical example (though it could work the same way with, say, hospital or hotel furniture), the negotiation process starts as early as the preliminary design phase of a project with the development of typical generic office and workstation layouts or "types." An estimate is made in terms of how many of each type are likely to be required for the project or in a certain time period. At this point, either a bidding or a negotiating situation might be created. If the designer selects similar products by two or more manufacturers to be evaluated by the owner, those manufacturers can be asked to submit specifications and unit cost proposals for their products based on the generic drawings and quantity estimates prepared by the designer. The cost proposals would be based on the assumption that a separate contract will be negotiated with a local dealer to provide the owner with services that manufacturers do not provide, such as product specification, order entry, receipt, storage and delivery, installation, and warranty service. The owner would select the manufacturer based on those comparative costs in addition to quality, design, stablity and response factors. This is an example of a combination of methods for approaching a purchasing contract, where the manufacturers are engaged in the bidding but a contract is negotiated with the dealer. It is advantageous to the owner because manufacturers have more flexibility with regard to setting prices and may have considerable product exposure incentives to offer the best price they can to be awarded the contract. Therefore, the owner is likely to pay the lowest possible price for the furniture, without sacrificing the service on a local level that can make or break the success of the project or of the ongoing purchasing agreement.

It should be evident that the decisions a designer makes in the early stages of the design process can influence how the cost of furnishing a project is established. There are many possible variations in combinations. In the example above, the contract could have been negotiated with the manufacturer, then local dealers could have been asked to bid on the costs to service the contract. No one method is best for all projects. A method must be selected based on the unique circumstances surrounding each project.

Limitations in Vendor Selection

Today, product selection influences and is influenced by the eventual source of the manufactured furniture portion of commercial interiors projects. When the commercial furnishings industry began to expand in the late 1950s, manufacturers sold products to just about any dealer that was financially sound and limited accounts only when an area became so saturated with dealers that competition between them became counter productive; the dealers would lose interest in spending time promoting the product because they were getting smaller and smaller pieces of the pie. Before long, major manufacturers protected the dealerships that represented them by limiting the number of dealerships they would sell to in an area, based on market size. This allowed the dealerships to invest in showroom samples and stock, knowing limited competition would ensure them a percentage of the business that would support this kind of investment. Other manufacturers kept their product lines open, meaning their products were still available through a larger number of dealerships.

Designers encountered very few limitations for 25 years or so, being able to select products from any combination of manufacturers and then invite at least three and sometimes more authorized dealers of the products to submit competitive bids. Then, as certain major manufacturers — particularly of steel casegoods — began to wield more clout in the industry, they began to prohibit the dealers that sold their products from selling competing manufacturers' products. Unwilling to cut off the source of their bread and butter, dealers agreed; these dealers soon became identified with one of a select group of major steel casegoods, then systems furniture, manufacturers. Designers wishing to solicit pricing for and purchase products by one manufacturer had to go elsewhere to obtain products from another manufacturer. Especially for smaller projects, it was inconvenient and time consuming to have to coordinate work between multiple vendors, and prices were not as low as if one vendor supplied all of the merchandise.

Designers learned to limit the range of manufacturers from whose products they selected to those available to the dealer(s) who sold the major steel or wood or systems furniture product line they proposed to their client for any given project. For a while they could still find at least two dealers from whom to get comparative pricing. Eventually, the major manufacturers limited their dealerships to only one in a given market area and almost simultaneously forged alignments with, if not actual purchases of, manufacturers of products commonly specified as part of a complete commercial interior. Today the major systems furniture manufacturers own, produce, and market a full complement of interior furnishings including task and lounge seating, wood casegoods, freestanding metal casegoods, metal file and storage cabinets, conference and training tables, textiles, and accessories. Although a wide variety of choices is still available, designers must consider the details of the eventual furniture purchasing situation before the first catalog is opened.

One technique designers may use in reponse to the development of these furniture conglomerates is to develop their design, bidding, and contract documents to create a bidding situation between vendors of these package offerings. A limited open proprietary specification can name the products of one of the major systems manufacturers, allowing the substitution of one or two other named manufacturer's products along with their associated family of product offerings. The client must, of course, be willing to accept any of the resulting products. For units requiring assembly, drawings that correspond to the products of each named manufacturer must be included in the bid package. The designer must also evaluate how the differing products might affect the interior construction documents. If the effect would be substantial, either alternates would need to be included in the construction documents or the furniture bidding would need to be completed before the construction documents were completed and released for bidding. This example illustrates how the nature of the furniture purchasing process affects not only the type of agreement and bidding documents employed in a project's contract documents, but also the way specifications are written and drawings are developed.

FURNITURE SPECIFICATIONS

Specifications for the purchase and installation of furniture, or for any product or service, have two purposes:

- To establish a basis for obtaining a price from a contractor or vendor for the product or service.
- To serve as instructions for fabricating, providing, and/or installing the product or service.

The five types of construction specifications (proprietary, descriptive, reference standard, cash allowance, and performance) were covered in Chapter 10. Those specification types also apply to furniture, for the same reasons listed in Chapter 10, with the same inherent advantages and disadvantages.

Descriptive specifications for furniture are typically used only for public projects, when every possible vendor must be allowed an opportunity to submit a bid. The process involves describing materials and fabrication methods in exhaustive detail. Sometimes an antique or unique piece is only loosely described for the purpose of budgeting or bidding purposes when services associated with it must be included in an overall scope of work. Descriptive specifications are most often used for custom drapery, particularly when competitive bidding will be the basis for selecting a fabricator. *Reference standard* and *performance standard* specifications are often incorporated into descriptive specifications and are also employed when specifying custom-built furniture when it's included in the furniture contract and not part of the custom casework portion of the construction specifications. *Proprietary* specifications are used for "manufactured" products—which are the majority of items specified for most privately-funded commercial interiors projects. Certain items could be specified by *cash allowance* but this specifying technique is seldom used.

An interiors project often includes requirements for items besides those typically thought of as "furniture," such as planters and other accessory items. They may all be provided by one vendor, but they usually are not. For flexibility in this regard, specifications may be handled in two ways:

- The specifications can be divided into groups with their own applicable products, instructions, and pertinent information. This allows a vendor to bid either all or part(s) of a bid package, depending on the vendor's capabilities.
- The designer can divide the bid package beforehand, sending only parts of the package to some vendors. If the client prefers a certain vendor for some items, specifications for those items can be sent to that vendor only.

Specifications for Services

Some requirements are not for products at all but for *services* related to existing furniture, such as upholstery cleaning. Including them in the specification package reduces the likelihood that they will be overlooked and includes the associated costs in the overall project cost. Information about such services are then conveniently organized within the specifications – in this way, vendors may gain a better overall understanding of the project as a whole. You may also realize some savings opportunities if a vendor can combine sections, thereby increasing efficiency. For example, a reupholsterer may also offer a wood refinishing or upholstery cleaning service. Items requiring those services would then need to be picked up and delivered only once.

Specifications for Smaller Projects

For projects requiring only a small amount of new furniture and delivery and no installation, a simple list indicating the quantity of each item and manufacturers' model numbers and selected options is sufficient. Vendors can be invited to submit proposals based on this list. A cover sheet should indicate the following:

- When the product must be delivered.
- The name and address of the project.

- Whether or not substitutions will be accepted.
- To whom the proposal should be addressed.
- When the proposal is due.

You may wish to include a drawing indicating the locations of the items, keying the item numbers to the symbols on the drawing for use by the vendor upon delivery, but this is not necessary if someone will be on hand to give instructions at the time.

Vendors will respond with their proposals (bids) printed on their own proposal forms or letterhead accompanied by a list of the terms and conditions under which they agree to *sell* the merchandise, one signature line with a signature from an authorized representative of their organization, and another line for the owner's signature.

A vendor is selected by comparing the price against the totals quoted. Returning a copy of that proposal with the owner's signature, along with a check in the amount of the requested deposit, authorizes the vendor to place the order. The owner's signature on the vendor's proposal form indicates that the owner agrees to purchase the items described under the terms and conditions included in the vendor's proposal or "selling contract."

Purchase Orders

If the owner must issue a purchase order, a copy of the vendor's proposal can usually be attached and the purchase order can be worded "per the attached proposal" — referencing the proposal number, date, vendor, and a brief description of what is being ordered. Be aware, however, that purchase orders are, in essence, "purchasing contracts," including the terms and conditions under which the owner agrees to *buy* the described items. Since only one contract can be in force for one order, the owner who issues a signed purchase order stating terms and conditions can not also sign the vendor's proposal. Also, you and/or your client will need to closely compare the language of the purchase order with that of the vendor's terms and conditions to identify any possible conflicts. Minor discrepancies can usually be negotiated between the vendor and the owner.

Issuing a purchase order instead of signing the vendor's proposal indicates that the terms of the purchase order supersede those of the proposal. To avoid this, the purchase order can be amended (just as supplementary conditions amend general conditions of a contract) with a line stating that the owner agrees to the vendor's standard terms and conditions. Serious conflicts that cannot be easily resolved should be referred to the owner's attorney.

The Procurement Contract

The proposal or purchase order described above becomes a simple "procurement" contract. The contract is between the vendor and the owner and, unless designer and vendor are one entity, there is no mention of the role of the designer in the vendor's and owner's agreement documents and very limited statements of the owner's and vendor's responsibilities. Statements regarding insurance are very brief. There is usually no mention of bonds. Also, unless *specifically instructed to do so* in the general notes or the body of the specifications, the vendor probably will not visit the site to verify dimensions or site conditions. The burden of accuracy is completely on the shoulders of the specifier, including whether the owner's elevator is large enough to accept that 10 foot long conference table!

Specifications for Larger Projects

When projects involve a large number and variety of interior furnishings, including significant on-site assembly and installation to be coordinated with interior construction, the complexity of the contract documents, including the drawings and specifications, increases accordingly. Too many people and too much money are involved for anything to be left to chance. Everyone's roles and responsibilities, and methods of communication, must be clearly defined. Preprinted agreements, general conditions, and bid forms such as those offered by the AIA and ASID are appropriate, particularly if a related document was used for the owner/designer agreement.

Especially for large, complex projects, the specifications for products and their delivery, storage, handling, application, or installation must be logically organized. If the logic and clarity of the CSI format for construction specifications has revolutionized that industry, doesn't it make sense to use it for furniture specifications? If you grasp the essentials of that system, you can create a number of broadscope sections that address furniture and related items just as construction specifications are divided into sections. For example, see Figure 14.1. Broadscope sections might include the titles shown in boldface type. Listed below each broadscope section title are items that might either be included or become separate narrowscope sections, depending on the scope of the project — similar to the way "Wallcovering," a broadscope section in Division 9 — Finishes, could be broken into narrowscope sections such as vinyl wallcovering, textile wallcovering, and wood veneer wallcovering.

Grouping products by manufacturer is a popular method of organizing sections since it makes the pricing and evaluation process more convenient. While some of the sections shown in Figure 14.1 might be included under the general construction contract, most of them represent portions of work that are normally under a separate contract.

While Figure 14.1 indicates permanently assigned sections, there may be additional narrowscope sections you may wish to generate for a specific project. For example, under FURNITURE it may be advantageous to add a section to specify pieces of antique furniture. Also, if existing furniture is being reused, you might have extensive requirements for refurbishing it. To accomplish this you could write individual sections concerning such topics as:

- Reupholstering
- Upholstery Cleaning
- Drapery Cleaning
- Stain Protection Treatment
- Wood Refinishing, Touch-up, and Repair
- Recaning
- Electrostatic Painting
- Relaminating (Plastic Laminate Tops)
- Protective Glass Tops
- Slipcovers

Writing Furniture Specifications

Once you've developed a list of the sections required for a particular project you can structure your specifications by writing three-part sections in the same procedure used for construction specifications. Part 1 — General would include:

- A brief summary listing the items covered in the section.

Division 12—Furnishings

Section Number	Title	Section Number	Title
12050	**Fabrics**	**12500**	**Window Treatment**
	Drapery and upholstery materials. Note: This section is used for data filing of information on fabrics. The application of these materials is usually specified in the section where used.	-510	Blinds *Horizontal Louver Blinds* *Vertical Louver Blinds*
		-520	Shades *Insulating Shades* *Lightproof Shades* *Woven Wood Shades*
12100	**Artwork**	-525	Solar Control Film
-110	Murals	-530	Drapery and Curtain Hardware
-120	Wall Hangings	-540	Draperies and Curtains
-130	Paintings	**12600**	**Furniture and Accessories**
-140	Carved or Cast Statuary	-610	Landscape Partitions and Components
-150	Carved or Cast Relief Work		
-160	Custom Chancel Fittings	-620	Furniture
-170	Stained Glass Work	-640	Furniture Systems
12300	**Manufactured Casework**	-650	Furniture Accessories
-301	Metal Casework	**12670**	**Rugs and Mats**
-302	Wood Casework	-675	Rugs
-304	Plastic Laminate-faced Casework	-680	Foot Grilles
-310	Bank Fixtures and Casework	-690	Floor Mats and Frames
-315	Library Casework	**12700**	**Multiple Seating**
-320	Restaurant and Cafeteria Casework	-705	Chairs
		-710	Auditorium and Theater Seating
-325	Educational Casework	-730	Stadium and Arena Seating
-330	Dormitory Casework	-740	Booths and Tables
-335	Medical and Laboratory Casework	-750	Multiple-Use Fixed Seating *Pedestal Table Armchairs*
-340	Pharmacy Casework		
-345	Laboratory Casework	-760	Telescoping Stands
-350	Hospital Casework	-770	Pews and Benches
-355	Dental Casework	**12800**	**Interior Plants and Planters**
-360	Optical Casework	-810	Interior Plants
-365	Veterinary Casework	-815	Planters
-370	Hotel and Motel Casework	-820	Interior Plants Maintenance
-375	Ecclesiastical Casework		
-380	Display Casework		
-390	Residential Casework		

Figure 14.1

- Description of any required submittals (such as samples from the current dye lots of upholstery fabrics for approvals and installation drawings for systems furniture).
- Installer qualifications.
- Coordination with work by others.
- Applicable information regarding site conditions.
- Delivery and handling requirements.
- Warranties required.
- Other similar requirements.

Part 2 – Products would specify the actual products with:

- Manufacturers
- Model numbers
- Quantities
- Finishes
- Options
- Fabrics
- Additional accessory items required for installation

Part 3 – Execution would set forth the installation or assembly procedures to be observed.

Once you have fleshed out the technical sections of the furnishings specifications, use them to identify any overall requirements and information that should be covered in a first section like Division 1 – General Requirements in construction specifications. See Figure 14.2.

For certain projects, it may be more suitable for some furnishings to be included under the general construction contract rather than the furniture contract(s). Except for possible local union rules, there are no hard and fast rules for what products and services are included under which contract(s). You must think through the alternatives with every project and make decisions based on the particular requirements and conditions of each situation. Some of these considerations might be:

- Is there any price advantage to assigning or awarding more of the work to any particular vendor or contractor? Some vendors may offer a lower price if awarded all or a stated portion of the work.

- Coordination between vendors (contractors) becomes more complex when the number of different vendors increases.

- Do local union rules (or owner policy) require that all work done on the project site be performed by union workers? If so, how can your specifications be structured so you can use the vendors you prefer and still comply with the rules? For example, the fabrication of some custom built-in furniture could be done off-site and be part of a furniture contract to provide and deliver only. The installation of that work could then be included under the general construction contract.

- Does a previously negotiated contract include all of the services required for this project? A large corporation's national buying agreement for furniture entered into directly with the manufacturer usually does not include installation services.

Checklist of Responsibilities to be Assigned in Division 1 of Furniture Specifications

Verification of dimensions and site conditions
Specifications of the product
Order entry
Acknowledgement review
Expediting
Scheduling of shipping
Delivery and installation
Delivery only
Installation only
Installation drawings
Receipt of product at their facility
Inspection for freight damage
Freight damage claims as required
Reorder or repair of damaged or defective products
Storage until customer is ready to accept delivery
Verification of receipt of all items ordered
End user orientation/product demonstration
Invoicing
Service during warranty period
Service after warranty period
Regular maintenance

Figure 14.2

Furniture receipt and installation might need to be included under the general construction contract. For smaller quantities, the manufacturer may arrange with a local dealer to provide receipt, storage, and delivery storage services even though the owner pays the manufacturer directly.

FURNITURE DRAWINGS

The furniture plan drawing is a major element in the furniture contract documents and, while not actually part of the interior construction documents, is usually also included in the set with the other construction drawings for use as a reference.

Depending on the scope of the project, there are other drawings that may be required as part of the furniture contract documents. If existing furniture is to be relocated or reconfigured, an accurate existing furniture plan, coded to coordinate with the proposed furniture plan, should be included as a graphic illustration of the scope of the changes involved. For projects involving the relocation of a large quantity of existing furniture, separate relocation charts similar to the chart for coding new furniture shown in the Furniture Code Schedule in Figure 14.3 should be developed to track the destination of each piece. Drawings also should be prepared to illustrate the design of special window treatments, placement of art, and placement of plants. Signage systems require a plan drawing showing locations of signs coded to individual sign type drawings and elevations showing height and relationship to building elements.

When furniture items are to be assembled on site to create a whole unit, as in the case of modular casegoods and seating, it is important to include as part of the specification package large-scale detail drawings of the finished assembly (in plan view, elevation, isometric, or all three), with each piece coded to the specifications. Assigning the whole assembly a code and then giving the separate parts sub-codes (MD-1 for Modular Desk, Type 1, then MD-1-a for the desk part, MD-1-b for the bridge part, MD-1-c for the credenza part) has several advantages. On the furniture plan drawing, the unit can be identified with only the main code (MD-1), eliminating the problem of limited space for codes on small scale drawings. Also, it is unnecessary to change that code on the furniture plan in the event that adjustments are made in the

Furniture Code Schedule

Code	Item	Qty	Description	Location	Source	Contract	Del./Inst.	Spec. Section	Dwg. Smp.	Notes
D-0	Desk	1	Custom built U shape, wood	Reception	Cabinetmaker	Gen. Const.	Inst.	Custom Casework	D, S	
CH-1-A	Desk Chair	1	With arms, black fab., black plas.	Reception	Hag	Furn./Dealer	Del.	Freestanding Furniture	S	
S-1	Sofa	2	3 seat trad., beige/blue, cherry	Reception	HBF	Furn./Dealer	Del.	Freestanding Furniture	S	
OT-1	Occas. Table	2	Coffee table, trad., cherry, oval, 24" × 36"	Reception	HBF	Furn./Dealer	Del.	Freestanding Furniture		
AX	Vase	1	Clear glass vase, 8"h	Reception	Sarried	Furn./Dealer	Inst.	Accessories		
CC-0	Planter	1	Custom casework—built-in planter	Reception	Cabinetmaker	Gen. Const.	Inst.	Custom Casework	D, S	
PL-1	Plant	10	Pothos, 8"h	Reception	Plant Vendor	Plants	Inst.	Plants		
ART-1	Art	2	Original, 36" × 48"	Reception	Art Vendor	Art	Inst.	Art		
SN-1	Sign	1	Informational, custom brass applied logo	Reception	Signage Vendor	Signage	Inst.	Signage	D	
SN-2	Sign	2	Informational, silk screened acrylic plaque, wall mounted	Reception	Signage Vendor	Signage	Inst.	Signage	D	
CT-1	Conf. Table	1	Cherry, boat shape, 144" × 54", 3 chrome cyl. bases, 2 pc. top	Conf. 1	Intrex	Furn./Dealer	Inst.	Freestanding Furniture		Assemble, weight bases, field inst. grommet
CH-2-A	Conf. Chair	10	With arms, swiv./tilt, fixed height, black leather, chrome base	Conf. 1	Brayton	Furn./Mfr.	Del.	Freestanding Furniture	S	
PS	Pres. Syst.		Modular presentation system	Conf. 1	Egan Visual	Furn./Dealer	Inst.	Accessories	D	Install track, hang components
PL-2	Plant	2	Floor plant in 18" dia. chrome container, 60"h	Conf. 1	Plant Vendor	Plants	Inst.	Plants		
LF-3	Lateral File	3	3 dwr., 36" × 18", beige metal	Storage 1	Steelcase	Furn./Mfr.	Del.	Freestanding Furniture		Key alike
SC-1	Storage Cabinet	2	5 shelf, 36" × 18", beige metal	Storage 1	Existing	Furn./Dealer	Del.	Furn. Rep.—Elec. Pntg.		Key alike
CH-3-A	Side Chair	2	With arms, trad., cherry, tapestry	Exec. Sec'y 1	HBF	Furn./Dealer	Del.	Freestanding Furniture	S	
OT-2	Occas. Table	1	Side table, chrome cyl., beige marble top, 15" dia., 20"h	Exec. Sec'y 1	Intrex	Furn./Dealer	Del.	Freestanding Furniture		

Figure 14.3

Furniture Code Schedule

Code	Item	Qty	Description	Location	Source	Contract	Del./Inst.	Spec. Section	Dwg. Smp.	Notes
WS-C	Type C Wrkstat.	1	"Places" system, wood ext., fab. int., cherry 9' × 9'	Exec. Sec'y 1	Haworth	Furn./Mfr.	Inst.	Systems Furniture	D	Key alike, drill for wire mgmt clips & kybrd arm
CH-1-B	Desk Chair	1	With arms, beige fab., black plas.	Exec. Sec'y 1	Hag	Furn./Dealer	Del.	Freestanding Furniture	S	
D-0	Desk	1	Custom built U shape, wood	Senior Partner 1	Cabinetmaker	Gen. Const	Inst.	Custom Casework	D, S	
CH-4	Desk Chair	1	Steelcase "Breton", black leather, chrome base	Senior Partner 1	Existing	Moving	Del.	NA		
S-2	Sofa	1	Contemp., 3 seat, beige tweed	Senior Partner 1	Existing	Furn./Dealer	Del.	Furn. Repair –Reuph.	S	
CH-5	Lounge Chair	1	Contemp., beige tweed	Senior Partner 1	Existing	Furn./Dealer	Del.	Furn. Repair –Reuph.	S	
OT-3	Occas. Table	1	Coffee table, trad., cherry, 36" × 18", scratched	Senior Partner 1	Existing	Furn./Dealer	Del.	Furn. Repair –Refin.		
OT-4	Occas. Table	1	Side table, trad., cherry, 28" × 18", scratched	Senior Partner 1	Existing	Furn./Dealer	Del.	Furn. Repair –Refin.		
LP-1	Table Lamp	1	Brass with beige silk shade, 28"h	Senior Partner 1	Frederick Cooper	Furn./Dealer	Del.	Accessories		
PL-3	Plant	1	Flowering plant in porcelain container provided by owner	Senior Partner 1	Plant Vendor	Plants	Inst.	Plants		
MC-B	Office Type B	1	Wood modular casegoods with wall mtd overhead cabs, cherry	Lawyer 1	Bernhardt	Furn./Dealer	Inst.	Modular Furniture	D,S	Assemble, hang wall cabs (blocking—G.C.)
BC-1	Bookcase	1	5 shelf, cherry, 36" × 11" × 72"h	Lawyer 1	Bernhardt	Furn./Dealer	Del.	Freestanding Furniture		
CH-6	Side Chair	1	Cherry, blue	Lawyer 1	Bernhardt	Furn./Dealer	Del.	Freestanding Furniture	S	
OT-5	Occas. Table	1	Black laq. cyl., glass top, 15" dia., 22"h	Lawyer 1	Intrex	Furn./Dealer	Del.	Freestanding Furniture		
PL-4	Plant	1	Floor plant in 15" black fiberglass container, 4'-6"h	Lawyer 1	Plant Vendor	Plants	Inst.	Plants	D	
MFS	Mobile files		High density mobile file system, mech. assist., 84"h	Files	Spacesaver	Furn./Dealer	Inst.	Mobile Stor. Systems	D	Build platform (Floor bracing—G.C.)
WS-D	Type D Wrkstat.	4	"Places" system cluster of 4, beige fab., lt. bge. lam.	Paralegals	Haworth	Furn./Mfr.	Inst.	Systems Furniture	D	

Figure 14.3 (continued)

components that comprise the unit — only the specifications and detail drawings need to be changed. In addition, the codes can be assigned so that the the sub-code "a", for instance, is always used for the same component. In this way, when a furniture code schedule is developed, the sub-codes can be sorted to show the total quantity of each component required for the entire project and re-sorted to double-check that all components for a given unit have been specified.

When a project involves large areas of systems furniture, it is common practice to develop a separate furniture plan showing only the layout of the panels. Strings of dimensions locating each cluster of workstations in relationship to fixed building elements and each other are included on this plan, as well as locations for electrical infeeds for powered panels. A similar plan drawing showing the components is usually prepared as well, indicating workstation type codes. This drawing is used to show the locations of separate clusters of workstations keyed to large-scale detail drawings of each cluster. The large-scale detail drawings bear the model numbers and finish information for each part of the system. To allow room for the numbers, sometimes the large-scale detail drawings of the clusters are also divided into a panel plan and a separate component plan. These drawings are used to develop the specifications for the systems furniture as well as for installation.

Computer software used by major systems furniture manufacturers creates specifications (bill of materials) automatically as these detail drawings are created. Because of this capability, the responsibility for generating the specifications and installation drawings varies from project to project. A design firm without this software may develop panel, component, and typical workstation plans and then ask the vendor or manufacturer to develop the specifications and installation drawings as part of the service they provide. Obviously, this is another example in which advance planning is necessary in developing the scope of work specified in the furniture contract documents.

TOOLS FOR ORGANIZATION

A Furniture Code Schedule like the one shown in Figure 14.3 is a tool that can be developed during the preliminary and design development phases of a project. It is most useful when created on a computer using a spreadsheet application. It becomes the link between the specifications and the furniture plan drawings. Both the product part of the specifications and smaller detail drawings showing the configuration of modular and systems furniture components should be keyed to the furniture plan drawing through the use of codes. Codes that have some relationship to the name of the item are the most useful, reducing the need to refer to a legend to identify the item. They also can be used by the owner for inventory purposes in the future—in fact, if the owner already has an inventory coding system in place, incorporating that in your coding for the project will ensure a smooth transition. Coded plans are used by the vendor and installer and also by the mover when existing items are to be relocated.

As items are approved in the design stages of a project, assigning them a code and entering the manufacturer, description, and quantity information on the Furniture Code Schedule by location, and entering the corresponding code on the furniture plan for every item, including existing items to be relocated and/or refurbished, will help avoid omissions and duplication. As the design is finalized, information can be added regarding:

- Under what contract the item will be purchased.
- Whether the item requires assembly and installation, or delivery only.
- In what section of the specifications the item should appear.
- Whether any submittals in the way of samples or installation or shop drawings (or even mock ups) will be required of the vendor.
- Notes referring to execution requirements, or an alert that the item influences work to be done under another contract.

It is a simple matter, then, to sort the information by various categories to produce checklists. Such lists are especially valuable communication tools when the project is being produced by a team.

SUMMARY

While furniture is a significant part of the project, it is normally separate from the construction contract. As such, the furniture contract requires a separate and distinct set of documents, which ideally should be organized in the same manner as the construction contract documents. The contract documents for furniture must contain the same elements as those for general construction. See Figure 14.4 for a detailed furniture contract checklist. This list is only a sample—responsibilities for a specific project might be quite different.

Although furniture "specifications" have often existed as merely materials lists or schedules, interior designers can benefit from recognizing that a convenient form already exists to organize these documents. CSI MasterFormat is the tool that gives life to *all* specifications; Division 12 is the primary residence of specifications related to the furniture contract. Again, it is important to realize that this is a highly flexible tool. Topics under this heading may be combined when that approach makes sense or they can be further subdivided when that tactic produces more responsive documents for specific circumstances.

Furniture Contract Checklist

Activity	Design Firm	Design Firm/Dealer	Dealer	Manu-facturer	Mfr's Rep.	Owner	Indep. Installer	Bldg Mgmt	Gen. Cntrctr	Other	Notes
Product specifications	S		P		S	S					
Product price negotiation	X		P		S	S					
Product price bid	X		P		S						
Product proposals			P								
Order entry			P		S						
Installation drawings	X		P	S							
Acknowledgement review	S		P		S						
Expediting	S		P								
Shipping	X		X	P	S	S					
Coord. recvng (dock, freight elev.)	X		P			S		X			
Receive/unload at warehouse			P								
Verification of order receipt	X		P			S					
Inspect product for freight damage	S		P								
Initiate freight damage claims	X		P								
Reorder damaged product	X		P	S		S					
Storage before delivery			P								
Delivery to building	X		P								
Receive/unload at building			P			S		X	X		Dealer's own installers
Repair damaged product	X		P					X	P		
Delivery to project site			P						X		
Coord. furn. install. w/other work	X		S								Coordinate w/sub-contractors
Supervise installation	S		P								
Assembly/Installation			P								
Inspection of installation/punch list	P		P			S					
Reorder defective product	X		P								
End user orientation/prod. demo	S		P			X					
Invoicing	S		P		S						
Service during warranty period	S		P								
Service after warranty period			P								
Periodic maintenance			P					S			

P = Primary responsibility   S = Secondary responsibility   X = Coordination

Figure 14.4

Furniture Contract Checklist

Product (Mfr, description)	Shipped By				Shipped To				Date Req.		Notes
	Mfr's Trucks	Indep. Carrier	UPS/ Fedex	Other	Project Site	Owner's Whse	Dealer's Whse	Other	Ship	Del.	
ABC Co.- Seating		P					P		1/28	2/6	
XYZ Inc.- Systems	P						P		2/1	2/3	
JEM Refinishers	P				P				2/5	2/5	Owner's exist'g furniture

P = Primary responsibility   S = Secondary responsibility   X = Coordination

Figure 14.4 (continued)

CHAPTER 15

THE SAMPLE PROJECT

Books that deal with theories and procedures often dwell too much on "what" and not enough on "how" and "why." Background theory is useful, but if the explanations tend to be peripheral to what you really want to know, the information will have little continuing value. For this reason, we have chosen to present a sample project that draws on the explanations in the text and demonstrates *how* and *why* the concepts presented throughout this book are applied. The elements we have provided to illustrate this sample project include a project manual and drawings, which begin on page 309 following this chapter.

The sample project is developed to explore as many conditions and options as possible. This gives us an opportunity to show a wide variety of solutions, but the fact that we created the sample project gave us the luxury of determining what problems we thought were worthwhile to include for illustrative purposes. Unfortunately, real projects don't work that way. While you may encounter many of the conditions we have elected to include, the real projects you take on will have unique conditions that make them more difficult to solve. We hope, however, that the thought processes and problem-solving techniques we've attempted to bring to this example will help you in handling most problems.

DESCRIPTION OF THE PROJECT

The sample project is a law office. We have chosen this project because it has some unique requirements but also maintains typical conditions that are similar for most professional and corporate offices. Although it's a relatively small project, we've elected to include, for illustrative purposes, conditions that might not be normally associated with such a small project. For example, we've indicated a dense filing system that might typically appear in more extensive projects.

The sample project occupies an entire floor of a small speculative office building. The firm includes two senior partners, who will occupy special offices with private toilets. One of the senior partners is physically handicapped and requires the toilet facility to be designed to accommodate wheelchair access; the other senior partner desires a shower and a built-in bar. Special facilities such as these are not uncommon in professional and corporate executive offices; they give us the opportunity to further illustrate special conditions.

In addition to a variety of private offices, we have programmed spaces for conference, a library, and the usual range of support facilities found in offices of this type.

The basic mechanical and electrical systems are in place as part of the base building; the work of this contract includes extending and adapting those systems to serve the resulting space. We would prefer to have appropriate engineering professionals design and specify these systems, but we have elected to have this work done under a design-build contract. Design-build contracts for this work are quite common and, in some cases, may actually be dictated by the building owner who wants to retain specific contractors to do the work—often those with whom the owner has continuing maintenance contracts. Making this assumption for the sample project gives us a convenient way to show how this work can be handled in ways that give the designer some control.

The floor structure has been reinforced to support the loads we are imposing. Although we are using some "heavy" materials and equipment that result in concentrated loads, we do not mean to imply that similar installations can be used with impunity. If you are contemplating something similar, you should recognize the potential problems and obtain the approval of a qualified structural engineer before you proceed.

The sample project calls for a wide array of finish materials—probably more than most designers would consider for a single project. We've done this purely for illustrative purposes and to show how a variety of similar conditions can be handled in several ways.

You will find instances in which varied materials and products have been incorporated when a more consistent choice could have been made. If this troubles you, remember that our purpose is not to comment on design decisions or their appropriateness. It is to provide an opportunity to illustrate a more comprehensive whole.

While we have attempted to prepare appropriate documents and have no qualms about your borrowing any ideas contained in the sample project for use in your own work, we must caution you to use your own professional judgment in doing so. Again, just because we've done something in a particular way doesn't mean that it's appropriate for another project.

THE DRAWINGS

The drawings provided are not a *complete* set of drawings for the sample project. The full range of required drawings would contain many additional graphics that would contribute little to the reader's understanding of the project. We have presented a floor plan that is essentially complete, since this is the principal and controlling drawing for every project. Other drawings that are subordinate to the base plan have been developed only to the point where they begin to illustrate the basic concepts they are intended to convey.

Designation of Finish Materials

Since the selection and designation of finish materials is a primary concern for the interior designer, it is important to discuss the approach we've taken to accomplish this task.

There are several schools of thought about how the documents should indicate finishes. Many designers prefer a *Finish Plan,* in which each finish is given a key designation. The keys are indicated directly on a plan drawing with arrows to show which surfaces will receive specific finishes, and the extent of each particular finish. The distinct advantage of the Finish Plan is that it allows the designer to show specific transition points where finishes change. For example, it is easy to show finishes that occur in recesses or on features that project from another surface. It is also ideal for distinguishing transitions in flooring materials and indicating flooring patterns, insets, and borders. The Finish Plan's major weakness is that it cannot easily show horizontal transitions and must rely on supplementary elevations to do so. Also, when a project has many different finishes occurring at the same time within a relatively small space, the Finish Plan tends to become confusing.

In cases where a Finish Plan is insufficient, many design professionals prefer to prepare a *Finish Schedule* in tabular form. This method allows the designer to tailor the schedule to include all the information that is pertinent to a specific project. The Finish Schedule's major disadvantage is that it is difficult to indicate termination points, and floor finish changes must be indicated on a supplementary plan drawing.

When using either method, it is usually easier to adopt symbols for various finishes than to write out each one. For example, if you have several different types of carpet, you may distinguish them as CPT1, CTP2, and so on. Then you must define just what "CPT1" and "CPT2" are. There are two approaches that are generally used. Some designers — those who strictly subscribe to the principle that the specific attributes of all materials fall within the province of the specifications — believe that such information belongs in the specifications and nowhere else. A significant number of designers, however, prefer to call out specific products, colors, and patterns directly on the drawings, particularly if the design is predicated on particular proprietary products and no substitutions will be accepted. Because including such data within the Finish Schedule itself would be unwieldy, most designers prepare a separate *Material and Color Schedule* that works in conjunction with either a Finish Schedule or a Finish Plan. Thus all material, color, and pattern selections are coordinated in one spot and not scattered among the drawings and specifications. This approach also simplifies the specifications, allowing them to concentrate on the physical properties of the materials and their methods of installation or application. Keep in mind that only the ultimate finish material is called out on the drawings — therefore, the specifications must identify all accessory products such as the required cushion for various carpets, primers for paint materials, and similar items.

The dual schedule method described above is used to illustrate finish designations for the sample project. For most surfaces included in the Finish Schedule, we list both the base material and the applied finish, since the application of the finish usually depends on the substrate. The schedule may be expanded as necessary to accommodate finishes that may be particular to your specific project. For example, if you had many wainscots or similar features, you could add a wainscot column with subcolumns to indicate material, finish, and height. Likewise, if you had several types of trim within a given space and each type was to be painted a different color, you could expand the trim column to reflect this condition.

Because the schedule system we're using should be reasonably self-explanatory, we've completed only a representative portion of it — just enough to indicate how it's utilized. Other schedules are only partially completed for the same reason.

A project of this scope would have many more details than those included here. Again, our intent is to show only a representative sample. To include more might encourage inexperienced designers to copy them without understanding the basic considerations that underlie their development.

We have made a reasonable attempt to coordinate the drawings and the specifications. Even so, discrepancies may exist. We suggest to the reader that it is fruitful to use the information presented only to expand and clarify your own thinking.

THE SAMPLE PROJECT MANUAL

As discussed in Chapter 11, the project manual contains three types of documents:

- Documents that relate to bidding requirements
- Documents that set forth the contract conditions
- The specifications

While all of these are bound together in a single volume, commonly called the "specs," each serves a function and must be seen as separate and distinct. Perhaps the most common error made by design professionals is assuming that the bidding requirements are part of the Contract Documents. Unless they are specifically enumerated in the

Agreement and included by reference, the Invitation to Bid, the Instructions to Bidders, and the Bid Form become void when bids are received. While the stipulations made on the Bid Form become the basis for the Agreement, the form itself is not part of the Contract Documents.

Bidding Requirements and Conditions of the Contract

The sample project manual includes examples of typical bidding requirements and Conditions of the Contract documents. They include an Invitation to Bid; preprinted Instructions to Bidders; a Bid Form; a Supplement to the Bid Form; a standard preprinted Agreement Form (included so each bidder will know what will be required if he or she is the successful bidder); preprinted General Conditions; and Supplementary Conditions showing typical modifications to the General Conditions. The types of documents included here are required for virtually all projects. For a specific project, you may have to include additional documents. Those can be so varied that it's not possible to include samples that respond to all situations. As a designer you should understand the required documents for a given project, whether they relate to bidding requirements or contract conditions, and be able to include them in the proper place.

Sample Specifications

You will notice that the specification sections we've written for illustrative purposes are very brief—rarely more than a page or two. If you are accustomed to seeing much longer and more comprehensive specifications, you might suspect that we've taken unwarranted liberties by paring down each topic to the absolute essentials. Perhaps we have—and if this were a real project with potential liabilities, we would probably succumb to uneasiness about the potential risks and fluff up the specs a bit by adding more stringent provisions and going into more detail on each topic. Would that approach give us and the owner greater protection? Probably. But we can't say for certain, since experience indicates that more problems and conflicts arise from overspecifying than from underspecifying.

Lengthy specifications often produce "static" that gets in the way of clear communication. If the bidder has difficulty locating essential information, two things will invariably happen. First, the bid will increase to cover for all the extraneous information you've included that the bidder can't immediately comprehend and evaluate. Second, if you decide to enforce an obscure provision that's buried somewhere within the excess verbiage, the contractor will find a comparable loophole to exploit in retaliation.

In preparing the specifications we have held to the time-honored practice of making all references to parties as singular in number and masculine in gender. The specification sections in the sample project manual indicate specific products by trade name and model number. To the best of our knowledge they are current and accurate as of the time they were committed to paper. This doesn't mean that they're appropriate for other projects or even the best choices for our sample project. In many cases they are included simply because the information concerning them is readily accessible and convenient to use. We don't necessarily endorse the use of these products. Please do not copy them. Select materials and products with the same professional care you've always exercised. Also, and this may be even more important, do not copy ASTM or other numbers applying to code or association standards. Those numbers are probably changing as you're reading this. If you repeat them, it is almost inevitable that you'll be referencing inapplicable or obsolete requirements.

Section Organization

Part 1 of each sample specification section begins with a summary that lists the major components of work that appear in that section. This enables the bidder to quickly locate items for a takeoff and helps the project superintendent to find pertinent data. The summary is typically followed by the requirements for submittals relating to the specific section. In some sections we include additional requirements for quality assurance and other items that may be unique to the specific trade. The balance of each section includes Parts 2 and 3, which specify products and set forth the standards for execution.

Part 2 is often very brief since it simply references specific products indicated on the drawings. Purists may object to this practice, arguing that the drawings should not contain information that is the province of the specifications. However, our own experience indicates that designers are more comfortable calling out specific products on the drawings and will continue to do so even though the practice is frowned upon. Rather than repeat information and run the risk of creating conflicts, we merely reference the selections that are indicated on the drawings.

In Part 3 of each section, we often call for the installation of the specified products to be done in accordance with the manufacturer's instructions. This saves us the effort of repeating those instructions and possibly omitting something important.

You should be able to use the sample specification sections as a guide in preparing your own specifications; we hope that they will be useful for that purpose. We must reiterate, however, that in instances where we have specified particular products, those selections were made for the purpose of illustration only and may be wholly inappropriate for another situation. Further, those products may be unavailable, updated, or renumbered by the manufacturer when this book goes to press.

Our own experience, coupled with input from a wide variety of sources, forms the basis for writing the specifications. Although we have written mostly "from scratch," we have also used our own previous work, manufacturers' suggested specifications, and the work of others as guidelines.

The balance of this chapter is devoted to a division-by-division summary of the content of the specifications. The sample project manual and drawings follow these summaries.

Division 1 — General Requirements

Division 1 — General Requirements is the foundation on which all other specification sections rest. The General Conditions, which may be supplemented by the Supplementary Conditions, establish the rules that broadly govern construction projects. Division 1 enumerates the "ground rules" that are in effect for your particular project.

If your Division 1 sections cover the significant items that may apply in one way or another to virtually every other section, you're relieved of having to repeat those provisions in every specification section. For example, by detailing how submittals are to be handled in Division 1, it is sufficient to call for pertinent submittals in subsequent sections without going into detail about how each submittal is to be made.

The primary sections that are assigned to Division 1 include the following:

01010 Summary of Work
01020 Allowances
01026 Unit Prices
01027 Applications for Payment
01030 Alternates
01035 Modification Procedures
01040 Coordination
01045 Cutting and Patching
01050 Field Engineering
01095 Reference Standards and Definitions
01200 Project Meetings
01300 Submittals
01400 Quality Control
01500 Construction Facilities and Temporary Controls
01600 Materials and Equipment
01631 Substitutions
01700 Contract Closeout
01740 Warranties

Many of these sections address issues that are rarely encountered in interior work; and some of the ones that do apply have such limited application that they seldom warrant treatment as a complete section. There is nothing wrong with writing your own broadscope section that pulls related items from what might be several smaller sections. For instance, we like to combine elements of Sections 01035, 01300, 01600, and 01631 into one section called Products, Submittals, and Substitutions. It is here that we can effectively deal with all the issues that surround product specifications and how the contract can be modified to incorporate changes to specified products without having that information scattered among several sections.

Divisions 2, 3, 4, & 5—Sitework, Concrete, Masonry, and Metals

CSI Divisions 2, 3, 4, and 5 are rarely used in interior work since the specification sections they encompass usually address base building conditions.

Included in the sample project manual are short specification sections within Divisions 2, 3, and 4 to cover items that frequently find their way into interior design. Division 5 — Metals is almost never used by interior designers unless they have occasion to specify some type of ornamental metalwork.

Division 6 — Wood and Plastics

Often the interior designer will need to write a section for rough carpentry to cover miscellaneous wood blocking, as we have done in section 06100. Occasionally the rough carpentry section will be more comprehensive if wood framing is being used, but most of the other sections reserved under Division 6 relating primarily to structural carpentry are never needed.

The exceptions are the sections for finish carpentry and architectural woodwork. We've included two brief sections that address these sections. Since the distinction between these topics for small projects is slight, you may prefer to combine them into a single section. Plastic laminate usually occurs in conjunction with casework, so the specification for plastic laminate is typically included under architectural woodwork. If the project is large enough and plastic laminate products are very extensive, you may want to devote a stand-alone section for laminate only.

Division 7 — Thermal and Moisture Protection

CSI Division 7 deals almost exclusively with the building's exterior envelope. It covers waterproofing, insulation, roofing, and a wide variety of related topics. The interior designer rarely, if ever, needs to deal with the items included in Division 7.

Interior work frequently calls for sound-isolated items within the sections directly related to their use. For example, acoustic insulation and sealant is specified with the drywall section because they are integral to that work. To try to include them in Division 7 sections would increase the likelihood that they would be overlooked.

The sample project manual does not include a specification for this division.

Division 8 — Doors and Windows

Specifications for doors and windows fall under CSI Division 8. While overhead doors, curtain walls, and skylights virtually never appear in interior projects, standard doors, interior glazing, and hardware almost always do.

For the sample project we have included specifications for steel door frames that are required for fire-rated openings, wood doors, tempered glass doors and sidelights, finish hardware specified as an allowance, and interior glazing.

In the wood door section you will notice that we have specified factory finishing and premachining for hardware. It is our experience that this procedure produces the best results, particularly when the doors are to receive a natural transparent finish. If you intend to paint doors on your project, you may want to have them field finished so that they match other trim finishes. In this case, you may elect to call only for factory priming.

Note: Although steel frames fall under Division 8, wood door frames are normally covered under the Division 6 section devoted to finish carpentry, as we have done.

Division 9 — Finishes

Division 9 is the special province of the interior designer. What is specified here has the greatest impact on the finished space.

Listed below are the sections used in the sample project specifications.

09250 Gypsum Drywall
09300 Tile
09510 Acoustical Ceilings
09550 Wood Flooring
09600 Interior Stonework
09650 Resilient Flooring
09680 Carpeting
09900 Painting
09950 Wall Coverings

In addition to the sections selected for the sample project, other sections that might apply to a particular project are listed below. Note that many of them are "narrowscope" sections that typically describe very specific products that, in many cases, can be included in related sections unless their application is extensive enough to warrant a separate section.

09200 Lath and Plaster
09215 Veneer Plaster

09400 Terrazzo

09513 Metal Acoustical Ceilings

09521 Acoustical Panels

09678 Resilient Base and Accessories

09690 Carpet Tile

09800 Special Coatings

09960 Vinyl Wallcoverings

09970 Wallpaper

09975 Textile Wallcovering

09980 Wood Veneer Wallcovering

To illustrate the foregoing, note that we have elected to include resilient base in Section 09650 rather than use a separate narrowscope section numbered 09678.

Division 10 — Specialties

Division 10 covers a wide range of items that are typically used in interior work. It is here that you can specify such disparate products as chalkboards, toilet partitions, access flooring, bulletin boards, metal lockers, and demountable partitions.

Included in the sample project manual are brief specification sections for fire extinguisher cabinets and toilet accessories, two items that are incorporated into many interior projects.

Division 11 — Equipment

CSI Division 11 includes a vast array of equipment that might appear in a building, ranging from loading dock equipment to laboratory fume hoods. Most of these items fall outside the realm of the interior designer.

The sample project manual includes short sections specifying an electric projection screen for the conference room and appliances for the kitchenette and lunch room, which are typical inclusions in interior projects. While you can include all appliances under the general contract, it is more common to include only those that will be built in. Freestanding appliances are usually excluded and simply purchased by the owner directly.

Division 12 — Furnishings

Division 12 — Furnishings can, of course, be used for specifying furniture, but since furniture is normally covered under a separate contract, this division typically covers fixed furnishings such as auditorium seating, gymnasium bleachers, and various other types of built-in seating that might be included under the general contract. It is also used for specifying items such as manufactured casework used in laboratories, medical facilities, and similar types of specialized installations. Division 12 is also the location for floor mats and window coverings such as blinds, shades, shutters, and drapery and curtain hardware.

The sample project manual includes a section to cover window blinds, specifying both horizontal and vertical blinds. In normal practice, however, it is probably more common to create a separate contract for window covering.

Divisions 13 & 14—Special Construction and Conveying Systems

Interior designers rarely deal with Division 13, which covers such topics as air-supported structures, pre-engineered buildings, radiation protection, saunas, and swimming pools.

Likewise, Division 14, which encompasses dumbwaiters, elevators, escalators, and similar conveying devices, seldom enters into interior design projects.

Since the sample project does not include any work under these two divisions, there are no sample specification sections included in the project manual.

Division 15—Mechanical

In a great deal of tenant work, mechanical systems are installed under design-build contracts where the mechanical contractors design and install their systems to meet simple performance specifications. This is done primarily because the basic systems are already in place and building management often has maintenance agreements with selected contractors. For this reason, management may require that the work be performed by those contractors so that single-source responsibility for each of the building's systems is preserved.

Specific items of material and equipment may be designated as "building standard" and maintained in stock. Since the selected contractors are familiar with all of these parameters, it often makes sense to enter into design-build contracts for each system. The specification sections in the sample project manual for plumbing, fire protection, and heating, ventilating and air conditioning systems reflect this arrangement. They are very brief since they only set forth the scope of work and hold the contractors responsible for the satisfactory functioning of their systems.

If your scope of services and fee arrangement support professional design, working with a qualified consulting mechanical engineer is almost always a better course of action than making the contractor responsible for design. This arrangement gives you more control over the finished product, as well as the peace of mind that comes from knowing that your consultant's design is responsive to your client's needs rather than being driven by a profit motive.

Division 16 — Electrical

Electrical work is often covered under a design-build contract in the same way mechanical work is done and for the same basic reasons. Therefore, a brief specification similar to the ones in Division 15 of the sample project, summarizing the work to be completed and setting forth pertinent provisions to be met, is sufficient.

While a brief specification may be sufficient, again our preference is to avoid this arrangement whenever possible. The electrical contractor has an inherent conflict of interest. The electrical contractor has design responsibility but his or her real interest lies in making a profit on the installed work.

SUMMARY

As we pointed out at the beginning of this chapter, the sample project has been developed to show the *hows* and *whys* of putting together Contract Documents, illustrating the principles discussed in previous chapters. Remember, the sample project is purely hypothetical. It is included for illustrative purposes only and is intended to show how all the elements of the Contract Documents relate to each other. We hope that it will bring the principles and procedures we've discussed into sharper focus.

The sample project manual begins on the next page.

LAW OFFICES FOR
ANDERSON CALDWELL
& ASSOCIATES
FISK BUILDING
1400 TENTH AVENUE
PITTSBURGH, PA 15233

Project Number 95207.04

THE   DESIGN   GROUP

432 CATALPA ST.
PITTSBURGH
PA 15263
(412) 555-1234

June 5, 1995

TABLE OF CONTENTS

DOCUMENT 00020 - INVITATION TO BID

Anderson Caldwell & Associates, Attorneys at Law, will receive sealed bids for a project entitled:

Law Offices for
ANDERSON CALDWELL & ASSOCIATES
Fisk Building
1400 Tenth Avenue
Pittsburgh, PA 15233

The Contract Documents for which require the furnishing of all labor, materials, equipment, and services for the project until 3:00 p.m. prevailing local time on _____, 19___, at the office of The Design Group, 432 Catalpa St., Pittsburgh, PA 15263 at which time and place all bids will be privately opened.

Contract Documents, including drawings and specifications, are on file at the office of the Designer and bidders may obtain one set without charge. Additional sets may be obtained for the cost of their reproduction.

The successful bidder may be required to furnish and pay for satisfactory Performance and Payment Bonds.

The Owner reserves the right to reject any or all bids or to waive any informalities in the bidding.

No bid shall be withdrawn for a period of thirty (30) days subsequent to the opening of bids.

END OF DOCUMENT 00020

AIA Document A701

Instructions to Bidders

1987 EDITION

TABLE OF ARTICLES

1. DEFINITIONS

2. BIDDER'S REPRESENTATIONS

3. BIDDING DOCUMENTS

4. BIDDING PROCEDURES

5. CONSIDERATION OF BIDS

6. POST-BID INFORMATION

7. PERFORMANCE BOND AND PAYMENT BOND

8. FORM OF AGREEMENT BETWEEN OWNER AND CONTRACTOR

ARTICLE 1
DEFINITIONS

1.1 Bidding Documents include the Bidding Requirements and the proposed Contract Documents. The Bidding Requirements consist of the Advertisement or Invitation to Bid, Instructions to Bidders, Supplementary Instructions to Bidders, the bid form, and other sample bidding and contract forms. The proposed Contract Documents consist of the form of Agreement between the Owner and Contractor, Conditions of the Contract (General, Supplementary and other Conditions), Drawings, Specifications and all Addenda issued prior to execution of the Contract.

1.2 Definitions set forth in the General Conditions of the Contract for Construction, AIA Document A201, or in other Contract Documents are applicable to the Bidding Documents.

1.3 Addenda are written or graphic instruments issued by the Architect prior to the execution of the Contract which modify or interpret the Bidding Documents by additions, deletions, clarifications or corrections.

1.4 A Bid is a complete and properly signed proposal to do the Work for the sums stipulated therein, submitted in accordance with the Bidding Documents.

1.5 The Base Bid is the sum stated in the Bid for which the Bidder offers to perform the Work described in the Bidding Documents as the base, to which Work may be added or from which Work may be deleted for sums stated in Alternate Bids.

1.6 An Alternate Bid (or Alternate) is an amount stated in the Bid to be added to or deducted from the amount of the Base Bid if the corresponding change in the Work, as described in the Bidding Documents, is accepted.

1.7 A Unit Price is an amount stated in the Bid as a price per unit of measurement for materials, equipment or services or a portion of the Work as described in the Bidding Documents.

1.8 A Bidder is a person or entity who submits a Bid.

1.9 A Sub-bidder is a person or entity who submits a bid to a Bidder for materials, equipment or labor for a portion of the Work.

ARTICLE 2
BIDDER'S REPRESENTATIONS

2.1 The Bidder by making a Bid represents that:

2.1.1 The Bidder has read and understands the Bidding Documents and the Bid is made in accordance therewith.

2.1.2 The Bidder has read and understands the Bidding Documents or contract documents, to the extent that such documentation relates to the Work for which the Bid is submitted, for other portions of the Project, if any, being bid concurrently or presently under construction.

2.1.3 The Bidder has visited the site, become familiar with local conditions under which the Work is to be performed and

has correlated the Bidder's personal observations with the requirements of the proposed Contract Documents.

2.1.4 The Bid is based upon the materials, equipment and systems required by the Bidding Documents without exception.

ARTICLE 3
BIDDING DOCUMENTS

3.1 COPIES

3.1.1 Bidders may obtain complete sets of the Bidding Documents from the issuing office designated in the Advertisement or Invitation to Bid in the number and for the deposit sum, if any, stated therein. The deposit will be refunded to Bidders who submit a bona fide Bid and return the Bidding Documents in good condition within ten days after receipt of Bids. The cost of replacement of missing or damaged documents will be deducted from the deposit. A Bidder receiving a Contract award may retain the Bidding Documents and the Bidder's deposit will be refunded.

3.1.2 Bidding Documents will not be issued directly to Sub-bidders or others unless specifically offered in the Advertisement or Invitation to Bid, or in supplementary instructions to bidders.

3.1.3 Bidders shall use complete sets of Bidding Documents in preparing Bids; neither the Owner nor Architect assumes responsibility for errors or misinterpretations resulting from the use of incomplete sets of Bidding Documents.

3.1.4 In making copies of the Bidding Documents available on the above terms, the Owner and the Architect do so only for the purpose of obtaining Bids on the Work and do not confer a license or grant permission for any other use of the Bidding Documents.

3.2 INTERPRETATION OR CORRECTION OF BIDDING DOCUMENTS

3.2.1 The Bidder shall carefully study and compare the Bidding Documents with each other, and with other work being bid concurrently or presently under construction to the extent that it relates to the Work for which the Bid is submitted, shall examine the site and local conditions, and shall at once report to the Architect errors, inconsistencies or ambiguities discovered.

3.2.2 Bidders and Sub-bidders requiring clarification or interpretation of the Bidding Documents shall make a written request which shall reach the Architect at least seven days prior to the date for receipt of Bids.

3.2.3 Interpretations, corrections and changes of the Bidding Documents will be made by Addendum. Interpretations, corrections and changes of the Bidding Documents made in any other manner will not be binding, and Bidders shall not rely upon them.

3.3 SUBSTITUTIONS

3.3.1 The materials, products and equipment described in the Bidding Documents establish a standard of required function, dimension, appearance and quality to be met by any proposed substitution.

3.3.2 No substitution will be considered prior to receipt of Bids unless written request for approval has been received by the Architect at least ten days prior to the date for receipt of Bids. Such requests shall include the name of the material or equipment for which it is to be substituted and a complete description of the proposed substitution including drawings, performance and test data, and other information necessary for an evaluation. A statement setting forth changes in other materials, equipment or other portions of the Work including changes in the work of other contracts that incorporation of the proposed substitution would require shall be included. The burden of proof of the merit of the proposed substitution is upon the proposer. The Architect's decision of approval or disapproval of a proposed substitution shall be final.

3.3.3 If the Architect approves a proposed substitution prior to receipt of Bids, such approval will be set forth in an Addendum. Bidders shall not rely upon approvals made in any other manner.

3.3.4 No substitutions will be considered after the Contract award unless specifically provided in the Contract Documents.

3.4   ADDENDA

3.4.1 Addenda will be mailed or delivered to all who are known by the issuing office to have received a complete set of Bidding Documents.

3.4.2 Copies of Addenda will be made available for inspection wherever Bidding Documents are on file for that purpose.

3.4.3 No Addenda will be issued later than four days prior to the date for receipt of Bids except an Addendum withdrawing the request for Bids or one which includes postponement of the date for receipt of Bids.

3.4.4 Each Bidder shall ascertain prior to submitting a Bid that the Bidder has received all Addenda issued, and the Bidder shall acknowledge their receipt in the Bid.

ARTICLE 4

BIDDING PROCEDURES

4.1   FORM AND STYLE OF BIDS

4.1.1 Bids shall be submitted on forms identical to the form included with the Bidding Documents.

4.1.2 All blanks on the bid form shall be filled in by typewriter or manually in ink.

4.1.3 Where so indicated by the makeup of the bid form, sums shall be expressed in both words and figures, and in case of discrepancy between the two, the amount written in words shall govern.

4.1.4 Interlineations, alterations and erasures must be initialed by the signer of the Bid.

4.1.5 All requested Alternates shall be bid. If no change in the Base Bid is required, enter "No Change."

4.1.6 Where two or more Bids for designated portions of the Work have been requested, the Bidder may, without forfeiture

of the bid security, state the Bidder's refusal to accept award of less than the combination of Bids stipulated by the Bidder. The Bidder shall make no additional stipulations on the bid form nor qualify the Bid in any other manner.

4.1.7 Each copy of the Bid shall include the legal name of the Bidder and a statement that the Bidder is a sole proprietor, partnership, corporation or other legal entity. Each copy shall be signed by the person or persons legally authorized to bind the Bidder to a contract. A Bid by a corporation shall further give the state of incorporation and have the corporate seal affixed. A Bid submitted by an agent shall have a current power of attorney attached certifying the agent's authority to bind the Bidder.

4.2   BID SECURITY

4.2.1 If so stipulated in the Advertisement or Invitation to Bid, or supplementary instructions to bidders, each Bid shall be accompanied by a bid security in the form and amount required, pledging that the Bidder will enter into a Contract with the Owner on the terms stated in the Bid and will, if required, furnish bonds covering the faithful performance of the Contract and payment of all obligations arising thereunder. Should the Bidder refuse to enter into such Contract or fail to furnish such bonds if required, the amount of the bid security shall be forfeited to the Owner as liquidated damages, not as a penalty. The amount of the bid security shall not be forfeited to the Owner in the event the Owner fails to comply with Subparagraph 6.2.1.

4.2.2 If a surety bond is required, it shall be written on AIA Document A310, Bid Bond, unless otherwise provided in the Bidding Documents, and the attorney-in-fact who executes the bond on behalf of the surety shall affix to the bond a certified and current copy of the power of attorney.

4.2.3 The Owner will have the right to retain the bid security of Bidders to whom an award is being considered until either (a) the Contract has been executed and bonds, if required, have been furnished, or (b) the specified time has elapsed so that Bids may be withdrawn, or (c) all Bids have been rejected.

4.3   SUBMISSION OF BIDS

4.3.1 All copies of the Bid, the bid security, if any, and other documents required to be submitted with the Bid shall be enclosed in a sealed opaque envelope. The envelope shall be addressed to the party receiving the Bids and shall be identified with the Project name, the Bidder's name and address and, if applicable, the designated portion of the Work for which the Bid is submitted. If the Bid is sent by mail, the sealed envelope shall be enclosed in a separate mailing envelope with the notation "SEALED BID ENCLOSED" on the face thereof.

4.3.2 Bids shall be deposited at the designated location prior to the time and date for receipt of Bids. Bids received after the time and date for receipt of Bids will be returned unopened.

4.3.3 The Bidder shall assume full responsibility for timely delivery at the location designated for receipt of Bids.

4.3.4 Oral, telephonic or telegraphic Bids are invalid and will not receive consideration.

4.4   MODIFICATION OR WITHDRAWAL OF BID

4.4.1 A Bid may not be modified, withdrawn or canceled by the Bidder during the stipulated time period following the time

AIA DOCUMENT A701 • INSTRUCTIONS TO BIDDERS • FOURTH EDITION • AIA® • ©1987 • THE AMERICAN INSTITUTE OF ARCHITECTS, 1735 NEW YORK AVENUE, N.W., WASHINGTON, D.C. 20006 and date designated for the receipt of Bids, and each Bidder so agrees in submitting a Bid.

4.4.2 Prior to the time and date designated for receipt of Bids, a Bid submitted may be modified or withdrawn by notice to the party receiving Bids at the place designated for receipt of Bids. Such notice shall be in writing over the signature of the Bidder or by telegram; if by telegram, written confirmation over the signature of the Bidder shall be mailed and postmarked on or before the date and time set for receipt of Bids. A change shall be so worded as not to reveal the amount of the original Bid.

4.4.3 Withdrawn Bids may be resubmitted up to the date and time designated for the receipt of Bids provided that they are then fully in conformance with these Instructions to Bidders.

4.4.4 Bid security, if required, shall be in an amount sufficient for the Bid as modified or resubmitted.

ARTICLE 5
CONSIDERATION OF BIDS

5.1 OPENING OF BIDS

5.1.1 Unless stated otherwise in the Advertisement or Invitation to Bid, the properly identified Bids received on time will be opened publicly and will be read aloud. An abstract of the Bids will be made available to Bidders. When it has been stated that Bids will be opened privately, an abstract of the same information may, at the discretion of the Owner, be made available to the Bidders within a reasonable time.

5.2 REJECTION OF BIDS

5.2.1 The Owner shall have the right to reject any or all Bids, reject a Bid not accompanied by a required bid security or by other data required by the Bidding Documents, or reject a Bid which is in any way incomplete or irregular.

5.3 ACCEPTANCE OF BID (AWARD)

5.3.1 It is the intent of the Owner to award a Contract to the lowest responsible Bidder provided the Bid has been submitted in accordance with the requirements of the Bidding Documents and does not exceed the funds available. The Owner shall have the right to waive informalities or irregularities in a Bid received and to accept the Bid which, in the Owner's judgment, is in the Owner's own best interests.

5.3.2 The Owner shall have the right to accept Alternates in any order or combination, unless otherwise specifically provided in the Bidding Documents, and to determine the low Bidder on the basis of the sum of the Base Bid and Alternates accepted.

ARTICLE 6
POST-BID INFORMATION

6.1 CONTRACTOR'S QUALIFICATION STATEMENT

6.1.1 Bidders to whom award of a Contract is under consideration shall submit to the Architect, upon request, a properly executed AIA Document A305, Contractor's Qualification Statement, unless such a Statement has been previously

required and submitted as a prerequisite to the issuance of Bidding Documents.

6.2 OWNER'S FINANCIAL CAPABILITY

6.2.1 The Owner shall, at the request of the Bidder to whom award of a Contract is under consideration and no later than seven days prior to the expiration of the time for withdrawal of Bids, furnish to the Bidder reasonable evidence that financial arrangements have been made to fulfill the Owner's obligations under the Contract. Unless such reasonable evidence is furnished, the Bidder will not be required to execute the Agreement between the Owner and Contractor.

6.3 SUBMITTALS

6.3.1 The Bidder shall, as soon as practicable after notification of selection for the award of a Contract, furnish to the Owner through the Architect in writing:

   .1 a designation of the Work to be performed with the Bidder's own forces;

   .2 names of the manufacturers, products and the suppliers of principal items or systems of materials and equipment proposed for the Work; and

   .3 names of persons or entities (including those who are to furnish materials or equipment fabricated to a special design) proposed for the principal portions of the Work.

6.3.2 The Bidder will be required to establish to the satisfaction of the Architect and Owner the reliability and responsibility of the persons or entities proposed to furnish and perform the Work described in the Bidding Documents.

6.3.3 Prior to the award of the Contract, the Architect will notify the Bidder in writing if either the Owner or Architect, after due investigation, has reasonable objection to a person or entity proposed by the Bidder. If the Owner or Architect has reasonable objection to a proposed person or entity, the Bidder may, at the Bidder's option, (1) withdraw the Bid, or (2) submit an acceptable substitute person or entity with an adjustment in the Base Bid or Alternate Bid to cover the difference in cost occasioned by such substitution. The Owner may accept the adjusted bid price or disqualify the Bidder. In the event of either withdrawal or disqualification, bid security will not be forfeited.

6.3.4 Persons and entities proposed by the Bidder and to whom the Owner and Architect have made no reasonable objection must be used on the Work for which they were proposed and shall not be changed except with the written consent of the Owner and Architect.

ARTICLE 7
PERFORMANCE BOND AND
PAYMENT BOND

7.1 BOND REQUIREMENTS

7.1.1 If stipulated in the Bidding Documents, the Bidder shall furnish bonds covering the faithful performance of the Contract and payment of all obligations arising thereunder. Bonds may be secured through the Bidder's usual sources.

7.1.2 If the furnishing of such bonds is stipulated in the Bidding Documents, the cost shall be included in the Bid. If the furnishing of such bonds is required after receipt of bids and before execution of the Contract, the cost of such bonds shall be added to the Bid in determining the Contract Sum.

7.1.3 If the Owner requires that bonds be secured from other than the Bidder's usual sources, changes in cost will be adjusted as provided in the Contract Documents.

7.2 TIME OF DELIVERY AND FORM OF BONDS

7.2.1 The Bidder shall deliver the required bonds to the Owner not later than three days following the date of execution of the Contract. If the Work is to be commenced prior thereto in response to a letter of intent, the Bidder shall, prior to commencement of the Work, submit evidence satisfactory to the Owner that such bonds will be furnished and delivered in accordance with this Subparagraph 7.2.1.

7.2.2 Unless otherwise provided, the bonds shall be written on AIA Document A312, Performance Bond and Payment Bond. Both bonds shall be written in the amount of the Contract Sum.

7.2.3 The bonds shall be dated on or after the date of the Contract.

7.2.4 The Bidder shall require the attorney-in-fact who executes the required bonds on behalf of the surety to affix thereto a certified and current copy of the power of attorney.

ARTICLE 8

FORM OF AGREEMENT BETWEEN OWNER AND CONTRACTOR

8.1 FORM TO BE USED

8.1.1 Unless otherwise required in the Bidding Documents, the Agreement for the Work will be written on AIA Document A101, Standard Form of Agreement Between Owner and Contractor Where the Basis of Payment Is a Stipulated Sum.

AIA DOCUMENT A701 • INSTRUCTIONS TO BIDDERS • FOURTH EDITION • AIA® • ©1987 • THE AMERICAN INSTITUTE OF ARCHITECTS, 1735 NEW YORK AVENUE, N.W., WASHINGTON, D.C. 20006

DOCUMENT 00300 - BID FORM

DATE: _____

SUBMITTED BY: _____

_____

_____

_____

Address of Bidder

_____

Telephone Number of Bidder

TO: Anderson Caldwell & Associates

PROJECT: Law Offices for
ANDERSON CALDWELL & ASSOCIATES
Fisk Building
1400 Tenth Avenue
Pittsburgh, PA 15233

1. Stipulated Sum Bid
In compliance with the Invitation to Bid inviting proposals for the work named, the undersigned, having become thoroughly familiar with the terms and conditions of the proposed Contract Documents and with conditions affecting the performance and cost of the work, and having fully examined existing site conditions in all particulars, hereby proposes and agrees to fully perform the work in strict accordance with the proposed Contract Documents, including the furnishing of any and all labor, materials, services, equipment, and other means of construction in whatever manner and sequence required to complete said work for the Stipulated Sum of:

_____ Dollars ($_____)
(Words)   (Figures)

If the Owner requires the furnishing of Performance and Labor and Material Payment Bonds, add to the Stipulated Sum _____ Dollars ($_____).

2.   Addenda

The undersigned Bidder acknowledges receipt of the following addenda:

Addendum Number _____ Date _____

Addendum Number _____ Date _____

Addendum Number _____ Date _____

and further acknowledges its/their inclusion in the proposed Contract Documents.

3.   Rejection of Bid

In submitting this Bid, the Bidder understands that the right is reserved by the Owner to reject any or all bids without explanation.

4.   Acceptance of Bid and Award of Contract

When written notice of the acceptance of this Bid is mailed or delivered to the undersigned within thirty (30) days after the opening thereof, or at any time thereafter prior to written notice that the Proposal is withdrawn, the undersigned agrees to execute and deliver a Contract in the prescribed form and furnish bonds, if required, within ten (10) days after the Contract is presented to him for signature.

5.   Contract Time

The undersigned proposes to commence work under the Contract within ten (10) calendar days of the receipt of the "Notice to Proceed."

And further proposes to substantially complete the work of the Contract within 120 calendar days thereafter.

Date: _____

Signed: _____

SEAL:

By: _____
                          (Print or Type Name)

Title: _____

Name of Firm: _____

Attested: _____
                          (Notary)

My Term Expires: _____

END OF DOCUMENT 00300

DOCUMENT 00400 - SUPPLEMENT TO BID FORM

INSTRUCTIONS:
Fill out in its entirety either Section A or Section B (whichever corresponds to Bidder's form of business organization) and complete Section C (signature must be same as on Bid Form).

(Supplemental Information Required if a Corporation)

A.   Names of Officers:
President _____
Address _____
Secretary _____
Address _____
Treasurer _____
Address _____
Corporation is organized under the laws of the State of _____

(Supplemental Information Required if an Individual, Partnership, or Non-Incorporated Organization)

B. Names and Addresses of Members of Firm:

_____
_____
_____
_____

C. SIGNATURES
Date: _____
Signed: _____
Title: _____
Name of Firm: _____
Telephone: _____

END OF DOCUMENT 00400

Copies of the current edition of this AIA document may be purchased from The American Institute of Architects or its local distributors. The text of this document is not "model language" and is not intended for use in other documents without permission of the AIA.

AIA Document A101

Standard Form of Agreement Between Owner and Contractor

where the basis of payment is a

STIPULATED SUM

1987 EDITION

THIS DOCUMENT HAS IMPORTANT LEGAL CONSEQUENCES; CONSULTATION WITH AN ATTORNEY IS ENCOURAGED WITH RESPECT TO ITS COMPLETION OR MODIFICATION.

The 1987 Edition of AIA Document A201, General Conditions of the Contract for Construction, is adopted in this document by reference. Do not use with other general conditions unless this document is modified.

This document has been approved and endorsed by The Associated General Contractors of America.

AGREEMENT

made as of the   day of   in the year of
Nineteen Hundred and

BETWEEN the Owner:
(Name and address)

and the Contractor:
(Name and address)

The Project is:
(Name and location)

The Architect is:
(Name and address)

The Owner and Contractor agree as set forth below.

ARTICLE 1
THE CONTRACT DOCUMENTS

The Contract Documents consist of this Agreement, Conditions of the Contract (General, Supplementary and other Conditions), Drawings, Specifications, Addenda issued prior to execution of this Agreement, other documents listed in this Agreement and Modifications issued after execution of this Agreement; these form the Contract, and are as fully a part of the Contract as if attached to this Agreement or repeated herein. The Contract represents the entire and integrated agreement between the parties hereto and supersedes prior negotiations, representations or agreements, either written or oral. An enumeration of the Contract Documents, other than Modifications, appears in Article 9.

ARTICLE 2
THE WORK OF THIS CONTRACT

The Contractor shall execute the entire Work described in the Contract Documents, except to the extent specifically indicated in the Contract Documents to be the responsibility of others, or as follows:

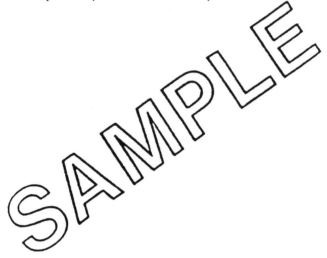

ARTICLE 3
DATE OF COMMENCEMENT AND SUBSTANTIAL COMPLETION

3.1 The date of commencement is the date from which the Contract Time of Paragraph 3.2 is measured, and shall be the date of this Agreement, as first written above, unless a different date is stated below or provision is made for the date to be fixed in a notice to proceed issued by the Owner.

(Insert the date of commencement, if it differs from the date of this Agreement or, if applicable, state that the date will be fixed in a notice to proceed.)

Unless the date of commencement is established by a notice to proceed issued by the Owner, the Contractor shall notify the Owner in writing not less than five days before commencing the Work to permit the timely filing of mortgages, mechanic's liens and other security interests.

3.2 The Contractor shall achieve Substantial Completion of the entire Work not later than

(Insert the calendar date or number of calendar days after the date of commencement. Also insert any requirements for earlier Substantial Completion of certain portions of the Work, if not stated elsewhere in the Contract Documents.)

, subject to adjustments of this Contract Time as provided in the Contract Documents.

(Insert provisions, if any, for liquidated damages relating to failure to complete on time.)

ARTICLE 4
CONTRACT SUM

4.1 The Owner shall pay the Contractor in current funds for the Contractor's performance of the Contract the Contract Sum of
Dollars
($), subject to additions and deductions as provided in the Contract Documents.

4.2 The Contract Sum is based upon the following alternates, if any, which are described in the Contract Documents and are hereby accepted by the Owner:

(State the numbers or other identification of accepted alternates. If decisions on other alternates are to be made by the Owner subsequent to the execution of this Agreement, attach a schedule of such other alternates showing the amount for each and the date until which that amount is valid.)

4.3 Unit prices, if any, are as follows:

ARTICLE 5
PROGRESS PAYMENTS

5.1 Based upon Applications for Payment submitted to the Architect by the Contractor and Certificates for Payment issued by the Architect, the Owner shall make progress payments on account of the Contract Sum to the Contractor as provided below and elsewhere in the Contract Documents.

5.2 The period covered by each Application for Payment shall be one calendar month ending on the last day of the month, or as follows:

5.3 Provided an Application for Payment is received by the Architect not later than the   day of a month, the Owner shall make payment to the Contractor not later than the   day of the   month. If an Application for Payment is received by the Architect after the application date fixed above, payment shall be made by the Owner not later than   days after the Architect receives the Application for Payment.

5.4 Each Application for Payment shall be based upon the Schedule of Values submitted by the Contractor in accordance with the Contract Documents. The Schedule of Values shall allocate the entire Contract Sum among the various portions of the Work and be prepared in such form and supported by such data to substantiate its accuracy as the Architect may require. This Schedule, unless objected to by the Architect, shall be used as a basis for reviewing the Contractor's Applications for Payment.

5.5 Applications for Payment shall indicate the percentage of completion of each portion of the Work as of the end of the period covered by the Application for Payment.

5.6 Subject to the provisions of the Contract Documents, the amount of each progress payment shall be computed as follows:

5.6.1 Take that portion of the Contract Sum properly allocable to completed Work as determined by multiplying the percentage completion of each portion of the Work by the share of the total Contract Sum allocated to that portion of the Work in the Schedule of Values, less retainage of   percent (%). Pending final determination of cost to the Owner of changes in the Work, amounts not in dispute may be included as provided in Subparagraph 7.3.7 of the General Conditions even though the Contract Sum has not yet been adjusted by Change Order;

5.6.2 Add that portion of the Contract Sum properly allocable to materials and equipment delivered and suitably stored at the site for subsequent incorporation in the completed construction (or, if approved in advance by the Owner, suitably stored off the site at a location agreed upon in writing), less retainage of   percent (%);

5.6.3 Subtract the aggregate of previous payments made by the Owner; and

5.6.4 Subtract amounts, if any, for which the Architect has withheld or nullified a Certificate for Payment as provided in Paragraph 9.5 of the General Conditions.

5.7 The progress payment amount determined in accordance with Paragraph 5.6 shall be further modified under the following circumstances:

5.7.1 Add, upon Substantial Completion of the Work, a sum sufficient to increase the total payments to   percent (%) of the Contract Sum, less such amounts as the Architect shall determine for incomplete Work and unsettled claims; and

5.7.2 Add, if final completion of the Work is thereafter materially delayed through no fault of the Contractor, any additional amounts payable in accordance with Subparagraph 9.10.3 of the General Conditions.

5.8 Reduction or limitation of retainage, if any, shall be as follows:

(If it is intended, prior to Substantial Completion of the entire Work, to reduce or limit the retainage resulting from the percentages inserted in Subparagraphs 5.6.1 and 5.6.2 above, and this is not explained elsewhere in the Contract Documents, insert here provisions for such reduction or limitation.)

ARTICLE 6
FINAL PAYMENT

Final payment, constituting the entire unpaid balance of the Contract Sum, shall be made by the Owner to the Contractor when (1) the Contract has been fully performed by the Contractor except for the Contractor's responsibility to correct nonconforming Work as provided in Subparagraph 12.2.2 of the General Conditions and to satisfy other requirements, if any, which necessarily survive final payment; and (2) a final Certificate for Payment has been issued by the Architect; such final payment shall be made by the Owner not more than 30 days after the issuance of the Architect's final Certificate for Payment, or as follows:

ARTICLE 7
MISCELLANEOUS PROVISIONS

7.1 Where reference is made in this Agreement to a provision of the General Conditions or another Contract Document, the reference refers to that provision as amended or supplemented by other provisions of the Contract Documents.

7.2 Payments due and unpaid under the Contract shall bear interest from the date payment is due at the rate stated below, or in the absence thereof, at the legal rate prevailing from time to time at the place where the Project is located.

(Insert rate of interest agreed upon, if any.)

(Usury laws and requirements under the Federal Truth in Lending Act, similar state and local consumer credit laws and other regulations at the Owner's and Contractor's principal places of business, the location of the Project and elsewhere may affect the validity of this provision. Legal advice should be obtained with respect to deletions or modifications, and also regarding requirements such as written disclosures or waivers.)

7.3 Other provisions:

ARTICLE 8
TERMINATION OR SUSPENSION

8.1 The Contract may be terminated by the Owner or the Contractor as provided in Article 14 of the General Conditions.

8.2 The Work may be suspended by the Owner as provided in Article 14 of the General Conditions.

ARTICLE 9
ENUMERATION OF CONTRACT DOCUMENTS

9.1 The Contract Documents, except for Modifications issued after execution of this Agreement, are enumerated as follows:

9.1.1 The Agreement is this executed Standard Form of Agreement Between Owner and Contractor, AIA Document A101, 1987 Edition.

9.1.2 The General Conditions are the General Conditions of the Contract for Construction, AIA Document A201, 1987 Edition.

9.1.3 The Supplementary and other Conditions of the Contract are those contained in the Project Manual dated
, and are as follows:

Document   **Title**   **Pages**

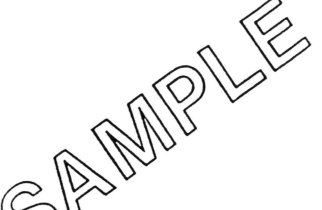

9.1.4 The Specifications are those contained in the Project Manual dated as in Subparagraph 9.1.3, and are as follows:

(Either list the Specifications here or refer to an exhibit attached to this Agreement.)

Section   **Title**   **Pages**

9.1.5 The Drawings are as follows, and are dated   unless a different date is shown below:

(Either list the Drawings here or refer to an exhibit attached to this Agreement.)

Number   **Title**   **Date**

9.1.6 The Addenda, if any, are as follows:

Number   **Date**   **Pages**

Portions of Addenda relating to bidding requirements are not part of the Contract Documents unless the bidding requirements are also enumerated in this Article 9.

9.1.7 Other documents, if any, forming part of the Contract Documents are as follows:

(List here any additional documents which are intended to form part of the Contract Documents. The General Conditions provide that bidding requirements such as advertisement or invitation to bid, Instructions to Bidders, sample forms and the Contractor's bid are not part of the Contract Documents unless enumerated in this Agreement. They should be listed here only if intended to be part of the Contract Documents.)

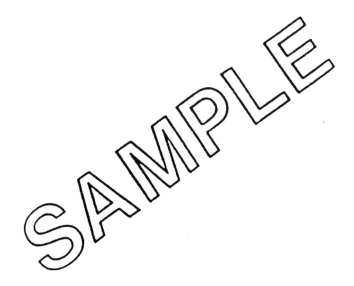

This Agreement is entered into as of the day and year first written above and is executed in at least three original copies of which one is to be delivered to the Contractor, one to the Architect for use in the administration of the Contract, and the remainder to the Owner.

OWNER   CONTRACTOR

_____   _____
(Signature)   *(Signature)*

_____   _____
(Printed name and title)   *(Printed name and title)*

AIA Document A201

General Conditions of the Contract for Construction

THIS DOCUMENT HAS IMPORTANT LEGAL CONSEQUENCES; CONSULTATION WITH AN ATTORNEY IS ENCOURAGED WITH RESPECT TO ITS MODIFICATION

1987 EDITION
TABLE OF ARTICLES

1. GENERAL PROVISIONS

2. OWNER

3. CONTRACTOR

4. ADMINISTRATION OF THE CONTRACT

5. SUBCONTRACTORS

6. CONSTRUCTION BY OWNER OR BY SEPARATE CONTRACTORS

7. CHANGES IN THE WORK

8. TIME

9. PAYMENTS AND COMPLETION

10. PROTECTION OF PERSONS AND PROPERTY

11. INSURANCE AND BONDS

12. UNCOVERING AND CORRECTION OF WORK

13. MISCELLANEOUS PROVISIONS

14. TERMINATION OR SUSPENSION OF THE CONTRACT

This document has been approved and endorsed by the Associated General Contractors of America.

 CAUTION: You should use an original AIA document which has this caution printed in red. An original assures that changes will not be obscured as may occur when documents are reproduced.

INDEX

AIA DOCUMENT A201 • GENERAL CONDITIONS OF THE CONTRACT FOR CONSTRUCTION • FOURTEENTH EDITION
AIA® • ©1987 THE AMERICAN INSTITUTE OF ARCHITECTS, 1735 NEW YORK AVENUE, N.W., WASHINGTON, D.C. 20006

ARTICLE 1

GENERAL PROVISIONS

1.1 BASIC DEFINITIONS

1.1.1 THE CONTRACT DOCUMENTS

The Contract Documents consist of the Agreement between Owner and Contractor (hereinafter the Agreement), Conditions of the Contract (General, Supplementary and other Conditions), Drawings, Specifications, addenda issued prior to execution of the Contract, other documents listed in the Agreement and Modifications issued after execution of the Contract. A Modification is (1) a written amendment to the Contract signed by both parties, (2) a Change Order, (3) a Construction Change Directive or (4) a written order for a minor change in the Work issued by the Architect. Unless specifically enumerated in the Agreement, the Contract Documents do not include other documents such as bidding requirements (advertisement or invitation to bid, Instructions to Bidders, sample forms, the Contractor's bid or portions of addenda relating to bidding requirements).

1.1.2 THE CONTRACT

The Contract Documents form the Contract for Construction. The Contract represents the entire and integrated agreement between the parties hereto and supersedes prior negotiations, representations or agreements, either written or oral. The Contract may be amended or modified only by a Modification. The Contract Documents shall not be construed to create a contractual relationship of any kind (1) between the Architect and Contractor, (2) between the Owner and a Subcontractor or Subsubcontractor or (3) between any persons or entities other than the Owner and Contractor. The Architect shall, however, be entitled to performance and enforcement of obligations under the Contract intended to facilitate performance of the Architect's duties.

1.1.3 THE WORK

The term "Work" means the construction and services required by the Contract Documents, whether completed or partially completed, and includes all other labor, materials, equipment and services provided or to be provided by the Contractor to fulfill the Contractor's obligations. The Work may constitute the whole or a part of the Project.

1.1.4 THE PROJECT

The Project is the total construction of which the Work performed under the Contract Documents may be the whole or a part and which may include construction by the Owner or by separate contractors.

1.1.5 THE DRAWINGS

The Drawings are the graphic and pictorial portions of the Contract Documents, wherever located and whenever issued, showing the design, location and dimensions of the Work, generally including plans, elevations, sections, details, schedules and diagrams.

1.1.6 THE SPECIFICATIONS

The Specifications are that portion of the Contract Documents consisting of the written requirements for materials, equip-ment, construction systems, standards and workmanship for the Work, and performance of related services.

1.1.7 THE PROJECT MANUAL

The Project Manual is the volume usually assembled for the Work which may include the bidding requirements, sample forms, Conditions of the Contract and Specifications.

1.2 EXECUTION, CORRELATION AND INTENT

1.2.1 The Contract Documents shall be signed by the Owner and Contractor as provided in the Agreement. If either the Owner or Contractor or both do not sign all the Contract Documents, the Architect shall identify such unsigned Documents upon request.

1.2.2 Execution of the Contract by the Contractor is a representation that the Contractor has visited the site, become familiar with local conditions under which the Work is to be performed and correlated personal observations with requirements of the Contract Documents.

1.2.3 The intent of the Contract Documents is to include all items necessary for the proper execution and completion of the Work by the Contractor. The Contract Documents are complementary, and what is required by one shall be as binding as if required by all; performance by the Contractor shall be required only to the extent consistent with the Contract Documents and reasonably inferable from them as being necessary to produce the intended results.

1.2.4 Organization of the Specifications into divisions, sections and articles, and arrangement of Drawings shall not control the Contractor in dividing the Work among Subcontractors or in establishing the extent of Work to be performed by any trade.

1.2.5 Unless otherwise stated in the Contract Documents, words which have well-known technical or construction industry meanings are used in the Contract Documents in accordance with such recognized meanings.

1.3 OWNERSHIP AND USE OF ARCHITECT'S DRAWINGS, SPECIFICATIONS AND OTHER DOCUMENTS

1.3.1 The Drawings, Specifications and other documents prepared by the Architect are instruments of the Architect's service through which the Work to be executed by the Contractor is described. The Contractor may retain one contract record set. Neither the Contractor nor any Subcontractor, Subsubcontractor or material or equipment supplier shall own or claim a copyright in the Drawings, Specifications and other documents prepared by the Architect, and unless otherwise indicated the Architect shall be deemed the author of them and will retain all common law, statutory and other reserved rights, in addition to the copyright. All copies of them, except the Contractor's record set, shall be returned or suitably accounted for to the Architect, on request, upon completion of the Work. The Drawings, Specifications and other documents prepared by the Architect, and copies thereof furnished to the Contractor, are for use solely with respect to this Project. They are not to be used by the Contractor or any Subcontractor, Subsubcontractor or material or equipment supplier on other projects or for additions to this Project outside the scope of the

Work without the specific written consent of the Owner and Architect. The Contractor, Subcontractors, Sub-subcontractors and material or equipment suppliers are granted a limited license to use and reproduce applicable portions of the Drawings, Specifications and other documents prepared by the Architect appropriate to and for use in the execution of their Work under the Contract Documents. All copies made under this license shall bear the statutory copyright notice, if any, shown on the Drawings, Specifications and other documents prepared by the Architect. Submittal or distribution to meet official regulatory requirements or for other purposes in connection with this Project is not to be construed as publication in derogation of the Architect's copyright or other reserved rights.

1.4 CAPITALIZATION

1.4.1 Terms capitalized in these General Conditions include those which are (1) specifically defined, (2) the titles of numbered articles and identified references to Paragraphs, Subparagraphs and Clauses in the document or (3) the titles of other documents published by the American Institute of Architects.

1.5 INTERPRETATION

1.5.1 In the interest of brevity the Contract Documents frequently omit modifying words such as "all" and "any" and articles such as "the" and "an," but the fact that a modifier or an article is absent from one statement and appears in another is not intended to affect the interpretation of either statement.

ARTICLE 2

OWNER

2.1 DEFINITION

2.1.1 The Owner is the person or entity identified as such in the Agreement and is referred to throughout the Contract Documents as if singular in number. The term "Owner" means the Owner or the Owner's authorized representative.

2.1.2 The Owner upon reasonable written request shall furnish to the Contractor in writing information which is necessary and relevant for the Contractor to evaluate, give notice of or enforce mechanic's lien rights. Such information shall include a correct statement of the record legal title to the property on which the Project is located, usually referred to as the site, and the Owner's interest therein at the time of execution of the Agreement and, within five days after any change, information of such change in title, recorded or unrecorded.

2.2 INFORMATION AND SERVICES REQUIRED OF THE OWNER

2.2.1 The Owner shall, at the request of the Contractor, prior to execution of the Agreement and promptly from time to time thereafter, furnish to the Contractor reasonable evidence that financial arrangements have been made to fulfill the Owner's obligations under the Contract. *[Note: Unless such reasonable evidence were furnished on request prior to the execution of the Agreement, the prospective contractor would not be required to execute the Agreement or to commence the Work.]*

2.2.2 The Owner shall furnish surveys describing physical characteristics, legal limitations and utility locations for the site of the Project, and a legal description of the site.

2.2.3 Except for permits and fees which are the responsibility of the Contractor under the Contract Documents, the Owner shall secure and pay for necessary approvals, easements, assess-

ments and charges required for construction, use or occupancy of permanent structures or for permanent changes in existing facilities.

2.2.4 Information or services under the Owner's control shall be furnished by the Owner with reasonable promptness to avoid delay in orderly progress of the Work.

2.2.5 Unless otherwise provided in the Contract Documents, the Contractor will be furnished, free of charge, such copies of Drawings and Project Manuals as are reasonably necessary for execution of the Work.

2.2.6 The foregoing are in addition to other duties and responsibilities of the Owner enumerated herein and especially those in respect to Article 6 (Construction by Owner or by Separate Contractors), Article 9 (Payments and Completion) and Article 11 (Insurance and Bonds).

2.3 OWNER'S RIGHT TO STOP THE WORK

2.3.1 If the Contractor fails to correct Work which is not in accordance with the requirements of the Contract Documents as required by Paragraph 12.2 or persistently fails to carry out Work in accordance with the Contract Documents, the Owner, by written order signed personally or by an agent specifically so empowered by the Owner in writing, may order the Contractor to stop the Work, or any portion thereof, until the cause for such order has been eliminated; however, the right of the Owner to stop the Work shall not give rise to a duty on the part of the Owner to exercise this right for the benefit of the Contractor or any other person or entity, except to the extent required by Subparagraph 6.1.3.

2.4 OWNER'S RIGHT TO CARRY OUT THE WORK

2.4.1 If the Contractor defaults or neglects to carry out the Work in accordance with the Contract Documents and fails within a seven-day period after receipt of written notice from the Owner to commence and continue correction of such default or neglect with diligence and promptness, the Owner may after such seven-day period give the Contractor a second written notice to correct such deficiencies within a second seven-day period. If the Contractor within such second seven-day period after receipt of such second notice fails to commence and continue to correct any deficiencies, the Owner may, without prejudice to other remedies the Owner may have, correct such deficiencies. In such case an appropriate Change Order shall be issued deducting from payments then or thereafter due the Contractor the cost of correcting such deficiencies, including compensation for the Architect's additional services and expenses made necessary by such default, neglect or failure. Such action by the Owner and amounts charged to the Contractor are both subject to prior approval of the Architect. If payments then or thereafter due the Contractor are not sufficient to cover such amounts, the Contractor shall pay the difference to the Owner.

ARTICLE 3

CONTRACTOR

3.1 DEFINITION

3.1.1 The Contractor is the person or entity identified as such in the Agreement and is referred to throughout the Contract Documents as if singular in number. The term "Contractor" means the Contractor or the Contractor's authorized representative.

3.2 REVIEW OF CONTRACT DOCUMENTS AND FIELD CONDITIONS BY CONTRACTOR

3.2.1 The Contractor shall carefully study and compare the Contract Documents with each other and with information furnished by the Owner pursuant to Subparagraph 2.2.2 and shall at once report to the Architect errors, inconsistencies or omissions discovered. The Contractor shall not be liable to the Owner or Architect for damage resulting from errors, inconsistencies or omissions in the Contract Documents unless the Contractor recognized such error, inconsistency or omission and knowingly failed to report it to the Architect. If the Contractor performs any construction activity knowing it involves a recognized error, inconsistency or omission in the Contract Documents without such notice to the Architect, the Contractor shall assume appropriate responsibility for such performance and shall bear an appropriate amount of the attributable costs for correction.

3.2.2 The Contractor shall take field measurements and verify field conditions and shall carefully compare such field measurements and conditions and other information known to the Contractor with the Contract Documents before commencing activities. Errors, inconsistencies or omissions discovered shall be reported to the Architect at once.

3.2.3 The Contractor shall perform the Work in accordance with the Contract Documents and submittals approved pursuant to Paragraph 3.12.

3.3 SUPERVISION AND CONSTRUCTION PROCEDURES

3.3.1 The Contractor shall supervise and direct the Work, using the Contractor's best skill and attention. The Contractor shall be solely responsible for and have control over construction means, methods, techniques, sequences and procedures and for coordinating all portions of the Work under the Contract, unless Contract Documents give other specific instructions concerning these matters.

3.3.2 The Contractor shall be responsible to the Owner for acts and omissions of the Contractor's employees, Subcontractors and their agents and employees, and other persons performing portions of the Work under a contract with the Contractor.

3.3.3 The Contractor shall not be relieved of obligations to perform the Work in accordance with the Contract Documents either by activities or duties of the Architect in the Architect's administration of the Contract, or by tests, inspections or approvals required or performed by persons other than the Contractor.

3.3.4 The Contractor shall be responsible for inspection of portions of Work already performed under this Contract to determine that such portions are in proper condition to receive subsequent Work.

3.4 LABOR AND MATERIALS

3.4.1 Unless otherwise provided in the Contract Documents, the Contractor shall provide and pay for labor, materials, equipment, tools, construction equipment and machinery, water, heat, utilities, transportation, and other facilities and services necessary for proper execution and completion of the Work, whether temporary or permanent and whether or not incorporated or to be incorporated in the Work.

3.4.2 The Contractor shall enforce strict discipline and good order among the Contractor's employees and other persons carrying out the Contract. The Contractor shall not permit employment of unfit persons or persons not skilled in tasks assigned to them.

3.5 WARRANTY

3.5.1 The Contractor warrants to the Owner and Architect that materials and equipment furnished under the Contract will be of good quality and new unless otherwise required or permitted by the Contract Documents, that the Work will be free from defects not inherent in the quality required or permitted, and that the Work will conform with the requirements of the Contract Documents. Work not conforming to these requirements, including substitutions not properly approved and authorized, may be considered defective. The Contractor's warranty excludes remedy for damage or defect caused by abuse, modifications not executed by the Contractor, improper or insufficient maintenance, improper operation, or normal wear and tear under normal usage. If required by the Architect, the Contractor shall furnish satisfactory evidence as to the kind and quality of materials and equipment.

3.6 TAXES

3.6.1 The Contractor shall pay sales, consumer, use and similar taxes for the Work or portions thereof provided by the Contractor which are legally enacted when bids are received or negotiations concluded, whether or not yet effective or merely scheduled to go into effect.

3.7 PERMITS, FEES AND NOTICES

3.7.1 Unless otherwise provided in the Contract Documents, the Contractor shall secure and pay for the building permit and other permits and governmental fees, licenses and inspections necessary for proper execution and completion of the Work which are customarily secured after execution of the Contract and which are legally required when bids are received or negotiations concluded.

3.7.2 The Contractor shall comply with and give notices required by laws, ordinances, rules, regulations and lawful orders of public authorities bearing on performance of the Work.

3.7.3 It is not the Contractor's responsibility to ascertain that the Contract Documents are in accordance with applicable laws, statutes, ordinances, building codes, and rules and regulations. However, if the Contractor observes that portions of the Contract Documents are at variance therewith, the Contractor shall promptly notify the Architect and Owner in writing, and necessary changes shall be accomplished by appropriate Modification.

3.7.4 If the Contractor performs Work knowing it to be contrary to laws, statutes, ordinances, building codes, and rules and regulations without such notice to the Architect and Owner, the Contractor shall assume full responsibility for such Work and shall bear the attributable costs.

3.8 ALLOWANCES

3.8.1 The Contractor shall include in the Contract Sum all allowances stated in the Contract Documents. Items covered by allowances shall be supplied for such amounts and by such persons or entities as the Owner may direct, but the Contractor shall not be required to employ persons or entities against which the Contractor makes reasonable objection.

3.8.2 Unless otherwise provided in the Contract Documents:

.1 materials and equipment under an allowance shall be selected promptly by the Owner to avoid delay in the Work;

.2 allowances shall cover the cost to the Contractor of materials and equipment delivered at the site and all required taxes, less applicable trade discounts;

.3 Contractor's costs for unloading and handling at the site, labor, installation costs, overhead, profit and other expenses contemplated for stated allowance amounts shall be included in the Contract Sum and not in the allowances;

.4 whenever costs are more than or less than allowances, the Contract Sum shall be adjusted accordingly by Change Order. The amount of the Change Order shall reflect (1) the difference between actual costs and the allowances under Clause 3.8.2.2 and (2) changes in Contractor's costs under Clause 3.8.2.3.

3.9 SUPERINTENDENT

3.9.1 The Contractor shall employ a competent superintendent and necessary assistants who shall be in attendance at the Project site during performance of the Work. The superintendent shall represent the Contractor, and communications given to the superintendent shall be as binding as if given to the Contractor. Important communications shall be confirmed in writing. Other communications shall be similarly confirmed on written request in each case.

3.10 CONTRACTOR'S CONSTRUCTION SCHEDULES

3.10.1 The Contractor, promptly after being awarded the Contract, shall prepare and submit for the Owner's and Architect's information a Contractor's construction schedule for the Work. The schedule shall not exceed time limits current under the Contract Documents, shall be revised at appropriate intervals as required by the conditions of the Work and Project, shall be related to the entire Project to the extent required by the Contract Documents, and shall provide for expeditious and practicable execution of the Work.

3.10.2 The Contractor shall prepare and keep current, for the Architect's approval, a schedule of submittals which is coordinated with the Contractor's construction schedule and allows the Architect reasonable time to review submittals.

3.10.3 The Contractor shall conform to the most recent schedules.

3.11 DOCUMENTS AND SAMPLES AT THE SITE

3.11.1 The Contractor shall maintain at the site for the Owner one record copy of the Drawings, Specifications, addenda, Change Orders and other Modifications, in good order and marked currently to record changes and selections made during construction, and in addition approved Shop Drawings, Product Data, Samples and similar required submittals. These shall be available to the Architect and shall be delivered to the Architect for submittal to the Owner upon completion of the Work.

3.12 SHOP DRAWINGS, PRODUCT DATA AND SAMPLES

3.12.1 Shop Drawings are drawings, diagrams, schedules and other data specially prepared for the Work by the Contractor or a Subcontractor, Sub-subcontractor, manufacturer, supplier or distributor to illustrate some portion of the Work.

3.12.2 Product Data are illustrations, standard schedules, performance charts, instructions, brochures, diagrams and other information furnished by the Contractor to illustrate materials or equipment for some portion of the Work.

3.12.3 Samples are physical examples which illustrate materials, equipment or workmanship and establish standards by which the Work will be judged.

3.12.4 Shop Drawings, Product Data, Samples and similar submittals are not Contract Documents. The purpose of their submittal is to demonstrate for those portions of the Work for which submittals are required the way the Contractor proposes to conform to the information given and the design concept expressed in the Contract Documents. Review by the Architect is subject to the limitations of Subparagraph 4.2.7.

3.12.5 The Contractor shall review, approve and submit to the Architect Shop Drawings, Product Data, Samples and similar submittals required by the Contract Documents with reasonable promptness and in such sequence as to cause no delay in the Work or in the activities of the Owner or of separate contractors. Submittals made by the Contractor which are not required by the Contract Documents may be returned without action.

3.12.6 The Contractor shall perform no portion of the Work requiring submittal and review of Shop Drawings, Product Data, Samples or similar submittals until the respective submittal has been approved by the Architect. Such Work shall be in accordance with approved submittals.

3.12.7 By approving and submitting Shop Drawings, Product Data, Samples and similar submittals, the Contractor represents that the Contractor has determined and verified materials, field measurements and field construction criteria related thereto, or will do so, and has checked and coordinated the information contained within such submittals with the requirements of the Work and of the Contract Documents.

3.12.8 The Contractor shall not be relieved of responsibility for deviations from requirements of the Contract Documents by the Architect's approval of Shop Drawings, Product Data, Samples or similar submittals unless the Contractor has specifically informed the Architect in writing of such deviation at the time of submittal and the Architect has given written approval to the specific deviation. The Contractor shall not be relieved of responsibility for errors or omissions in Shop Drawings, Product Data, Samples or similar submittals by the Architect's approval thereof.

3.12.9 The Contractor shall direct specific attention, in writing or on resubmitted Shop Drawings, Product Data, Samples or similar submittals, to revisions other than those requested by the Architect on previous submittals.

3.12.10 Informational submittals upon which the Architect is not expected to take responsive action may be so identified in the Contract Documents.

3.12.11 When professional certification of performance criteria of materials, systems or equipment is required by the Contract Documents, the Architect shall be entitled to rely upon the accuracy and completeness of such calculations and certifications.

3.13 USE OF SITE

3.13.1 The Contractor shall confine operations at the site to areas permitted by law, ordinances, permits and the Contract Documents and shall not unreasonably encumber the site with materials or equipment.

3.14 CUTTING AND PATCHING

3.14.1 The Contractor shall be responsible for cutting, fitting or patching required to complete the Work or to make its parts fit together properly.

3.14.2 The Contractor shall not damage or endanger a portion of the Work or fully or partially completed construction of the Owner or separate contractors by cutting, patching or otherwise altering such construction, or by excavation. The Contractor shall not cut or otherwise alter such construction by the

Owner or a separate contractor except with written consent of the Owner and of such separate contractor; such consent shall not be unreasonably withheld. The Contractor shall not unreasonably withhold from the Owner or a separate contractor the Contractor's consent to cutting or otherwise altering the Work.

3.15 CLEANING UP

3.15.1 The Contractor shall keep the premises and surrounding area free from accumulation of waste materials or rubbish caused by operations under the Contract. At completion of the Work the Contractor shall remove from and about the Project waste materials, rubbish, the Contractor's tools, construction equipment, machinery and surplus materials.

3.15.2 If the Contractor fails to clean up as provided in the Contract Documents, the Owner may do so and the cost thereof shall be charged to the Contractor.

3.16 ACCESS TO WORK

3.16.1 The Contractor shall provide the Owner and Architect access to the Work in preparation and progress wherever located.

3.17 ROYALTIES AND PATENTS

3.17.1 The Contractor shall pay all royalties and license fees. The Contractor shall defend suits or claims for infringement of patent rights and shall hold the Owner and Architect harmless from loss on account thereof, but shall not be responsible for such defense or loss when a particular design, process or product of a particular manufacturer or manufacturers is required by the Contract Documents. However, if the Contractor has reason to believe that the required design, process or product is an infringement of a patent, the Contractor shall be responsible for such loss unless such information is promptly furnished to the Architect.

3.18 INDEMNIFICATION

3.18.1 To the fullest extent permitted by law, the Contractor shall indemnify and hold harmless the Owner, Architect, Architect's consultants, and agents and employees of any of them from and against claims, damages, losses and expenses, including but not limited to attorneys' fees, arising out of or resulting from performance of the Work, provided that such claim, damage, loss or expense is attributable to bodily injury, sickness, disease or death, or to injury to or destruction of tangible property (other than the Work itself) including loss of use resulting therefrom, but only to the extent caused in whole or in part by negligent acts or omissions of the Contractor, a Subcontractor, anyone directly or indirectly employed by them or anyone for whose acts they may be liable, regardless of whether or not such claim, damage, loss or expense is caused in part by a party indemnified hereunder. Such obligation shall not be construed to negate, abridge, or reduce other rights or obligations of indemnity which would otherwise exist as to a party or person described in this Paragraph 3.18.

3.18.2 In claims against any person or entity indemnified under this Paragraph 3.18 by an employee of the Contractor, a Subcontractor, anyone directly or indirectly employed by them or anyone for whose acts they may be liable, the indemnification obligation under this Paragraph 3.18 shall not be limited by a limitation on amount or type of damages, compensation or benefits payable by or for the Contractor or a Subcontractor under workers' or workmen's compensation acts, disability benefit acts or other employee benefit acts.

3.18.3 The obligations of the Contractor under this Paragraph 3.18 shall not extend to the liability of the Architect, the Architect's consultants, and agents and employees of any of them arising out of (1) the preparation or approval of maps, drawings, opinions, reports, surveys, Change Orders, designs or specifications, or (2) the giving of or the failure to give directions or instructions by the Architect, the Architect's consultants, and agents and employees of any of them provided such giving or failure to give is the primary cause of the injury or damage.

ARTICLE 4

ADMINISTRATION OF THE CONTRACT

4.1 ARCHITECT

4.1.1 The Architect is the person lawfully licensed to practice architecture or an entity lawfully practicing architecture identified as such in the Agreement and is referred to throughout the Contract Documents as if singular in number. The term "Architect" means the Architect or the Architect's authorized representative.

4.1.2 Duties, responsibilities and limitations of authority of the Architect as set forth in the Contract Documents shall not be restricted, modified or extended without written consent of the Owner, Contractor and Architect. Consent shall not be unreasonably withheld.

4.1.3 In case of termination of employment of the Architect, the Owner shall appoint an architect against whom the Contractor makes no reasonable objection and whose status under the Contract Documents shall be that of the former architect.

4.1.4 Disputes arising under Subparagraphs 4.1.2 and 4.1.3 shall be subject to arbitration.

4.2 ARCHITECT'S ADMINISTRATION OF THE CONTRACT

4.2.1 The Architect will provide administration of the Contract as described in the Contract Documents, and will be the Owner's representative (1) during construction, (2) until final payment is due and (3) with the Owner's concurrence, from time to time during the correction period described in Paragraph 12.2. The Architect will advise and consult with the Owner. The Architect will have authority to act on behalf of the Owner only to the extent provided in the Contract Documents, unless otherwise modified by written instrument in accordance with other provisions of the Contract.

4.2.2 The Architect will visit the site at intervals appropriate to the stage of construction to become generally familiar with the progress and quality of the completed Work and to determine in general if the Work is being performed in a manner indicating that the Work, when completed, will be in accordance with the Contract Documents. However, the Architect will not be required to make exhaustive or continuous on-site inspections to check quality or quantity of the Work. On the basis of on-site observations as an architect, the Architect will keep the Owner informed of progress of the Work, and will endeavor to guard the Owner against defects and deficiencies in the Work.

4.2.3 The Architect will not have control over or charge of and will not be responsible for construction means, methods, techniques, sequences or procedures, or for safety precautions and programs in connection with the Work, since these are solely the Contractor's responsibility as provided in Paragraph 3.3. The Architect will not be responsible for the Contractor's failure to carry out the Work in accordance with the Contract Documents. The Architect will not have control over or charge of and will not be responsible for acts or omissions of the Con-

AIA DOCUMENT A201 • GENERAL CONDITIONS OF THE CONTRACT FOR CONSTRUCTION • FOURTEENTH EDITION
AIA® • ©1987 THE AMERICAN INSTITUTE OF ARCHITECTS, 1735 NEW YORK AVENUE, N.W., WASHINGTON, D.C. 20006

tractor, Subcontractors, or their agents or employees, or of any other persons performing portions of the Work.

4.2.4 Communications Facilitating Contract Administration. Except as otherwise provided in the Contract Documents or when direct communications have been specially authorized, the Owner and Contractor shall endeavor to communicate through the Architect. Communications by and with the Architect's consultants shall be through the Architect. Communications by and with Subcontractors and material suppliers shall be through the Contractor. Communications by and with separate contractors shall be through the Owner.

4.2.5 Based on the Architect's observations and evaluations of the Contractor's Applications for Payment, the Architect will review and certify the amounts due the Contractor and will issue Certificates for Payment in such amounts.

4.2.6 The Architect will have authority to reject Work which does not conform to the Contract Documents. Whenever the Architect considers it necessary or advisable for implementation of the intent of the Contract Documents, the Architect will have authority to require additional inspection or testing of the Work in accordance with Subparagraphs 13.5.2 and 13.5.3, whether or not such Work is fabricated, installed or completed. However, neither this authority of the Architect nor a decision made in good faith either to exercise or not to exercise such authority shall give rise to a duty or responsibility of the Architect to the Contractor, Subcontractors, material and equipment suppliers, their agents or employees, or other persons performing portions of the Work.

4.2.7 The Architect will review and approve or take other appropriate action upon the Contractor's submittals such as Shop Drawings, Product Data and Samples, but only for the limited purpose of checking for conformance with information given and the design concept expressed in the Contract Documents. The Architect's action will be taken with such reasonable promptness as to cause no delay in the Work or in the activities of the Owner, Contractor or separate contractors, while allowing sufficient time in the Architect's professional judgment to permit adequate review. Review of such submittals is not conducted for the purpose of determining the accuracy and completeness of other details such as dimensions and quantities, or for substantiating instructions for installation or performance of equipment or systems, all of which remain the responsibility of the Contractor as required by the Contract Documents. The Architect's review of the Contractor's submittals shall not relieve the Contractor of the obligations under Paragraphs 3.3, 3.5 and 3.12. The Architect's review shall not constitute approval of safety precautions or, unless otherwise specifically stated by the Architect, of any construction means, methods, techniques, sequences or procedures. The Architect's approval of a specific item shall not indicate approval of an assembly of which the item is a component.

4.2.8 The Architect will prepare Change Orders and Construction Change Directives, and may authorize minor changes in the Work as provided in Paragraph 7.4.

4.2.9 The Architect will conduct inspections to determine the date or dates of Substantial Completion and the date of final completion, will receive and forward to the Owner for the Owner's review and records written warranties and related documents required by the Contract and assembled by the Contractor, and will issue a final Certificate for Payment upon compliance with the requirements of the Contract Documents.

4.2.10 If the Owner and Architect agree, the Architect will provide one or more project representatives to assist in carrying out the Architect's responsibilities at the site. The duties, responsibilities and limitations of authority of such project representatives shall be as set forth in an exhibit to be incorporated in the Contract Documents.

4.2.11 The Architect will interpret and decide matters concerning performance under and requirements of the Contract Documents on written request of either the Owner or Contractor. The Architect's response to such requests will be made with reasonable promptness and within any time limits agreed upon. If no agreement is made concerning the time within which interpretations required of the Architect shall be furnished in compliance with this Paragraph 4.2, then delay shall not be recognized on account of failure by the Architect to furnish such interpretations until 15 days after written request is made for them.

4.2.12 Interpretations and decisions of the Architect will be consistent with the intent of and reasonably inferable from the Contract Documents and will be in writing or in the form of drawings. When making such interpretations and decisions, the Architect will endeavor to secure faithful performance by both Owner and Contractor, will not show partiality to either and will not be liable for results of interpretations or decisions so rendered in good faith.

4.2.13 The Architect's decisions on matters relating to aesthetic effect will be final if consistent with the intent expressed in the Contract Documents.

4.3   CLAIMS AND DISPUTES

4.3.1 Definition. A Claim is a demand or assertion by one of the parties seeking, as a matter of right, adjustment or interpretation of Contract terms, payment of money, extension of time or other relief with respect to the terms of the Contract. The term "Claim" also includes other disputes and matters in question between the Owner and Contractor arising out of or relating to the Contract. Claims must be made by written notice. The responsibility to substantiate Claims shall rest with the party making the Claim.

4.3.2 Decision of Architect. Claims, including those alleging an error or omission by the Architect, shall be referred initially to the Architect for action as provided in Paragraph 4.4. A decision by the Architect, as provided in Subparagraph 4.4.4, shall be required as a condition precedent to arbitration or litigation of a Claim between the Contractor and Owner as to all such matters arising prior to the date final payment is due, regardless of (1) whether such matters relate to execution and progress of the Work or (2) the extent to which the Work has been completed. The decision by the Architect in response to a Claim shall not be a condition precedent to arbitration or litigation in the event (1) the position of Architect is vacant, (2) the Architect has not received evidence or has failed to render a decision within agreed time limits, (3) the Architect has failed to take action required under Subparagraph 4.4.4 within 30 days after the Claim is made, (4) 45 days have passed after the Claim has been referred to the Architect or (5) the Claim relates to a mechanic's lien.

4.3.3 Time Limits on Claims. Claims by either party must be made within 21 days after occurrence of the event giving rise to such Claim or within 21 days after the claimant first recognizes the condition giving rise to the Claim, whichever is later. Claims must be made by written notice. An additional Claim made after the initial Claim has been implemented by Change Order will not be considered unless submitted in a timely manner.

4.3.4 Continuing Contract Performance. Pending final resolution of a Claim including arbitration, unless otherwise agreed in writing the Contractor shall proceed diligently with performance of the Contract and the Owner shall continue to make payments in accordance with the Contract Documents.

4.3.5 Waiver of Claims: Final Payment. The making of final payment shall constitute a waiver of Claims by the Owner except those arising from:

    .1 liens, Claims, security interests or encumbrances arising out of the Contract and unsettled;

    .2 failure of the Work to comply with the requirements of the Contract Documents; or

    .3 terms of special warranties required by the Contract Documents.

4.3.6 Claims for Concealed or Unknown Conditions. If conditions are encountered at the site which are (1) subsurface or otherwise concealed physical conditions which differ materially from those indicated in the Contract Documents or (2) unknown physical conditions of an unusual nature, which differ materially from those ordinarily found to exist and generally recognized as inherent in construction activities of the character provided for in the Contract Documents, then notice by the observing party shall be given to the other party promptly before conditions are disturbed and in no event later than 21 days after first observance of the conditions. The Architect will promptly investigate such conditions and, if they differ materially and cause an increase or decrease in the Contractor's cost of, or time required for, performance of any part of the Work, will recommend an equitable adjustment in the Contract Sum or Contract Time, or both. If the Architect determines that the conditions at the site are not materially different from those indicated in the Contract Documents and that no change in the terms of the Contract is justified, the Architect shall so notify the Owner and Contractor in writing, stating the reasons. Claims by either party in opposition to such determination must be made within 21 days after the Architect has given notice of the decision. If the Owner and Contractor cannot agree on an adjustment in the Contract Sum or Contract Time, the adjustment shall be referred to the Architect for initial determination, subject to further proceedings pursuant to Paragraph 4.4.

4.3.7 Claims for Additional Cost. If the Contractor wishes to make Claim for an increase in the Contract Sum, written notice as provided herein shall be given before proceeding to execute the Work. Prior notice is not required for Claims relating to an emergency endangering life or property arising under Paragraph 10.3. If the Contractor believes additional cost is involved for reasons including but not limited to (1) a written interpretation from the Architect, (2) an order by the Owner to stop the Work where the Contractor was not at fault, (3) a written order for a minor change in the Work issued by the Architect, (4) failure of payment by the Owner, (5) termination of the Contract by the Owner, (6) Owner's suspension or (7) other reasonable grounds, Claim shall be filed in accordance with the procedure established herein.

4.3.8 Claims for Additional Time

4.3.8.1 If the Contractor wishes to make Claim for an increase in the Contract Time, written notice as provided herein shall be given. The Contractor's Claim shall include an estimate of cost and of probable effect of delay on progress of the Work. In the case of a continuing delay only one Claim is necessary.

4.3.8.2 If adverse weather conditions are the basis for a Claim for additional time, such Claim shall be documented by data substantiating that weather conditions were abnormal for the period of time and could not have been reasonably anticipated, and that weather conditions had an adverse effect on the scheduled construction.

4.3.9 Injury or Damage to Person or Property. If either party to the Contract suffers injury or damage to person or property because of an act or omission of the other party, of any of the other party's employees or agents, or of others for whose acts such party is legally liable, written notice of such injury or damage, whether or not insured, shall be given to the other party within a reasonable time not exceeding 21 days after first observance. The notice shall provide sufficient detail to enable the other party to investigate the matter. If a Claim for additional cost or time related to this Claim is to be asserted, it shall be filed as provided in Subparagraphs 4.3.7 or 4.3.8.

4.4   RESOLUTION OF CLAIMS AND DISPUTES

4.4.1 The Architect will review Claims and take one or more of the following preliminary actions within ten days of receipt of a Claim: (1) request additional supporting data from the claimant, (2) submit a schedule to the parties indicating when the Architect expects to take action, (3) reject the Claim in whole or in part, stating reasons for rejection, (4) recommend approval of the Claim by the other party or (5) suggest a compromise. The Architect may also, but is not obligated to, notify the surety, if any, of the nature and amount of the Claim.

4.4.2 If a Claim has been resolved, the Architect will prepare or obtain appropriate documentation.

4.4.3 If a Claim has not been resolved, the party making the Claim shall, within ten days after the Architect's preliminary response, take one or more of the following actions: (1) submit additional supporting data requested by the Architect, (2) modify the initial Claim or (3) notify the Architect that the initial Claim stands.

4.4.4 If a Claim has not been resolved after consideration of the foregoing and of further evidence presented by the parties or requested by the Architect, the Architect will notify the parties in writing that the Architect's decision will be made within seven days, which decision shall be final and binding on the parties but subject to arbitration. Upon expiration of such time period, the Architect will render to the parties the Architect's written decision relative to the Claim, including any change in the Contract Sum or Contract Time or both. If there is a surety and there appears to be a possibility of a Contractor's default, the Architect may, but is not obligated to, notify the surety and request the surety's assistance in resolving the controversy.

4.5   ARBITRATION

4.5.1 Controversies and Claims Subject to Arbitration. Any controversy or Claim arising out of or related to the Contract, or the breach thereof, shall be settled by arbitration in accordance with the Construction Industry Arbitration Rules of the American Arbitration Association, and judgment upon the award rendered by the arbitrator or arbitrators may be entered in any court having jurisdiction thereof, except controversies or Claims relating to aesthetic effect and except those waived as provided for in Subparagraph 4.3.5. Such controversies or Claims upon which the Architect has given notice and rendered a decision as provided in Subparagraph 4.4.4 shall be subject to arbitration upon written demand of either party. Arbitration may be commenced when 45 days have passed after a Claim has been referred to the Architect as provided in Paragraph 4.3 and no decision has been rendered.

AIA DOCUMENT A201 • GENERAL CONDITIONS OF THE CONTRACT FOR CONSTRUCTION • FOURTEENTH EDITION
AIA® • ©1987 THE AMERICAN INSTITUTE OF ARCHITECTS, 1735 NEW YORK AVENUE, N.W., WASHINGTON, D.C. 20006

4.5.2 Rules and Notices for Arbitration. Claims between the Owner and Contractor not resolved under Paragraph 4.4 shall, if subject to arbitration under Subparagraph 4.5.1, be decided by arbitration in accordance with the Construction Industry Arbitration Rules of the American Arbitration Association currently in effect, unless the parties mutually agree otherwise. Notice of demand for arbitration shall be filed in writing with the other party to the Agreement between the Owner and Contractor and with the American Arbitration Association, and a copy shall be filed with the Architect.

4.5.3 Contract Performance During Arbitration. During arbitration proceedings, the Owner and Contractor shall comply with Subparagraph 4.3.4.

4.5.4 When Arbitration May Be Demanded. Demand for arbitration of any Claim may not be made until the earlier of (1) the date on which the Architect has rendered a final written decision on the Claim, (2) the tenth day after the parties have presented evidence to the Architect or have been given reasonable opportunity to do so, if the Architect has not rendered a final written decision by that date, or (3) any of the five events described in Subparagraph 4.3.2.

4.5.4.1 When a written decision of the Architect states that (1) the decision is final but subject to arbitration and (2) a demand for arbitration of a Claim covered by such decision must be made within 30 days after the date on which the party making the demand receives the final written decision, then failure to demand arbitration within said 30 days' period shall result in the Architect's decision becoming final and binding upon the Owner and Contractor. If the Architect renders a decision after arbitration proceedings have been initiated, such decision may be entered as evidence, but shall not supersede arbitration proceedings unless the decision is acceptable to all parties concerned.

4.5.4.2 A demand for arbitration shall be made within the time limits specified in Subparagraphs 4.5.1 and 4.5.4 and Clause 4.5.4.1 as applicable, and in other cases within a reasonable time after the Claim has arisen, and in no event shall it be made after the date when institution of legal or equitable proceedings based on such Claim would be barred by the applicable statute of limitations as determined pursuant to Paragraph 13.7.

4.5.5 Limitation on Consolidation or Joinder. No arbitration arising out of or relating to the Contract Documents shall include, by consolidation or joinder or in any other manner, the Architect, the Architect's employees or consultants, except by written consent containing specific reference to the Agreement and signed by the Architect, Owner, Contractor and any other person or entity sought to be joined. No arbitration shall include, by consolidation or joinder or in any other manner, parties other than the Owner, Contractor, a separate contractor as described in Article 6 and other persons substantially involved in a common question of fact or law whose presence is required if complete relief is to be accorded in arbitration. No person or entity other than the Owner, Contractor or a separate contractor as described in Article 6 shall be included as an original third party or additional third party to an arbitration whose interest or responsibility is insubstantial. Consent to arbitration involving an additional person or entity shall not constitute consent to arbitration of a dispute not described therein or with a person or entity not named or described therein. The foregoing agreement to arbitrate and other agreements to arbitrate with an additional person or entity duly consented to by parties to the Agreement shall be specifically enforceable under applicable law in any court having jurisdiction thereof.

4.5.6 Claims and Timely Assertion of Claims. A party who files a notice of demand for arbitration must assert in the demand all Claims then known to that party on which arbitration is permitted to be demanded. When a party fails to include a Claim through oversight, inadvertence or excusable neglect, or when a Claim has matured or been acquired subsequently, the arbitrator or arbitrators may permit amendment.

4.5.7 Judgment on Final Award. The award rendered by the arbitrator or arbitrators shall be final, and judgment may be entered upon it in accordance with applicable law in any court having jurisdiction thereof.

ARTICLE 5

SUBCONTRACTORS

5.1   DEFINITIONS

5.1.1 A Subcontractor is a person or entity who has a direct contract with the Contractor to perform a portion of the Work at the site. The term "Subcontractor" is referred to throughout the Contract Documents as if singular in number and means a Subcontractor or an authorized representative of the Subcontractor. The term "Subcontractor" does not include a separate contractor or subcontractors of a separate contractor.

5.1.2 A Sub-subcontractor is a person or entity who has a direct or indirect contract with a Subcontractor to perform a portion of the Work at the site. The term "Sub-subcontractor" is referred to throughout the Contract Documents as if singular in number and means a Sub-subcontractor or an authorized representative of the Sub-subcontractor.

5.2   AWARD OF SUBCONTRACTS AND OTHER CONTRACTS FOR PORTIONS OF THE WORK

5.2.1 Unless otherwise stated in the Contract Documents or the bidding requirements, the Contractor, as soon as practicable after award of the Contract, shall furnish in writing to the Owner through the Architect the names of persons or entities (including those who are to furnish materials or equipment fabricated to a special design) proposed for each principal portion of the Work. The Architect will promptly reply to the Contractor in writing stating whether or not the Owner or the Architect, after due investigation, has reasonable objection to any such proposed person or entity. Failure of the Owner or Architect to reply promptly shall constitute notice of no reasonable objection.

5.2.2 The Contractor shall not contract with a proposed person or entity to whom the Owner or Architect has made reasonable and timely objection. The Contractor shall not be required to contract with anyone to whom the Contractor has made reasonable objection.

5.2.3 If the Owner or Architect has reasonable objection to a person or entity proposed by the Contractor, the Contractor shall propose another to whom the Owner or Architect has no reasonable objection. The Contract Sum shall be increased or decreased by the difference in cost occasioned by such change and an appropriate Change Order shall be issued. However, no increase in the Contract Sum shall be allowed for such change unless the Contractor has acted promptly and responsively in submitting names as required.

5.2.4 The Contractor shall not change a Subcontractor, person or entity previously selected if the Owner or Architect makes reasonable objection to such change.

5.3 SUBCONTRACTUAL RELATIONS

5.3.1 By appropriate agreement, written where legally required for validity, the Contractor shall require each Subcontractor, to the extent of the Work to be performed by the Subcontractor, to be bound to the Contractor by terms of the Contract Documents, and to assume toward the Contractor all the obligations and responsibilities which the Contractor, by these Documents, assumes toward the Owner and Architect. Each subcontract agreement shall preserve and protect the rights of the Owner and Architect under the Contract Documents with respect to the Work to be performed by the Subcontractor so that subcontracting thereof will not prejudice such rights, and shall allow to the Subcontractor, unless specifically provided otherwise in the subcontract agreement, the benefit of all rights, remedies and redress against the Contractor that the Contractor, by the Contract Documents, has against the Owner. Where appropriate, the Contractor shall require each Subcontractor to enter into similar agreements with Sub-sub-contractors. The Contractor shall make available to each proposed Subcontractor, prior to the execution of the subcontract agreement, copies of the Contract Documents to which the Subcontractor will be bound, and, upon written request of the Subcontractor, identify to the Subcontractor terms and conditions of the proposed subcontract agreement which may be at variance with the Contract Documents. Subcontractors shall similarly make copies of applicable portions of such documents available to their respective proposed Sub-subcontractors.

5.4 CONTINGENT ASSIGNMENT OF SUBCONTRACTS

5.4.1 Each subcontract agreement for a portion of the Work is assigned by the Contractor to the Owner provided that:

  .1 assignment is effective only after termination of the Contract by the Owner for cause pursuant to Paragraph 14.2 and only for those subcontract agreements which the Owner accepts by notifying the Subcontractor in writing; and

  .2 assignment is subject to the prior rights of the surety, if any, obligated under bond relating to the Contract.

5.4.2 If the Work has been suspended for more than 30 days, the Subcontractor's compensation shall be equitably adjusted.

ARTICLE 6

CONSTRUCTION BY OWNER OR BY SEPARATE CONTRACTORS

6.1 OWNER'S RIGHT TO PERFORM CONSTRUCTION AND TO AWARD SEPARATE CONTRACTS

6.1.1 The Owner reserves the right to perform construction or operations related to the Project with the Owner's own forces, and to award separate contracts in connection with other portions of the Project or other construction or operations on the site under Conditions of the Contract identical or substantially similar to these including those portions related to insurance and waiver of subrogation. If the Contractor claims that delay or additional cost is involved because of such action by the Owner, the Contractor shall make such Claim as provided elsewhere in the Contract Documents.

6.1.2 When separate contracts are awarded for different portions of the Project or other construction or operations on the site, the term "Contractor" in the Contract Documents in each case shall mean the Contractor who executes each separate Owner-Contractor Agreement.

6.1.3 The Owner shall provide for coordination of the activities of the Owner's own forces and of each separate contractor with the Work of the Contractor, who shall cooperate with them. The Contractor shall participate with other separate contractors and the Owner in reviewing their construction schedules when directed to do so. The Contractor shall make any revisions to the construction schedule and Contract Sum deemed necessary after a joint review and mutual agreement. The construction schedules shall then constitute the schedules to be used by the Contractor, separate contractors and the Owner until subsequently revised.

6.1.4 Unless otherwise provided in the Contract Documents, when the Owner performs construction or operations related to the Project with the Owner's own forces, the Owner shall be deemed to be subject to the same obligations and to have the same rights which apply to the Contractor under the Conditions of the Contract, including, without excluding others, those stated in Article 3, this Article 6 and Articles 10, 11 and 12.

6.2 MUTUAL RESPONSIBILITY

6.2.1 The Contractor shall afford the Owner and separate contractors reasonable opportunity for introduction and storage of their materials and equipment and performance of their activities and shall connect and coordinate the Contractor's construction and operations with theirs as required by the Contract Documents.

6.2.2 If part of the Contractor's Work depends for proper execution or results upon construction or operations by the Owner or a separate contractor, the Contractor shall, prior to proceeding with that portion of the Work, promptly report to the Architect apparent discrepancies or defects in such other construction that would render it unsuitable for such proper execution and results. Failure of the Contractor so to report shall constitute an acknowledgment that the Owner's or separate contractors' completed or partially completed construction is fit and proper to receive the Contractor's Work, except as to defects not then reasonably discoverable.

6.2.3 Costs caused by delays or by improperly timed activities or defective construction shall be borne by the party responsible therefor.

6.2.4 The Contractor shall promptly remedy damage wrongfully caused by the Contractor to completed or partially completed construction or to property of the Owner or separate contractors as provided in Subparagraph 10.2.5.

6.2.5 Claims and other disputes and matters in question between the Contractor and a separate contractor shall be subject to the provisions of Paragraph 4.3 provided the separate contractor has reciprocal obligations.

6.2.6 The Owner and each separate contractor shall have the same responsibilities for cutting and patching as are described for the Contractor in Paragraph 3.14.

6.3 OWNER'S RIGHT TO CLEAN UP

6.3.1 If a dispute arises among the Contractor, separate contractors and the Owner as to the responsibility under their respective contracts for maintaining the premises and surrounding area free from waste materials and rubbish as described in Paragraph 3.15, the Owner may clean up and allocate the cost among those responsible as the Architect determines to be just.

AIA DOCUMENT A201 • GENERAL CONDITIONS OF THE CONTRACT FOR CONSTRUCTION • FOURTEENTH EDITION
AIA® • ©1987 THE AMERICAN INSTITUTE OF ARCHITECTS, 1735 NEW YORK AVENUE, N.W., WASHINGTON, D.C. 20006

ARTICLE 7

CHANGES IN THE WORK

7.1 CHANGES

7.1.1 Changes in the Work may be accomplished after execution of the Contract, and without invalidating the Contract, by Change Order, Construction Change Directive or order for a minor change in the Work, subject to the limitations stated in this Article 7 and elsewhere in the Contract Documents.

7.1.2 A Change Order shall be based upon agreement among the Owner, Contractor and Architect; a Construction Change Directive requires agreement by the Owner and Architect and may or may not be agreed to by the Contractor; an order for a minor change in the Work may be issued by the Architect alone.

7.1.3 Changes in the Work shall be performed under applicable provisions of the Contract Documents, and the Contractor shall proceed promptly, unless otherwise provided in the Change Order, Construction Change Directive or order for a minor change in the Work.

7.1.4 If unit prices are stated in the Contract Documents or subsequently agreed upon, and if quantities originally contemplated are so changed in a proposed Change Order or Construction Change Directive that application of such unit prices to quantities of Work proposed will cause substantial inequity to the Owner or Contractor, the applicable unit prices shall be equitably adjusted.

7.2 CHANGE ORDERS

7.2.1 A Change Order is a written instrument prepared by the Architect and signed by the Owner, Contractor and Architect, stating their agreement upon all of the following:

.1 a change in the Work;

.2 the amount of the adjustment in the Contract Sum, if any; and

.3 the extent of the adjustment in the Contract Time, if any.

7.2.2 Methods used in determining adjustments to the Contract Sum may include those listed in Subparagraph 7.3.3.

7.3 CONSTRUCTION CHANGE DIRECTIVES

7.3.1 A Construction Change Directive is a written order prepared by the Architect and signed by the Owner and Architect, directing a change in the Work and stating a proposed basis for adjustment, if any, in the Contract Sum or Contract Time, or both. The Owner may by Construction Change Directive, without invalidating the Contract, order changes in the Work within the general scope of the Contract consisting of additions, deletions or other revisions, the Contract Sum and Contract Time being adjusted accordingly.

7.3.2 A Construction Change Directive shall be used in the absence of total agreement on the terms of a Change Order.

7.3.3 If the Construction Change Directive provides for an adjustment to the Contract Sum, the adjustment shall be based on one of the following methods:

.1 mutual acceptance of a lump sum properly itemized and supported by sufficient substantiating data to permit evaluation;

.2 unit prices stated in the Contract Documents or subsequently agreed upon;

.3 cost to be determined in a manner agreed upon by the parties and a mutually acceptable fixed or percentage fee; or

.4 as provided in Subparagraph 7.3.6.

7.3.4 Upon receipt of a Construction Change Directive, the Contractor shall promptly proceed with the change in the Work involved and advise the Architect of the Contractor's agreement or disagreement with the method, if any, provided in the Construction Change Directive for determining the proposed adjustment in the Contract Sum or Contract Time.

7.3.5 A Construction Change Directive signed by the Contractor indicates the agreement of the Contractor therewith, including adjustment in Contract Sum and Contract Time or the method for determining them. Such agreement shall be effective immediately and shall be recorded as a Change Order.

7.3.6 If the Contractor does not respond promptly or disagrees with the method for adjustment in the Contract Sum, the method and the adjustment shall be determined by the Architect on the basis of reasonable expenditures and savings of those performing the Work attributable to the change, including, in case of an increase in the Contract Sum, a reasonable allowance for overhead and profit. In such case, and also under Clause 7.3.3.3, the Contractor shall keep and present, in such form as the Architect may prescribe, an itemized accounting together with appropriate supporting data. Unless otherwise provided in the Contract Documents, costs for the purposes of this Subparagraph 7.3.6 shall be limited to the following:

.1 costs of labor, including social security, old age and unemployment insurance, fringe benefits required by agreement or custom, and workers' or workmen's compensation insurance;

.2 costs of materials, supplies and equipment, including cost of transportation, whether incorporated or consumed;

.3 rental costs of machinery and equipment, exclusive of hand tools, whether rented from the Contractor or others;

.4 costs of premiums for all bonds and insurance, permit fees, and sales, use or similar taxes related to the Work; and

.5 additional costs of supervision and field office personnel directly attributable to the change.

7.3.7 Pending final determination of cost to the Owner, amounts not in dispute may be included in Applications for Payment. The amount of credit to be allowed by the Contractor to the Owner for a deletion or change which results in a net decrease in the Contract Sum shall be actual net cost as confirmed by the Architect. When both additions and credits covering related Work or substitutions are involved in a change, the allowance for overhead and profit shall be figured on the basis of net increase, if any, with respect to that change.

7.3.8 If the Owner and Contractor do not agree with the adjustment in Contract Time or the method for determining it, the adjustment or the method shall be referred to the Architect for determination.

7.3.9 When the Owner and Contractor agree with the determination made by the Architect concerning the adjustments in the Contract Sum and Contract Time, or otherwise reach agreement upon the adjustments, such agreement shall be effective immediately and shall be recorded by preparation and execution of an appropriate Change Order.

7.4 MINOR CHANGES IN THE WORK

7.4.1 The Architect will have authority to order minor changes in the Work not involving adjustment in the Contract Sum or extension of the Contract Time and not inconsistent with the intent of the Contract Documents. Such changes shall be effected by written order and shall be binding on the Owner and Contractor. The Contractor shall carry out such written orders promptly.

ARTICLE 8

TIME

8.1 DEFINITIONS

8.1.1 Unless otherwise provided, Contract Time is the period of time, including authorized adjustments, allotted in the Contract Documents for Substantial Completion of the Work.

8.1.2 The date of commencement of the Work is the date established in the Agreement. The date shall not be postponed by the failure to act of the Contractor or of persons or entities for whom the Contractor is responsible.

8.1.3 The date of Substantial Completion is the date certified by the Architect in accordance with Paragraph 9.8.

8.1.4 The term "day" as used in the Contract Documents shall mean calendar day unless otherwise specifically defined.

8.2 PROGRESS AND COMPLETION

8.2.1 Time limits stated in the Contract Documents are of the essence of the Contract. By executing the Agreement the Contractor confirms that the Contract Time is a reasonable period for performing the Work.

8.2.2 The Contractor shall not knowingly, except by agreement or instruction of the Owner in writing, prematurely commence operations on the site or elsewhere prior to the effective date of insurance required by Article 11 to be furnished by the Contractor. The date of commencement of the Work shall not be changed by the effective date of such insurance. Unless the date of commencement is established by a notice to proceed given by the Owner, the Contractor shall notify the Owner in writing not less than five days or other agreed period before commencing the Work to permit the timely filing of mortgages, mechanic's liens and other security interests.

8.2.3 The Contractor shall proceed expeditiously with adequate forces and shall achieve Substantial Completion within the Contract Time.

8.3 DELAYS AND EXTENSIONS OF TIME

8.3.1 If the Contractor is delayed at any time in progress of the Work by an act or neglect of the Owner or Architect, or of an employee of either, or of a separate contractor employed by the Owner, or by changes ordered in the Work, or by labor disputes, fire, unusual delay in deliveries, unavoidable casualties or other causes beyond the Contractor's control, or by delay authorized by the Owner pending arbitration, or by other causes which the Architect determines may justify delay, then the Contract Time shall be extended by Change Order for such reasonable time as the Architect may determine.

8.3.2 Claims relating to time shall be made in accordance with applicable provisions of Paragraph 4.3.

8.3.3 This Paragraph 8.3 does not preclude recovery of damages for delay by either party under other provisions of the Contract Documents.

ARTICLE 9

PAYMENTS AND COMPLETION

9.1 CONTRACT SUM

9.1.1 The Contract Sum is stated in the Agreement and, including authorized adjustments, is the total amount payable by the Owner to the Contractor for performance of the Work under the Contract Documents.

9.2 SCHEDULE OF VALUES

9.2.1 Before the first Application for Payment, the Contractor shall submit to the Architect a schedule of values allocated to various portions of the Work, prepared in such form and supported by such data to substantiate its accuracy as the Architect may require. This schedule, unless objected to by the Architect, shall be used as a basis for reviewing the Contractor's Applications for Payment.

9.3 APPLICATIONS FOR PAYMENT

9.3.1 At least ten days before the date established for each progress payment, the Contractor shall submit to the Architect an itemized Application for Payment for operations completed in accordance with the schedule of values. Such application shall be notarized, if required, and supported by such data substantiating the Contractor's right to payment as the Owner or Architect may require, such as copies of requisitions from Subcontractors and material suppliers, and reflecting retainage if provided for elsewhere in the Contract Documents.

9.3.1.1 Such applications may include requests for payment on account of changes in the Work which have been properly authorized by Construction Change Directives but not yet included in Change Orders.

9.3.1.2 Such applications may not include requests for payment of amounts the Contractor does not intend to pay to a Subcontractor or material supplier because of a dispute or other reason.

9.3.2 Unless otherwise provided in the Contract Documents, payments shall be made on account of materials and equipment delivered and suitably stored at the site for subsequent incorporation in the Work. If approved in advance by the Owner, payment may similarly be made for materials and equipment suitably stored off the site at a location agreed upon in writing. Payment for materials and equipment stored on or off the site shall be conditioned upon compliance by the Contractor with procedures satisfactory to the Owner to establish the Owner's title to such materials and equipment or otherwise protect the Owner's interest, and shall include applicable insurance, storage and transportation to the site for such materials and equipment stored off the site.

9.3.3 The Contractor warrants that title to all Work covered by an Application for Payment will pass to the Owner no later than the time of payment. The Contractor further warrants that upon submittal of an Application for Payment all Work for which Certificates for Payment have been previously issued and payments received from the Owner shall, to the best of the Contractor's knowledge, information and belief, be free and clear of liens, claims, security interests or encumbrances in favor of the Contractor, Subcontractors, material suppliers, or other persons or entities making a claim by reason of having provided labor, materials and equipment relating to the Work.

9.4 CERTIFICATES FOR PAYMENT

9.4.1 The Architect will, within seven days after receipt of the Contractor's Application for Payment, either issue to the

AIA DOCUMENT A201 • GENERAL CONDITIONS OF THE CONTRACT FOR CONSTRUCTION • FOURTEENTH EDITION
AIA® • ©1987 THE AMERICAN INSTITUTE OF ARCHITECTS, 1735 NEW YORK AVENUE, N.W., WASHINGTON, D.C. 20006

Owner a Certificate for Payment, with a copy to the Contractor, for such amount as the Architect determines is properly due, or notify the Contractor and Owner in writing of the Architect's reasons for withholding certification in whole or in part as provided in Subparagraph 9.5.1.

9.4.2 The issuance of a Certificate for Payment will constitute a representation by the Architect to the Owner, based on the Architect's observations at the site and the data comprising the Application for Payment, that the Work has progressed to the point indicated and that, to the best of the Architect's knowledge, information and belief, quality of the Work is in accordance with the Contract Documents. The foregoing representations are subject to an evaluation of the Work for conformance with the Contract Documents upon Substantial Completion, to results of subsequent tests and inspections, to minor deviations from the Contract Documents correctable prior to completion and to specific qualifications expressed by the Architect. The issuance of a Certificate for Payment will further constitute a representation that the Contractor is entitled to payment in the amount certified. However, the issuance of a Certificate for Payment will not be a representation that the Architect has (1) made exhaustive or continuous on-site inspections to check the quality or quantity of the Work, (2) reviewed construction means, methods, techniques, sequences or procedures, (3) reviewed copies of requisitions received from Subcontractors and material suppliers and other data requested by the Owner to substantiate the Contractor's right to payment or (4) made examination to ascertain how or for what purpose the Contractor has used money previously paid on account of the Contract Sum.

9.5 DECISIONS TO WITHHOLD CERTIFICATION

9.5.1 The Architect may decide not to certify payment and may withhold a Certificate for Payment in whole or in part, to the extent reasonably necessary to protect the Owner, if in the Architect's opinion the representations to the Owner required by Subparagraph 9.4.2 cannot be made. If the Architect is unable to certify payment in the amount of the Application, the Architect will notify the Contractor and Owner as provided in Subparagraph 9.4.1. If the Contractor and Architect cannot agree on a revised amount, the Architect will promptly issue a Certificate for Payment for the amount for which the Architect is able to make such representations to the Owner. The Architect may also decide not to certify payment or, because of subsequently discovered evidence or subsequent observations, may nullify the whole or a part of a Certificate for Payment previously issued, to such extent as may be necessary in the Architect's opinion to protect the Owner from loss because of:

.1 defective Work not remedied;

.2 third party claims filed or reasonable evidence indicating probable filing of such claims;

.3 failure of the Contractor to make payments properly to Subcontractors or for labor, materials or equipment;

.4 reasonable evidence that the Work cannot be completed for the unpaid balance of the Contract Sum;

.5 damage to the Owner or another contractor;

.6 reasonable evidence that the Work will not be completed within the Contract Time, and that the unpaid balance would not be adequate to cover actual or liquidated damages for the anticipated delay; or

.7 persistent failure to carry out the Work in accordance with the Contract Documents.

9.5.2 When the above reasons for withholding certification are removed, certification will be made for amounts previously withheld.

9.6 PROGRESS PAYMENTS

9.6.1 After the Architect has issued a Certificate for Payment, the Owner shall make payment in the manner and within the time provided in the Contract Documents, and shall so notify the Architect.

9.6.2 The Contractor shall promptly pay each Subcontractor, upon receipt of payment from the Owner, out of the amount paid to the Contractor on account of such Subcontractor's portion of the Work, the amount to which said Subcontractor is entitled, reflecting percentages actually retained from payments to the Contractor on account of such Subcontractor's portion of the Work. The Contractor shall, by appropriate agreement with each Subcontractor, require each Subcontractor to make payments to Sub-subcontractors in similar manner.

9.6.3 The Architect will, on request, furnish to a Subcontractor, if practicable, information regarding percentages of completion or amounts applied for by the Contractor and action taken thereon by the Architect and Owner on account of portions of the Work done by such Subcontractor.

9.6.4 Neither the Owner nor Architect shall have an obligation to pay or to see to the payment of money to a Subcontractor except as may otherwise be required by law.

9.6.5 Payment to material suppliers shall be treated in a manner similar to that provided in Subparagraphs 9.6.2, 9.6.3 and 9.6.4.

9.6.6 A Certificate for Payment, a progress payment, or partial or entire use or occupancy of the Project by the Owner shall not constitute acceptance of Work not in accordance with the Contract Documents.

9.7 FAILURE OF PAYMENT

9.7.1 If the Architect does not issue a Certificate for Payment, through no fault of the Contractor, within seven days after receipt of the Contractor's Application for Payment, or if the Owner does not pay the Contractor within seven days after the date established in the Contract Documents the amount certified by the Architect or awarded by arbitration, then the Contractor may, upon seven additional days' written notice to the Owner and Architect, stop the Work until payment of the amount owing has been received. The Contract Time shall be extended appropriately and the Contract Sum shall be increased by the amount of the Contractor's reasonable costs of shut-down, delay and start-up, which shall be accomplished as provided in Article 7.

9.8 SUBSTANTIAL COMPLETION

9.8.1 Substantial Completion is the stage in the progress of the Work when the Work or designated portion thereof is sufficiently complete in accordance with the Contract Documents so the Owner can occupy or utilize the Work for its intended use.

9.8.2 When the Contractor considers that the Work, or a portion thereof which the Owner agrees to accept separately, is substantially complete, the Contractor shall prepare and submit to the Architect a comprehensive list of items to be completed or corrected. The Contractor shall proceed promptly to complete and correct items on the list. Failure to include an item on such list does not alter the responsibility of the Contractor to complete all Work in accordance with the Contract Documents. Upon receipt of the Contractor's list, the Architect will make an inspection to determine whether the Work or designated portion thereof is substantially complete. If the Architect's inspection discloses any item, whether or not included on the Contractor's list, which is not in accordance with the requirements of the Contract Documents, the Contractor shall, before issuance of the Certificate of Substantial Completion, complete or correct such item upon notification by the Architect. The Contractor shall then submit a request for another inspection by the Architect to determine Substantial Completion. When the Work or designated portion thereof is substantially complete, the Architect will prepare a Certificate of Substantial Completion which shall establish the date of Substantial Completion, shall establish responsibilities of the Owner and Contractor for security, maintenance, heat, utilities, damage to the Work and insurance, and shall fix the time within which the Contractor shall finish all items on the list accompanying the Certificate. Warranties required by the Contract Documents shall commence on the date of Substantial Completion of the Work or designated portion thereof unless otherwise provided in the Certificate of Substantial Completion. The Certificate of Substantial Completion shall be submitted to the Owner and Contractor for their written acceptance of responsibilities assigned to them in such Certificate.

9.8.3 Upon Substantial Completion of the Work or designated portion thereof and upon application by the Contractor and certification by the Architect, the Owner shall make payment reflecting adjustment in retainage, if any, for such Work or portion thereof as provided in the Contract Documents.

9.9 PARTIAL OCCUPANCY OR USE

9.9.1 The Owner may occupy or use any completed or partially completed portion of the Work at any stage when such portion is designated by separate agreement with the Contractor, provided such occupancy or use is consented to by the insurer as required under Subparagraph 11.3.11 and authorized by public authorities having jurisdiction over the Work. Such partial occupancy or use may commence whether or not the portion is substantially complete, provided the Owner and Contractor have accepted in writing the responsibilities assigned to each of them for payments, retainage if any, security, maintenance, heat, utilities, damage to the Work and insurance, and have agreed in writing concerning the period for correction of the Work and commencement of warranties required by the Contract Documents. When the Contractor considers a portion substantially complete, the Contractor shall prepare and submit a list to the Architect as provided under Subparagraph 9.8.2. Consent of the Contractor to partial occupancy or use shall not be unreasonably withheld. The stage of the progress of the Work shall be determined by written agreement between the Owner and Contractor or, if no agreement is reached, by decision of the Architect.

9.9.2 Immediately prior to such partial occupancy or use, the Owner, Contractor and Architect shall jointly inspect the area to be occupied or portion of the Work to be used in order to determine and record the condition of the Work.

9.9.3 Unless otherwise agreed upon, partial occupancy or use of a portion or portions of the Work shall not constitute acceptance of Work not complying with the requirements of the Contract Documents.

9.10 FINAL COMPLETION AND FINAL PAYMENT

9.10.1 Upon receipt of written notice that the Work is ready for final inspection and acceptance and upon receipt of a final Application for Payment, the Architect will promptly make

such inspection and, when the Architect finds the Work acceptable under the Contract Documents and the Contract fully performed, the Architect will promptly issue a final Certificate for Payment stating that to the best of the Architect's knowledge, information and belief, and on the basis of the Architect's observations and inspections, the Work has been completed in accordance with terms and conditions of the Contract Documents and that the entire balance found to be due the Contractor and noted in said final Certificate is due and payable. The Architect's final Certificate for Payment will constitute a further representation that conditions listed in Subparagraph 9.10.2 as precedent to the Contractor's being entitled to final payment have been fulfilled.

9.10.2 Neither final payment nor any remaining retained percentage shall become due until the Contractor submits to the Architect (1) an affidavit that payrolls, bills for materials and equipment, and other indebtedness connected with the Work for which the Owner or the Owner's property might be responsible or encumbered (less amounts withheld by Owner) have been paid or otherwise satisfied, (2) a certificate evidencing that insurance required by the Contract Documents to remain in force after final payment is currently in effect and will not be cancelled or allowed to expire until at least 30 days' prior written notice has been given to the Owner, (3) a written statement that the Contractor knows of no substantial reason that the insurance will not be renewable to cover the period required by the Contract Documents, (4) consent of surety, if any, to final payment and (5), if required by the Owner, other data establishing payment or satisfaction of obligations, such as receipts, releases and waivers of liens, claims, security interests or encumbrances arising out of the Contract, to the extent and in such form as may be designated by the Owner. If a Subcontractor refuses to furnish a release or waiver required by the Owner, the Contractor may furnish a bond satisfactory to the Owner to indemnify the Owner against such lien. If such lien remains unsatisfied after payments are made, the Contractor shall refund to the Owner all money that the Owner may be compelled to pay in discharging such lien, including all costs and reasonable attorneys' fees.

9.10.3 If, after Substantial Completion of the Work, final completion thereof is materially delayed through no fault of the Contractor or by issuance of Change Orders affecting final completion, and the Architect so confirms, the Owner shall, upon application by the Contractor and certification by the Architect, and without terminating the Contract, make payment of the balance due for that portion of the Work fully completed and accepted. If the remaining balance for Work not fully completed or corrected is less than retainage stipulated in the Contract Documents, and if bonds have been furnished, the written consent of surety to payment of the balance due for that portion of the Work fully completed and accepted shall be submitted by the Contractor to the Architect prior to certification of such payment. Such payment shall be made under terms and conditions governing final payment, except that it shall not constitute a waiver of claims. The making of final payment shall constitute a waiver of claims by the Owner as provided in Subparagraph 4.3.5.

9.10.4 Acceptance of final payment by the Contractor, a Subcontractor or material supplier shall constitute a waiver of claims by that payee except those previously made in writing and identified by that payee as unsettled at the time of final Application for Payment. Such waivers shall be in addition to the waiver described in Subparagraph 4.3.5.

AIA DOCUMENT A201 • GENERAL CONDITIONS OF THE CONTRACT FOR CONSTRUCTION • FOURTEENTH EDITION
AIA® • ©1987 THE AMERICAN INSTITUTE OF ARCHITECTS, 1735 NEW YORK AVENUE, N.W., WASHINGTON, D.C. 20006

ARTICLE 10

PROTECTION OF PERSONS AND PROPERTY

10.1 SAFETY PRECAUTIONS AND PROGRAMS

10.1.1 The Contractor shall be responsible for initiating, maintaining and supervising all safety precautions and programs in connection with the performance of the Contract.

10.1.2 In the event the Contractor encounters on the site material reasonably believed to be asbestos or polychlorinated biphenyl (PCB) which has not been rendered harmless, the Contractor shall immediately stop Work in the area affected and report the condition to the Owner and Architect in writing. The Work in the affected area shall not thereafter be resumed except by written agreement of the Owner and Contractor if in fact the material is asbestos or polychlorinated biphenyl (PCB) and has not been rendered harmless. The Work in the affected area shall be resumed in the absence of asbestos or polychlorinated biphenyl (PCB), or when it has been rendered harmless, by written agreement of the Owner and Contractor, or in accordance with final determination by the Architect on which arbitration has not been demanded, or by arbitration under Article 4.

10.1.3 The Contractor shall not be required pursuant to Article 7 to perform without consent any Work relating to asbestos or polychlorinated biphenyl (PCB).

10.1.4 To the fullest extent permitted by law, the Owner shall indemnify and hold harmless the Contractor, Architect, Architect's consultants and agents and employees of any of them from and against claims, damages, losses and expenses, including but not limited to attorneys' fees, arising out of or resulting from performance of the Work in the affected area if in fact the material is asbestos or polychlorinated biphenyl (PCB) and has not been rendered harmless, provided that such claim, damage, loss or expense is attributable to bodily injury, sickness, disease or death, or to injury to or destruction of tangible property (other than the Work itself) including loss of use resulting therefrom, but only to the extent caused in whole or in part by negligent acts or omissions of the Owner, anyone directly or indirectly employed by the Owner or anyone for whose acts the Owner may be liable, regardless of whether or not such claim, damage, loss or expense is caused in part by a party indemnified hereunder. Such obligation shall not be construed to negate, abridge, or reduce other rights or obligations of indemnity which would otherwise exist as to a party or person described in this Subparagraph 10.1.4.

10.2 SAFETY OF PERSONS AND PROPERTY

10.2.1 The Contractor shall take reasonable precautions for safety of, and shall provide reasonable protection to prevent damage, injury or loss to:

   .1 employees on the Work and other persons who may be affected thereby;

   .2 the Work and materials and equipment to be incorporated therein, whether in storage on or off the site, under care, custody or control of the Contractor or the Contractor's Subcontractors or Sub-subcontractors; and

   .3 other property at the site or adjacent thereto, such as trees, shrubs, lawns, walks, pavements, roadways, structures and utilities not designated for removal, relocation or replacement in the course of construction.

10.2.2 The Contractor shall give notices and comply with applicable laws, ordinances, rules, regulations and lawful orders of public authorities bearing on safety of persons or property or their protection from damage, injury or loss.

10.2.3 The Contractor shall erect and maintain, as required by existing conditions and performance of the Contract, reasonable safeguards for safety and protection, including posting danger signs and other warnings against hazards, promulgating safety regulations and notifying owners and users of adjacent sites and utilities.

10.2.4 When use or storage of explosives or other hazardous materials or equipment or unusual methods are necessary for execution of the Work, the Contractor shall exercise utmost care and carry on such activities under supervision of properly qualified personnel.

10.2.5 The Contractor shall promptly remedy damage and loss (other than damage or loss insured under property insurance required by the Contract Documents) to property referred to in Clauses 10.2.1.2 and 10.2.1.3 caused in whole or in part by the Contractor, a Subcontractor, a Sub-subcontractor, or anyone directly or indirectly employed by any of them, or by anyone for whose acts they may be liable and for which the Contractor is responsible under Clauses 10.2.1.2 and 10.2.1.3, except damage or loss attributable to acts or omissions of the Owner or Architect or anyone directly or indirectly employed by either of them, or by anyone for whose acts either of them may be liable, and not attributable to the fault or negligence of the Contractor. The foregoing obligations of the Contractor are in addition to the Contractor's obligations under Paragraph 3.18.

10.2.6 The Contractor shall designate a responsible member of the Contractor's organization at the site whose duty shall be the prevention of accidents. This person shall be the Contractor's superintendent unless otherwise designated by the Contractor in writing to the Owner and Architect.

10.2.7 The Contractor shall not load or permit any part of the construction or site to be loaded so as to endanger its safety.

10.3 EMERGENCIES

10.3.1 In an emergency affecting safety of persons or property, the Contractor shall act, at the Contractor's discretion, to prevent threatened damage, injury or loss. Additional compensation or extension of time claimed by the Contractor on account of an emergency shall be determined as provided in Paragraph 4.3 and Article 7.

ARTICLE 11

INSURANCE AND BONDS

11.1 CONTRACTOR'S LIABILITY INSURANCE

11.1.1 The Contractor shall purchase from and maintain in a company or companies lawfully authorized to do business in the jurisdiction in which the Project is located such insurance as will protect the Contractor from claims set forth below which may arise out of or result from the Contractor's operations under the Contract and for which the Contractor may be legally liable, whether such operations be by the Contractor or by a Subcontractor or by anyone directly or indirectly employed by any of them, or by anyone for whose acts any of them may be liable:

   .1 claims under workers' or workmen's compensation, disability benefit and other similar employee benefit acts which are applicable to the Work to be performed;

.2 claims for damages because of bodily injury, occupational sickness or disease, or death of the Contractor's employees;

.3 claims for damages because of bodily injury, sickness or disease, or death of any person other than the Contractor's employees;

.4 claims for damages insured by usual personal injury liability coverage which are sustained (1) by a person as a result of an offense directly or indirectly related to employment of such person by the Contractor, or (2) by another person;

.5 claims for damages, other than to the Work itself, because of injury to or destruction of tangible property, including loss of use resulting therefrom;

.6 claims for damages because of bodily injury, death of a person or property damage arising out of ownership, maintenance or use of a motor vehicle; and

.7 claims involving contractual liability insurance applicable to the Contractor's obligations under Paragraph 3.18.

11.1.2 The insurance required by Subparagraph 11.1.1 shall be written for not less than limits of liability specified in the Contract Documents or required by law, whichever coverage is greater. Coverages, whether written on an occurrence or claims-made basis, shall be maintained without interruption from date of commencement of the Work until date of final payment and termination of any coverage required to be maintained after final payment.

11.1.3 Certificates of Insurance acceptable to the Owner shall be filed with the Owner prior to commencement of the Work. These Certificates and the insurance policies required by this Paragraph 11.1 shall contain a provision that coverages afforded under the policies will not be cancelled or allowed to expire until at least 30 days' prior written notice has been given to the Owner. If any of the foregoing insurance coverages are required to remain in force after final payment and are reasonably available, an additional certificate evidencing continuation of such coverage shall be submitted with the final Application for Payment as required by Subparagraph 9.10.2. Information concerning reduction of coverage shall be furnished by the Contractor with reasonable promptness in accordance with the Contractor's information and belief.

11.2 OWNER'S LIABILITY INSURANCE

11.2.1 The Owner shall be responsible for purchasing and maintaining the Owner's usual liability insurance. Optionally, the Owner may purchase and maintain other insurance for self-protection against claims which may arise from operations under the Contract. The Contractor shall not be responsible for purchasing and maintaining this optional Owner's liability insurance unless specifically required by the Contract Documents.

11.3 PROPERTY INSURANCE

11.3.1 Unless otherwise provided, the Owner shall purchase and maintain, in a company or companies lawfully authorized to do business in the jurisdiction in which the Project is located, property insurance in the amount of the initial Contract Sum as well as subsequent modifications thereto for the entire Work at the site on a replacement cost basis without voluntary deductibles. Such property insurance shall be maintained, unless otherwise provided in the Contract Documents or otherwise agreed in writing by all persons and entities who are beneficiaries of such insurance, until final payment has been made as provided in Paragraph 9.10 or until no person or entity

other than the Owner has an insurable interest in the property required by this Paragraph 11.3 to be covered, whichever is earlier. This insurance shall include interests of the Owner, the Contractor, Subcontractors and Sub-subcontractors in the Work.

11.3.1.1 Property insurance shall be on an all-risk policy form and shall insure against the perils of fire and extended coverage and physical loss or damage including, without duplication of coverage, theft, vandalism, malicious mischief, collapse, falsework, temporary buildings and debris removal including demolition occasioned by enforcement of any applicable legal requirements, and shall cover reasonable compensation for Architect's services and expenses required as a result of such insured loss. Coverage for other perils shall not be required unless otherwise provided in the Contract Documents.

11.3.1.2 If the Owner does not intend to purchase such property insurance required by the Contract and with all of the coverages in the amount described above, the Owner shall so inform the Contractor in writing prior to commencement of the Work. The Contractor may then effect insurance which will protect the interests of the Contractor, Subcontractors and Sub-subcontractors in the Work, and by appropriate Change Order the cost thereof shall be charged to the Owner. If the Contractor is damaged by the failure or neglect of the Owner to purchase or maintain insurance as described above, without so notifying the Contractor, then the Owner shall bear all reasonable costs properly attributable thereto.

11.3.1.3 If the property insurance requires minimum deductibles and such deductibles are identified in the Contract Documents, the Contractor shall pay costs not covered because of such deductibles. If the Owner or insurer increases the required minimum deductibles above the amounts so identified or if the Owner elects to purchase this insurance with voluntary deductible amounts, the Owner shall be responsible for payment of the additional costs not covered because of such increased or voluntary deductibles. If deductibles are not identified in the Contract Documents, the Owner shall pay costs not covered because of deductibles.

11.3.1.4 Unless otherwise provided in the Contract Documents, this property insurance shall cover portions of the Work stored off the site after written approval of the Owner at the value established in the approval, and also portions of the Work in transit.

11.3.2 Boiler and Machinery Insurance. The Owner shall purchase and maintain boiler and machinery insurance required by the Contract Documents or by law, which shall specifically cover such insured objects during installation and until final acceptance by the Owner; this insurance shall include interests of the Owner, Contractor, Subcontractors and Sub-subcontractors in the Work, and the Owner and Contractor shall be named insureds.

11.3.3 Loss of Use Insurance. The Owner, at the Owner's option, may purchase and maintain such insurance as will insure the Owner against loss of use of the Owner's property due to fire or other hazards, however caused. The Owner waives all rights of action against the Contractor for loss of use of the Owner's property, including consequential losses due to fire or other hazards however caused.

11.3.4 If the Contractor requests in writing that insurance for risks other than those described herein or for other special hazards be included in the property insurance policy, the Owner shall, if possible, include such insurance, and the cost thereof shall be charged to the Contractor by appropriate Change Order.

11.3.5 If during the Project construction period the Owner insures properties, real or personal or both, adjoining or adjacent to the site by property insurance under policies separate from those insuring the Project, or if after final payment property insurance is to be provided on the completed Project through a policy or policies other than those insuring the Project during the construction period, the Owner shall waive all rights in accordance with the terms of Subparagraph 11.3.7 for damages caused by fire or other perils covered by this separate property insurance. All separate policies shall provide this waiver of subrogation by endorsement or otherwise.

11.3.6 Before an exposure to loss may occur, the Owner shall file with the Contractor a copy of each policy that includes insurance coverages required by this Paragraph 11.3. Each policy shall contain all generally applicable conditions, definitions, exclusions and endorsements related to this Project. Each policy shall contain a provision that the policy will not be cancelled or allowed to expire until at least 30 days' prior written notice has been given to the Contractor.

11.3.7 Waivers of Subrogation. The Owner and Contractor waive all rights against (1) each other and any of their subcontractors, sub-subcontractors, agents and employees, each of the other, and (2) the Architect, Architect's consultants, separate contractors described in Article 6, if any, and any of their subcontractors, sub-subcontractors, agents and employees, for damages caused by fire or other perils to the extent covered by property insurance obtained pursuant to this Paragraph 11.3 or other property insurance applicable to the Work, except such rights as they have to proceeds of such insurance held by the Owner as fiduciary. The Owner or Contractor, as appropriate, shall require of the Architect, Architect's consultants, separate contractors described in Article 6, if any, and the subcontractors, sub-subcontractors, agents and employees of any of them, by appropriate agreements, written where legally required for validity, similar waivers each in favor of other parties enumerated herein. The policies shall provide such waivers of subrogation by endorsement or otherwise. A waiver of subrogation shall be effective as to a person or entity even though that person or entity would otherwise have a duty of indemnification, contractual or otherwise, did not pay the insurance premium directly or indirectly, and whether or not the person or entity had an insurable interest in the property damaged.

11.3.8 A loss insured under Owner's property insurance shall be adjusted by the Owner as fiduciary and made payable to the Owner as fiduciary for the insureds, as their interests may appear, subject to requirements of any applicable mortgagee clause and of Subparagraph 11.3.10. The Contractor shall pay Subcontractors their just shares of insurance proceeds received by the Contractor, and by appropriate agreements, written where legally required for validity, shall require Subcontractors to make payments to their Sub-subcontractors in similar manner.

11.3.9 If required in writing by a party in interest, the Owner as fiduciary shall, upon occurrence of an insured loss, give bond for proper performance of the Owner's duties. The cost of required bonds shall be charged against proceeds received as fiduciary. The Owner shall deposit in a separate account proceeds so received, which the Owner shall distribute in accordance with such agreement as the parties in interest may reach, or in accordance with an arbitration award in which case the procedure shall be as provided in Paragraph 4.5. If after such loss no other special agreement is made, replacement of damaged property shall be covered by appropriate Change Order.

11.3.10 The Owner as fiduciary shall have power to adjust and settle a loss with insurers unless one of the parties in interest shall object in writing within five days after occurrence of loss to the Owner's exercise of this power; if such objection be made, arbitrators shall be chosen as provided in Paragraph 4.5. The Owner as fiduciary shall, in that case, make settlement with insurers in accordance with directions of such arbitrators. If distribution of insurance proceeds by arbitration is required, the arbitrators will direct such distribution.

11.3.11 Partial occupancy or use in accordance with Paragraph 9.9 shall not commence until the insurance company or companies providing property insurance have consented to such partial occupancy or use by endorsement or otherwise. The Owner and the Contractor shall take reasonable steps to obtain consent of the insurance company or companies and shall, without mutual written consent, take no action with respect to partial occupancy or use that would cause cancellation, lapse or reduction of insurance.

11.4 PERFORMANCE BOND AND PAYMENT BOND

11.4.1 The Owner shall have the right to require the Contractor to furnish bonds covering faithful performance of the Contract and payment of obligations arising thereunder as stipulated in bidding requirements or specifically required in the Contract Documents on the date of execution of the Contract.

11.4.2 Upon the request of any person or entity appearing to be a potential beneficiary of bonds covering payment of obligations arising under the Contract, the Contractor shall promptly furnish a copy of the bonds or shall permit a copy to be made.

ARTICLE 12

UNCOVERING AND CORRECTION OF WORK

12.1 UNCOVERING OF WORK

12.1.1 If a portion of the Work is covered contrary to the Architect's request or to requirements specifically expressed in the Contract Documents, it must, if required in writing by the Architect, be uncovered for the Architect's observation and be replaced at the Contractor's expense without change in the Contract Time.

12.1.2 If a portion of the Work has been covered which the Architect has not specifically requested to observe prior to its being covered, the Architect may request to see such Work and it shall be uncovered by the Contractor. If such Work is in accordance with the Contract Documents, costs of uncovering and replacement shall, by appropriate Change Order, be charged to the Owner. If such Work is not in accordance with the Contract Documents, the Contractor shall pay such costs unless the condition was caused by the Owner or a separate contractor in which event the Owner shall be responsible for payment of such costs.

12.2 CORRECTION OF WORK

12.2.1 The Contractor shall promptly correct Work rejected by the Architect or failing to conform to the requirements of the Contract Documents, whether observed before or after Substantial Completion and whether or not fabricated, installed or completed. The Contractor shall bear costs of correcting such rejected Work, including additional testing and inspections and compensation for the Architect's services and expenses made necessary thereby.

12.2.2 If, within one year after the date of Substantial Completion of the Work or designated portion thereof, or after the date for commencement of warranties established under Subparagraph 9.9.1, or by terms of an applicable special warranty required by the Contract Documents, any of the Work is found to be not in accordance with the requirements of the Contract Documents, the Contractor shall correct it promptly after receipt of written notice from the Owner to do so unless the Owner has previously given the Contractor a written acceptance of such condition. This period of one year shall be extended with respect to portions of Work first performed after Substantial Completion by the period of time between Substantial Completion and the actual performance of the Work. This obligation under this Subparagraph 12.2.2 shall survive acceptance of the Work under the Contract and termination of the Contract. The Owner shall give such notice promptly after discovery of the condition.

12.2.3 The Contractor shall remove from the site portions of the Work which are not in accordance with the requirements of the Contract Documents and are neither corrected by the Contractor nor accepted by the Owner.

12.2.4 If the Contractor fails to correct nonconforming Work within a reasonable time, the Owner may correct it in accordance with Paragraph 2.4. If the Contractor does not proceed with correction of such nonconforming Work within a reasonable time fixed by written notice from the Architect, the Owner may remove it and store the salvable materials or equipment at the Contractor's expense. If the Contractor does not pay costs of such removal and storage within ten days after written notice, the Owner may upon ten additional days' written notice sell such materials and equipment at auction or at private sale and shall account for the proceeds thereof, after deducting costs and damages that should have been borne by the Contractor, including compensation for the Architect's services and expenses made necessary thereby. If such proceeds of sale do not cover costs which the Contractor should have borne, the Contract Sum shall be reduced by the deficiency. If payments then or thereafter due the Contractor are not sufficient to cover such amount, the Contractor shall pay the difference to the Owner.

12.2.5 The Contractor shall bear the cost of correcting destroyed or damaged construction, whether completed or partially completed, of the Owner or separate contractors caused by the Contractor's correction or removal of Work which is not in accordance with the requirements of the Contract Documents.

12.2.6 Nothing contained in this Paragraph 12.2 shall be construed to establish a period of limitation with respect to other obligations which the Contractor might have under the Contract Documents. Establishment of the time period of one year as described in Subparagraph 12.2.2 relates only to the specific obligation of the Contractor to correct the Work, and has no relationship to the time within which the obligation to comply with the Contract Documents may be sought to be enforced, nor to the time within which proceedings may be commenced to establish the Contractor's liability with respect to the Contractor's obligations other than specifically to correct the Work.

12.3 ACCEPTANCE OF NONCONFORMING WORK

12.3.1 If the Owner prefers to accept Work which is not in accordance with the requirements of the Contract Documents, the Owner may do so instead of requiring its removal and correction, in which case the Contract Sum will be reduced as appropriate and equitable. Such adjustment shall be effected whether or not final payment has been made.

ARTICLE 13

MISCELLANEOUS PROVISIONS

13.1 GOVERNING LAW

13.1.1 The Contract shall be governed by the law of the place where the Project is located.

13.2 SUCCESSORS AND ASSIGNS

13.2.1 The Owner and Contractor respectively bind themselves, their partners, successors, assigns and legal representatives to the other party hereto and to partners, successors, assigns and legal representatives of such other party in respect to covenants, agreements and obligations contained in the Contract Documents. Neither party to the Contract shall assign the Contract as a whole without written consent of the other. If either party attempts to make such an assignment without such consent, that party shall nevertheless remain legally responsible for all obligations under the Contract.

13.3 WRITTEN NOTICE

13.3.1 Written notice shall be deemed to have been duly served if delivered in person to the individual or a member of the firm or entity or to an officer of the corporation for which it was intended, or if delivered at or sent by registered or certified mail to the last business address known to the party giving notice.

13.4 RIGHTS AND REMEDIES

13.4.1 Duties and obligations imposed by the Contract Documents and rights and remedies available thereunder shall be in addition to and not a limitation of duties, obligations, rights and remedies otherwise imposed or available by law.

13.4.2 No action or failure to act by the Owner, Architect or Contractor shall constitute a waiver of a right or duty afforded them under the Contract, nor shall such action or failure to act constitute approval of or acquiescence in a breach thereunder, except as may be specifically agreed in writing.

13.5 TESTS AND INSPECTIONS

13.5.1 Tests, inspections and approvals of portions of the Work required by the Contract Documents or by laws, ordinances, rules, regulations or orders of public authorities having jurisdiction shall be made at an appropriate time. Unless otherwise provided, the Contractor shall make arrangements for such tests, inspections and approvals with an independent testing laboratory or entity acceptable to the Owner, or with the appropriate public authority, and shall bear all related costs of tests, inspections and approvals. The Contractor shall give the Architect timely notice of when and where tests and inspections are to be made so the Architect may observe such procedures. The Owner shall bear costs of tests, inspections or approvals which do not become requirements until after bids are received or negotiations concluded.

13.5.2 If the Architect, Owner or public authorities having jurisdiction determine that portions of the Work require additional testing, inspection or approval not included under Subparagraph 13.5.1, the Architect will, upon written authorization from the Owner, instruct the Contractor to make arrangements for such additional testing, inspection or approval by an entity acceptable to the Owner, and the Contractor shall give timely notice to the Architect of when and where tests and inspections are to be made so the Architect may observe such procedures.

AIA DOCUMENT A201 • GENERAL CONDITIONS OF THE CONTRACT FOR CONSTRUCTION • FOURTEENTH EDITION
AIA® • ©1987 THE AMERICAN INSTITUTE OF ARCHITECTS, 1735 NEW YORK AVENUE, N.W., WASHINGTON, D.C. 20006

The Owner shall bear such costs except as provided in Sub-paragraph 13.5.3.

13.5.3 If such procedures for testing, inspection or approval under Subparagraphs 13.5.1 and 13.5.2 reveal failure of the portions of the Work to comply with requirements established by the Contract Documents, the Contractor shall bear all costs made necessary by such failure including those of repeated procedures and compensation for the Architect's services and expenses.

13.5.4 Required certificates of testing, inspection or approval shall, unless otherwise required by the Contract Documents, be secured by the Contractor and promptly delivered to the Architect.

13.5.5 If the Architect is to observe tests, inspections or approvals required by the Contract Documents, the Architect will do so promptly and, where practicable, at the normal place of testing.

13.5.6 Tests or inspections conducted pursuant to the Contract Documents shall be made promptly to avoid unreasonable delay in the Work.

13.6 INTEREST

13.6.1 Payments due and unpaid under the Contract Documents shall bear interest from the date payment is due at such rate as the parties may agree upon in writing or, in the absence thereof, at the legal rate prevailing from time to time at the place where the Project is located.

13.7 COMMENCEMENT OF STATUTORY LIMITATION PERIOD

13.7.1 As between the Owner and Contractor:

.1 **Before Substantial Completion.** As to acts or failures to act occurring prior to the relevant date of Substantial Completion, any applicable statute of limitations shall commence to run and any alleged cause of action shall be deemed to have accrued in any and all events not later than such date of Substantial Completion;

.2 **Between Substantial Completion and Final Certificate for Payment.** As to acts or failures to act occurring subsequent to the relevant date of Substantial Completion and prior to issuance of the final Certificate for Payment, any applicable statute of limitations shall commence to run and any alleged cause of action shall be deemed to have accrued in any and all events not later than the date of issuance of the final Certificate for Payment; and

.3 **After Final Certificate for Payment.** As to acts or failures to act occurring after the relevant date of issuance of the final Certificate for Payment, any applicable statute of limitations shall commence to run and any alleged cause of action shall be deemed to have accrued in any and all events not later than the date of any act or failure to act by the Contractor pursuant to any warranty provided under Paragraph 3.5, the date of any correction of the Work or failure to correct the Work by the Contractor under Paragraph 12.2, or the date of actual commission of any other act or failure to perform any duty or obligation by the Contractor or Owner, whichever occurs last.

ARTICLE 14

TERMINATION OR SUSPENSION OF THE CONTRACT

14.1 TERMINATION BY THE CONTRACTOR

14.1.1 The Contractor may terminate the Contract if the Work is stopped for a period of 30 days through no act or fault of the Contractor or a Subcontractor, Sub-subcontractor or their agents or employees or any other persons performing portions of the Work under contract with the Contractor, for any of the following reasons:

.1 issuance of an order of a court or other public authority having jurisdiction;

.2 an act of government, such as a declaration of national emergency, making material unavailable;

.3 because the Architect has not issued a Certificate for Payment and has not notified the Contractor of the reason for withholding certification as provided in Subparagraph 9.4.1, or because the Owner has not made payment on a Certificate for Payment within the time stated in the Contract Documents;

.4 if repeated suspensions, delays or interruptions by the Owner as described in Paragraph 14.3 constitute in the aggregate more than 100 percent of the total number of days scheduled for completion, or 120 days in any 365-day period, whichever is less; or

.5 the Owner has failed to furnish to the Contractor promptly, upon the Contractor's request, reasonable evidence as required by Subparagraph 2.2.1.

14.1.2 If one of the above reasons exists, the Contractor may, upon seven additional days' written notice to the Owner and Architect, terminate the Contract and recover from the Owner payment for Work executed and for proven loss with respect to materials, equipment, tools, and construction equipment and machinery, including reasonable overhead, profit and damages.

14.1.3 If the Work is stopped for a period of 60 days through no act or fault of the Contractor or a Subcontractor or their agents or employees or any other persons performing portions of the Work under contract with the Contractor because the Owner has persistently failed to fulfill the Owner's obligations under the Contract Documents with respect to matters important to the progress of the Work, the Contractor may, upon seven additional days' written notice to the Owner and the Architect, terminate the Contract and recover from the Owner as provided in Subparagraph 14.1.2.

14.2 TERMINATION BY THE OWNER FOR CAUSE

14.2.1 The Owner may terminate the Contract if the Contractor:

.1 persistently or repeatedly refuses or fails to supply enough properly skilled workers or proper materials;

.2 fails to make payment to Subcontractors for materials or labor in accordance with the respective agreements between the Contractor and the Subcontractors;

.3 persistently disregards laws, ordinances, or rules, regulations or orders of a public authority having jurisdiction; or

.4 otherwise is guilty of substantial breach of a provision of the Contract Documents.

14.2.2 When any of the above reasons exist, the Owner, upon certification by the Architect that sufficient cause exists to justify such action, may without prejudice to any other rights or remedies of the Owner and after giving the Contractor and the Contractor's surety, if any, seven days' written notice, terminate employment of the Contractor and may, subject to any prior rights of the surety:

   .1 take possession of the site and of all materials, equipment, tools, and construction equipment and machinery thereon owned by the Contractor;

   .2 accept assignment of subcontracts pursuant to Paragraph 5.4; and

   .3 finish the Work by whatever reasonable method the Owner may deem expedient.

14.2.3 When the Owner terminates the Contract for one of the reasons stated in Subparagraph 14.2.1, the Contractor shall not be entitled to receive further payment until the Work is finished.

14.2.4 If the unpaid balance of the Contract Sum exceeds costs of finishing the Work, including compensation for the Architect's services and expenses made necessary thereby, such excess shall be paid to the Contractor. If such costs exceed the unpaid balance, the Contractor shall pay the difference to the Owner. The amount to be paid to the Contractor or Owner, as the case may be, shall be certified by the Architect, upon application, and this obligation for payment shall survive termination of the Contract.

14.3 SUSPENSION BY THE OWNER FOR CONVENIENCE

14.3.1 The Owner may, without cause, order the Contractor in writing to suspend, delay or interrupt the Work in whole or in part for such period of time as the Owner may determine.

14.3.2 An adjustment shall be made for increases in the cost of performance of the Contract, including profit on the increased cost of performance, caused by suspension, delay or interruption. No adjustment shall be made to the extent:

   .1 that performance is, was or would have been so suspended, delayed or interrupted by another cause for which the Contractor is responsible; or

   .2 that an equitable adjustment is made or denied under another provision of this Contract.

14.3.3 Adjustments made in the cost of performance may have a mutually agreed fixed or percentage fee.

AIA DOCUMENT A201 • GENERAL CONDITIONS OF THE CONTRACT FOR CONSTRUCTION • FOURTEENTH EDITION
AIA® • ©1987 THE AMERICAN INSTITUTE OF ARCHITECTS, 1735 NEW YORK AVENUE, N.W., WASHINGTON, D.C. 20006

DOCUMENT 00800 - SUPPLEMENTARY CONDITIONS

The following supplements modify the "General Conditions of the Contract for Construction" (AIA Document A201, 1987 Edition). Where a portion of the General Conditions is modified by these Supplementary Conditions, the unaltered portions of the General Conditions shall remain in effect.

ARTICLE 8 -TIME

8.1 DEFINITIONS

Add Clause 8.1.4.1

> **8.1.4.1** The term "day" does not intend any specific time nor any fixed number of hours for trade union, subcontract, or any other purpose. With prior consent of the Owner, the Contractor is permitted to work any reasonable schedule the Contractor finds necessary.

Add Paragraph 8.4.

8.4 OWNER-REQUESTED EARLY COMPLETION

> **8.4.1** The Owner may request that the Work be performed in such a manner as to become Substantially Complete prior to the date of Substantial Completion in the Agreement. Upon such request the Contractor shall respond promptly, informing the Owner of what measures could be employed to achieve early completion. Adjustment to the Contract Sum for early completion will be based solely on the added costs to the Contractor with no allowance for overhead and profit.

ARTICLE 11 - INSURANCE AND BONDS

11.1 CONTRACTOR'S LIABILITY INSURANCE

Replace Subparagraph 11.1.2

> **11.1.2** The insurance required by Subparagraph 11.1.1 shall be written for not less than the limits of liability specified or that required by law, whichever is greater. Coverages must be written on an occurrence basis and shall be maintained without interruption from the date of the commencement of the Work until the date of final payment and the termination of those coverages required to be maintained after the final payment.

Add Clauses 11.1.2.1 through 11.1.2.3

11.1.2.1 Entities performing work at the site who are exempt from any statutory coverages shall maintain voluntary coverages.

11.1.2.2 Insurance shall include all major divisions of coverage and be on a comprehensive basis including:

.1 Premises Operations, including explosion, collapse, underground damage and elevator.

.2 Independent Contractors' Protective.

.3 Products and Completed Operations, maintained for two years after Final Payment.

.4 Personal Injury, with Employment Exclusion deleted.

.5 Contractual, including those required by "Indemnification," Paragraph 3.18.

.6 Motor Vehicles, including owned, non-owned, and hired.

.7 Broad Form Property Damage, including Completed Operations.

.8 Incidental Medical Malpractice.

.9 Workers' Compensation, including Employer's Liability. Extend coverage to Longshoremen and Harbor Workers, if employed in the performance of this Agreement.

.10 Aircraft and Watercraft, including owned, non-owned, and hired if used in the performance of this Agreement.

.11 Owner's Protective Liability, as identified in Paragraph 11.2.1.

.12 Property Insurance, as identified in Paragraph 11.3.1.4.

11.1.2.3 The specified limits of liability insurance are:

.1 Workers' Compensation

.1 State statutory requirement.

.2 Employer's Liability: $100,000.

.2 General Liability:

.1 Bodily Injury: $1,000,000 each occurrence and aggregate.

.2 Property Damage: $500,000 each occurrence and aggregate.

.3 Coverages provided by a Commercial Liability Policy shall have the aggregate of not less than $1,000,000, and it shall apply solely to this Project.

.3 Auto Liability:

.1 Bodily Injury: $500,000 each person/$1,000,000 each occurrence.

.2 Property Damage: $250,000 each occurrence.

.4 Excess Liability: $5,000,000 per occurrence, over primary, in umbrella form.

Add Clause 11.1.3.1

11.1.3.1 Insurance written on the Comprehensive General Liability policy form shall use AIA Document G705, Certificate of Insurance. Insurance written on a Commercial General Liability policy form shall use ACORD form 25S.

11.2 OWNER'S LIABILITY INSURANCE

Replace 11.2.1

11.2.1 The Owner shall be responsible for purchasing and maintaining the Owner's usual liability insurance. The Contractor is to purchase and maintain other insurance, Owner's Protective Liability, to protect the Owner against claims that may arise from operations under this Agreement.

11.3 PROPERTY INSURANCE

Replace Clause 11.3.1.4

11.3.1.4 The Contractor shall provide insurance coverage for portions of the work in transit and portions stored off the site.

END OF DOCUMENT 00800

SECTION 01010 - SUMMARY OF WORK

PART 1 GENERAL

1.1 Summary

Project title: Offices for Anderson Caldwell & Associates, Attorneys at Law.

Project location: Fourth floor, Fisk Building, 1400 Tenth Avenue, Pittsburgh, PA 15233.

Project consists of interior finishing of existing vacant office space. Major systems include architectural, plumbing, fire protection, HVAC, and electrical work.

1.2 Codes

Code governing project work: BOCA 1993 with amendments as adopted by the City of Pittsburgh.

Occupancy: Use group B

Construction type: 1

1.3 Schedule

Work shall commence within ten (10) days of the Owner's written Notice to Proceed and the project shall be substantially completed within 120 calendar days thereafter.

PART 2 PRODUCTS (Not Applicable)

PART 3 EXECUTION (Not Applicable)

END OF SECTION 01010

SECTION 01020 - ALLOWANCES

PART 1 GENERAL

1.1 Summary

Include all costs related to specified lump sum allowances and unit price allowances in the project cost. Allowance and unit price amounts are for materials only. Include installation costs in the stipulated sum.

1.2 Lump Sum Allowance

Include a lump sum allowance of $5,000 for the selection of finish hardware. Refer to Section 08710.

1.3 Unit Price Allowance

Include a unit price allowance of $28 per square yard for the selection of carpet. Refer to Section 09690.

PART 2 PRODUCTS (Not Applicable)

PART 3 EXECUTION (Not Applicable)

END OF SECTION 01020

SECTION 01027 - APPLICATIONS FOR PAYMENT

PART 1 GENERAL

1.1 Summary

Follow procedures established in the Contract and as specified herein in the preparation of Applications for Payment.

1.2 Schedule of Values

Prepare and submit to the Designer a Schedule of Values not less than ten (10) days prior to the submittal of the initial Application for Payment.

Arrange schedule in tabular form to indicate units of work related to specification sections. Indicate the dollar amount of each unit of work, including its prorated share of overhead and profit and its percentage of the Contract sum.

1.3 Applications for Payment

Form: AIA document G702 and Continuation Sheet G703. Computer-generated continuation sheet may be used.

Payment dates are established in the Agreement. Submit Applications for Payment corresponding to established periods.

Each application shall be consistent with previous applications and approved Schedule of Values.

Submit three (3) fully executed copies to the Designer for certification within five (5) days of the end of the period covered.

Complete all required Contract closeout procedures prior to submitting final Application for Payment.

PART 2 PRODUCTS (Not Applicable)

PART 3 EXECUTION (Not Applicable)

END OF SECTION 01027

SECTION 01040 - COORDINATION

PART 1 GENERAL

1.1 Summary

Provide project coordination and general supervision as specified herein.

1.2 Project Coordination

The General Contractor shall arrange and schedule all work and shall assume the responsibility to coordinate the work of his subcontractors.

Each subcontractor shall be thoroughly familiar with all provisions governing the work of other contractors and shall obtain from such contractors all information as may be required to coordinate work with theirs.

Where items are to be furnished by one contractor and installed by another or installed by one and connected by another, careful coordination shall be maintained so that such items are installed properly.

1.3 Job Site Administration

The Contractor shall provide continuous supervision of all work by a competent superintendent acceptable to the Owner and the Designer, and shall continue in that capacity for the duration of the contract unless employment is terminated.

The Contractor shall, at all times, enforce good order and conduct among his employees.

1.4 Field Conditions

Before ordering material or commencing work, the Contractor shall check and verify all dimensions and conditions. Notify the Designer of any omissions or discrepancies at once.

Field measurements shall be furnished in a timely manner to suppliers and/or fabricators who require them to complete their work. The Contractor shall ascertain the requirement for such measurements at the earliest practical date and shall make every reasonable effort to expedite the affected work.

<u>1.5 Conflicts</u>

The Designer and his consultants have exercised reasonable professional care to ensure that there are no conflicts between the work of the various trades. Such conflicts, however, may exist and no warranty to the contrary is made or implied.

<u>PART 2 PRODUCTS</u> (Not Applicable)

<u>PART 3 EXECUTION</u> (Not Applicable)

END OF SECTION 01040

SECTION 01045 - CUTTING AND PATCHING

PART 1 GENERAL

1.1 Summary

Provide necessary labor and equipment to execute required cutting and patching in manner specified.

PART 2 PRODUCT (Not Applicable)

PART 3 EXECUTION

3.1 Execution of Cutting and Patching

Do not endanger the stability or integrity of any structural part by cutting or drilling without the Designer's approval of both the operation and the intended method to rectify any damage.

Patching shall be done using the material and trade involved in providing the original finish. The mechanics of one trade shall not attempt to patch the work of another.

All patching shall restore the specific location to its original appearance and shall match adjacent finish.

END OF SECTION 01045

SECTION 01200 - PROJECT MEETINGS

PART 1 GENERAL

1.1 Preconstruction Conference

Either before or soon after the actual award of contract, at a time and place designated by the Designer, a preconstruction conference shall be held.

A representative of the Owner, the Designer, and the General Contractor, along with each subcontractor whose portion of the work represents ten percent (10%) of the contract, shall attend.

The purpose of the conference shall be to acquaint the participants with the methods of contract administration and specific requirements under which the construction operation is to proceed.

1.2 Progress Meeting

At weekly intervals throughout the course of the work there shall be progress meetings for the purpose of reviewing and promoting the progress of the work.

A representative of the Owner, the Designer, the Contractor, and each subcontractor currently engaged on the work shall attend. Material suppliers and others may be invited to attend those meetings in which their aspects of the work are involved.

1.3 Attendance

To the maximum extent possible, assign the same person or persons to represent the Contractor and subcontractors at all meetings throughout the construction period.

Persons designated by any participant to attend and participate in project meetings shall have the authority to act in the participant's behalf and to make commitments relative to actions taken.

1.4 Agenda Items

Meeting discussion will be strictly limited to analysis of problems encountered or anticipated in the execution of the work and review of the progress of the project.

The Contractor's relations with his subcontractors and suppliers, and discussions relative thereto, are the Contractor's responsibility and are not part of project meeting content.

1.5 Reports

The Designer will prepare a brief written report of each project meeting prior to the next regularly scheduled meeting.

Reports will be in outline form and will note individuals in attendance, the items discussed, and the agreed upon or directed disposition of such items.

Copies of each report will be distributed to the Owner and the Contractor. The Contractor may make and distribute such additional copies as he wishes.

If any participant disagrees with the conclusions reached in any report or notes discrepancies or omissions therein, the participant shall call such to the attention of the Designer in writing.

PART 2 PRODUCTS (Not Applicable)

PART 3 EXECUTION (Not Applicable)

END OF SECTION 01200

SECTION 01300 - PRODUCTS, SUBMITTALS, AND SUBSTITUTIONS

PART 1 GENERAL

1.1 Summary

This section describes the selection of materials, assemblies, and items of equipment required for the execution of the work, how those items are to be submitted for approval, and the provisions for making substitutions.

1.2 Specified Materials and Equipment

Unless otherwise specifically indicated, all items shall be new, unused, and of the quantities and quality required by the Contract Documents in accordance with the provisions of the General Conditions.

Except as the drawings and specifications are modified by Addenda or Change Order, the Contractor will be held to furnish all work as specified. Substitutions will be allowed only by procedures described herein.

Where the specifications describe or list several items, the Contractor may choose and utilize any of those so described or listed, except that unity shall be maintained throughout the project to facilitate maintenance, repairs, and replacements.

Where the specifications list a single item, that item has been determined to be the only item that fulfills the intent of the documents. Provide only that item unless it can be demonstrated that it cannot be successfully incorporated in the project.

1.3 Substitutions Proposed by Contractor

The Contractor, as hereinafter provided, may propose substitutions for specified items or methods for reasons of economy, durability, availability, or ease of maintenance. Neither the Owner nor the Designer, however, has any obligation to accept such proposals.

All requests for substitution shall include a statement of the reason for such request along with all basic data and characteristics of the proposed item so that a direct comparison can be made. It is the sole responsibility of the Contractor to submit complete descriptive and technical information so that the Designer can make a proper and informed appraisal. The Designer reserves the right to exercise his judgment in making all determinations concerning the merit of the proposed substitution.

If any proposed substitution will or may affect adjacent construction, the work of other trades, or the functioning of a related item, such changes, modifications, or coordination that will or may be required for its proper incorporation into the work shall be considered to be an integral part of the proposed substitution and shall be completely accomplished at no additional cost.

1.4 Substitutions Proposed Before Submission of Bids

Before submission of bids, any bidder may request approval of items other than those specified by submitting a request in writing to the Designer not later than ten (10) days prior to the date set for the opening of bids.

If the proposed substitution is rejected, the bidder submitting the request will be promptly notified.

If the proposed substitution is accepted, all bidders will be notified by Addendum.

1.5 Substitutions Proposed After Award of Contract

After execution of the Contract, substitutions for specified items shall constitute changes in the work and may be proposed only on the condition that the specified item cannot be delivered and incorporated in the work in the time allowed due to conditions beyond the control of the Contractor, or that the manufacturer of the specified item has discontinued its manufacture, or that the Owner will benefit by a reduced cost or in some other material way.

All requests shall be made in writing to the Designer setting forth all pertinent details of the proposed substitution including documentary evidence of the merit of the proposal. State also, if applicable, any proposed changes in contract price or time.

Approved substitutions will be incorporated into the Contract Documents by issuance of a Change Order.

1.6 Approval of Specified Items

Where specified, submit shop drawings, samples, or other data as required for approval.

Shop drawings, specifically prepared for this project, shall be fully reviewed and annotated by the Contractor. Submit one reproducible and one print. Designer will review and return reproducible. Contractor may make as many copies as required for distribution.

Submit product data, samples, and other required documents in sufficient quantity that Designer may retain one copy.

Shop drawings shall show sufficient information to indicate conformance with the Contract Documents. Where submittals contain manufacturer's catalog pages, clearly indicate the precise item(s) submitted for approval.

Incomplete, unclear, or erroneous submissions will be returned without action.

Samples that represent products having a pattern or variation in color or texture shall be large enough to indicate the complete pattern, full range of color, or variation in texture.

Samples for large or cumbersome products may be less than full size provided such samples clearly indicate all salient features of the product they represent.

Where samples, color charts, or other data are submitted for the Designer's review and selection of colors or patterns, it will be assumed, unless specifically noted to the contrary, that all available colors and patterns have identical costs and performance characteristics, and are identically suited to the installation.

1.7 Certificate of Compliance

Where certificates of compliance, affidavits, or other supporting data are required, they shall accompany the submissions of the items for which they apply.

1.8 Method of Submission

Submittals shall be made only through the General Contractor. Material received from subcontractors or suppliers, unless previously authorized by the Designer, will not be considered.

Submissions of any item will be construed as evidence that the Contractor has thoroughly checked the submittal and that the submission represents what the Contractor intends to furnish under the Contract.

1.9 Designer's Review

The Designer will review each submittal promptly for general arrangement and design conformance only.

Action by the Designer shall not relieve the Contractor of full compliance with the terms of the Contract.

Approval of an item shall not be construed as prior acceptance of the item before its incorporation into the work.

The Designer will stamp each submittal clearly indicating its status. Do not use or permit to be used any submittal requiring resubmittal for approval.

When action on one or more submittals is contingent upon receipt of another submittal, each as sub-assemblies of a larger item or system, the Designer may, with notification to the Contractor, withhold action on the submitted item(s) until receipt of associated items.

1.10 Disposition of Submittals

The Contractor shall distribute approved copies of all submittals to the appropriate subcontractors, fabricators, manufacturers, and suppliers.

One copy of each approved shop drawing shall be retained at the project site and shall be available for review by all interested parties.

After approval, samples shall be maintained at the site until completion of the work and shall serve as the standard of quality for similar products incorporated in the work.

With the approval of the Designer, undamaged samples may be built into work after a substantial quantity of the materials they represent has been built in and approved.

PART 2 PRODUCTS (Not Applicable)

PART 3 EXECUTION (Not Applicable)

END OF SECTION 01300

SECTION 01400 - QUALITY CONTROL

PART 1 GENERAL

1.1 Summary

Institute and maintain a quality control program to protect all components of the work.

1.2 Delivery and Handling

All items shall be appropriately packaged, crated, boxed, or otherwise protected to prevent damage during delivery and handling.

All packaged items shall be delivered in their original containers with the manufacturer's labels thereon.

All unpackaged or loose items shall be delivered with the manufacturer's label affixed to the item, or the appropriate association grade stamp thereon, or the supplier's delivery ticket showing the quality of the item and the quantity of the item or lot.

Inspect all items upon receipt. Do not accept items damaged in transit.

1.3 Storage and Protection

Provide and maintain suitable temporary storage facilities either on the project site or at such off-site locations as may be required to adequately protect all items.

Do not store any items in areas that might impede access.

Keep storage areas neat and orderly. Observe all pertinent regulations regarding the storage of flammable materials.

Any item damaged by improper storage shall be rejected and promptly removed from the project site.

1.4 Incorporation into the Work

All items shall be erected, installed, applied, connected, and incorporated into the finished work in strict compliance with all provisions of the Contract Documents, applicable codes and standards, and the recommendations or specifications of the manufacturer.

Do not use damaged items on the work. Remove and replace all items that become damaged by subsequent construction operations.

1.5 Markings

Do not affix name plates or other identifying markings on exposed surfaces of items incorporated in finished spaces.

Only name plates permanently affixed by the manufacturer, or other identifying markings required by the Contract Documents to be placed in concealed locations, will be permitted to remain as part of the finished work.

Removed all temporary markings, protective wrappers, stickers, or tags from all items after they have been inspected and approved.

PART 2 PRODUCTS (Not Applicable)

PART 3 EXECUTION (Not Applicable)

END OF SECTION 01400

SECTION 01500 - CONSTRUCTION FACILITIES AND TEMPORARY CONTROL

PART 1 GENERAL

1.1 Summary

Provide construction facilities and temporary control as specified herein.

1.2 Project Office

During the course of construction, furnish and maintain a temporary office for the use of all authorized persons within the project space.

Furniture shall include a table for the laying out of drawings, files for the storage of project documents, and furniture suitable for the conduct of project meetings.

1.3 Temporary Utilities

Temporary heat, light, power, and water will be available from existing sources at no cost to the Contractor. Provide extension cords, hoses, other devices as may be required.

1.4 Sanitary Facilities

Workers may use existing toilet facilities and the Contractor shall assume responsibility for the maintenance and cleaning thereof. Do not permit the use of toilet facilities in other occupied areas of the building.

1.5 Deliveries

Conform to building management policies concerning scheduling of deliveries, use of loading dock, and use of elevators.

1.6 Temporary Enclosures

Provide, install, and maintain all temporary enclosures, barricades, etc., as required for the proper execution of the work.

Provide dust barriers in finished interior spaces to separate existing work from work under construction. Barriers shall be polyethylene film or other approved material and maintained in such a manner as to fully protect existing finished surfaces and equipment.

PART 2 PRODUCTS (Not Applicable)

PART 3 EXECUTION

3.1 Installation of Protective Facilities

Install temporary barricades, guardrails, handrails, and the like at all openings as required by the scope and magnitude of the work.

The movement of protective facilities, if required for another contractor to perform his work, shall be the responsibility of the contractor requiring the movement and shall include the satisfactory replacement thereof.

3.2 Removal

Maintain all temporary facilities and controls as long as needed for the safe and proper completion of the work. Remove all such temporary facilities and controls as rapidly as the progress of the work will permit.

END OF SECTION 01500

SECTION 01700 - CONTRACT CLOSEOUT

PART 1 GENERAL

1.1 Summary

Notify the Designer when the project is substantially complete and ready for final inspection.

Submit record documents and all other documents enumerated herein.

Correct all deficiencies in the work prior to submitting an Application for Final Payment.

1.2 Final Inspection

At the time of final inspection, submit to the Designer a list of all items that remain incomplete along with the following:
· Operation and maintenance manuals along with all guarantees, warranties, and bonds whether required by the Contracts Documents or issued by various manufacturers for specific products.
· Record documents.
· Legal copies of all certificates attesting to approval of the work by various jurisdictions and code inspectors.
· Keys to all locks to the Owner except for those that may, by mutual agreement, be temporarily retained by the Contractor for the purpose of acquiring access for the correction of deficiencies.

All items found to be in non-compliance or deficient in any respect will be noted and included on a "punch list" prepared by the Designer.

The "punch list" will indicate each deficient item, noting the specific deficiency and the acceptable correction thereof if applicable, and its location. If one or more items is found to be generally deficient throughout the project in several locations, it shall become the Contractor's responsibility to correct such at all locations, whether each is specifically noted or not.

Failure of the Designer or other inspectors to observe deficiencies at the time of final inspection shall not be construed as approval or acceptance of such.

If any item or items cannot be corrected within thirty (30) calendar days due to conditions or circumstances beyond the control of the Contractor, notify the Designer in writing, stating the reason(s) for any delays and the approximate date when such corrections can be made. In such instances, the Designer will estimate the cost of such corrections and that amount shall be withheld from the final payment until the corrections are fully made, approved, and accepted.

1.3 Final Payment: Release of Retainages

Final payment and release of retainages shall be made in accordance with the provisions of the General Conditions and the further conditions of this section.

Application for final payment shall not be submitted until all other documents and submittals required herein have been submitted and approved by the Designer and correction of deficiencies has been made, approved, and accepted.

1.4 Record Documents

One set of drawings and specifications shall be maintained on the project site for the specific purpose of recording changes in the work.

The Designer will furnish one set of reproducible drawings for the purpose of recording changes. Changes to or deviations from the original drawings shall be accurately detailed and dimensioned records rendered by accepted drafting conventions and neatly lettered notes and figures.

Changes in specification requirements shall be neatly written or typed notations documented by reference to Change Orders if applicable.

The Contractor may make copies of record documents for his own use.

1.5 Operation and Maintenance Manuals

Furnish three (3) complete sets of catalog data of the items incorporated in the work requiring maintenance and/or operating instructions.

Data shall include the manufacturers' recommendations and instructions for the proper maintenance and operation of each item of equipment or apparatus furnished under the contract. Where available, include the manufacturer's current replacement parts list and the name and address of the nearest service representative.

Where catalog pages depict or describe more than one item, clearly mark the precise item(s) actually incorporated in the work.

Where a single item is a component part of a larger assembly or system, provide notation and cross reference to other related items.

Manuals shall contain a table of contents, be indexed, and be suitably bound, preferably in hard-back three-ring binders.

1.6 Approval Certificates; Tests

Prior to the final inspection, arrange for all required inspections by other authorities required for the issuance of approval certificates. Arrange and pay for all tests or demonstrations required by such inspectors.

If a temporary or permanent Occupancy Permit is required by law, arrange for inspections by authorities having jurisdiction.

Pay all fees required for inspections.

1.7 Warranties

In addition to warranties mandated by the provisions of the General Conditions, furnish all other extended warranties required under the various sections of the specifications.

All documents shall be properly executed and drawn in the Owner's favor.

PART 2 PRODUCTS (Not Applicable)

PART 3 EXECUTION (Not Applicable)

END OF SECTION 01700

SECTION 02070 - SELECTIVE DEMOLITION

PART 1 GENERAL

1.1 Summary

Demolish existing building components not designated to remain in the finished work.

Protect existing improvements affected by selective demolition.

Remove and legally dispose of demolished materials.

PART 2 PRODUCTS (Not Applicable)

PART 3 EXECUTION

3.1 Demolition

Do not damage building elements and improvements indicated to remain. Items of salvage value must be removed from structure. Storage or sale of items at project site is prohibited.

Do not close or obstruct occupied spaces or facilities without the written permission of the Owner. Do not interrupt utilities serving occupied or used facilities without the written permission of the Owner and authorities having jurisdiction. If necessary, provide temporary utilities.

Cease operations if public safety or remaining improvements are endangered. Perform temporary corrective measures until operations can be continued properly.

END OF SECTION 02070

SECTION 03320 - CONCRETE FLOOR TOPPING

PART 1 GENERAL

1.1 Summary

Provide concrete floor topping over existing concrete slabs to repair and provide level substrate for the application of floor finishes.

1.2 Quality Assurance

Installation of this work shall be by applicator approved by the material manufacturer, using mixing equipment and tools approved by the manufacturer.

1.3 Submittals

Submit product data and test reports for the Designer's review.

PART 2 PRODUCTS

2.1 Materials

Floor topping: Ardex K-15 self-leveling cement topping mix with a minimum compressive strength of 4,000 psi at 28 days. Primer: Ardex P-51.

PART 3 EXECUTION

3.1 Preparation

Clean and prepare surfaces in strict accordance with the manufacturer's instructions.

Prime surfaces following manufacturer's instructions.

3.2 Installation

Mix topping mix in ratios following manufacturer's instructions. Pour and spread topping following manufacturer's recommendations.

Level surfaces to within 1/8" in 10' in any direction.

Cure and protect.

END OF SECTION 03320

SECTION 04270 - GLASS BLOCK

PART 1 GENERAL

1.1 Summary

Provide interior glass block partition.

1.2 Submittals

Submit product data and samples for the Designer's review.

1.3 Storage and Handling

Deliver, handle, and store materials in accordance with the manufacturer's instructions. Reject chipped or damaged units.

PART 2 PRODUCTS

2.1 Materials

Hollow glass block: 8" x 8" x 3-1/2" thinline series, "Delphi" pattern as manufactured by Pittsburgh Corning.

Mortar: Portland cement lime mortar, type S.

Accessories: Expansion strips, panel reinforcing, panel anchors, sealant, and other required accessory materials as manufactured by or approved by the glass block manufacturer.

PART 3 EXECUTION

3.1 Installation

Install materials and systems in accordance with manufacturer's instructions and approved submittals. Install materials and systems in proper relation with adjacent construction and with uniform appearance.

Clean and protect completed work from damage.

END OF SECTION 04270

SECTION 06100 - ROUGH CARPENTRY

PART 1 GENERAL

1.1 Summary

Provide fire retardant treated wood nailers, grounds, blocking, furring, plywood backing panels, and similar members.

1.2 Submittals

Submit certification by treating plant that fire-retardant-treated material complies with standards acceptable to authorities having jurisdiction.

PART 2 PRODUCTS

2.1 Lumber

Lumber: No. 3 Common or Standard boards of any commercially available species.

2.2 Plywood

Plywood backing panels for mounting electrical or telephone equipment: 15/32" APA C-D PLUGGED INT with exterior glue.

PART 3 EXECUTION

3.1 Installation

Work lumber into shapes and dimensions indicated or required using maximum practicable lengths.

Discard material that is cupped, bowed, or has other defects that might impair quality of work.

Securely attach carpentry work to required lines and levels with members plumb and aligned.

Shim as required for tolerance for finished work.

END OF SECTION 06100

SECTION 06200 - FINISH CARPENTRY

PART 1 GENERAL

1.1 Summary

Provide finish carpentry and millwork for interior standing and running trim, door and window frames and casings, and wood shelving.

1.2 Submittals

Submit millwork shop drawings for approval.

1.3 Quality Assurance

Conform to Architectural Woodwork Institute Quality Standards, Premium grade, unless specifically noted otherwise.

PART 2 PRODUCTS

2.1 Materials

All woodwork: Clear white pine.

Shelving: Hardwood or medium density particleboard with hardwood edges.

Mill all trim to clean accurate profiles.

PART 3 EXECUTION

3.1 Installation

Backprime all work before installation.

Install all work plumb, level, straight, and in true alignment.

Scribe, cope, and fit all work to produce tight hairline joints.

Set nails, fill holes, and leave ready for finish painting.

END OF SECTION 06200

SECTION 06400 - ARCHITECTURAL WOODWORK

PART 1 GENERAL

1.1 Summary

Provide shop fabricated wood casework and plastic laminate countertops.

1.2 Submittals

Submit shop drawings for approval.

1.3 Quality Assurance

Conform to Architectural Woodwork Institute Quality Standards, Premium grade, unless noted otherwise.

PART 2 PRODUCTS

2.1 Cabinet Materials

Wood: Rift-sawn red oak for solid wood, rift-cut red oak for plywood.

Casework type: Flush overlay conforming to details shown for profile.

Finish: Catalyzed polyurethane, AWI finish system No. 5, premium grade.

Hardware: Steel or brass with chrome plated finish as selected the Designer; ball bearing side-mounted drawer slides.

2.2 Countertops

Plastic laminate: NEMA LD-3, 0.050" horizontal grade on 45 pound density particleboard.

Type: Integral coved splash and radius self-edge at front lip.

Colors and patterns of laminate: As scheduled or as selected by the Designer.

PART 3   EXECUTION

3.1 Installation

Install work plumb, level, true, and straight. Scribe to fit. Anchor securely with concealed fasteners.

Repair or replace damaged work; clean, lubricate, and adjust hardware; protect work until final acceptance.

END OF SECTION 06400

SECTION 08110 - STEEL DOOR FRAMES

PART 1 GENERAL

1.2 Summary

Provide fire-rated steel door frames.

1.2 Sumittals

Submit for approval shop drawings and product data.

PART 2 PRODUCTS

Frames: Welded construction with mitered corners, 16 gauge, UL labeled, with rust inhibiting primer compatible with paint finish specified.

Fabricate frames to be rigid, free from defects and exposed fasteners.

Secure finish hardware templates and accurately install, or make provision for, finish hardware at the factory.

Provide three silencers on each frame.

PART 3 EXECUTION

3.1 Installation

Install frames plumb, rigid, and in true alignment.

Anchor securely so that frames retain their position and clearance.

Sand smooth rusted or damaged areas of primer and apply touch-up primer; leave ready for hanging of doors and finish painting of frames.

END OF SECTION 08110

SECTION 08210 - FLUSH WOOD DOORS

PART 1   GENERAL

1.1 Summary

Provide solid core factory-finished flush wood doors premachined for fitting of selected hardware.

1.2 Submittals

Submit product data for approval.

Submit two samples indicating specified factory finish. Prepare samples on panels of actual material large enough to indicate full range of grain pattern and finish characteristics.

1.3 Quality Assurance

Comply with "Architectural Woodwork Quality Standards" of the Architectural Woodwork Institute for grade of door, core construction, and finish.

For fire-rated doors provide units identical to units tested in assemblies which are labeled and listed for ratings of testing and inspection agency acceptable to authorize having jurisdiction.

1.4 Handling

Deliver prefinished doors in manufacturer's original packaging.

PART 2   PRODUCTS

2.1 Materials

Flush wood doors: Sizes as indicated on door schedule and as follows:

Faces: Red Oak, plain sliced.

AWI Grade: Premium

Construction: PC-4 or PC-7.

2.2 Fabrication

Factory prefit and premachine doors to fit frame opening sizes with uniform clearances and bevels.

Obtain hardware schedule and templates. Machine doors to conform.

For doors to be installed in metal frames, coordinate hardware mortises in frames to verify dimensions and alignment.

2.3 Factory Finishing

Comply with following:

AWI Grade: Premium.

Finish: Manufacturer's standard finish comparable to AWI System #2 catalyzed lacquer or AWI System #3 alkyd urea conversion varnish.

Staining: None required.

Effect: Filled finish.

Sheen: Satin medium rubbed.

PART 3   EXECUTION

3.1 Surface Conditions

Prior to installation of wood doors, carefully inspect the installed work of all other trades and verify that all such work is complete.

Install doors after completion of all other work that would raise the moisture content of wood doors or damage door surfaces.

3.2 Installation

Fit, hang, and trim all doors so that they hang square, plumb, straight with required clearances, and firmly anchored into position.

Adjust all hardware as required so that doors operate easily, close, and latch without binding.

END OF SECTION 08210

SECTION 08450 - GLASS DOORS AND SIDELIGHTS

PART 1 GENERAL

1.1 Summary

Provide tempered glass doors and sidelights.

1.2 Submittals

Submit shop drawings and product data for approval.

Submit samples of glass and exposed metal finishes.

1.3 Quality Assurance

Provide doors, sidelights, and hardware produced by a single manufacturer.

All work shall be installed by an experienced installer approved by the manufacturer.

PART 2 PRODUCTS

2.1 Acceptable Manufacturers

Provide complete assembly of Ellison Bronze Company, Falconer Glass Industries, PPG Industries, or Virginia Glass Products Corporation.

2.2 Glass

Provide 1/2" thick, clear tempered safety glass complying with ASTM C-1048.

2.3 Fittings

Provide approved manufacturer's standard fittings and hardware with all exposed metal polished chrome finish.

Hardware: Manufacturer's heavy-duty type, including overhead concealed holder with dead-stop setting, push-pull handles, deadbolt locks to accept cylinder keyed to other locks, and mill-finish extruded bronze threshold.

Where manufacturer offers option in design of any accessory, design shall be as selected by the Designer.

2.4 Fabrication

Take accurate field measurements before fabrication. Show measurements on shop drawings to ensure proper fitting.

Fabricate work to accommodate fittings and hardware.

Do not cut, drill, or alter glass in any way after tempering.

PART 3   EXECUTION

3.1 Installation

Install doors and sidelights in strict accordance with the manufacturer's printed instructions and recommendations.

Set units level, plumb, and in true alignment.

Adjust hardware to achieve proper operation.

3.2 Cleaning

At completion of installation clean and polish glass and metal surfaces. Protect completed installation from damage as required.

END OF SECTION 08450

SECTION 08710 - FINISH HARDWARE

PART 1   GENERAL

1.1 Summary

Provide and install finish hardware.

Refer to Section 01020 - Allowances.

1.2 Submittals

Submit for approval product data, hardware schedule, and material invoices.

PART 2   PRODUCTS

2.1 Hardware Allowance

The Contractor shall include in his contract a lump sum allowance of $5,000 for the furnishing of all hardware not covered by other trades.

The Owner and the Designer reserve the right to select and/or approve all hardware.

If the cost of the selected and approved hardware including applicable sales taxes and delivery charges exceeds the stated allowance, the Owner will pay the difference under a properly executed Change Order. If the cost of the hardware is less than the stated allowance, the difference shall be credited to the Contract.

On receipt of the hardware, the Contractor shall accept the material, store it securely, and be responsible for its distribution and installation.

2.2 Materials

Hinges, butts, and pivots: Full-mortise, 5 knuckle ball-bearing type; Stanley or approved equal.

Locksets and latchsets: Sargent 8100 series, Schlage D series or approved equal.

Lock cylinders and keying: Interchangeable-core pin tumbler lock cylinders and nickel silver keys.

Exit devices: Sargent 80 Series, Von Duprin or approved equal.

Stops: Ives or approved equal.

Closet and shelving hardware: Knape and Vogt or approved equal.

Finish: US 26D, Satin chrome.

PART 3 EXECUTION

3.1 Installation

For the Contractor's guidance in estimating his cost of installation, the hardware requirements generally will be as follows:

All doors shall be butt hung, three (3) hinges per door.

Locksets shall all be cylindrical or tubular type with lever handles.

Closers shall be modern surface-mounted type with painted plastic covers.

Door holders and stops shall be surface applied to floor or wall.

Hardware for glass doors shall be supplied and installed by the door manufacturer.

Stockpile all items sufficiently in advance to ensure their availability and make all necessary deliveries in a timely manner to ensure orderly progress of the total work.

Employ only skilled mechanics to install all hardware.

Adjust all hardware so that it operates smoothly and properly.

Clean, polish, and oil hardware; leave in first class working order.

3.2 Schedule

The following schedule is intended only as a guide in establishing the type and function of hardware required for each opening and is not to be construed as all inclusive or comprehensive.

Hardware Set #1
    1-1/2 Pair Butts
    1 Lockset
    1 Closer

Hardware Set #2
    1 Stop
    1-1/2 Pair Butts
    1 Exit Device
    1 Closer

Hardware Set #3
    1-1/2 Pair Butts
    1 Lockset
    1 Stop

Hardware Set #4
    1-1/2 Pair Butts
    1 Privacy Lock
    1 Closer
    1 Stop

Hardware Set #5
    1-1/2 Pair Butts
    1 Latchset
    1 Stop

END OF SECTION 08710

SECTION 08800 - GLASS AND GLAZING

PART 1 GENERAL

1.1 Summary

Provide interior glazing.

1.2 Submittals

Submit product data for approval.

PART 2 PRODUCTS

2.1 Glass Products

Glass: 1/4" clear float glass and 1/4" tempered safety glass where indicated or required.

2.2 Accessory Products

Acrylic glazing sealant; Tremco Mono or approved equal.

Preformed glazing tape; Tremco Polyshim Tape or approved equal.

Setting blocks, shims, and spacers as required.

PART 3 EXECUTION

3.1 Installation

Inspect framing and rectify unsatisfactory conditions.

Comply with FGMA "Glazing Manual" and manufacturers instructions and recommendations. Use manufacturer's recommended accessories.

Install glass with uniformity of pattern, draw, bow and roller marks.

Remove and replace damaged glass and glazing. Wash, polish and protect all glass.

END OF SECTION 08800

SECTION 09250 - GYPSUM DRYWALL

PART 1 GENERAL

1.1 Summary

Provide metal framing and gypsum drywall work.

1.2 Submittals

Submit product data for approval.

PART 2 PRODUCTS

2.1 Framing Materials

Steel studs: 3-5/8" 25 gauge screw type.

Ceiling suspension system: Approved manufacturer's standard grid comprised of runner channels and hat-shaped furring channels.

2.2 Gypsum Boards

Gypsum drywall panels: 5/8" thick regular and fire-rated types, tapered edges.

Backer board at ceramic tile: USG "Durock" glass mesh reinforced Portland Cement backer board.

Joint reinforcement: Paper tape and ready-mixed vinyl compound as manufactured by the gypsum board manufacturer.

Accessories: Galvanized steel corner beads and casing beads as indicated.

2.3 Other Materials

Acoustical insulation: Fiberglass batts cut to fill stud cavity.

Acoustical sealant: As manufactured by U.S. Gypsum or approved equal.

PART 3 EXECUTION

3.1 Installation

Comply with ASTM C 587 and manufacturer's instructions.

Extend fire-rated and sound control partitions to underside of structure above.

Extend other partitions at least 3" above finished ceilings and securely brace to structure above.

Verify that blocking for casework and accessories is in place before installing panels.

Provide fire-rated systems where indicated or where required by authorities.

Install boards vertically. Do not permit joints of cut edges to tapered edges, butt to butt joints, and joints that do not fall over framing members.

Install trim and joint treatment in strict compliance with the manufacturer's instructions.

Tolerances: Not more than 1/16" difference in true plane at joints between boards before finishing and not more than 1/8" in 10' deviation from true plane and plumb in finished surfaces.

After finishing joints shall be invisible. Sand and leave ready for finish painting.

END OF SECTION 09250

SECTION 09330 - TILE

PART 1 GENERAL

1.1 Summary

Provide ceramic tile work.

1.2 Submittals

Submit product data and samples for approval.

PART 2 PRODUCTS

2.1 Tile Materials

Glazed wall tile, unglazed ceramic mosaic floor tile and cove base, and glazed vitreous pavers: as indicated in finish schedule.

Trim: Match field tile color, size, and finish.

2.2 Mortars and Grout

Setting mortar: Latex Portland Cement type.

Grout: Latex Portland Cement in color selected by the Designer.

2.3 Other Materials

Thresholds: White marble.

Setting bed reinforcing: 2" x 2" 16/16 welded wire fabric.

Shower pan: 16 oz. lead coated copper.

Sealant: Silicone type in color selected by Designer.

PART 3 EXECUTION

3.1 Installation Methods

Tile floor in shower: Reinforced mortar setting bed over shower pan.

Tile floors and walls at all other locations: Adhesive thin set.

3.2 Installation

Comply with manufacturer's instructions and recommendations, and with Tile Council of America and ANSI Standard Specifications for Installation.

Lay tile in grid pattern with alignment of floor, base, walls and trim grids.

Lay out to provide uniform joint widths and to minimize cutting; do not use less than 1/2 tile units.

Accurately and neatly form intersections and returns. Cut and drill tile where required without damaging visible surfaces.

Fit tile closely to penetrations so that covers and flanges cover cut edges.

Provide sealant joints where recommended by TCA and approved by Designer.

Grout and cure, clean and protect.

END OF SECTION 09330

SECTION 09510 - ACOUSTIC PANEL CEILINGS

PART 1   GENERAL

1.1 Summary

Provide acoustic panel ceiling with exposed suspension system.

1.2 Quality Assurance

Obtain each type of product specified from a single manufacturer.

1.3 Submittals

Submit product data for specified products.

Submit the following samples:
- Two (2) 6-inch square samples of each type of acoustic panel and/or pattern.
- Two (2) 12-inch long samples of each type of exposed suspension system.

1.4 Extra Materials

Furnish quantity of full size acoustic panels equal to three percent (3%) of quantity installed. Package with protective covering, tag, and deliver to Owner's designated storage space.

PART 2 PRODUCTS

2.1 Acoustic Panels

Acoustic panel size, type, and design: As indicated in finish schedule.

2.2 Suspension System and Accessories

Provide a complete system of supporting members, anchors, wall angles, and accessories of every type required for a complete suspended tee grid system as indicated on the drawings.

Exposed grid: Armstrong "Prelude" exposed tee grid. Color: White.

Face dimension of exposed members: 15/16".

Where indicated or required by governing codes, provide suspension system components with appropriate fire rating classification.

Hanger wire: 12 gauge (minimum) galvanized carbon steel wire.

2.3 Other Materials

Provide non-hardening, non-skinning, non-staining acoustical sealant where indicated.

Provide hold-down clips as manufactured by the panel manufacturer where indicated.

Provide other materials required for a complete and satisfactory installation as selected by the Contractor, subject to the approval of the Designer.

PART 3 EXECUTION

3.1 Coordination

Carefully coordinate with other trades to accommodate installation of sprinklers, HVAC grilles, registers, diffusers, lighting fixtures, and other items penetrating acoustic panel ceilings.

3.2 Layout

Lay out all work in accordance with reflected ceiling plans.

Unless indicated otherwise, lay out acoustic units to balance border widths at opposite sides of each ceiling space and in a manner to avoid less than half-width units at borders.

3.3 Installation

Install acoustic ceiling systems in strict accordance with the approved manufacturer's installation instructions.

Suspend hangers from building structural members and anchor securely.

Where ceiling cavity obstructions interfere with location of hangers, install supplemental suspension members sized and braced to support loads.

Install all grid level and straight within a tolerance of 1/8" in 10 feet.

At sound control partitions and other indicated locations, set wall angles and adjacent acoustic panels in continuous beads of acoustical sealant.

Install acoustic panels with edges concealed by suspension members. Scribe and cut panels to fit neatly at borders and penetrations.

For directionally patterned units, install all panels with pattern in the same direction.

Comply with all requirements of governing codes for fire-rated systems.

3.4 Cleanup

Clean all exposed surfaces immediately upon completion of installation.

Touch up minor finish damage in conformance with manufacturer's instructions.

Remove and replace work that cannot be successfully cleaned or repaired.

END OF SECTION 09510

SECTION 09550 - WOOD FLOORING

PART 1 GENERAL

1.1 Summary

Provide solid prefinished wood parquet flooring.

1.2 Submittals

Submit product data and samples for approval.

PART 2 PRODUCTS

2.1 Wood Flooring

Hardwood parquet flooring: As indicated in finish schedule.

2.2 Adhesives

Adhesives for parquet flooring: As recommended by the manufacturer.

PART 3 EXECUTION

3.1 Layout

Lay out all work about space centerlines to produce equal spaces at edges. Avoid cuts that produce cut pieces less than 1/2 tile unit.

3.2 Installation

Install materials in strict accordance with the manufacturer's printed instructions and approved submittals.

Install material with uniform appearance and in proper relation to adjacent finishes.

3.3 Cleanup

Clean and protect work from damage. Restore damaged finishes.

END OF SECTION 09550

SECTION 09650 - RESILIENT FLOORING

PART 1 GENERAL

1.1 Summary

Provide resilient flooring and base.

1.2 Quality Assurance

Each type of resilient flooring and accessories shall be produced by a single manufacturer, including primers and adhesives.

1.3 Submittals

Submit samples of specified materials for Designer's verification.

1.4 Extra Materials

Furnish quantity of full-size tile units equal to three percent (3%) of amount installed for each type, color, and pattern. Material shall be set aside from actual cartons used on the project.

Package extra materials, tag, and deliver to Owner's designated storage space.

PART 2 PRODUCTS

2.1 Resilient Tile and Base

Resilient tile and base: As indicated in finish schedule.

Tile: Vinyl composition tile, 12" x 12" x 1/8", asbestos free.

Base: 4" high x 1/8" gauge, matte finish vinyl, standard top-set cove.

2.2 Accessories

Resilient edge strips: 1/8" thick vinyl, tapered edge, color to match flooring or as selected by the Designer from manufacturer's standard colors.

2.3 Other Materials

Adhesives: Waterproof type as recommended by the flooring manufacturer to suit material and substrate conditions.

Provide other materials including slab primer, if required, and leveling and patching compounds as recommended by the flooring manufacturer.

PART 3 EXECUTION

3.1 Preparation

Thoroughly clean substrate. Remove coatings that might prevent or reduce adhesive bond.

Fill small cracks, holes, and depressions with leveling and patching compound.

3.2 Installation

Install all work in strict accordance with manufacturer's printed instructions.

Lay tile from centerlines of space with tile at opposite edges of equal width. Adjust to avoid use of cut widths less than 1/2 tile.

Where borders, feature strips, or other patterns are indicated, lay out work prior to installation required to produce indicated pattern.

Use tile from cartons in same sequence as manufactured and packaged if so numbered.

Scribe, cut, and fit tiles neatly. Fit tightly to permanent fixtures and floor penetrations. Extend into recesses, closets and similar openings.

Lay tile with grain running in one direction.

Apply base to walls, columns, pilasters, casework, and other permanent fixtures in lengths as long as practicable. Tightly bond to substrate with continuous contact at each length.

At edges of flooring that would otherwise be exposed, place resilient edge strips tightly butted to flooring.

3.3 Cleaning and Protection

Clean all resilient flooring thoroughly using only products and methods specifically recommended by the flooring manufacturer.

Protect completed work from damage. Cover and prevent access to floors if required.

END OF SECTION 09650

SECTION 09680 - CARPETING

PART 1 GENERAL

1.1 Summary

Provide carpet under allowance and installation.

Refer to Section 01020 - Allowances.

1.2 Submittals

Submit for approval samples, product data, warranty, maintenance data, extra stock, material invoices, and delivery slips to show actual quantities of material delivered to the site in fulfillment of allowance.

PART 2 PRODUCTS

2.1 Allowance

Include a unit cost of $28.00 per square yard for the purchase of carpet to be selected by the Owner and the Designer. All carpet shall be the manufacturer's first quality from the same dye lot.

Allowance shall include quantity of carpet actually installed plus a quantity for   normal waste plus 5% extra stock for Owner's use.

If selection of carpet exceeds unit cost allowance, Owner will pay difference. If selection is less than unit cost allowance, the difference will be credited to the Contract.

Allowance includes carpet material only. Specified pad, accessories, installation, overhead, and profit shall be included in the Contractor's stipulated sum and not subject to any adjustment based on selected carpet.

2.2 Carpet Pad

Pad: 64 oz. flat sponge rubber, nominal 0.25 inch thick.

2.3 Accessories

Seaming cement: Type specifically recommended by the carpet manufacturer for butting cut edges at backing to form secure seams.

Carpet stripping: Type designed to grip and hold stretched carpet at backing, thickness to match pad.

Edge guard: Aluminum in color and finish as selected by Designer from manufacturer's standards.

PART 3 EXECUTION

3.1 Preparation

Inspect substrates for detrimental conditions. Beginning work means acceptance of substrate.

Prepare floors, install using method as recommended by carpet manufacturer.

3.2 Installation

Install all materials in strict accordance with the manufacturer's instructions.

Maintain uniformity of carpet direction and lay of pile. Center seams under doors in closed position.

Install carpet stripping securely. Locate to conceal carpet edge between stripping and base of wall.

Install pad seams at 90-degree angle with carpet seams. Place cushion face up as recommended by cushion manufacturer. Apply minimum 2-inch fabric-type adhesive tape on cushion seams.

Install carpet by trimming edges, butting cuts with seaming cement, and taping and/or sewing seams to provide sufficient strength for stretching and continued stresses during life of carpet.

Stretch carpet to provide smooth, ripple-free, taut, trim edges; secure to stripping and conceal behind edge of stripping.

3.3 Cleaning

Remove and dispose of debris and unusable scraps.

Remove spots from carpet surface using only products and methods recommended by the manufacturer.

Vacuum carpet and remove any protruding face yarns with sharp scissors.

END OF SECTION 09680

SECTION 09990 - PAINTING

PART 1 GENERAL

1.1 Summary

Provide surface preparation and painting for all unfinished surfaces.

1.2 Submittals

Submit product data and color charts for all specified products.

1.3 Extra Stock

Provide a minimum of one gallon of each color of finish coat applied. Clearly label and deliver to Owner's designated storage space.

PART 2 PRODUCTS

2.1 Paint Products

Paint: As indicated in the finish schedule. Colors indicated are those of PPG or Sherwin-Williams. Standard first quality products of other reputable manufacturers will be acceptable if approved by the Designer. Match specified colors.

2.2 Paint Systems

Drywall: Latex primer, two (2) coats acrylic latex, eggshell finish.

Drywall to receive wallcovering: One (1) coat latex primer.

Wood for opaque finish: Alkyd enamel undercoater, two (2) coats alkyd enamel finish.

Wood for transparent finish: Oil stain, sanding sealer, two (2) coats alkyd varnish finish.

Ferrous metal: Alkyd metal primer, two (2) coats alkyd enamel finish.

PART 3 EXECUTION

3.1 Preparation

Comply with manufacturer's recommendations for preparation and priming.

Rectify any unsatisfactory conditions as required.

3.2 Application

Comply with manufacturer's recommendations for the application of all material.

Before applying finish coats complete one space to serve as a mock-up of subsequent work. Obtain Designer's approval.

Match approved mock-up for color, texture, and coverage. Recoat work that does not match.

At completion clean up, touch up damaged surfaces, and protect work.

END OF SECTION 09990

SECTION 09950 - WALL COVERINGS

PART 1 GENERAL

1.1 Summary

Provide wall covering work.

1.2 Submittals

Submit product data for each type of product specified.

Submit samples of each type, color, texture, and pattern of wall covering specified. Samples: Full width long enough to indicate complete pattern repeat.

1.3 Extra Stock

Furnish quantity of full rolls equal to five percent (5%) of amount installed for each product used. Extra stock: Same production runs as product installed.

Wrap with protective covering, label, and deliver to Owner's designated storage space.

PART 2 PRODUCTS

2.1 Materials

Wall coverings: As indicated in finish schedule.

Adhesives: Manufacturer's standard mildew-resistant, nonstaining, and strippable adhesive formulated for use with specific wall covering and substrate.

PART 3   EXECUTION

3.1 Preparation

Follow manufacturer's printed instructions for surface preparation.

Acclimatize materials by removing them from packaging in areas of installation 24 hours before installation.

3.2 Installation

Follow manufacturer's printed instructions for installation.

Install wall coverings with no gaps or overlaps. Butt seams.

Match pattern six (6) feet above finish floor.

Install seams vertical and plumb at least six (6) inches from outside corners and three (3) inches from inside corners. No horizontal seams.

Remove air bubbles, wrinkles, blisters, and other defects.

Trim edges for color uniformity, pattern match, and tight closure at seams and edges.

3.3 Cleaning

Remove excess adhesive at finished seams, perimeter edges, and adjacent surfaces.

Use cleaning methods recommended by the wall covering manufacturer.

Replace strips that cannot be cleaned.

END OF SECTION 09950

SECTION 10520 - FIRE EXTINGUISHER CABINET

PART 1 GENERAL

1.1 Summary

Provide fire extinguisher cabinet indicated.

1.2 Submittals

Submit for approval product data, roughing in dimensions, and details indicating mounting methods and relationship to adjacent materials and finishes.

1.3 Quality Assurance

Conform to applicable code requirements.

Verify that fire extinguisher cabinet is of size to accommodate fire extinguisher indicated to be provided by Owner.

PART 2 PRODUCTS

2.1 Cabinet

Fire extinguisher cabinet: Semi-recessed, clear acrylic revolving turntable door, square stainless steel trim, similar to one of the following:
- J.L. Industries, "Clear Vu" series, model 2535
- Larsen Manufacturing Co., "Rota" series, model R-2409
- Potter-Roemer Co., "Loma" series, model 7365-BA

2.2 Identification

Provide approved manufacturer's standard diecut vinyl or silk screened lettering on cabinet door. Color: Red.

PART 3 EXECUTION

3.1 Surface Conditions

Examine areas and conditions under which work of this Section will be performed.

Verify that rough opening is of required dimensions and that blocking is in place. Correct conditions detrimental to proper installation of cabinet.

3.2 Installations

Coordinate with other trades to assure proper installation and finishing of adjacent surfaces.

Install fire extinguisher cabinet in strict compliance with the manufacturer's recommended installation procedures and in accordance with approved submittals.

Anchor all components securely using only hardware furnished by the manufacturer.

Clean and protect completed installation.

END OF SECTION 10520

SECTION 10800 - TOILET ACCESSORIES

PART 1 GENERAL

1.1 Summary

Provide toilet accessories at private toilet rooms.

1.2 Submittals

Submit product data and schedule of accessories for the Designer's review.

PART 2 PRODUCTS

2.1 Acceptable Products

Where products are specified by manufacturer and model number, that designation is to establish a standard of quality. Similar products by other reputable manufacturers may be submitted for the Designer's review.

2.2 Accessories

Toilet tissue dispenser: HallMack HM-675, one per toilet.

Soap dispenser: Deck-mounted push-type valve with 16 oz. capacity for dispensing liquid soap, one per lavatory.

Bath cabinets: NuTone 268R, one per toilet room mounted over lavatory.

Towel bars: HallMack HM-695-24, one per toilet room.

Shower curtain rod: 1-1/4" diameter heavy duty stainless steel.

Folding shower seat: American Standard R5010. Color: White.

Grab bars: HallMack HM-352-32, located in shower stall as indicated.

Finish for all accessories: Chrome-plated or polished stainless steel.

2.3 Mounting

Toilet accessories shall be recessed or surface mounted as required for specific accessory.

Locate accessories as directed by the Designer or as mandated by provisions of ADA standards.

PART 3 EXECUTION

3.1 Installation

Before commencing installation, verify that required blocking is in place.

Install accessories in accordance with the manufacturer's instructions using only hardware furnished by the manufacturer.

Clean and protect work from damage.

Remove damaged items and replace.

END OF SECTION 10800

SECTION 11132 - PROJECTION SCREEN

PART 1 GENERAL

1.1 Summary

Provide automatic electrically-operated projection screen.

1.2 Submittals

Submit for approval product data, including wiring diagrams to be furnished to electrical subcontractor.

PART 2 PRODUCTS

2.1 Projection Screen

Screen: Da-Lite "Boardroom Electrol," 70" x 70", glass beaded without borders, for recessed above-ceiling mounting in accordance with manufacturer's method "A" mounting.

PART 3 EXECUTION

3.1 Coordination

Coordinate electrical requirements.

3.2 Installation

Install screen according to manufacturer's written instructions.

Permanently support screen by anchoring screen case firmly to substrate.

Wire screen motor according to manufacturer's written instructions.

Adjust to operate properly.

END OF SECTION 11132

SECTION 11450 - APPLIANCES

PART 1 GENERAL

1.1 Summary

Provide built-in appliances indicated.

1.2 Submittals

Submit for approval manufacturer's product data.

PART 2 PRODUCTS

2.1 Appliances

Undercounter refrigerator: Sub-Zero model 249RP.

Undercounter dishwasher: General Electric model GSD2930TWW.

Hot water dispenser: KitchenAid "Instant-Hot" model KHWS160.

2.2 Trim Kits

Provide manufacturer's standard trim kits as required to face appliance doors with panels to match cabinets.

PART 3 EXECUTION

3.1 Installation

Install appliances plumb, level and true in strict accordance with the manufacturer's installation instructions. Include all required connections and components required for proper operation.

3.2 Testing

Test appliances after installation for proper functioning. Leave in proper order, cleaned and ready for Owner's use.

END OF SECTION 11450

SECTION 12500 - WINDOW TREATMENT

PART 1 GENERAL

1.1 Summary

Provide horizontal and vertical blinds as scheduled.

1.2 Submittals

Submit for approval samples and product data.

Prior to installation, prepare and install a full-size mock-up for each product specified. Mock-up shall be fully operable and complete in all details. Obtain Designer's approval before further installation.

PART 2 PRODUCTS

2.1 Materials

Horizontal blinds: Raising and tilting, wand and cord operation, "Riviera" 1/2" contract blinds as manufactured by Levelor Corp. Color: As selected by the Designer.

Vertical blinds: Traversing and rotating, cord and chain operations, type MR-CS as manufactured by LouverDrape Corp. Louvers spaced 1-3/4": 2" wide free-hang fabric, Architectural series II. Color: As selected by the Designer.

Track, hardware, and other accessories: Manufacturer's standards.

PART 3 EXECUTION

3.1 Installation

Install materials in strict accordance with the manufacturer's printed instructions, approved submittals, and mock-ups.

Restore damaged finishes and adjust for proper operation.

END OF SECTION 12500

SECTION 15400 - PLUMBING

PART 1 GENERAL

1.1 Summary

All plumbing work shall be performed under a "design-build" subcontract, which shall include complete engineering and construction in accordance with applicable codes and ordinances and building management standards.

Furnish and install plumbing fixtures and fittings indicated on schedules.

Install water, waste, soil, and vent piping required for plumbing fixtures and appliances.

Make plumbing connections to appliances specified in other sections or furnished by Owner.

1.2 Submittals

Submit for the Designer's review:
• Catalog cuts of all indicated fixtures and fittings.
• At completion of work, Plumbing Inspector's inspection report indicating approval of all work.

PART 2 PRODUCTS

2.1 Pipe and Fittings

Furnish and install all necessary pipe, fittings, traps, valves, and unions as required for a properly functioning plumbing system as indicated.

All materials: In strict accordance with governing plumbing codes.

2.2 Fixtures and Fittings

Fixtures and fittings are indicated in schedules on the drawings.

Furnish and install appropriate trim pieces not specifically indicated.

PART 3 EXECUTION

3.1 Installation

Design the plumbing system determining proper elevations for all components of the system and using only the minimum number of bends to produce a satisfactorily functioning system.

Lay out pipes to fall within partition or ceiling cavities, and to not require furring.

END OF SECTION 15400

SECTION 15500 - FIRE PROTECTION SPRINKLER SYSTEM

PART 1 GENERAL

1.1 Summary

All work under this Section shall be performed under a "design-build" subcontract, which shall include complete engineering and construction in accordance with NFPA 13 - Standards for the Installation of Sprinkler Systems and the requirements of governmental agencies having jurisdiction.

1.2 Quality Control

Use only skilled workers who are thoroughly trained and experienced in the necessary crafts and who are familiar with the requirements for proper performance of the work.

1.3 Submittals

Submit for the Designer's review:
· Design drawings approved by authorities having jurisdiction showing the location of sprinklers, control valves, and related items.
· Product data and samples of specified sprinklers.

PART 2 PRODUCTS

2.1 System Design

Provide a complete system design utilizing components that are UL listed and FM approved for the intended purpose.

Provide all required piping, valves, test and drain connections, and equipment supports for a satisfactorily functioning system.

2.2 Sprinklers

Exposed sprinklers: Star Model LD-2 upright or pendant type, chrome-plated finish. Temperature rating: 165°F.

Concealed sprinklers: Star Phantom Model PH-1 with cover plate color as selected by the Designer. Temperature rating: 165°F.

PART 3 EXECUTION

3.1 Installation

Coordinate the location of all sprinklers and piping with other trades to insure adequate space is available for installation.

Sprinkler layout shall be symmetrical with respect to walls and ceiling grid. Sprinklers in acoustic panel ceilings shall be located in the center of panels.

3.2 Testing

Upon completion, test the system in the presence of authorities, make adjustments as required, and secure all required approvals.

END OF SECTION 15500

SECTION 15600 - HEATING, VENTILATING, AND AIR CONDITIONING

PART 1 GENERAL

1.1 Summary

All HVAC work shall be performed under a "design-build" subcontract, which shall include complete engineering and construction in accordance with applicable codes and ordinances and building management standards.

The work shall include all items of mechanical equipment, including air handling units, ductwork, diffusers and other terminal devices, thermostats, controls, and all other items required to complete a fully operational and satisfactorily functioning system.

1.2 Quality Control

The selected mechanical subcontractor shall be thoroughly familiar with the functioning of the building's mechanical system and shall be acceptable to the Designer, the Owner, and Building Management.

Use adequate numbers of skilled workers who are thoroughly trained and experienced in the necessary crafts and who are completely familiar with the specified requirements and the methods needed for proper performance of the work of this Section.

Without additional cost to the Owner, provide such other labor and materials as are required to complete the work of this Section in accordance with the requirements of governmental agencies having jurisdiction, regardless of whether such materials and associated labor are called for elsewhere in these Contract Documents.

1.3 Submittals

Submit for the Designer's review:
• Design drawings, signed by a properly licensed engineer and showing proposed layout of equipment, ducts, registers, grilles, controls, and other components of the system.
• Calculations demonstrating the adequacy of the proposed system and its compliance with these Specifications.
• Manufacturers' catalogs, samples, and other items needed to fully demonstrate the quality of the proposed materials and equipment. The Designer specifically reserves the right to reject proposed items exposed to view in finished spaces for aesthetic reasons, provided comparable items, which are acceptable, can be furnished.

PART 2 PRODUCTS

2.1 Acceptable Products

All products shall be as selected by the approved subcontractor subject to the Designer's review.

PART 3 EXECUTION

3.1 Surface Conditions

Examine the areas and conditions under which work of this Section will be performed. Correct conditions detrimental to timely and proper completion of the Work. Do not proceed until unsatisfactory conditions are corrected.

3.2 Coordination

Coordinate, as required, with other trades to assure proper and adequate provision in the work of those trades for interface with the work of this Section.

3.3 Equipment Interface

Provide all required shutoff valves, unions, and final connections of piping to the work of this Section.

For electrically operated equipment, verify the electrical characteristics actually available for the work of this Section and provide equipment meeting those characteristics.

3.4 Instructions

Upon completion of this portion of the Work, and prior to its acceptance by the Owner, provide a qualified engineer and fully instruct maintenance personnel in the proper operation and maintenance of items provided under this Section.

3.5 Testing and Adjusting

Test and adjust each piece of equipment and each system as required to assure proper balance and operation.

Test and regulate ventilation and air conditioning systems to conform to the air volumes shown on the approved design drawings.

Make tests and adjustments in apparatus and ducts for securing the proper volume and face distribution of air for each grille and ceiling outlet.

Submit two sets of test and balance reports to the Designer.

Eliminate noise and vibration, and assure proper function of all controls, maintenance of temperature, and operation in accordance with the approved design.

END OF SECTION 15600

SECTION 16400 - POWER, LIGHTING, TELEPHONE, AND DATA

PART 1 GENERAL

1.1 Summary

All electrical work shall be performed under a "design-build" subcontract, which shall include complete engineering and construction in accordance with the National Electric Code, other applicable codes and ordinances, and building management standards.

1.2 Quality Control

The selected electrical contractor shall be thoroughly familiar with the building's electrical system and shall be acceptable to the Designer, the Owner, and Building Management.

Use only skilled workers who are thoroughly trained and experienced in the necessary crafts and who are familiar with the requirements for proper performance of the work.

Without additional cost to the Owner, provide such other labor and materials as required to complete the work of this Section in accordance with the requirements of governmental agencies having jurisdiction, regardless of whether such materials and associated labor are called for elsewhere in the Contract Documents.

1.3 Submittals

Submit for the Designer's review:
  • Catalog cuts of all fixtures and devices.
  • When so requested, samples of items scheduled to be exposed in the final structure.

When requested by the Contractor, samples will be returned to the Contractor for installation on the Work.

1.4 Warranty

In addition to standard one-year warranty on all labor and materials, provide extended warranties where such are provided by manufacturers or suppliers.

PART 2 PRODUCTS

2.1 General

Provide only materials that are new, of the typed and quality specified. Where Underwriters' Laboratories, Inc. has established standards for such materials, provide only materials bearing the UL label.

2.2 Acceptable Products

Other than products specifically designated by manufacturer and model number on the drawings, all products shall be as selected by the approved subcontractor subject to the Designer's review.

Products shall include, but shall not be limited to, the following as may apply:
1. Distribution and/or lighting panels, if required
2. Circuit breakers, fuses, and similar components
3. Grounding devices
4. Wiring devices and cover plates
5. Conduit, raceways, and metal clad cable
6. Conductors
7. Lighting fixtures
8. Transformers, if required
9. Telephone and data, except for such items and equipment furnished by under separate contracts

PART 3 EXECUTION

3.1 Surface Conditions

Examine the areas and conditions under which work of this Section will be performed. Correct conditions detrimental to timely and proper completion of the Work. Do not proceed until unsatisfactory conditions are corrected.

3.2 Preparation

Coordinate, as necessary, with other trades to assure proper and adequate provision in the work of those trades for interface with the work of this Section.

Coordinate the installation of electrical items with the schedule for work of other trades to prevent unnecessary delays in the total Work.

Where lighting fixtures and other electrical items are shown in conflict with locations of structural members and mechanical or other equipment, provide required supports and wiring to clear the encroachment.

Where outlets are not specifically located on the Drawings, locate as determined in the field by the Designer. Where outlets are installed without such specific direction, relocate as directed by the Designer and at no additional cost to the Owner.

Verify all measurements at the building. No extra compensation will be allowed because of differences between work shown on the Drawings and actual measurements.

The Electrical Drawings are diagrammatic, but are required to be followed as closely as actual construction and work of other trades will permit. Notify the Designer of any conflicts. Do not proceed with any work until conflict is resolved.

3.3 Installation

All installation shall be in strict conformance with governing codes and regulations and best practices of the trade.

Securely and rigidly support all conduit, raceways, and cable.

Install lighting fixtures complete and ready for service in accordance with the Lighting Fixture Schedule shown on the Drawings.

Install proper size lamps in all fixtures.

Install all lighting fixtures, including those mounted in continuous rows, so that the weight of the fixture is supported, either directly or indirectly, by a sound and safe structural member of the building, using adequate number and type of fastenings to assure safe installation.

Wire to, and connect to, all items of building equipment not specifically described but to which electrical power is required.

Coordinate as necessary with other trades and suppliers to verify types, numbers, and locations of equipment.

3.4 Testing and Inspection

Provide personnel and equipment, make required tests, and secure required approvals from government agencies having jurisdiction.

When material and/or workmanship is found to not comply with the specified requirements, within three days after receipt of notice of such non-compliance, remove the noncomplying items and replace them with items complying with the specified requirements, all at no additional cost to the Owner.

3.5 Project Completion

Upon completion of the work of this Section, thoroughly clean all exposed portions of the electrical installation, removing all traces of soil, labels, grease, oil, and other foreign material, and using only the type cleaner recommended by the manufacturer of the item being cleaned.

END OF SECTION 16400

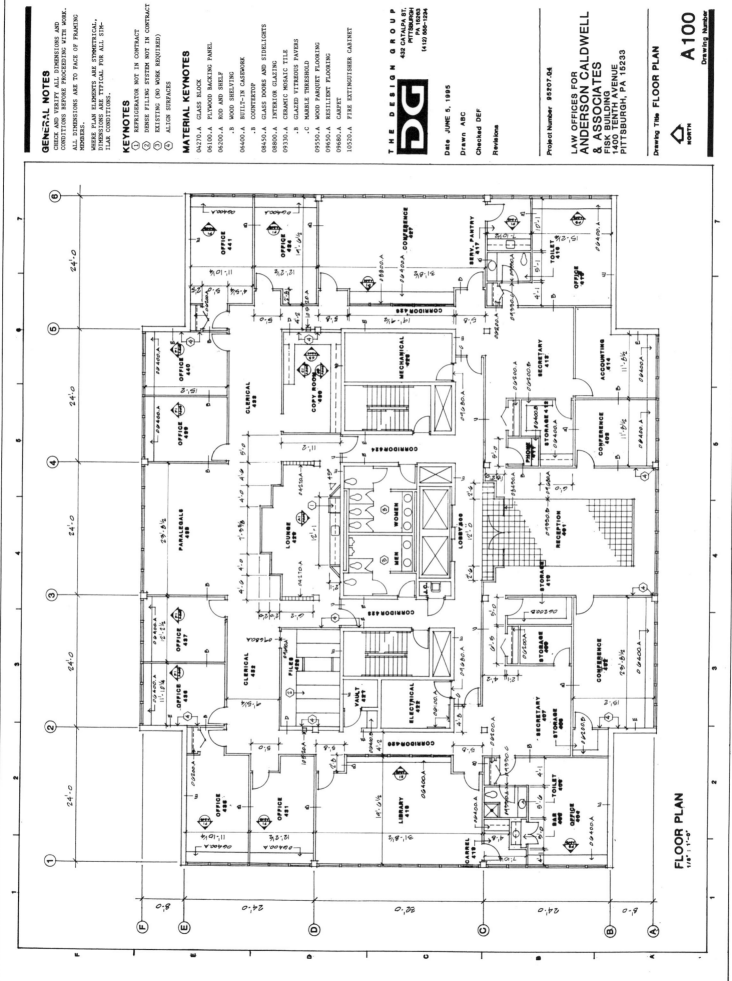

GENERAL NOTES

CHECK AND VERIFY ALL DIMENSIONS AND
CONDITIONS BEFORE PROCEEDING WITH WORK.

ALL DIMENSIONS ARE TO FACE OF FRAMING
MEMBERS.

WHERE PLAN ELEMENTS ARE SYMMETRICAL,
DIMENSIONS ARE TYPICAL FOR ALL SIM-
ILAR CONDITIONS.

KEYNOTES

1. REFRIGERATOR NOT IN CONTRACT
2. DENSE FILING SYSTEM NOT IN CONTRACT
3. EXISTING (NO WORK REQUIRED)
4. ALIGN SURFACES

MATERIAL KEYNOTES

04270.A GLASS BLOCK
06100.A PLYWOOD BACKING PANEL
06200.A ROD AND SHELF
     .B WOOD SHELVING
06400.A BUILT-IN CASEWORK
     .B COUNTERTOP
08450.A GLASS DOORS AND SIDELIGHTS
08800.A INTERIOR GLAZING
09330.A CERAMIC MOSAIC TILE
     .B GLAZED VITREOUS PAVERS
     .C MARBLE THRESHOLD
09550.A WOOD PARQUET FLOORING
09650.A RESILIENT FLOORING
09680.A CARPET
10520.A FIRE EXTINGUISHER CABINET

THE DESIGN GROUP

432 CATALPA ST.
PITTSBURGH,
PA 15263
(412) 555-1234

Date JUNE 5, 1995

Drawn ABC

Checked DEF

Revisions

Project Number 95207.04

LAW OFFICES FOR
ANDERSON CALDWELL
& ASSOCIATES
FISK BUILDING
1400 TENTH AVENUE
PITTSBURGH, PA 15233

Drawing Title FLOOR PLAN

NORTH

A100
Drawing Number

FLOOR PLAN
1/8" : 1'-0"

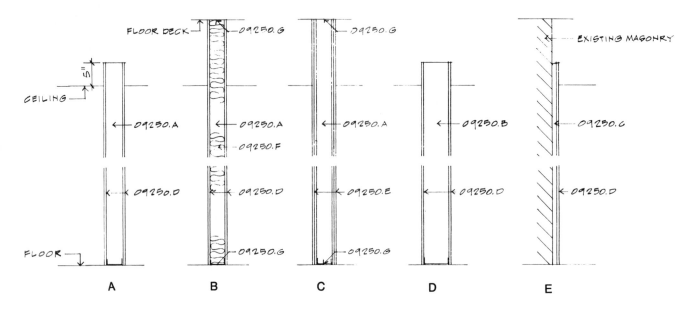

FLOOR DECK

5"

CEILING

09250.A   09250.G   09250.G   EXISTING MASONRY

09250.A   09250.A   09250.A   09250.B   09250.C

09250.F

09250.D   09250.D   09250.E   09250.D   09250.D

FLOOR

09250.G   09250.G

A   B   C   D   E

PARTITION TYPES

ALL PARTITIONS: TYPE A UNLESS NOTED OTHERWISE.

MATERIAL KEYNOTES

09250.A 3-5/8" METAL STUDS 16" O.C.

   .B 6" METAL STUDS 16" O.C.

   .C 7/8" METAL FURRING CHANNELS
      24" O.C.

   .D 5/8" GYPSUM WALLBOARD

   .E 2 LAYERS 5/8" FIRE-RATED
      GYPSUM WALLBOARD

   .F SOUND ATTENUATION BLANKET

   .G SEALANT

FINISH SCHEDULE

Space No.	Space Name	Floor Mat.	Floor Fin.	Base Mat.	Base Fin.	Walls North Mat.	Walls North Fin.	Walls East Mat.	Walls East Fin.	Walls South Mat.	Walls South Fin.	Walls West Mat.	Walls West Fin.	Trim Mat.	Trim Fin.	Doors Fin.	Frames Fin.	Ceiling Mat.	Ceiling Fin.	Ceiling Hgt.	Remarks
400	LOBBY	XCONC	CPT	WD	PT1	GWB	WC1	GWB	WC1	GWB	WC1	GWB	WC1	NONE	—	PT1	PT1	GWB	PT2	9'-0"	
401	RECEPTION	XCONC	GVP CPT	WD	PT1	GWB	WC2	GWB	WC2	GWB	WC2	GWB	WC2	WD	PT1	PT1	PT1	SAC	—	9'-0"	CHAIR RAIL @ 2'-8" A.F.F.
402	CONFERENCE	XCONC	CPT	WD	PT1	GWB	WC2	GWB	WC2	GWB	WC2	GWB	WC2	NONE	–	PT1	PT1	SAC	—	9'-0"	
403	CONFERENCE	XCONC	CPT	WD	PT1	GWB	WC2	GWB	WC2	GWB	WC2	GWB	WC2	NONE	–	PT1	PT1	SAC	—	9'-0"	
404	OFFICE	XCONC	CPT	WD	PT1	GWB	WC3	GWB	WC3	GWB	WC2	GWB	WC2	NONE	–	PT1	PT1	SAC	—	9'-0"	
405	BAR	XCONC	CPT	WD	PT1	GWB	WC3	GWB	WC3	GWB	WC3	GWB	WC3	NONE	–	PT1	PT1	GWB	PT2	8'-0"	
406	TOILET	XCONC	CT1	GWB	CT1	GWB	CT2	GWB	CT2	GWB	CT2	GWB	CT2	NONE	–	PT1	PT1	GWB	PT2	8'-0"	

FINISH MATERIAL AND COLOR SCHEDULE

Mark	Material/Product/Trade Name	Manufacturer	Pattern	Mfg. No.	Color/Finish	Remarks
CPT	BROADLOOM CARPET	—	—	—	—	ALLOWANCE - SEE SPECS
GVP	12" x 12" GLAZED VITREOUS PAVERS	DAL·TILE	—	2803	GRAY	
PT1	ALKYD ENAMEL	PPG	—	2759	METALLIC/SATIN	
PT2	LATEX WALL PAINT	PPG	—	2537	BLOSSOM WH./FLAT	
WC1	TEXTILE WALL COVERING	DESIGNTEX	BERLIN	6033-801	—	NO SUBSTITUTION
WC2	TEXTILE WALL COVERING	DESIGNTEX	PRAGUE	6023-101	—	NO SUBSTITUTION
CT1	2" x 2" CERAMIC MOSAIC TILE	AMERICAN OLEAN	—	A52	BUFF GRANITE	
CT2	4¼" x 4¼" GLAZED CERAMIC TILE	AMERICAN OLEAN	—	S13	CLASSIC BONE	S19 TEAL ACCENT - SEE ELEV.
SAC	2' x 2' SUSPENDED ACOUSTIC PANEL	ARMSTRONG	FINETEX	1709	WHITE	

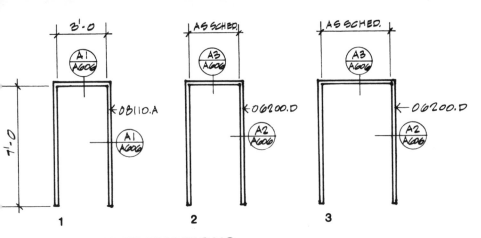

FRAME ELEVATIONS

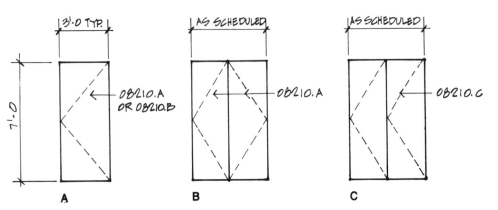

DOOR ELEVATIONS

DOOR SCHEDULE

No.	Door Opening Size			Frame				Door				Remarks
	Width	Hgt.	Thk.	Mat.	Elev.	Jamb	Head	Mat.	Elev.	Label	Hdw Set	
400A	6'-0	9'-0	1/2"	–	–	–	–	GLASS	–	–	–	FRAMELESS TEMP. GL., HDW. BY MFG.
400B	3'-0	7'-0	1¾"	H.M.	1	A1 A606	A1 A606	WOOD	A	"B"	2	1½ HR. F/R ASSEMBLY
400C	3'-0	7'-0	1¾"	H.M.	1	A1 A606	A1 A606	WOOD	A	"B"	2	1½ HR. F/R ASSEMBLY
402	3'-0	7'-0	1¾	WOOD	2	A2	A3	WOOD	A	–	5	
403	3'-0	7'-0	1¾"	WOOD	2	A2 A606	A3 A606	WOOD	A	–	5	
404A	3'-0	7'-0	1¾"	WOOD	2	A2 A606	A3 A606	WOOD	A	–	1	
404B	3'-6	7'-0	1¾"	–	–	–	A4 A606	WOOD	C	–	–	PR. BIFOLD, FRAME AT HEAD ONLY
405	4'-0	7'-0	1¾"	WOOD	3	A2	A3	WOOD	B	–	5	PR. SWINGING
406	3'-0	7'-0	1¾"	WOOD	2	A2 A606	A3 A606	WOOD	A	–	4	
408	3'-0	7'-0	1¾"	WOOD	2	A2 A606	A3 A606	WOOD	A	–	5	
409	3'-0	7'-0	1¾"	WOOD	2	A2 A606	A3 A606	WOOD	A	–	3	
410	3'-0	7'-0	1¾"	WOOD	2	A2 A606	A3 A606	WOOD	A	–	3	

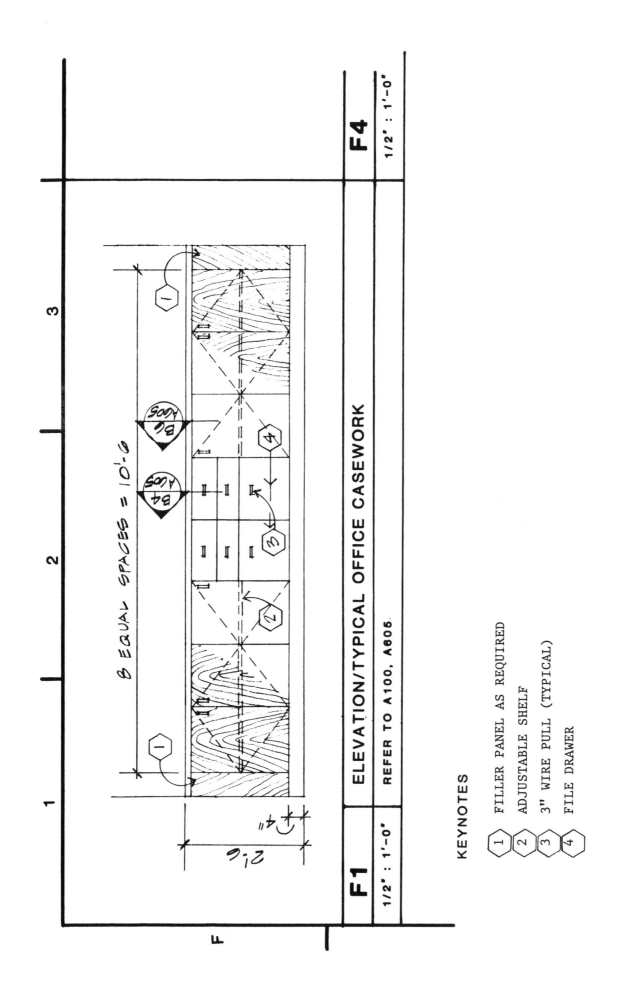

F1	ELEVATION/TYPICAL OFFICE CASEWORK
1/2" : 1'-0"	REFER TO A100, A605.

F4
1/2" : 1'-0"

KEYNOTES

1 FILLER PANEL AS REQUIRED
2 ADJUSTABLE SHELF
3 3" WIRE PULL (TYPICAL)
4 FILE DRAWER

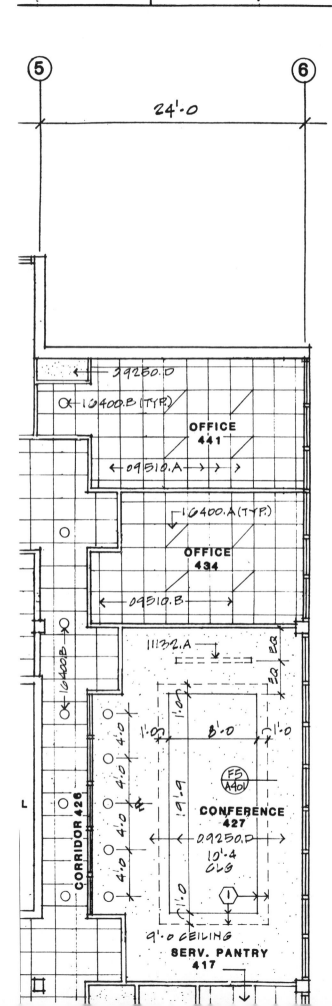

GENERAL NOTES

CHECK AND VERIFY ALL DIMENSIONS AND
CONDITIONS BEFORE PROCEEDING WITH WORK.

ALL DIMENSIONS ARE TO FACE OF FRAMING
MEMBERS.

VERIFY ADEQUATE SUPPORT FOR ALL CEILING
MOUNTED ELEMENTS.

KEYNOTES

1   LIGHT COVE, SEE DETAIL.

MATERIAL KEYNOTES

09250.D   5/8" GYPSUM WALLBOARD

09510.A   2' x 2' ACOUSTIC PANEL

   .B   CEILING SUSPENSION GRID

11132.A   ELECTRICALLY-OPERATED
          PROJECTION SCREEN

16400.A   2' x 2' FLUORESCENT
          LIGHTING FIXTURE

   .B   RECESSED INCANDESCENT
          LIGHTING FIXTURE

THE DESIGN GROUP

432 CATALPA ST.
PITTSBURGH
PA 15263
(412) 555-1234

Date JUNE 5, 1995

Drawn ABC

Checked DEF

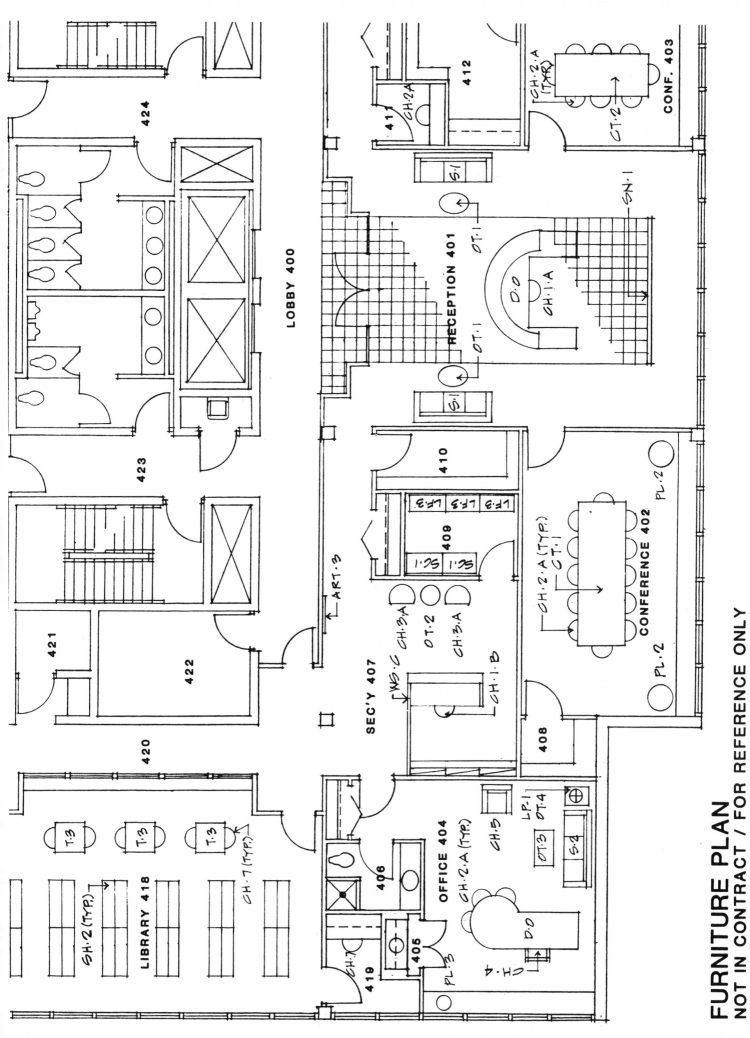

FURNITURE PLAN
NOT IN CONTRACT / FOR REFERENCE ONLY

APPENDIX

RECOMMENDED READINGS

Cohen, H. 1980. *You Can Negotiate Anything.* (Seacaucus, NJ: Lyle Stuart, Inc.)

DeChiara, J., Panero, J., & Zelnik, M. 1991. *Time-Saver Standards for Interior Design and Space Planning.* (NY: McGraw Hill.)

Farren, C. 1988. *Planning and Managing Interior Projects.* (Kingston, MA: R.S. Means Co., Inc.)

Heuer, C. 1989. *Means Legal Reference for Design and Construction.* (Kingston, MA: R.S. Means Co., Inc.)

Kearney, D. 1995. *The ADA in Practice.* (Revised edition of *The New ADA: Compliance and Costs.*) (Kingston, MA: R.S. Means Co., Inc.)

Knackstedt, M. 1992. *The Interior Design Business Handbook.* Second Edition. (NY: Van Nostrand Reinhold.)

Lew, A. 1987. *Means Interior Estimating.* (Kingston, MA: R.S. Means Co., Inc.)

Piotrowski, C. 1992. *Interior Design Management.* (NY: Van Nostrand Reinhold.)

Sampson, C. 1991. *Estimating for Interior Designers.* (NY: Whitney Library of Design.)

Staebler, W. 1988. *Architectural Detailing in Contract Interiors.* (NY: Whitney Library of Design.)

Stasiowski, F. 1985. *Negotiating Higher Design Fees.* (NY: Whitney Library of Design.)

Stitt, F. 1980. *Systems Drafting.* (NY: McGraw Hill.)

Thompson, J. (Ed.) 1992. *ASID Professional Practice Manual.* (NY: Whitney Library of Design.)

Manual of Practice. 1993. (Alexandria, VA: The Construction Specifications Institute.)

Means ADA Compliance Pricing Guide. 1994. (Kingston, MA: R.S. Means Co., Inc.)

Means Illustrated Construction Dictionary. 1991. (Kingston, MA: R.S. Means Co., Inc.)

Means Interior Cost Data 1995. (Kingston, MA: R.S. Means Co., Inc.)

INDEX

NOTES

NOTES

NOTES

NOTES

NOTES

NOTES

NOTES

NOTES

NOTES